St Antony's Series

Series Editors
Dan Healey, St Antony's College, University of Oxford, Oxford, UK
Leigh Payne, St Antony's College, University of Oxford, Oxford, UK

The St Antony's Series publishes studies of international affairs of contemporary interest to the scholarly community and a general yet informed readership. Contributors share a connection with St Antony's College, a world-renowned centre at the University of Oxford for research and teaching on global and regional issues. The series covers all parts of the world through both single-author monographs and edited volumes, and its titles come from a range of disciplines, including political science, history, and sociology. Over more than forty years, this partnership between St Antony's College and Palgrave Macmillan has produced about 400 publications.

This series is indexed by Scopus.

More information about this series at
https://link.springer.com/bookseries/15036

Barry Colfer
Editor

European Trade Unions in the 21st Century

The Future of Solidarity and Workplace Democracy

Editor
Barry Colfer
Department of Politics
and International Studies
University of Cambridge
Cambridge, UK

ISSN 2633-5964   ISSN 2633-5972 (electronic)
St Antony's Series
ISBN 978-3-030-88284-6   ISBN 978-3-030-88285-3 (eBook)
https://doi.org/10.1007/978-3-030-88285-3

© The Editor(s) (if applicable) and The Author(s), under exclusive license to Springer Nature Switzerland 2022
This work is subject to copyright. All rights are solely and exclusively licensed by the Publisher, whether the whole or part of the material is concerned, specifically the rights of translation, reprinting, reuse of illustrations, recitation, broadcasting, reproduction on microfilms or in any other physical way, and transmission or information storage and retrieval, electronic adaptation, computer software, or by similar or dissimilar methodology now known or hereafter developed.
The use of general descriptive names, registered names, trademarks, service marks, etc. in this publication does not imply, even in the absence of a specific statement, that such names are exempt from the relevant protective laws and regulations and therefore free for general use.
The publisher, the authors and the editors are safe to assume that the advice and information in this book are believed to be true and accurate at the date of publication. Neither the publisher nor the authors or the editors give a warranty, expressed or implied, with respect to the material contained herein or for any errors or omissions that may have been made. The publisher remains neutral with regard to jurisdictional claims in published maps and institutional affiliations.

Cover illustration: Hufton+Crow-VIEW/Alamy Stock Photo

This Palgrave Macmillan imprint is published by the registered company Springer Nature Switzerland AG
The registered company address is: Gewerbestrasse 11, 6330 Cham, Switzerland

Foreword

The last 18 months have demonstrated the power and value of trade unions. Across Europe, trade unions secured government support for new or extended short-time working schemes which protected millions of jobs in the face of the COVID-19 pandemic. They worked with government and employers to produce safe working guidance which kept millions safe at work. And they supported their members working in sectors as diverse as health, social care, retail, power supply, public transport and many more to ensure that the vital services we all rely on kept running even during periods of national lockdown.

But despite these achievements, it is clear that Europe's unions cannot face the post-COVID world with anything approaching complacency. As the contributors to this book note, union membership is declining even in those countries with high levels of collective bargaining coverage and well-established social partnership arrangements. Traditional links with social democratic parties—and by extension, governments—are under pressure. The emergence of the so-called gig economy represents just the latest effort by employers to rid themselves of their traditional employment obligations and shift risk from themselves to individual workers. Taken together with the need to decarbonise our economies and the inexorable rise of AI, digitalisation and automation, unions face a wave of industrial transformation that—if left unchecked—could have a profoundly negative impact on jobs, pay and terms and conditions of employment.

This book examines the response of trade unions to these fundamental challenges. It will not make easy reading for anyone—like me—who wants to see unions grow, thrive and effectively represent working people. But as a union activist and official for over 30 years, I know that we do ourselves no favours by pretending there is a silver bullet for rebuilding and recasting trade unionism. Instead—as this book clearly outlines—there are strategies and approaches that demonstrate ways that unions can still make important gains for workers.

Growing membership, extending collective bargaining rights and the ability to take industrial action will always be important. But so too are the ability to use the courts to take on bad employers; to form coalitions with other campaigning organisations and social movements; to develop new institutions that can bolster union efforts to raise wages or enforce labour standards; and to use social media and new technology to reach new audiences beyond our existing membership.

A post-Brexit Britain with a Conservative-led government in power for over a decade isn't the most fertile terrain for building a strong trade union movement. But a combination of these approaches outlined above has begun to show dividends. Trade union membership has risen (modestly) for four years in a row. We have secured breakthrough agreements with previously union averse or hostile companies such as Ryanair and Uber. We have won a seat at the political table to make the case for a just transition, and for green jobs to be good jobs, as the UK government seeks to meet its commitment to a net zero economy. And we have forged effective working relationships with the devolved governments in Wales and Scotland, and with sub-regional authorities across England.

It's these small steps forward, and many others featured in this book, which give me confidence that unions can organise, campaign and bargain their way back to effectively exerting power on behalf of working people. To do so, we will need to be ever more innovative. To take more chances. To be prepared to fail. And it will require us to learn from each other.

The contributors to this volume have captured and articulated some of those collective lessons. It's the job of trade unionists across Europe to take them on board and to redouble our efforts to win for workers.

August 2021

Paul Nowak
Deputy General Secretary of the
British Trade Union Congress
(TUC)
London, UK

Preface

> *If we want to make progress in key areas now, we have to build a multi-stakeholder process, harnessing the appropriate energies. So not only the politicians but also business, the wider civil society, and the trade union movement all have a contribution to make, whether it is at a national or at international level.*

—Mary Robinson, Former President of Ireland and Chair of The Elders

Work for this book began in the pre-pandemic era and came to completion at a point in time when our lives have been transformed by COVID-19. But even before the pandemic, the world that workers and unions inhabited was unrecognisable compared to even half a century ago, given the collapse of traditionally highly unionised industries, dramatic changes in technology and the erosion of collective rights seen throughout Europe and much of the world over recent decades. Taken together, this has resulted in a marked shift in power relations at work, typically away from workers and towards the owners of capital. This has made employment less stable and predictable for many, especially for those already on the margins of society, including among minorities, women, people with disabilities, migrants and young people.

However, while the ideas which underpin the contributions in this volume are timeless—relating to fairness, (in)equality, democracy, and dignity and respect at work among much else—they have been cast in new light through the prism of the pandemic. The introduction of restrictions on economic and social activity by governments in response to COVID-19 has highlighted the key roles played by frontline workers in health care, retail, transport and other essential services. Meanwhile, economic loss and disruption caused by the pandemic, including through the introduction of short-time working arrangements, have allowed many workers to appreciate the precarious nature of many forms of employment—often for the first time. At the same time, the shift towards remote working for many has presented both opportunities and threats for workers, unions and policy-makers alike. On the one hand, some in the growing army of remote workers risk slipping into the 'gig economy' by being reclassified as contract agents (as opposed to employees) by opportunistic employers, while the increasing rates of remote working raise important questions regarding liability at work and taxation. On the other hand, the pandemic highlights the possibility for some working people to strike a healthier balance between home and work life, and even to rejuvenate rural and peri-urban areas by transforming the nature and frequency of the commute to work. The planning and regulation of this new future will require ingenuity, creative policy-making and inclusive leadership.

Perhaps above all, when it comes to the future of work, the pandemic has shown the capacity of the state and organisations such as the European Union (EU) to tackle major challenges when they arise and when the political will can be mobilised. This book goes to print amid increasingly alarming calls by climate scientists and activists regarding the future of the planet and dire warnings about the consequences of man-made climate change. Under the auspices of the European Green Deal and the EU's pandemic recovery programme that are designed to support the green and digital transitions, the EU is attempting to assert itself as a global leader and trendsetter in the fight against climate change.

It is argued here that sustainable solutions to the many challenges that Europe and the world face—including when it comes to climate change, the technological revolution, COVID-19 and much besides—can only be reached with the meaningful involvement of trade unions, the oldest and biggest civil society movement in Europe. Thus, this book does not present a list of grievances but it rather points to evidence of how unions can contribute to making work more humane and sustainable while simultaneously acting as a 'sword of justice' by campaigning and agitating for a better society.

The COVID-19 pandemic crisis calls for a more assertive and coordinated response from unions. Unions will continue to play a key role in public discourse and debate but must continue to be open to change by, among much else: being innovative, reaching out to under-represented groups, forming alliances, leveraging the opportunities afforded by the network society and experimenting with new forms of legal and political instruments, as the contributions in this volume explore.

Florence, Italy
September 2021

Barry Colfer

Acknowledgements

This idea for this book originates at a workshop that was hosted in Oxford in June 2019. The workshop enjoyed the support of many within the Oxford community. In particular, the editor wishes to acknowledge the support of Frederic Thibault-Starzyk and the team at the Maison Francaise d'Oxford (MFO) for hosting the event at the wonderful MFO premises in Oxford and also Dr Hartmut Mayer, director of the European Studies Centre at St Antony's College, University of Oxford and executive chair of the Europaeum network, for their generous support and encouragement. Prof Leigh Payne and Prof Dan Healey at St Antony's College also provided invaluable support and guidance as the book took shape.

At Palgrave MacMillan, Ambra Finotello and Hemapriya Eswanth and their team were unwavering in their professionalism and kindness and helped to make the production and editing process an enjoyable one.

Above all else, this book has come into existence due to the energy, commitment and fellowship of a unique group of scholars from across a wide range of disciplines, including political science, sociology, law and business studies, writing with passion and expertise about a wide range of cases including the Czech Republic, Denmark, France, Finland, Germany, Spain, Sweden, Poland, the UK and the EU-level. The bulk of the work for this volume has come together under the shadow of the pandemic. Authors have thus delivered their contributions while balancing the many competing demands for their time and energies in their home and working lives under lockdown and I wish to wholeheartedly thank them and their families for their efforts.

Florence
September 2021

Barry Colfer

Contents

1	Introduction: European Trade Unions in the Twenty-First Century Barry Colfer and Thomas Prosser	1
2	The Right to Collective Bargaining for Economically Dependent Workers with a Self-Employed Status Pieter Pecinovsky	19
3	The European Court of Justice and Trade Union Power in Europe Lorenzo Cecchetti	45
4	Trade Unions and Migration in Europe Rolle Alho	71
5	Confronting a Moral Abyss: Unions and the Role of Law in the France Télécom Case Julia López López	95
6	The Renewal of Trade Unionism in France? Dominique Andolfatto and Dominique Labbé	109
7	France: Macron's Orders and Trade Union Power in the Field of Health at Work Sylvie Contrepois	129

8	Organised Labour and Fluid Organisations: Insights from the Gilets Jaunes Movement Barry Colfer and Yoann Bazin	149
9	The Decline of the Czech Trade Union Movement Martin Štefko	173
10	Trade Union Participation and New Forms of Collective Action: Pension Reform in Spain as a Case Study Eusebi Colàs-Neila	189
11	Danish Trade Unions and Young People: Using Media in the Battle for Hearts and Minds Torsten Geelan	209
12	German Trade Unions and The EU Minimum Wage Debate: Between National Elite and Transnational Working Class Mona Aranea	233
13	Workplace Democracy in the UK: Reviving Voice Institutions in Unpromising Times? David Coats	259
14	Polish Unions Towards Populism: Strategies and Dilemmas Jan Czarzasty and Adam Rogalewski	277
15	Conclusion: Multiple Challenges Confronting European Trade Unions Richard Hyman	297

Index   317

LIST OF CONTRIBUTORS

Rolle Alho University of Helsinki, Helsinki, Finland

Dominique Andolfatto Credespo (Law and Political Science Centre), Université de Bourgogne Franche-Comté, Dijon, France

Mona Aranea Hans Böckler Foundation, Düsseldorf, Germany

Yoann Bazin Human Resource Management, EM Normandie, Oxford, UK

Lorenzo Cecchetti Department of Law, LUISS University, Rome, Italy

David Coats Centre for Sustainable Work and Employment Futures, University of Leicester, Leicester, UK

Eusebi Colàs-Neila Faculty of Law, Univ. Pompeu Fabra, Barcelona, Spain

Barry Colfer Department of Politics and International Studies, University of Cambridge, Cambridge, UK

Sylvie Contrepois Centre de Recherches sociologiques et politiques de Paris (CNRS), Paris, France;
Institut régional du travail d'Occitanie, Université de Toulouse - Jean Jaurès, Toulouse, France

Jan Czarzasty Warsaw School of Economics, Warsaw, Poland

Torsten Geelan Department of Sociology, University of Copenhagen, Copenhagen, Denmark

Richard Hyman London School of Economics, London, UK

Dominique Labbé Pacte (Social Sciences Laboratory), Université de Grenoble-Alpes, Grenoble, France

Julia López López Labor Law and Social Security Law, University Pompeu Fabra, Barcelona, Spain

Pieter Pecinovsky Faculty of Law, KU Leuven, Institute for Labour Law, Leuven, Belgium

Thomas Prosser Cardiff Business School, Cardiff University, Cardiff, UK

Adam Rogalewski European Federation of Public Service Unions (EPSU), Brussels, Belgium

Martin Štefko Faculty of Law, Charles University, Prague, Czech Republic

LIST OF FIGURES

Chapter 5

Graph 1	Prevalence of bullying and harassment at work by country (*Source* Own elaboration from data of European Work Conditions Survey [2015] cited in European Parliament's Policy Department for Citizens' Rights and Constitutional Affairs [2018] *Bullying and sexual harassment at the workplace, in public spaces, and in political life in the EU, available at:* http://www.europarl.europa.eu/RegData/etudes/STUD/2018/604949/IPOL_STU(2018)604949_EN.pdf. Percentage of persons in national surveys who report having suffered harassment at the workplace)	99
Graph 2	Percentage of violations of Article 3 ECHR (Inhuman or degrading treatment) of total number of judgments and by state (1959–2018) (*Source* Own elaboration from data of Statistics on ECHR: Violations by Article and by State 1959–2018 [see: https://www.echr.coe.int/Pages/home.aspx?p=reports&c] This table has been generated using the metadata for each judgement contained in HUDOC, the Court's online case-law database)	99

Chapter 8

| Fig. 1 | Number of reported demonstrators November 2017–February 2018 (*Source* Ministère de l'Intérieur) | 163 |
| Fig. 2 | Public support for the Gilets Jaunes 2018–2019 | 165 |

| Image 1 | 'Colere 24' flyer calling for action on 17 February 2018 | 162 |

Chapter 11

Fig. 1	Average time spent daily on media platforms according to age (*Source* FDIM [2012, p. 8])	216
Fig. 2	Where have you seen or heard about the logo?/age	224
Fig. 3	The 'Are you OK?" Campaign Logo	229

Chapter 13

| Fig. 1 | Trade union density in the UK 1979–2018 (% employees) (*Source* BEIS, Trade Union Statistical Bulletin) | 260 |
| Fig. 2 | Trends in organisational influence 1992–2017 (% employees) (*Source* SES 2017) | 265 |

List of Tables

Chapter 6

Table 1	Unionisation in France in 2018	111
Table 2	The rate of unionisation in France (1949–2015)	112
Table 3	Scope and themes covered by collective bargaining in France about here-	119

Chapter 7

| Table 1 | Projection: the consequences of setting up CSEs | 138 |
| Table 2 | Projected situation at RTE | 140 |

Chapter 8

Table 1	Trade union membership in France, Germany, Sweden, UK, and USA	153
Table 2	French trade union confederations	153
Table 3	Number of days not worked due to strikes, Europe selected countries 2010–2018	155
Table 4	The characteristics of solid and liquid organisations	167

Chapter 11

| Table 1 | Have you heard of the campaign or seen the logo in the past three weeks? | 223 |
| Table 2 | Danish Union Membership 1985–2014 | 227 |

Table 3	The aim of the campaign is to inform the Danish public about collective agreements and their function. Do you agree or disagree that this is necessary?	228
Table 4	What do you think about the trade union movement doing this campaign?	228
Table 5	The campaign has made me more conscious of collective agreements and their function in the labour market?	228
Table 6	The campaign has made me more aware of the difference between LO unions and the ideological alternative unions?	229
Table 7	Has the campaign made you consider joining a trade union?	229

Chapter 12

Table 1	Organisations responding to first stage EC consultation	239
Table 2	Labour responses to the first stage Commission consultation on fair minimum wages	239

CHAPTER 1

Introduction: European Trade Unions in the Twenty-First Century

Barry Colfer and Thomas Prosser

Trade unions are intermediary organisations that help to mobilise workers' resources over those who exert power over them (Müller-Jentsch, 1985). It is possible to identify three key roles that unions seek to perform in Europe today: firstly, to promote collective voice and workplace democracy (Freeman & Medoff, 1984); secondly, to provide a 'countervailing power' to the socio-economic dominance of capital (Galbraith, 1952); and thirdly, a wider moral function as a 'sword of justice' by campaigning and agitating for a better society (Flanders, 1970; Thompson, 1963). Building on this, Gumbrell-McCormick and Hyman (2018) identify five key areas of union action, namely: matters of membership and mobilisation; organisational issues; bargaining and partnership; the formation

B. Colfer (✉)
Department of Politics and International Studies,
University of Cambridge, Cambridge, UK
e-mail: bc348@cam.ac.uk

T. Prosser
Cardiff Business School, Cardiff University, Cardiff, UK

© The Author(s), under exclusive license to Springer Nature Switzerland AG 2022
B. Colfer (ed.), *European Trade Unions in the 21st Century*,
St Antony's Series, https://doi.org/10.1007/978-3-030-88285-3_1

of alliances and politics; and transnational activities at the European and global levels, each of which are shaped and influenced by markets, institutions and other actors (Kelly, 1998).

However, the institutional arrangements that regulate employment relationships in Europe vary considerably (Hogan & Nolan, 2007). Crouch (1993) identifies the 'persistent variety' of labour market institutions, and their underlying dynamics and susceptibility to reform. Labour market institutions, and the socio-political context in which unions reside, are shaped by factors including the prevailing production (Hall & Soskice, 2001), welfare state (Esping-Andersen, 1990), employment (Gallie, 2007) and industrial relations (Visser & Dolvik, 2008) regimes. European Union (EU) legislation has had an important impact on each of these, albeit to varying degrees in different countries, but national industrial relations systems, traditions and practices remain central to labour regulation and social policy—and to the material and political conditions of European trade unions (Marginson & Sisson, 2004).

Meanwhile, it has become common to distinguish between different types of capitalism according to how far, and through which mechanisms, markets, including labour markets, are socially and politically regulated. In the varieties of capitalism conceptual framework, Hall and Soskice (2001) advance a dichotomy between Coordinated Market Economies (CMEs) and Liberal Market Economies (LMEs). This framework has become influential in comparative research and is useful for the analysis of employment and industrial relations systems and when trying to understand how unions now seek to exert influence (Hancké et al., 2007).

Regarding industrial relations, CMEs see more non-market forms of interaction between social partners, while social partner activities in LMEs are primarily coordinated through hierarchies and market mechanisms. These are partly distinguished by the ways the social partners interact and coordinate their behaviours.[1] CMEs typically have higher levels of membership in social partner organisations, and wage-bargaining tends to happen at the industrial, sectoral or national levels. In LMEs, unions and employer organisations tend to be less well organised, and wage negotiations tend to be decentralised. In CMEs, management and workers tend

---

[1] CMEs roughly coincide with North-western continental Europe and the Nordic countries, while the LMEs with the Anglo-Saxon countries.

to collaborate on key decisions while in LMEs, more adversarial relations tend to prevail, where managers are the primary decision-makers. This dichotomy has been extended to include a mixed-market economy group (MMEs) where unions and employers have traditionally used access to the state to maintain their position in society—what could also be called, a 'state-centred' group (Hancké et al. 2007; Molina & Rhodes 2007; Hassel 2014) which is characterised by a central role for the state in facilitating coordination between the social partners, which compensates for the lack of autonomous social partnership organisations.

In CMEs, strong unions often encounter strong employers' associations, especially in export sectors. The social partners often negotiate wages between a floor set by inflation and a ceiling set by productivity, which simultaneously safeguards wages and profitability. In MMEs, the state compensates for the lack of autonomous social partner bargaining by intervening directly in wage-setting. Notably, Baccaro and Howell (2017) argue that liberalisation is increasingly making CMEs more like LMEs, which creates further distinctive problems for unions in those countries.

Using similar language and ideas, Esping-Andersen (1990) developed a theory of welfare capitalism, identifying three 'worlds': a privatised (liberal) model, a state-led (conservative, inegalitarian social insurance) model and an egalitarian (social democratic model). In the liberal model, the state has a limited role in providing modest means-tested social transfers while emphasising that being in work should provide a benefit over social welfare payments. The conservative model seeks to provide more comprehensive unemployment insurance with transfers to the sick and unemployed based on contributions into the system. A social democratic approach is universal in outlook and seeks to provide cradle to grave care notwithstanding an individual's contributions, which is typically achieved through high levels of taxation—and with a central role afforded to unions in the administration of unemployment benefits in certain places, including in the Nordic countries and Belgium. Clearly whichever 'world' most closely approximates to a given industrial relations context has a major impact on union priorities, resources and capacities to act.

Employment regimes also differ in terms of the power relations that exist between the social partners, in how unions and employers are organised, in the levels and styles of bargaining which prevail, in whether social partners are involved in policy-making, and in the degree of government intervention in industrial relations. Gallie (2007) draws a distinction between three employment regimes, namely inclusive, dualist, and market-focused types. In inclusive regimes, employment rights are extended widely, unions tend to be strongly institutionalised within politics and decision-making processes, and there are strong welfare safety nets. In dualist regimes, unions are afforded a consultative role, and union involvement in politics tends to be contingent on what regime holds power. Unions tend to focus on members, being less concerned with the wider workforce and emphasise the distinctions between insiders and outsiders. In market regimes, unions are traditionally seen (at least by government and many employers) as unwelcome rigidities to efficiency, unions are typically excluded from decision-making, and there is minimal employment regulation. Relatedly, Schmidt (2002) advances the idea of a 'state-centred' regime where policies are made without systemic input from the social partners, with flexible implementation processes and where derogations are often provided through legislation. While the EU has been an important leveller with respect to employment regulation, important differences persist.

The contributions in this volume refer to unions and legislation that apply across each of these production, welfare state, employment, and industrial relations regimes. While it is by no means fully representative of the diversity that exists across European industrial relations regimes and trade union traditions, it presents a snapshot of how unions seek to exert influence across a broad range of economic, political and social contexts.

1 The Scope and Premise of This Volume

Our analysis happens as trade unions in Europe face a range of cross-cutting challenges. This includes the near universal contraction in union membership, the decline of traditionally highly unionised blue-collar industries, and the rise of automation, micro-processing and digitalisation (see Neufeind et al., 2018; Autor, 2019). The breakdown of the standard contract of employment and the increasing rates of precarious forms of employment have radically transformed the world of work which makes any collectivist vision of society, and the notion of solidarity upon which trade unionism is based, difficult to sustain. Meanwhile, especially since the 1980s, established linkages between unions and especially social democratic parties have almost universally weakened. All this serves to deprive unions and workers of what were once key sources of political power and influence.

All this raises tough questions for unions, policy-makers and commentators alike regarding the terms and conditions of employment, exploitation and control at work, and the role and nature of trade unions—the oldest and largest civil society movement in Europe. These challenging times coincide with a time of widespread discontent in modern societies vis-à-vis the political establishment more broadly, where unions are often seen as part of a discredited elite. How can unions change their practices and strategies to still be able to defend workers' rights in this changing workplace and political context? To what extent must unions reinvent their fundamental functions and must they renew and refine traditional methods of representation and action? In what ways can unions help to 'put the brakes' on the destruction of the standard contract of employment, on the reduction in the terms and conditions of employment, and on the breakdown of formal and informal forms of worker voice and workplace democracy that are making many workers poorer and less happy? These questions and more are considered in the contributions that follow. The contributiors to this volume also ask how and why union influence has diminished, and ultimately consider what prospects exist, if any, for its revival, as many of the traditional key demands of the union movement have now been met by legislation (see Wright et al., 2019).

In response to this challenging context, some unions have engaged in competition with European counterparts. Following the launch of the European Single Market, scholars noted the tendency for national unions to conclude pacts guaranteeing competitiveness (Streeck, 1998), often in anticipation of the EU single currency (Rhodes, 1998). In recent times, such trends have scarcely retreated, with Prosser (2019) emphasising the tendency of European labour movements to engage in competition during the sovereign debt crisis. Though we do not deny the existence of such processes, our emphasis in this book is more hopeful. We identify two processes which promote solidarity that are picked up in several of the chapters that follow, namely: (i) recourse to the law and (ii) the maximisation of opportunities associated with the network society.

Indeed, as union density rates have fallen over recent decades, many unions have been forced to rely on alternative strategies to mobilise influence. One of these is recourse to the law. Though this strategy can be problematic for a variety of reasons, including the fact that courts are often associated with technocratic solutions to the problems that unions face, this volume highlights several cases where such a strategy proved fruitful. Examining unions and the France Telecom case, for example,

Julia López López argues that the prosecution of managers for harassment represents a victory for unions over privatisation and commodification. Significantly, European legal interventions have also promoted solidarity. Pieter Pecinovsky asserts that the European Committee of Social Rights (ECSR) clarifies the rights of economically dependent workers to be covered by collective bargaining, while Lorenzo Cecchetti details Court of Justice of the EU (CJEU) jurisprudence relating to working time that unions have relied upon to defend workers' interests.

But the law is no substitute for effective mobilisation. The decline in mobilisation capacity is often associated with structural economic change, with globalisation having eroded the traditional sectors where unions in Europe were traditionally strong, including in manufacturing. Yet recent changes also present new opportunities. The 'information age' is characterised by the rise of networks over hierarchies. This has increased the ability of social actors to interconnect and to organise across the internet and via information and communication technologies (ICT) and beyond the boundaries of established institutions, surveillance, discipline and control. The COVID-19 pandemic crisis has only increased such tendencies, atomising society and increasing reliance on ICT for communications.

In these circumstances, we may ask whether solidarity, social cohesion and productive relations can be established within such networked structures. There are grounds for pessimism, yet we emphasise some reasons for optimism. Building on Zygmunt Bauman's analysis of 'liquid modernity' and the growing body of work on 'fluid organizations', Barry Colfer and Yoann Bazin show how movements like the 'Gilets Jaunes' (yellow vests) in France challenge the previously clear questions of leadership and purpose within social movement organisations. Other contributions also build on this theme, with Rolle Alho emphasising the capacity of unions to react positively to immigration and with David Coats discussing union responses to the gig economy in the UK. While such trends are not decisive proof that unions are thriving in their new economic environments, they may offer models which can inspire unions and researchers in the future.

Many of the ideas for these chapters were conceived in the aftermath of the 2008 financial crisis, and the EU's 'silent revolution' of new economic governance that institutionalises (or constitutionalises) neoliberalism in the EU (Lehndorff et al., 2018) and were written following the onset of the COVID-19 pandemic, which has had a transformative impact on labour markets, workplace democracy and the role of the state (Colfer, 2020). This volume thus hopes to contribute to the academic and public policy discourse regarding workplace democracy and worker power in the post-COVID world.

Other individual chapters consider trade unionism and union power in a range of different contexts, including in France in response to President Emmanuel Macron's labour reforms with Dominique Andolfatto and Dominique Labbé and separately from Sylvie Contrepois, under Poland's populist government with Jan Czarzasty and Adam Rogalewski, and amid pension reforms in Spain, with Eusebi Colàs-Neila. Torsten Geelan analyses the recent union campaign in Denmark to engage with young workers, Martin Štefko considers the state of the Czech labour movement with a focus on the mining sector and Mona Aranea examines the role of German unions in the EU minimum wage debate. This interdisciplinary volume thereby includes contributions covering the Czech Republic, Denmark, France, Finland, Germany, Spain, Poland, the UK and the EU-level, with scholars coming from a range of academic and intellectual backgrounds including from history, law, political science, public policy and sociology.

2 Outline of the Rest of the Book

Our collection begins with **Pieter Pecinovsky's** chapter that reviews the right to collective bargaining for self-employed yet economically dependent workers in Europe. One of the primary means for workers and trade unions to exert countervailing power over employers and capital is through collective bargaining, which is protected in Europe as a fundamental right. While the scope of the right to collective bargaining was traditionally restricted to employees, this position has become untenable, as new types of workers which do not easily fit the classical qualification of an employee have entered the labour market in great numbers. These new types of workers are often regarded as self-employed persons, even when they are economically dependent on certain employers or companies (e.g. freelancers and platform workers in the gig economy). As these workers are presumed to be self-employed, there is a clear risk that they do not fall within the traditional exceptions to the EU's competition rules that the CJEU has long since granted to collective bargaining agreements. This chapter discusses the conflict between competition law and the right to collective bargaining and finds a possible solution in the case law of the European Committee of Social Rights (ECSR).

Lorenzo Cecchetti's chapter defines and contextualises the legal approach taken by the CJEU in its case law relating to trade unions in the twenty-first century. Most notably, it explores the extent to which the judicialisation of social rights in the EU, particularly after the entry into force of the EU's Charter of Fundamental Rights (CFR) as a binding instrument in 2009 following the adoption of the Treaty of Lisbon, can be seen as a manifestation of trade union power. This analysis thus considers the recourse to law by unions as a way for unions to promote solidarity by taking a closer look at the CJEU's case law, with a focus on cases where unions have been involved in proceedings which relate to EU social law and fundamental rights as enshrined in Title III ('Equality') and Title IV ('Solidarity') of the CFR. Specific attention is devoted to a recent judgement of the Court in 2019, Case C-55/18, *Federación de Servicios de Comisiones Obreras (CCOO) v Deutsche Bank SAE*. This judgement is characterised by important factors with immediate relevance for the trade union movement, including the court's examination of the CFR's provisions which, in conjunction with relevant EU secondary law provisions, have been used by CJEU as the basis for the effective implementation of certain social rights, including as regards the limitation of working time on both a daily and weekly basis. This has resulted in an increase in the standard of protection of social rights in the EU vis-à-vis the national level, since, for example, according to the *Tribunal Supremo* (Supreme Court of Spain)'s case law, Spanish law did not previously lay down any obligation of general application on employers to establish a system that would enable the duration of time worked each day by each worker to be measured. This judgement will be presented against the backdrop of the now notorious case law on the interaction and balancing operation between economic freedoms and collective social rights, in the *Laval-quartet* as well as in some more recent cases.

Rolle Alho's chapter discusses trade union responses to labour migration in Europe since the turn of the millennium. This has been an era of substantial change in migration patterns, which has also seen the increased salience of migration in political discourse in many parts of Europe. Unions in an increasing number of countries have moved to consider what migration means to them and how they should react to it. Unions have increasingly accepted that people move across national borders, and, in many cases, have shown solidarity and have adopted policies aimed at integrating migrant workers within their ranks and by defending their interests. Typically, a key union demand is that employers do not undercut wages and working conditions when employing migrants in order to prevent a 'race to the bottom' in working conditions. However, union responses to labour migration have not been uniform: in some countries unions have defended restrictive national-level labour migration policies, while others have favoured a more liberal approach. This chapter explores this variation and seeks to illustrate trade union approaches to migration at the national level in a variety of European countries. Labour migration is understood here as encompassing work-based cross-country migration, which is governed by state labour migration policies, and includes short-term work-based migration, including posted workers.

The following four chapters provide an analysis of a particular case—France, a case that has traditionally been difficult to classify given that it has features of both the CME and MME groups. Firstly, **Julia López López's** contribution analyses the spillover effects of strategies forged by French trade unions to defend the rights of workers against the brutal process of collective dismissals implemented by France Télécom (now Orange) and the spate of suicides among employees that occurred between 2008 and 2011 in the wake of those dismissals. The analysis presented here emphasises the role that labour protests along with legal action (and legal actors, including judges) can play in union strategies. In this examination, López López highlights the role of solidarity both when it comes to relevant legislation and in the actions of organised labour. In the story analysed here, after a long period of negotiation between labour and management, the judicial efforts of unions met with success when judges condemned the firm for institutional harassment (Hatzfeld, 2016). The judicial sentence reinforced labour rights relating to dignity and health and safety at work, conceptualising these rights from a collective perspective. The sentence cites EU law extensively, presenting a legal foundation that includes major references to collective rights and various efforts to foster the principle of solidarity. Indeed, the Charter of Fundamental Rights of the European Union protects the freedom of association, collective bargaining and the right to strike under its title IV on solidarity. However, the institutional basis for the defence of collective rights is only part of the story told here, as collective action by workers involving various strategies is a crucial element of the process of achieving solidarity and defending labour rights.

Following this, **Dominique Andolfatto and Dominique Labbé** review the current state of trade unionism in France. For Andolfatto, French trade unionism often appears to be relatively dynamic which (for outsiders at least) may present an image of unions being in a relatively strong position. In fact, the rate of unionisation in France has fallen substantially in recent decades and has become one of the lowest in the industrialised world. This can be at least partly explained by a number of factors which, while not unique to France, are particularly marked in that country. First of all, there are exogenous reasons related to the system of production (that go beyond mere unemployment), trade union discrimination (which, while limited and subject to criminal sanctions, remains present in some workplaces) and cultural changes (given the rise of individualism and new forms of management and activism). Meanwhile, important endogenous influences are often minimised or overlooked. This includes the gradual distinction of stable workplace teams and the ambience they created in many workplaces. A further factor relates to the increased professionalisation of many trade union representatives which has resulted in the emergence of a gap between union officers and grassroots members and a perceived politicisation and lack of independence on the part of unions by many workers. As French unions have reached such a low ebb, these authors ask if there are signs that this period of 'deunionisation' has ended? While membership levels remain weak, which can only reduce the influence of unions in the social arena, it is also clear that unions remain intimately involved in collective bargaining processes and social policy-making. This implies a change in the very nature of trade union organisations in France, which challenge the image of French unions as mass member organisations. Ideological motivations for union membership are also declining, while more utilitarian motivations for membership are on the rise, as the authors explore in this chapter.

Sylvie Contrepois explores some of the reforms introduced by French President Emmanuel Macron in 2017 that undermine trade union action, especially in the field of health and safety at work where unions used to be highly effective. The chapter explores the effects of these reforms in the energy sector—one of the leading union strongholds in France. For this contribution, Contrepois first makes projections of the number of employee representatives who could be elected within the framework of the new CSE (Comité social et économique/Social and economic committee) in nine companies in the electricity and gas industries. From this analysis, it becomes clear that setting up a CSE on the strict basis of legal texts would lead to a reduction in the number of seats of permanent delegates ranging from 53.5% to just below 80%. The rate of reduction would be particularly high in the case of companies where the number of CHSCTs (Commissions de hygiène santé, sécurité et conditions de travail/hygiene, safety and working conditions committees) had been extended by collective agreement. The chapter then analyses the negotiation processes and the collective agreements that effectively established the new CSEs. From this analysis, it appears that the unions have only very marginally succeeded in negotiating more favourable provisions than what had been provided by the law, which highlights a clear risk of further union decline at the local level.

In their chapter, **Barry Colfer and Yoann Bazin** consider the emergence of the 'Gilets Jaunes' (yellow vest) movement in France in 2018 and the implications this has for trade unions. This disparate movement initially formed primarily to protest against the introduction of a new petrol tax alongside what would become a long list of grievances associated with President Macron's reform agenda following his election in 2017. After describing the emergence of this movement, the chapter reviews its initial successes, as the aforementioned fuel tax was dropped. Notably, the movement manifested without the support and beyond the structures of any trade union, political party or civil society organisations, being coordinated almost exclusively online via social media. The activities of the Gilets Jaunes are contrasted with the strike that was coordinated by the CGT union at SNCF—the national railway—earlier in 2018 and considers how the looser, leaderless structure of the Gilets Jaunes allowed for an effective but potentially unsustainable movement to emerge in opposition to similar issues and grievances as the unions had opposed at SNCF. The chapter also considers how the emergence of the Gilets Jaunes challenges key elements of social movement organisation theory. Building on Zygmunt Bauman's analysis of 'liquid modernity' and the growing body of work on 'fluid organisations', this chapter shows how movements such as these challenge the traditional understanding of leadership and purpose within social movement organisations, and considers how this might present new ways to view distributed leadership in complex, fluid organisations more generally.

Moving away from France, **Martin Štefko's** contribution addresses the nature of trade unionism, industrial democracy and trade union power in the Czech Republic. The Czech trade union movement can be seen as a manifestation of that country's liberal market economic (LME) regime, as social partner activities are primarily coordinated through hierarchies and market mechanisms. From a broader historical perspective, the Czech trade union movement represents an unusual picture of a totalitarian unified model, with a single trade union organisation that has existed for decades and that has developed and adjusted since the country became an open democratic society after the fall of communism in 1989. However, the transition period was not fully successful, and since 1989 the Czech labour movement has experienced a sustained fall in membership. To reverse the trend, unions have sought to implement new strategies with varying levels of success. The miners' trade unions have been extremely successful in relative terms in this regard by relying on a range of novel strategies that this chapter explores. This includes by engaging in legal avenues and by successfully influencing the development of the country's emergent welfare state to their members' benefit.

Eusebi Colàs-Neila considers trade union participation and new forms of collective action in Spain, using recent pension reforms as a case study. There are several factors that weaken the influence and traditional position of Spanish trade unions as relevant political and socio-economic actors. Despite this, their efforts to adapt to the new context must be emphasised, as they have explored and implemented new strategies and instruments, thus promoting solidarity through the creation of new networked alliances with other stakeholders. This contribution is focused on the democratic mechanisms of participation in regulatory processes used by unions and how they have adapted their approaches and tools of collective action to continue having an influence in this field. In particular, the role that unions have played in the reforms of Spain's public pension system is analysed as a case study, using a diachronic perspective as it helps to combine tradition and innovation as regards the actors involved and instruments used. The unions' participation has traditionally been articulated through the so-called Toledo Pact system of corporatist decision-making. Although the government departed from this mechanism, disrupting the unions' capacity to mobilise influence, organised labour has been able to create new alliances with NGOs and other associations, and have collectively explored the use of alternative legislative procedures, such as the popular legislative initiative. Additionally, the rise of new grassroots movements of pensioners in response to the discontent generated with pension reforms and the role of the most representative trade unions in the country in this regard are also considered as new manifestations of solidarity and influence on the part of organised labour in Spain.

Torsten Geelan looks at Denmark, which has often been considered the industrial relations (IR) model par excellence with high levels of union membership, union density and collective bargaining coverage (Due & Madsen, 2008). Over recent decades, however, the institutional context has transformed considerably. One of the most worrying trends for unions is the decline in membership, after many years as one of the few advanced European economies in which union membership remained steady (Blanchflower, 2007). This paper presents a case study of the '*Are you OK?*' campaign launched in 2012 by the Danish national-level social partners that aimed to increase knowledge of collective bargaining and collective organisation among the public, with a focus on people aged 20–40 with a view to improving union membership among this cohort. This contribution examines the campaign's main messages and the forms of communication used, and ultimately assesses how effective the initiative was at connecting with young people.

Mona Aranea's chapter focuses on German trade unions' engagement with the European Commission initiative for fair minimum wages in Europe. The minimum wage initiative constitutes an attempt for a countermovement from above against an unregulated and thus unsustainable European labour market (Harriss, 2010; Seeliger & Sommer, 2019). The research considers how far German unions can formulate political positions at EU-level that are distinct from or opposed to employer views. In the current context of widespread worker discontent towards the EU, trade unions are often perceived as members of discredited elites rather than defenders of working-class interests. Indeed, in Germany, trade unions are deeply embedded within the traditional national elite. Trade union representatives participate in company management as members of supervisory boards. Employees enjoy comparatively high levels of representation through works councils and via collective bargaining mechanisms. German multinational corporations also benefit disproportionately from Europe's integrated yet disembedded labour market (Hardy, 2014). Within this context, German unions have managed to secure partial benefits for workers. For example, the powerful alliance between unions and employers in metal and chemical sectors has in the past regularly resulted in comparatively high wage increases despite high sectoral exposure to global competition (Lehndorff, 2012, p. 94; see also Schulten, 2018). The large industry unions IG Metall and IG BCE tend to operate as part of a distributional coalition with employers (Höpner, 2007). This chapter considers how the deep embeddedness of German unions' among national industrial elites generates relatively high levels of influence on the part of organised labour, but also high levels of sensitivity for employer demands within a national competitive alliance.

David Coats charts the decline in trade union membership and influence in the United Kingdom (UK). For Coats, this is arguably the most striking and far-reaching change in the UK labour market over the last 40 years. In 1979 one in every two employees was a member of a trade union and almost four in every five had their pay and conditions of employment determined by a collective agreement. Today, fewer than one in four employees (23.4%) is a trade union member and collective bargaining covers a similar proportion of the workforce. Trade union members tend to be older than the general working population and are concentrated in the public sector. Fewer than one in seven employees in the private sector is a trade union member (13.2%). Contrary to the established stereotypes, most trade union members are women (56%), largely because professionals and associate professionals in the public sector are relatively well organised (BEIS, 2019). Within this context, Coats does not outline any detailed programme of reform for unions but rather highlights some possibilities for the revival of workplace voice institutions in the UK in these unpromising times.

Jan Czarzasty and Adam Rogalewski explore the orientation of Polish trade unions vis-a-vis the rise of populism in that country. During the last five years, Polish trade unions have operated under the right-wing populist PiS (Prawo i Sprawiedliwość/Law and Justice) Party-led government, elected in 2015. Although the party came to power on the basis of a robust social agenda, mirroring to a large extent the unions' own policies, the government has shown strong authoritarian tendencies, which have left their mark on social dialogue in Poland. The chapter analyses the strategies of the Polish labour movement in their response to the populist government by focusing on both the European and national contexts. The contribution examines unions' response to the revision of the Posted Workers directive and the important role of European trade union solidarity in supporting Polish unions' stance against the government. Secondly, the chapter focuses on the protests of public service workers, including: uniform services, teachers and civil servants employed by the Ministry of Justice. In particular, a protest by teachers was one the largest strikes in the recent history of Polish industrial relations, which maximised the opportunities associated with the network society by allowing unions to evolve into a more civic movement. In spite of the fact the PiS has 'hijacked' some major union postulates including, for example, increasing the minimum wage, the labour movement has been able to deploy some successful resistance strategies. For example, the unions have tried to use the European context of industrial legislation by challenging the government at that level. Unions have also focused on pay rise campaigns for public service workers to underline the hypocrisy of the PiS-led government, which was willing to increase the wages of workers but not those directly employed by its own government in the public sector.

In the concluding chapter, **Richard Hyman** draws together the themes and ideas presented in this volume and offers a reading of the current context of trade unions in the third decade of the twenty-first century. Hyman first discusses the extent to which 'varieties of capitalism' still persist and the implications of changes in industrial relations regimes for trade unions. Second, the author considers some of the ambiguities of EU regulation and whether 'Social Europe' is (still) a bulwark against market liberalisation. Third, drawing on Karl Polanyi, Hyman examines the rise of precarious work situations, including the emergence of the 'platform economy'. Fourth, Hyman comments on the impact of COVID-19 and the climate crisis, before offering some final remarks about trade union responses in Europe today.

BIBLIOGRAPHY

Autor, D.H. 2019. What Works in the Future? *NBER, Working Paper 25588*, available at: http://www.nber.org/papers/w25588, accessed on 30 April 2021.

Baccaro & Howell. 2017. *Trajectories of Neoliberal Transformation*, Cambridge, UK: CUP.

Colfer, B. 2020. Public policy responses to COVID-19 in Europe, *European Policy Analysis*, 06(02), pp. 126–137, https://doi.org/10.1002/epa2.1097.

Crouch, C. 1993. *Industrial Relations and European State Traditions*, Oxford: OUP.

Esping-Andersen, G. 1990. *The Three Worlds of Welfare Capitalism*, Cambridge: Polity Press.

Freeman, R.B. & Medoff, J.L. 1984. *What Do Unions Do?*, Cambridge MA: National Bureau of Economic Research.

Flanders, A. 1970. *Management and Unions: The Theory and Reform of Industrial Relations*, London: Faber.

Galbraith, J.K. 1952. *American Capitalism: The Concept of Countervailing Power*, Boston: Houghton Mifflin Company.

Gallie, D. 2007. Production regimes and the quality of employment in Europe. *Annual Review of Sociology*, 33(1), pp. 85–104.

Gumbrell-McCormick, R. & Hyman, R. 2018. *Trade Unions in Western Europe; Hard Times, Hard Choices*, Oxford: OUP.

Hall, P. & Soskice, D. 2001. *Varieties of Capitalism: The Institutional Foundations of Comparative Advantage*, Oxford: OUP.

Hancké, B., Rhodes, M. & Thatcher, M. 2007. *Beyond Varieties of Capitalism: Conflict, Contradictions, and Complementarities in the European Economy*, Oxford: OUP.

Hassel, A. 2014. *Adjustments in the Eurozone: Varieties of Capitalism and the Crisis in Southern Europe*, LEQS Paper No. 76/2014. London: LSE. 01 May. Available at: http://www.lse.ac.uk/europeanInstitute/LEQS_Discussion_Paper_Series/LEQSPaper76.pdf [Accessed 30 April 2021].

Hogan, J. & Nolan., P., 2007. Industrial Relations. In *Blackwell Encyclopedia of Sociology*. Ritzer, G (ed.), London: Blackwell.

Kelly, J. 1998. *Rethinking Industrial Relations: Mobilization, Collectivism and Long Waves*, London: Routledge.

Lehndorff, S., Dribbusch, H. & Schulten, T. (eds). 2018. *Rough waters European trade unions in a time of crises*, Brussels: ETUI.

Marginson, P. & Sisson, K. 2004. *European Integration and Industrial Relations: Multi-Level Governance in the Making*, London: Palgrave MacMillan.

Molina, O. & Rhodes, M. 2007. The Political Economy of Adjustment in Mixed Market Economies: A Study of Spain and Italy. In Hancke, B., Rhodes, M. & Thatcher, M. (eds.) *Beyond Varieties of Capitalism: Conflict, Contradictions, and Complementarities in the European Economy*. Oxford: OUP.

Müller-Jentsch, W. 1985. Trade unions as intermediary organizations. *Economic and Industrial Democracy*, 6(1), pp. 3–33.

Neufeind, M., Ranft, F., & O'Reilly, J. (eds.). 2018, *Work in the Digital Age: Challenges of the Fourth Industrial Revolution*, Rowman & Littlefield; London.

Prosser, T. 2019. *European Labour Movements in Crisis: From Indecision to Indifference* (1st ed.). Manchester University Press.

Schmidt, V.A. 2002. *The Futures of European Capitalism*, Oxford: OUP.

Streeck, W. 1998. The internationalization of industrial relations in Europe: prospects and problems. *Politics & Society*, 26(4), pp. 429–459.

Thompson, E.P. 1963. *The Making of the English Working Class*, London: Penguin.

Visser, J. & Dølvik, J.E. 2008. *The difficult birth of a European industrial relations system*, Formula (Free movement, labour market regulation, and multilevel governance in the enlarged EU/EEA - a Nordic and Comparative perspective No.5, University of Oslo. Available at: https://www.jus.uio.no/ifp/english/research/projects/freemov/publications/papers/WP5-Visser-2008.pdf [Accessed 30 April 2021].

Wright, C., Wood, A., Trevor, J., McLaughlin, C., Huang, C., Geelan, T., Colfer, B., Brown, W. 2019. Towards a new web of rules: An international review of institutional experimentations to strengthen labour standards, *Employee Relations*, 39(2), pp. 313-330.

CHAPTER 2

The Right to Collective Bargaining for Economically Dependent Workers with a Self-Employed Status

Pieter Pecinovsky

1 Introduction

As stated in the introduction to this book, one of the key functions of trade unions is to provide a "countervailing power" to the socio-economic dominance of capital. One of the important means to exert a countervailing power is by way of collective bargaining, which is protected in Europe by a fundamental right.[1] The right to collective bargaining evolved during the twentieth and twenty-first centuries as an important fundamental right and one of the primordial international labour standards as asserted by the International Labour Organisation (ILO). However, industrial relations have changed radically over recent decades. Perhaps most notably, the working patterns and the nature of

[1] See part 2.

P. Pecinovsky (✉)
Faculty of Law, KU Leuven, Institute for Labour Law, Leuven, Belgium
e-mail: pieter.pecinovsky@vow.be

© The Author(s), under exclusive license to Springer Nature Switzerland AG 2022
B. Colfer (ed.), *European Trade Unions in the 21st Century*, St Antony's Series, https://doi.org/10.1007/978-3-030-88285-3_2

the employment relationship have undergone a process of flexibilisation in the post-fordist era since the 1970s.[2] The promotion of the concept of "flexicurity"[3] (reference?), the growth of temporary and part-time work, and the digitalisation of the economy, which, taken together, have given rise to the on-demand or platform economy which has created a new set of challenges for workers and representatives in the world of work. Today, the labour market is no longer a simple dichotomy between capital (employers) and labour (employees) with traditional full-time employed workers on one side and the wide spectrum of independent workers on the other, who, in a traditional view, would not fall under the scope of the right to collective bargaining, as their relationship with companies or employees is of a purely contractual nature. Today, quasi-independent freelancers, consultants, crowd workers and platform workers are often strongly economically dependent on a certain employer and the divide between them and real employees has become unclear. This raises the question whether these economically dependent workers, who are characterised by a similar precarious power ratio as traditional employees are, should not be awarded collective bargaining rights. Such a move could strike a better and fairer balance in the power relationship between economically dependent workers and their client-companies.

This contribution will first look at the sources and content of the right to collective bargaining. Next, we will study the personal scope of this fundamental right, which will naturally lead to the case law of the Court of Justice of the European Union with regard to the question of whether collective bargaining is compatible with the economic freedoms and primacy of competition within the European Union. However, the

---

[2] See i.a., A. Amin, *Post-fordism: a reader*, Oxford, Oxford Blackwell, 1994, 435 p.; R. Blanpain, "The world of work in the XXI Century. From globalization to flexicurity" in F. Hendrickx (ed.), *Flexicurity and the Lisbon agenda*, Antwerpen, Intersentia, 2008, 1–19; M. DE VOS, "Arbeidsrecht in transitie" in I. Boone, I. Claeys and L. Laurysen (eds.), *Liber amoricum Hubert Bocken*, Brugge, die Keure, 2009, 591–593; A.J.M. Roobeek, "The crisis in fordism and the rise of a new technological paradigm", *Futures* 1987, vol. 19, afl. 2, 130–132; A. Tauss, "Contextualizing the Current Crisis: Post-Fordism, Neoliberal Restructuring, and Financialization", *Colombia Internacional* 2012, vol. 76, 54–55; F. Traxler, "Bargaining (de)centralization, macroeconomic performance and control over the employment relationship", *British Journal of Industrial Relations* 2003, vol. 23, afl. 1, 2.

[3] T. Wilthagen, F. Tros, H. Van Lieshout, "Towards 'Flexicurity'? Balancing Flexibility and Security in EU Member States, *European Journal of Social Security* 2004, vol. 6, no. 2, 113–136.

piece de resistance is left for the end: the ECSR's 2018 decision in the case of the Irish Congress of Trade Unions (ICTU) vs. Ireland (Complaint No.123/2016)[4] has given a good indication towards a definitive answer to the question of whether economically dependent workers should be awarded collective bargaining rights or not.

2 THE RIGHT TO COLLECTIVE BARGAINING

There is no single definition of "collective bargaining". Bamber, Sheldon and Gan (2010) broadly define collective bargaining as "*a process of accommodation of interests, covering all types of bipartite or tripartite discussions, concerning labour and industrial relations which may have a direct or indirect impact on the interests of employees or groups of employees*".[5] This process normally takes place between the social partners (bipartite), in particular employers' organisations and employees' organisations (trade unions). In the case of tripartite collective bargaining, the government is also involved.

The right to collective bargaining has a legal basis in many national constitutional traditions, but this contribution will restrict itself to the most important international and European legal sources of the right. With regard to the ILO, it can be found in the important Convention no. 98 concerning the Application of the Principles of the Right to Organise and to Bargain Collectively of 1949, one of the eight fundamental international labour standards of the ILO. The provisions of this convention are rather vague, and the scope is limited to the private sector. Therefore, Recommendation 91 concerning collective agreements of 1951, the Labour Administration Convention (no. 150) of 1978 and Convention no. 154 concerning the promotion of collective bargaining of 1989 provide some clarifications. Next, Convention no. 151 concerning the Protection of the Right to Organise and the Procedures for Determining Conditions of Employment in the Public Service of 1978 lays down the more limited collective bargaining right for workers in the public sector.

---

[4] European Committee of Social Rights, Decision on the merits of 12 September 2018, Irish Congress of Trade Unions (ICTU) v. Ireland, Complaint No.123/2016.

[5] G. Bamber, P. Sheldon and B. Gan, "Collective Bargaining: international developments and challenges" in R. Blanpain (ed.), *Comparative Labour Law and Industrial Relations in Industrialized Market Economies,* Alphen aan den Rijn, Kluwer Law International, 2010, 613–614.

These latter instruments do not have the same importance as Convention no. 98 and have been ratified by fewer of the ILO member states.

Next the Council of Europe has two legal instruments of importance to the right. First there is Article 6 of the (revised) European Social Charter (ESC) which contains provisions on social dialogue, conciliation and arbitration procedures and collective action. Article 6(2) ESC provides a clear right to collective bargaining where it states that the Charter entails *"an obligation to promote, where necessary and appropriate, machinery for voluntary negotiations between employers or employers' organisations and workers' organisations, with a view to the regulation of terms and conditions of employment by means of collective agreements"*. Also, ESC's more renowned sibling, the European Convention of Human Rights (ECHR), offers protection to the right to collective bargaining through its Article 11 on the freedom of association. Although this article does not refer explicitly to the right to collective bargaining, the European Court of Human Rights (ECtHR) has recognised that the right to collective bargaining is an essential element of article 11 ECHR in the famous *Demir and Baykara* case of 2008.[6]

Finally, the EU has included the right to collective bargaining in article 28 of the Charter of Fundamental Rights of the EU and in the 8th principle of the European Pillar of Social Rights. However, the scope of the Charter is limited to measures which fall under the scope of EU law and the Social Pillar is not a legally binding instrument. Also, the Social Policy chapter of the Treaty on the Functioning of the European Union (TFEU) refers explicitly to the importance of social dialogue and articles 144 and 154 TFEU set up a system of EU collective bargaining, which makes it possible for European social partners to conclude framework agreements at EU level.

The right to collective bargaining includes both a positive obligation to promote collective bargaining and a negative obligation on the part

---

[6] ECtHR 12 November 2008, no. 34503/97, Demir and Bakaya/Turkey; F. Dorssemont, "The Right to Form and to Join Trade Unions for the Protection of His Interests under Article 11 ECHR", *ELLJ* 2010, vol. 1, no. 2, 220–222; K.D. Ewing and J. Hendy, "The dramatic implications of Demir and Baykara", *Industrial Law Journal* 2010, vol. 39, no. 1, 2–4; A. Jacobs, "Article 11 ECHR: The right to bargain collectively under article 11 ECHR" in F. Dorssemont, K. Lörcher and I. Schömann (eds.), *The European Convention on Human Rights and the employment Relation*, Oxford, Hart Publishing, 2013, 311–314; R. Nordeide, "Demir & Baykara V. Turkey. App. No. 34503/97", *American Journal Of international Law* 2009, vol. 103, no. 3, 567–574.

of public authorities not to intervene in negotiations (under the principle of the autonomy of the social partners and the voluntary nature of negotiations). By examining the different legal instruments, the case law of the supervisory mechanisms and the relevant legal doctrine together with industrial relations research, it is possible to distinguish the different elements of the fundamental right.[7] These elements are referred to as "indicators" and are useful in identifying possible restrictions on the right to collective bargaining. Below, a precise overview of the twenty-two identifiable indicators of collective bargaining is provided, in order to give the reader a clear idea of the basic content of the right as it stands.

1. Collective bargaining is a precondition of freedom of association. It must be possible for voluntary, free, independent and representative trade unions and employers' organisations to be set up and grow (with public support where necessary) and to not be undermined.[8]
2. The condition of representativeness entails that social partners or governments shall install objective procedures for recognising the most representative organisations (in so far as only these may bargain collectively) with reasonable quotas if representative quotas are imposed.[9]

---

[7] See P. Pecinovsky, *EU economic governance en het recht op collectief onderhandelen*, Bruges, die Keure, 2019, 305–316; P. Pecinovsky, "EU economic governance and the right to collective bargaining, part. 1: Standard and extreme governance and the indicators and limits of the right to collective bargaining", *ELLJ* 2018, vol. 9, no. 4, 381–384.

[8] Art. 20 and 23 Universal Declaration of Fundamental Rights; ILO Convention no. 87; ILO Convention no. 98; ILO Recommendation no. 163, art. 11 ECHR; art. 5 and 6 ESC; art. 12 and 28 EU Charter; ECtHR 27 October 1975, no. 4464/70, National Union of Belgian Police/Belgium, §38; ECtHR 2 February 1976, no. 5614/72, Swedish Engine Driver's Union/Sweden, §39; ECtHR 12 November 2008, no. 34503/97, Demir and Bakaya/Turkey, §109; ILO, Freedom of Association Compilation of decisions 2018, 1232; ILO, General Survey 2012, 239–241; ECSR, Digest 2018, 94–97; ILO CFA, 363th report, case no. 2780 (Ireland), 809; ECSR, Conclusions XVI-1, Ireland, 419; ECSR, Conclusions XI-1, Denmark, 72; D. HARRIS and J. DARCY, *The European Social Charter*, Ardsley, Transnational Publishers, 2001, 101–102; A.M. Swiatkowski, *Charter of Social Rights of the Council of Europe*, Alphen aan den Rijn, Kluwer Law International, 2007, 216.

[9] ILO Convention no. 98; ILO Recommendation no. 163; art. 6, §2 ESC; ILO, General Survey 2012, 224; ILO, Freedom of Association Compilation of Decisions 2018, 1350 an 1354–1356; ECSR, Digest 2018, 95 and 100; ILO Committee of experts, Observation, adopted 2016, published 106th ILC session (2017), Croatia; ECSR, Conclusions

3. Collective bargaining with employees' organisations (i.e. trade unions) should be preferred to negotiations with non-organised employees.[10]
4. The personal scope of the right should not be interpreted too strictly (e.g. as only applying to workers in the private sector).[11]
5. The material scope of the negotiations is not limited to traditional working conditions and is, in principle, determined by the parties (i.e. there should be no restrictive interpretation).[12]
6. The social partners are free to determine their own relationship and procedures. If this is not done spontaneously, the state shall promote and support it.[13]
7. Collective bargaining can take place at any level (national/industry/sectoral/company/...), and it is up to the

---

2006, Albanië, 41–42; ECSR, Conclusie XV-1, Frankrijk, ESCEx 2000, 254–257; P. Pecinovsky, "Het recht op collectief onderhandelen en het recht op collectieve actie in het Europees Sociaal Handvest" in S. Van Drooghenbroeck, F. Dorssemont and G. Van Limberghen (eds.), *Europees Sociaal Handvest, Sociale rechten and grondrechten op de werkvloer*, Bruges, die Keure, 2016, 248.

[10] ILO Convention no. 98; art. 3 ILO Convention no. 154; art. 6, §2 ESC; §2, 1) ILO Recommendation no. 91; ILO, Freedom of Association Compilation of Decisions 2018, 1342–1349; ILO CFA, 340th report, case no. 2079 (Colombia), 68; ECSR, Conclusions XI-1, United Kingdom, art. 6, §2; ECSR, Conclusions 2014, Armenia, art. 6, §2; B. Gernigon, A. Oderon and H. Guido, "ILO Principles concerning collective bargaining", *International Labour Review* 2000, vol. 139, no. 1, 50–52.

[11] ILO Convention no. 98; ILO Recommendation no. 91; art. 6, §2 ESC; ECtHR 12 November 2008, no. 34503/97, Demir and Bakaya/Turkey, §96–108; ECSR, Collective complaint no. 83/2012, decision on the admissibility and the merits of 2 December 2013, European Confederation of Police (EuroCOP)/Ireland; ILO, General Survey 2012, 168; ILO, Freedom of Association Compilation of Decisions 2018, 1239–1260; ECSR, Conclusions I, Statement of Interpretation; B. Creighton, "Freedom of Association" in R. Blanpain and C. Engels (eds.), *Comparative Labour Law and Industrial Relations in Industrialized Market Economies*, Alphen aan den Rijn, Kluwer Law International, 2010, 300.

[12] ILO Convention no. 98; ILO Convention no. 151; ILO Convention no. 154; ILO Recommendation no. 91; art. 6, §2 ESC; ILO, General Survey 2012, 215; ILO, Freedom of Association Compilation of Decisions 2018, 1289–1312; ILO CFA, 344th report, case no. 2502 (Griekenland), 1022; ECSR, Conclusions 2014, Montenegro, art. 6, §2 ESC; B. GERNIGON, A. ODERON and H. GUIDO, "ILO Principles concerning collective bargaining", *International Labour Review* 2000, vol. 139, no. 1, 50–52.

[13] ILO Convention no. 98; ILO Convention no. 154; art. 6, §2 ESC; ILO, General Survey 2012, 241–242; ECSR, Digest 2018, 99.

social partners to choose the appropriate level.[14] This indicator also addresses the issue of forced decentralisation.

8. The hierarchy (legal coordination) of the negotiation levels shall be established.[15]
9. Collective agreements take legal precedence over individual employment agreements (unless the social partners agree otherwise).[16]
10. Negotiators shall have access to appropriate training and information, which are deemed necessary for the negotiations.[17]

---

[14] ILO Convention no. 98; Art. 6, §2 ESC; ILO Recommendation no. 163; ILO CFA, 321th report, case no. 1975 (Canada), 117; ILO CFA, 340th report, case no. 2267 (Nigeria), 152; ILO CFA, 371th report, case no. 2947 (Spain), 454; ILO CFA, 365th report, case no. 2820 (Greece), 997; ILO Committee of experts, Observation—adopted 2012, published 102nd ILC session (2013), Right to Organise and Collective Bargaining Convention, 1949 (No. 98), Greece; see follow-up in ILO Committee of experts, Observation—adopted 2013, published 103rd ILC session (2014), Right to Organise and Collective Bargaining Convention, 1949 (No. 98), Greece; ILO, General Survey 2012, 222; ILO Freedom of Association Compilation of Decisions 2018, 1404–1412; ECSR, Conclusions 2010, Italy, art. 6, § 2 ESC; B. Gernigon, "ILO Convention No. 98: An instrument still topical 50 years after its adoption" in M. Ozaki and U. Fleschenhar (eds.), *Collective bargaining: A fundamental principle, a right, a Convention, Labour Education* 1999, vol. 1–2, no. 114–115, 29; A. LO FARO, "Italian labour law in recession: legislative actions and judicial reactions", *European Journal of Social Law* 2014, no. 1, 84–85; K. Lörcher, "Legal and judicial international avenues: the (Revised) European Social Charter" in N. Bruun, K. Lörcher and I. Schömann (eds.), *The economic and financial crisis and collective labour law in Europe*, Oxford, Hart Publishing, 2014, 282–288; S. Clauwaert and I. Schömann, "The crisis and national labour reforms", *ELLJ* 2012, vol. 2, no. 1, 58 and 63; M.L. Rodríguez, "Labour rights in crisis in the Eurozone: the Spanish case", *European Journal of Social Law* 2014, no. 1, 136; M. Yannakourou, "Legal challenges to austerity measures affecting work rights at domestic and international level. The case of Greece", *European Journal of Social Law* 2014, no. 1–2, 32.

[15] ILO Convention no. 98; ILO Recommendation no. 163; Art. 6, §2 ESC; ILO, General Survey 2012, 223; ECSR, Conclusions 2006, 2010 and 2014, Slovenia, art. 6, §2; ECSR, Conclusions 2004, Estonia, art. 6, § 2 ESC; ECSR, Conclusions 2006, Albania, art. 6, § 2 ESC; ECSR, Conclusions 2010, Armenia, art. 6, § 2 ESC; Conclusions XVII-1, The Netherlands, art. 6, § 2 ESC.

[16] ILO Convention no. 98; Art. 6, §2 ESC; ILO Recommendation no. 91; ILO Recommendation no. 163; ILO CFA, 330th report, case no. 2178 (Denmark), 582; ILO CFA, 295th report, case no. 1698 (New Zealand), 255; 329th Report, Case no. 2172, 354; ILO, Freedom of Association Compilation of Decisions 2018, 1510–1513; ECSR, Conclusions 2010, Georgia, art. 6, §2 ESC.

[17] ILO Convention no. 98; ILO Convention no. 153; ILO Recommendation no. 163; Art. 6, §2 ESC; Art. 6, §2 ESC; ILO, General Survey 2012, 241 and 244; ECSR,

11. Any maximum period of time imposed for the negotiations should be proportionate.[18]
12. Only voluntary procedures can be laid down in order to help the parties find a solution in the most autonomous way possible in the event of a conflict during the negotiations (i.e. there should be no compulsory arbitration).[19]
13. Encouraging (usually by the employer) renunciations by the employees of their right to collective bargaining are problematic (e.g. promising additional benefits for employees who do not support/join a trade unions in order to make collective bargaining impossible).[20]
14. The parties should (in principle) not be forced to negotiate (or to stay at the negotiation table, as an initial government order for the social partners to sit together is often deemed acceptable).[21]

Conclusions 2014, Lithuania, art. 6, §2 ESC; ECSR, Conclusions XX-3, Poland, art. 6, §2 ESC.

[18] ILO Convention no. 98; ILO, Freedom of Association Compilation of Decisions 2018, 1501.

[19] ILO Convention no. 98; ILO Convention no. 151; ILO Recommendation no. 163; art. 6, §3 and §3 ESC; ILO, General Survey 1994, 247; ILO, Freedom of Association Compilation of Decisions 2018, 1415–1419; ILO CFA, 330th report, case no. 2170 (Iceland), 888; ILO CFA, 378th report, case no. 3147 (Norway), 570–571; ECSR, Conclusions XX-3, The Netherlands—Curaçao, art. 6, §2; ECSR, Conclusions 2014, Cyprus, art. 6, §2 ESC; ECSR, Conclusions 2010, Bulgaria, art. 6, §3 ESC; B. Gernigon, A. Oderon and H. Guido, "ILO Principles concerning collective bargaining", *International Labour Review* 2000, vol. 139, no. 1, 50–52.

[20] ILO Convention no. 98; art. 6, §2 ESC; ECtHR 10 January 2002, no. 53574/99, Unison/United Kingdom, unpublished; ILO CFA, 306th report, Case no. 1845 (Peru), 517; ILO CFA, 363th report, case no. 2780 (Ireland), 813; ECSR, Conclusions 2010, United Kingdom, art. 6, §2 ESC; ECSR, Conclusions, XX-3, United Kingdom; ILO Freedom of Association Compilation of Decisions 2018, 1510.

[21] ILO Convention no. 98; art. 11 ECHR; art. 6, §2 ESC; ECtHR 2 February 1976, no. 5614/72, Swedish Engine Driver's Union/Sweden; ECSR 3 July 2013, Collective complaint no. 85/2012, decision on the merits, Swedish Trade Union Confederation (LO) and Swedish Confederation of Professional Employees (TCO) v. Sweden, §51; ILO, General Survey 2012, 200; ILO, Freedom of Association Compilation of Decisions 2018, 1313–1321; ECSR, Digest 2018, 99; ECSR, Conclusions 2006, Slovenia, art. 6, §2; B. Gernigon, "ILO Convention No. 98: An instrument still topical 50 years after its adoption" in M. Ozaki and U. Fleschenhar (eds.), *Collective bargaining: A fundamental principle, a right, a Convention*, Labour Education 1999, vol. 1–2, no. 114–115, 28.

15. The parties (and the state) must respect the principle of good faith and must implement collective agreements that have been concluded.[22]
16. The public authorities should not interfere with the content of collective agreements, e.g. in order to bring them into line with their socio-economic policies.[23]
17. In principle, legislation should not force the renegotiation of rights or conditions already acquired through social dialogue (or collective bargaining).[24]
18. Any restriction on (future) collective bargaining (e.g. setting wage standards, restricting wage indexation) can only be imposed under certain conditions (e.g. exceptional, temporary, necessary conditions or by previous consultation, etc.).[25]

---

[22] ILO Convention no. 98; ILO Recommendation no. 91; art. 11 ECHR; art. 6, §2 ESC; ECtHR 21 November 2006, no. 34503/97, Demir and Baykara/Turkey, §46; ILO, General Survey 2012, 208; ILO, Freedom of Association Compilation of Decisions 2018, 1324–1341; ILO CFA, 327th report, case no. 2118 (Hungary), 639; ILO CFA, 380th report, case no. 2986 (Colombia), 301; ILO CFA, 381th report, case no. 3047 (South-Korea), 171 ILO CFA, 382th report, case no. 1962 (Colombia), 26; The ECSR mentions positively the existence of the principle of good faith in the legislation of several member states in the conclusions on art. 6, §2 ESC: ECSR, Conclusions XIX-3, Former Yugoslav Republic; ECSR, Conclusions 2004, Lithuania; ECSR, Conclusions XV-I, Poland; ECSR, Conclusions XIII-3, Portugal; ECSR, Conclusions VI, Cyprus; B. Gernigon, A. Oderon and H. Guido, "ILO Principles concerning collective bargaining", *International Labour Review* 2000, vol. 139, no. 1, 50–52.

[23] ILO Convention no. 87; ILO Convention no. 98; art. 11 ECHR; art. 5 and 6, §2 ESC; ILO CFA, 320th report, case no. 2030 (Costa Rica), 596; ILO CFA, 344th report, case no. 2502 (Greece), 1018; ILO CFA, 350th report, case no. 2586 (Greece), 840; ILO CFA, 380th report, case no. 3138 (South-Korea), 356; ILO CFA, 381th report, case no. 2927 (Guatemala), 493; ILO CFA, 382th report, case no. 1865 (South-Korea), 96; ILO Freedom of Association Compilation of Decisions 2018, 1424–1436; ECSR, Conclusions XX-3, Spain, art. 6, §2; B. Creighton, "Freedom of Association" in R. Blanpain (ed.), *Comparative Labour Law and Industrial Relations in Industrialized Market Economies*, Alphen aan den Rijn, Kluwer Law International, 2010, 330; A. Pankert, "Government Influence on Wage Bargaining: The Limits Set by International Labour Standards", *International Labour Review* 1983, vol. 122, no. 5, 583–584; A. Schellart and L. Van Weth Rlaak, "De Geus and de loonpolitiek: is de geest weer in de fles?", *SMA* 2005, no. 7–8, 360.

[24] ILO Convention no. 98; ILO Freedom of Association Compilation of Decisions 2018, 1452–1453; B. Gernigon, A. Oderon and H. Guido, "ILO Principles concerning collective bargaining", *International Labour Review* 2000, vol. 139, no. 1, 50–52.

[25] ILO Convention no. 98; art. 6, §2 ESC; ILO, General Survey 2012, 220. ILO, Freedom of Association Compilation of Decisions 2018, 1448–1449 and 1456–1460;

19. The parties determine (in principle) the duration of the collective agreement.[26] However, the survival of the collective agreement (after the end of its term) does not fall under the protection of the right to collective bargaining.[27]
20. The compulsory automatic renewal (or prolongation) of the collective agreement is not permitted.[28]
21. The public authorities may not refuse administrative approval for the declaration of universal applicability (i.e. extension) on account of the collective agreement's content, but purely formal conditions may be imposed. The extension of collective agreements is only possible if the parties are actually the most representative, and sometimes a previous tripartite analysis is required.[29]
22. And finally, if the state itself is a party to the collective agreement, it can only exceptionally hide behind the budgetary situation in order to breach or adjust any agreement.[30]

ILO CFA, 380th report, case no. 3130 (Croatia), 398; ECSR, Conclusions XII-1, The Netherlands, 122–123; ECSR, Conclusions XIII-3, The Netherlands, 123; ECSR, Conclusions XII-1, Denmark, 118; B. Gernigon, A. Oderon and H. Guido, "ILO Principles concerning collective bargaining", *International Labour Review* 2000, vol. 139, no. 1, 50–52.

[26] ILO Convention no. 98; ILO CFA, 320th report, case no. 2047 (Bulgaria), 361; ILO Freedom of Association Compilation of Decisions 2018, 1502–1504.

[27] ILO CFA, 365th report, case no. 2820 (Greece), §996.

[28] ILO Convention no. 98; art. 6, §2 ESC; ILO CFA, 243th report, case no. 1338 (Denmark), 246; ILO Freedom of Association Compilation of Decisions 2018, 1455; ECSR, Conclusions XVII-1, vol. 2, Poland, 380; B. Gernigon, A. Oderon and H. Guido, "ILO Principles concerning collective bargaining", *International Labour Review* 2000, vol. 139, no. 1, 50–52.

[29] ILO Convention no. 98; art. 6, §2 ESC; ILO Recommendation no. 91; ILO, General Survey 2012, 245; ILO, Freedom of Association Compilation of Decisions 2018, 1505–1509; ECSR, Conclusions 2010, General introduction: statement of interpretation 12, 9; A.M. Swiatkowski, *Charter of Social Rights of the Council of Europe*, Alphen aan den Rijn, Kluwer Law International, 2007, 219.

[30] ILO Convention no. 98; art. 6, §2 ESC; ILO Freedom of Association Compilation of Decisions 2018, 1481–1496; ILO Committee of experts, Observation, adopted 2016, published 106th ILC session (2017), Croatia; ILO CFA, 381th report, case no. 3019 (Paraguay), 542; ILO CFA, 378th report, case no. 2183 (Japan), 465; ECSR, Conclusions XIX, Poland, art. 6, §2; ECSR, Conclusions 2014, Moldavia, art. 6, §2; ECSR, Conclusions XII-2, Cyprus, art. 6, §2 ECSR.

3 THE PERSONAL SCOPE OF THE RIGHT TO COLLECTIVE BARGAINING

The most important question for this contribution is whether the right to collective bargaining is restricted to employees "pur sang", meaning a worker in an employment relationship with an employer (usually through an employment contract) and under the supervision of the latter. This question does not focus on the application of the right to public sector employees or civil servants. But it does try to figure out if workers who are not in a (clear) employment relationship could benefit from the right to collective bargaining and if this fundamental right is fully or partially applicable to them.

For the ILO, the answer seems rather straightforward. Not only do the ILO's supervisory institutions award the right to collective bargaining to independent workers who are economically dependent, they also consider that true self-employed persons fall under its protection as well. The Committee of Experts of the ILO holds the view that the right to collective bargaining also applies to self-employed workers and that organisations representing self-employed workers can also invoke the right under Convention No 98.[31] For the ILO, collective bargaining systems that are not adapted to admit these organisations should be reformed.[32] Moreover, the Committee on Freedom of Association directs any government to take the necessary measures to ensure that workers who are self-employed could fully enjoy trade union rights for the purpose of furthering and defending their interest, including by the means of collective bargaining; and to identify, in consultation with the social partners concerned, the particularities of self-employed workers that have a bearing on collective bargaining so as to develop specific collective bargaining mechanisms relevant to self-employed workers, if appropriate.[33]

However, until recently, such a clear recognition was not to be found in the other important legal orders of the EU and the Council of Europe. While ECtHR has not yet had an opportunity to express its opinion on whether the scope of the right to collective bargaining in Article 11

---

[31] ILO, General Survey 2012, 209.

[32] ILO Conference Committee on the Application of Standards, Observations on individual cases—adopted 2016, published 105th ILC session (2016), Right to Organise and Collective Bargaining Convention, 1949 (No. 98), Ireland, 80.

[33] CFA Compilation 2018, § 1285; CFA, 376th Report, Case No. 2786, para. 349.

ECHR should be extended to cover independent workers, the Court of Justice of the European Union (CJEU) has touched upon the issue in relation to EU competition law, which is examined below.

4 The Right to Collective Bargaining versus EU Competition Law

As mentioned above, the CJEU has not directly addressed the question of whether the right to collective bargaining can be applied to independent workers. However, the issue has surfaced in its competition case law. First, it is necessary to remind the reader of the important *Albany* case of 1999[34] which has set forth the principal exemption for collective bargaining from EU competition rules. Next the CJEU has ventured into our discussion with the *FNV Kunsten* case in 2014.

4.1 The Albany Exception

The Albany case concerned a Dutch collective agreement which made it compulsory for companies in the textile sector to join a pension fund in favour of employees. The company—Albany—claimed that this was contrary to free competition that was guaranteed by (current) Article 101 TFEU. Advocate General (AG) Francis Jacobs denied the existence of any fundamental right to collective bargaining in the EU and argued that the collective bargaining agreement was contrary to free competition, which undermined the supremacy of competition policy.[35]

---

[34] CJEU 21 September 1999, no. C-67/96, ECLI:EU:C:1999:430, Albany International BV/Stichting Bedrijfspensioenfonds Textielindustrie, *Jur.* 1999 I-05751; see for similar CJEU case law rechtspraak: CJEU 21 September 2000, no. C-222/98, ECLI:EU:C:2000:475, Hendrik van der Woude/Stichting Beatrixoord, *Jur.* 2000 I-07111; S. EVJU, "The Collective Agreements and Competition Law. The Albany Puzzle, and van der Woude", *International Journal of Comparative Labour Law and Industrial Relations* 2001, vol. 17, no. 2, 165–184; K. Lenaerts and T. Heremans, "Het statuut van collectieve onderhandelingen in de Europese rechtspraak" in INSTITUUT VOOR ARBEIDSRECHT, *Arbeidsrecht tussen wel-zijn en niet-zijn: Liber amicorum Prof. Dr. Othmar Vanachter,* Antwerpen, Intersentia, 2009, 711–714; V. SMEJKAL, "Competition law and the social market economy goal of the EU", *International Comparative Jurisprudence* 2015, vol. 1, no.1, 33–43.

[35] Concl. Adv.-Gen. Jacobs 28 January 1999, no. C-67/96, ECLI:EU:C:1999:28, Albany, Jur. 1999, I-05751, §160–163.

However, the Court did not follow the AG's view and made it clear that the importance of the EU's social policy is equivalent to its competition policy, without, however, going into the existence of the fundamental right to collective bargaining.[36] It also noted that collective agreements are inherently contrary to free competition and should therefore be excluded from the scope of (current) Article 101 TFEU. The CJEU stated: "*It is beyond question that certain restrictions of competition are inherent in collective agreements between organisations representing employers and workers. However, the social policy objectives pursued by such agreements would be seriously undermined if management and labour were subject to Article 85(1) of the Treaty when seeking jointly to adopt measures to improve conditions of work and employment*".[37] With the Albany doctrine, the Court took an important step with regard to the protection of the right to collective bargaining in relation to free competition within the EU.

4.2 The FNV Kunsten Case

A second important case is *FNV Kunsten Informatie en Media* (FNV Arts Information and Media),[38] which concerned a collective agreement prescribing minimum rates for orchestral musicians who were members of the FNV (a major Dutch trade union). The collective agreement applied both to independent musicians who performed services via a contracting agreement and to musicians who performed (the same) work, but as employees of an employer (in this case, the orchestra). However, the Court ruled that the collective agreement can only benefit from the (Albany) exception of Article 101 TFEU if the artists who are not employees are bogusly self-employed (i.e. employees who have the status of self-employed, although in reality they exercise a professional activity

---

[36] CJEU 21 September 1999, Albany, §57–60.

[37] CJEU 21 September 1999, Albany, §59.

[38] CJEU 4 December 2014, no. C-413/13, ECLI:EU:C:2014:2411, FNV Kunsten Informatie en Media/Staat der Nederlanden; V. DE STEFANO, "Non-Standard Work and Limits on Freedom of Association: A Human Rights-Based Approach", *Industrial Law Journal* 2017, vol 46, afl. 2, 193; M. FREEDLAND anc N. COUNTOURIS, "Some Reflections on the 'Personal Scope' of Collective Labour Law", *Industrial Law Journal* 2017, vol. 46, afl. 1, 61–62.

under the authority of an employer). According to the Court, an employees' organisation that negotiates on behalf of and in the interest of genuinely self-employed persons is not a social partner within the context of the collective agreement exception that the Court had awarded in the Albany case, but rather an association of undertakings within the meaning of EU competition law.[39]

Therefore, it was up to the domestic Dutch court to ascertain whether or not the freelance musicians could benefit from the collective agreement without illegally distorting free competition. The *FNV Kunsten* case could, at first sight, be seen as a blowback for the defenders of a broad personal scope for the right to collective bargaining. However, the *FNV Kunsten* case can also be interpreted by highlighting the reasoning of the CJEU that the classification of a "self-employed person" under national law does not prevent this person from being classified as an employee within the meaning of EU law if his independence is merely notional, thereby disguising an employment relationship.[40] The CJEU gave certain criteria to ascertain the employment status of a worker, listing their freedom to choose the time, place and content of his work, the fact that they do not share in the employer's commercial risks, and, for the duration of that relationship, form an integral part of that employer's undertaking, thus forming an economic unit with that undertaking.[41]

The Court in The Hague, which had to deliver the final decision, followed a broad interpretation of the CJEU's reasoning and ruled that the musicians, although freelancers (and thus independent workers) under Dutch law, should qualify as bogus self-employed in the light of the reasoning of the CJEU and EU law.[42] Therefore, the workers could benefit from the provisions of the collective agreement without distorting free competition.

This might be seen as a rather positive outcome for the freelance workers concerned, but the *FNV Kunsten* case can still also be interpreted in a more restrictive way, leaving less room for workers to qualify as bogus self-employed. In any case, the CJEU did not make a clear extension of

---

[39] E.F. Grosheide, "Overheid en sociale partners op wenkbrauwgesprek bij Europa", *Tijdschrift voor Recht & Arbeid* 2015, no. 12, 98–108.

[40] CJEU 4 December 2014, FNV Kunsten, § 35; F. Dorssemont.

[41] CJEU 4 December 2014, FNV Kunsten, § 36.

[42] Court of The Hague 1 September 2015, no. 200.082.997/01, ECLI:NL:GHDHA:2015:2305.

the Albany exception to economically dependent workers and effectively excluded the true independent workers, which should be viewed as undertakings in the light of EU competition law. The CJEU's view is therefore not easy to reconcile with the opinion of the supervisory institutions of the ILO who, as has been seen, extended the scope of the right to collective bargaining to self-employed workers. In this sense, EU competition law forms a restriction of the right to collective bargaining, which is nowadays clearly established as a fundamental right of the legal order of the EU. It is thus to be expected that, when asked, the CJEU would easily find a justification for such a restriction with the EU's competition policy as a legitimate aim. However, it is far from certain that the ECSR, the ECtHR and the ILO institutions would come to the same conclusion.

Taking into account the framework outlined above of indicators of the right to collective bargaining, a strict interpretation of the personal scope as only a right for employees "pur sang" comes into conflict with the fourth indicator (on the personal scope of the right). This fourth indicator, which covers a wide range of workers, has traditionally originated from the frequently used exclusion of public sector employees, but can also serve to address the current question. Moreover, a possible exclusion should be examined cumulatively in the light of the fifth (relating to material scope) and sixth indicators (relating to how the social partners themselves define their mutual relations). If collective bargaining is recognised by the employer(s) and trade unions or workers' representatives, and clearly concerns working conditions and social aspects relating to work, there are additional elements that demonstrate that a unilateral interpretation of a collective bargaining agreement as an anti-competitive instrument would demonstrate an overly narrow view of the right to collective bargaining. The unconditional exclusion of such collective agreements might find a legitimate objective under the terms of free competition, but the requirement of proportionality seems to be very difficult to satisfy in order to justify such a far-reaching restriction of the right, especially for the ECtHR, the ECSR and the ILO, which do not regard free competition as a quasi-holy grail.

5 THE ECSR: COLLECTIVE COMPLAINT NO. 123/2016 ICTU v. IRELAND

The above-mentioned discussion leads us to the landmark decision of the ECSR of 18 September 2018 on the Collective Complaint No. 123/2016 ICTU v. Ireland.[43] The Irish Congress of Trade Unions (ICTU) had filed a complaint following a decision of the Irish Competition Authority of 31 August 2004[44] relating to the application of Section 4 of the Irish Competition Act of 2002, to certain categories of self-employed persons in Ireland, principally voice-over actors, journalists and musicians. ICTU argued that by reason of that decision, certain categories of self-employed persons were not entitled to enter into collective agreements negotiated through collective bargaining and consequently, Ireland was in breach of its obligations under Article 6(2) of the ESC which protects the right to collective bargaining.

5.1 Decision Relating to the Competition Act of 2002

Sector 4 of the Irish Competition Act of 2002 prohibited all agreements between undertakings, decisions by associations of undertakings and concerted practices which have as the object or effect the prevention, restriction or distortion of competition in trade in any goods or services. The Irish Competition Authority decided that a collective agreement of 2002 between an actors' union and the employers' association representing advertising agencies (who hire actors and voice-overs) was in breach of Section 4 of the 2002 Act for the sole reason that each actor was considered to be a business, or an "undertaking", and it was therefore unlawful for undertakings to agree to fix prices for the sale of their services. This decision also had consequences for other trade unions representing self-employed workers in Ireland regarding the conclusion of collective agreements, such as unions for journalists and musicians.

---

[43] See also N. Contouris and V. De Stefano, "New trade unions strategies for new forms of employment", ETUC, Brussels, 2019, 39; B. ROMBOUTS, "ICTU v. Ireland: Expanding the Scope of Self-employed Workers Entitled to Collective Bargaining Rights in Relation to Competition Law Prohibitions", *International Labor Rights Case Law* 2019, vol. 5, no. 1, 17–22.

[44] Reference Number E/04/002.

First, the ECSR reiterates that it has primarily considered the right to bargain collectively as applying to workers who are seen as dependent employees and had until this case never addressed the situation of self-employed workers.[45] However, the Committee recalled that the Charter in general does not state whether its employment-related provisions apply to the self-employed. Furthermore, the Committee has constantly held that in principle the provisions of Part II of the Charter apply to the self-employed except where the context requires that they be limited to employed persons. No such context pertains in a generalised way under Article 6(2) ESC.[46]

The ECSR also takes into account that the world of work is changing rapidly and fundamentally with a proliferation of contractual arrangements, often with the express aim of avoiding the obligations of contracts of employment under labour law, of shifting risk from the labour engager to the labour provider. This has resulted in an increasing number of workers falling outside the definition of a dependent employee, including many low-paid workers or service providers who are de facto "dependent" on one or more "labour engagers" or clients.[47]

Moreover, the ECSR emphasises that collective mechanisms in the field of work are justified by the comparably weak position of an individual supplier of labour in establishing the terms and conditions of their contract. The image of competition law, where companies collude with one other to endanger fair prices for consumers does not fit this picture. These dependent workers lack just as much individual bargaining power as employees do. In the light of this, the ECSR refers to the *Albany* case law of the CJEU, suggesting that the same exception seems appropriate.[48]

The ECSR deduces that, in establishing the scope of the right to collective bargaining, it is not sufficient to rely on the traditional distinctions between worker and self-employed. Instead, the ECSR contends that the decisive criterion is rather whether there is an imbalance of power between the providers and engagers of labour.[49] Where providers

---

[45] ECSR, ICTU v. Ireland, §35.
[46] ECSR, ICTU v. Ireland, §35.
[47] ECSR, ICTU v. Ireland, §37.
[48] ECSR, ICTU v. Ireland, §38.
[49] ECSR, ICTU v. Ireland, §38.

of labour have no substantial influence over the content of their contractual conditions, they must be given the possibility of improving the power imbalance through collective bargaining. This assertion is also in line with the view of the supervisory institutions of the ILO, which apply the right to collective bargaining to self-employed workers.[50]

The ECSR concludes that, although it does not deem it appropriate to elaborate a general definition of how self employed workers are covered under Article 6(2) ESC, even without developing the precise circumstances under which categories of self-employed workers fall under the personal scope of Article 6, §2, an outright ban on collective bargaining of all self-employed workers would be excessive as it would run counter to the object and purpose of this provision.[51]

As Section 4 of the Irish Competition Act prohibited all agreements between undertakings, and as the Irish Competition Authority decided that each actor should be seen as an undertaking (having implications for journalists and musicians too), the ECSR considers that the situation amounted to an outright ban on collective bargaining with respect to remuneration for voice-over actors, freelance journalists and certain musicians and thus to a restriction of the right guaranteed by Article 6(2) ESC.[52]

As nothing in the wording of Article 6 of the Charter entitles a state to impose restrictions on the right to bargain collectively of specific categories of workers, any restrictions should conform with Article G ESC. Although the restriction was provided for by law and could be said to pursue a legitimate aim of ensuring effective and undistorted competition in trade with a view to protecting the rights and freedoms of others, the ban was excessive and therefore not necessary in a democratic society in that the categories of persons included in the notion of "undertaking" were over-inclusive.[53] Therefore, the conditions for the justification of a restriction of a right under the ESC, as included in Article 6 ESC, were not fulfilled and the ban was indeed in violation of Article 6(2) ESC.

Besides, the ECSR considers it evident that the concerned workers cannot predominantly be characterised as being genuinely independent

---

[50] ECSR, ICTU v. Ireland, §39.
[51] ECSR, ICTU v. Ireland, §40.
[52] ECSR, ICTU v. Ireland, §98.
[53] ECSR, ICTU v. Ireland, §98 and 101.

and self-employed, meeting all or most of the relevant criteria such as having several clients, having the authority to hire staff, and having the authority to make important strategic decisions about how to run the business.[54] The self-employed workers concerned here are, according to the Committee, obviously not in a position to influence their conditions of pay once they have been denied the right to bargain collectively.

5.2 *Decision Relating to the Competition (Amendment) Act 2017*

However, the complaint by ICTU also concerned the subsequent amendments to the Irish Competition Act. Indeed, after the aforementioned decision of the Irish Competition Authority, many years of discussions between the Irish social partners and the Irish authorities led to the Act being amended in 2017.[55] During the preparation of the amendments, Ireland found itself within the auspices of the country's bailout agreement with the Troika of the EU Commission, the European Central Bank and the International Monetary Fund (IMF), as the state was rescued from bankruptcy with a loan of 85 billion euro.[56] Under the close supervision that went with this arrangement, it became clear that the Memorandum of Understanding between the Troika and Ireland, which listed the conditions demanded by the Troika in exchange for this financial support, precluded Ireland from granting any further exemptions from the Competition Act. What's more, the European Commission repeated that EU law would not permit self-employed workers to exercise the right to bargain collectively.[57] However, the amendment of the Irish Competition Act in 2017 took place well after the exit of the Irish State from its Economic Adjustment Programme (and thus the close surveillance of the Troika) on 15 December 2013.

---

[54] ECSR, ICTU v. Ireland, §99.

[55] ECSR, ICTU v. Ireland, §51–59.

[56] 21.7 billion euro of the EFSM; 17.7 billion euro of the EFSF and bilateral loans of the UK, Denmark and Sweden; 19.5 billion euro of the IMF and 17.5 billion euro of Ireland itself (Treasury and Pension fund); European Commission, "Financial assistance to Ireland", website Commission, https://ec.europa.eu/info/business-economy-euro/economic-and-fiscal-policy-coordination/eu-financial-assistance/which-eu-countries-have-received-assistance/financial-assistance-ireland_en (last consulted on 25 May 2019).

[57] Letter of the EU Commission to ICTU of 18 April 2013, as mentioned in ECSR, ICTU v. Ireland, §54.

The Competition (Amendment) Act 2017 provides for Section 4 of the Competition Act 2002 to not be applied to collective bargaining and agreements in respect of certain categories of workers, more specifically, relevant categories of self-employed workers. As a consequence, any worker who falls within a relevant category of self-employed worker is no longer subject to the restrictions contained in Section 4 of the Competition Act 2002 and may thus engage in collective bargaining.[58] The groups of self-employed workers that are explicitly named as falling under an applicable category are: actors engaged as voice-over actors, musicians engaged as session musicians and journalists engaged as freelance journalists. For other categories of false self-employed workers or fully dependant self-employed workers, the Amended Act of 2017 provides self-employed workers with the possibility to apply to the Minister for Jobs to be included on the list of exemptions.[59] Such an application can be done by a representative trade union.

ICTU claimed that the amended act still constitutes a violation of Article 6(2) ESC as, first, it does not offer any protection against EU competition law and, secondly, the coverage of the exemptions for collective bargaining is very limited (including only the three named professions) while there are many other categories of economically independent self-employed workers which are in the same precarious situation and would benefit substantially form the right to collective bargaining.[60]

With regard to the second claim, while acknowledging that the scope of the exemption remains vague, as no exact definition of false self-employed worker or fully dependant self-employed worker is provided, the Committee observes that the amended Act does not contain any explicit prohibition of collective bargaining for self-employed workers.[61] Next, it is of the view that the question of whether the preconditions establishing self-employed workers as belonging to the two specified categories are overly restrictive depends on the interpretation of these preconditions in practice by the Minister for Jobs.[62] In other words, there

---

[58] ECSR, ICTU v. Ireland, §105.
[59] ECSR, ICTU v. Ireland, §107.
[60] ECSR, ICTU v. Ireland, §61–70.
[61] ECSR, ICTU v. Ireland, §110.
[62] ECSR, ICTU v. Ireland, §110–111.

will only be a violation of Article 6(2) ESC if the application procedure turns out to be too restrictive or difficult in practice.

This view is not followed by Committee Members Petros Stangos and Barbara Kresal, who in a joint dissenting opinion claim that the application procedure for other categories of false self-employed workers or fully dependant self-employed workers is only a "quasi-exemption", as they fear that, in practice, this would lead to an overly restrictive interpretation by the Minister for Jobs.[63] They certainly have a point when they point out that the modified Competition Act gives a very large margin of appreciation to the executive power, while Article G requires that restrictions are prescribed by law and given the fact that the adapted Act fails to lay down any concrete objectives or clear criteria. Ireland gets away with this relatively easily. In view of the framework of the indicators of the right to collective bargaining, such a procedure not only seems problematic with regard to the fourth indicator regarding the personal scope of collective bargaining, especially when the Minister applies a strict interpretation in practice, but it can also affect the first indicator regarding the freedom of association, which may constitute a disproportionate obstacle to the creation and growth of trade unions for economically dependent workers. After all, a prior procedure can have an undermining effect because of the uncertainty that it creates. A less far-reaching option would be not to limit the scope of the competition exception in principle to the three groups of workers concerned, but to clearly define when this exception cannot be used.

Regarding the protection against EU competition law, the ECSR recalls that it is not competent to assess the conformity of national situations with EU law, nor to assess the compliance of EU law with the Charter.[64] Instead, it can only look at the national measures implementing EU law. Nevertheless, the Committee states that Article 101 TFEU is not likely, per se, to affect the implementation of the Charter, as it does not restrict collective bargaining rights for workers as such, and allows for the exemption of certain categories of self-employed workers.[65] As the domestic Competition Act in Ireland seems not to restrict the right

---

[63] ECSR, ICTU v. Ireland, Joint dissenting opinion of Petros Stangos and Barbara Kresal.

[64] ECSR, ICTU v. Ireland, §114.

[65] ECSR, ICTU v. Ireland, §115.

to collective bargaining, the ECSR did not support the claim of ICTU that the Competition (Amendment) Act 2017 violates Article 6(2) of the Charter.[66]

6 Conclusion

With its decision of 12 September 2018, the ECSR has made it very clear that economically dependent workers should be awarded the right to collective bargaining. Thereby, it supports the view of the ILO institutions, although it does not go as far as to open up the personal scope of the right to all self-employed persons. The main criterion of the ECSR to discern whether certain workers should be able to make use of the right to collective bargaining could be used as a general standard, namely: it is not sufficient to rely on distinctions between worker and self-employed. Rather, the decisive criterion is whether there is an imbalance of power between the providers and engagers of labour.[67] If the worker, even when self-employed, finds himself in a precarious situation and in an imbalanced power relationship vis à vis the employer or client, he and his or her peers should be able to enter into collective bargaining to restore the power imbalance. If the worker, even if he or she is legally self-employed, is in a precarious situation and an imbalance of power exists vis-à-vis the employer or client, he or she must be able to enter into collective bargaining with his or her colleagues (or through a trade union) in order to rectify the power imbalance. This vision certainly deserves to be followed: economically dependent workers, such as many freelancers and workers in the platform economy, such as Uber drivers and Deliveroo

---

[66] ECSR, ICTU v. Ireland, §115–116.
[67] The ECSR also included this in its Digest of 2018, 100.

couriers,[68] could use such a right effectively in times when the digitalisation of the economy brings with it much scope for the exploitation of workers and the deterioration of working conditions.

Whether the views of the ILO and the ECSR are fully consistent with the *FNV Kunsten* case law of the CJEU remains to be seen. A broad interpretation of *FNV Kunsten* can, as seen, lead to an exemption to EU competition law, which means that the economically dependent workers can freely make use of their right to collective bargaining. However, it cannot be ruled out that the CJEU would not support a broad interpretation of its reasoning in *FNV Kunsten* and would adhere to a stricter view in a future case that raised similar questions. Of course, this would lead to notable incoherence between the different legal orders of Europe, which could cause legal uncertainty and confusion for the member states and legal subjects. On the one hand, the CJEU's rulings are more enforceable than the rulings of the ILO's supervisory mechanisms and the ECSR, which are often both characterised as "soft-law" due to their lack of binding effect vis-à-vis the member states, but nevertheless the specialised expertise of the latter bodies is an important guide when it comes to fundamental social rights and they at least carry a high moral value.[69] Moreover, a "guerre des juges" could completely grow out of proportion if the ECtHR were to clash with the CJEU, given the importance of the ECHR for the EU[70] and given the fact that the ECtHR's rulings

---

[68] In so far they are not bogus self-employed, and therefore actually employees. But the qualification issue is not the subject of this contribution; see S. Albers en P. Maerten, "Het sociaal statuut van de digitaalplatformmedewerker: een status quo en een blik op de toekomst", *Or.* 2019, afl. 2, 26.: V. De Stefano en M. WOUTERS, "The Court of Justice of the EU, Uber and Labour Protection: A Labour Lawyers' Approach" in B. DEVOLDER, *The platform Economy*, Antwerpen, Intersentia 2018, 187; F. KEFER, Q. CORDIER en A. FARCY, "Quel statut juridique pour les travailleurs des plateformes numeriques?", *Tijdschrift voor Sociaal Recht* 2019, afl. 1, 31 e.v.; C. VAN OLMEN en N. SIMON, "Le lien de subordination à l'épreuve de l'ubérisation de l'économie?", *Chroniques de droit social* 2016, afl. 7, 273.

[69] C. DENEVE, "Internationaal collectief onderhandelen" in G. COX, M. RIGAUX en J. ROMBOUTS (eds.), *Collectief onderhandelen*, Mechelen, Kluwer, 2006, 382; G. MAES, "Collectief klachtenrecht bij het Europees Sociaal Handvest: overzicht van rechtspraak 1998-2002", *TSR* 2005, afl. 1, 37-40; P. PECINOVSKY, *EU economic governance en het recht op collectief onderhandelen*, Brugge, die Keure, 2019, 176-179; J.M. SERVAIS, "Les normes de l'OIT au XXIème siècle: légitimité, effectivité", *TSR* 2012, afl. 1, 117-118.

[70] P. CRAIG, "EU Accession to the ECHR: Competence, Procedure and Substance", *Fordham Int'l L.J.* 2013, vol. 36, 1114-1150; T. LOCK, "End of an Epic? The Draft

are also legally binding on the EU member states.[71] Therefore, a strict interpretation by the CJEU should be avoided.

The importance of the application of the right to collective bargaining to economically dependent workers also is highlighted in a European Trade Union Confederation (ETUC) report of N. CONTOURIS and V. DE STEFANO, in which they not only briefly assess the ECSR decision, but also refer to existing examples of economically dependent workers, including freelancers or platform workers, who are making use of their collective bargaining rights in several EU member states.[72] For example in Belgium, Deliveroo Riders are teaming up with the help of trade unions in order to resist their precarious and constantly changing working conditions, unilaterally laid down by the Deliveroo platform. In the Netherlands, the largest trade union FNV has a "FNV Riders Union" department which focuses on the social rights of bike couriers and similar workers in the platform economy. In June 2019, the Belgian trade union ACV also launched "United Freelancers", a new trade union for freelancers and the self-employed.[73] Such trade unions would be of very little use if they were not allowed to enter into collective bargaining.[74] Finally, in other countries, including Spain, the economically dependent workers with self-employed status are seen a special category of workers (TRADE), which are granted the right to collective bargaining.[75]

Agreement on the EU's Accession to the ECHR", *Yearbook of European Law* 2012, vol. 31, afl. 1, 162–197; J. ODERMATT, "The EU's Accession to the European Convention on Human Rights: An International Law Perspective", *New York University Journal of International Law and Politics* 2014, vol. 47, afl. 1, 26–28; P. PECINOVSKY, *EU economic governance en het recht op collectief onderhandelen*, Brugge, die Keure, 2019, 275–285; L.H. STORGAARD, "EU Law Autonomy versus European Fundamental Rights Protection – On EU Accession to the ECHR", *Human Rights Law Review* 2015, vol. 15, afl. 3, 485–502.

[71] Article 42 and 46, §1 ECHR.

[72] N. CONTOURIS and V. DE STEFANO, "New trade unions strategies for new forms of employment", ETUC, Brussels, 2019, 39–42.

[73] ACV, "ACV lanceert United Freelancers", persmededeling 4 juni 2019.

[74] For more information on trade union strategies with regard to new forms of labour, see the special edition of the *European Labour Law Journal* 2019, vol. 10, afl. 3, coordinated by V. DE STEFANO and N. CONTOURIS, "Special issue: Testing the 'Personal Work' Relation: New Trade Union Strategies for New Forms of Employment".

[75] Act 20/2007of 11 July 2007, on the Statute for Self-Employment; R. FLOREZ, "Spain" in C. VAN OLMEN and G. WAGOTT (eds.), *The On-demand Economy Report*, International Bar Association – Global Employment institute, 2019, 65–66.

In the meanwhile, the European Commission has shown a profound interest in the problem. Commission President Ursula Von der Leyen's mission letters addressed to Competition Commissioner, Margrethe Vestager, and Commissioner for work, Nicolas Schmit, underlined the importance in this mandate to "ensure the working conditions of platform workers are addressed".[76] This led to the European Commission launching a process on 30 June 2020 to ensure that the EU competition rules do not stand in the way of collective bargaining for those who need it.[77] The initiative seeks to ensure that working conditions can be improved through collective agreements not only for employees, but also for those self-employed workers who need protection. The European Commission is therefore now assessing whether it is necessary to adopt measures at the EU level in order to address the issue that, according to EU competition law, professionals including independent (platform) workers and freelancers can be considered "undertakings" and collective bargaining agreements they enter into may therefore be captured by EU competition rules. Stakeholders, including competition authorities and government bodies, academics, legal and economic practitioners, trade unions and employer organisations were invited to participate in a public consultation on the matter.[78] However, the ETUC were disappointed that the Commission is delaying the solution, while the EU *"should just confirm the correct interpretation of EU Competition Law to fully exclude collective agreements from the remit of Article 101 TFEU and national competition rules"*.[79]

---

[76] EU COMMISSION, Mission Letter of Ursula von der Leyen to Nicolas Schmit, Commissioner-designate for jobs, 10 September 2019, 5, https://ec.europa.eu/commission/sites/beta-political/files/mission-letter-nicolas-schmit_en.pdf; EU COMMISSION, Mission letter of Ursula von de Leyen to Margrethe Vestager, Executive Vice-President-designate for a Europe fit for the Digital Age, 10 September 2019, 5, https://ec.europa.eu/commission/sites/beta-political/files/mission-letter-margrethe-vestager_2019_en.pdf.

[77] EU COMMISSION, "Competition: The European Commission launches a process to address the issue of collective bargaining for the self-employed", Press Release 30 June 2020, IP/20/1237, https://ec.europa.eu/commission/presscorner/detail/en/IP_20_1237.

[78] This consultation is a part of the public consultation concerning the Digital Services Act, see A. Ponce Del Castillo, "The Digital Services Act package: Reflections on the EU Commission's policy options", ETUC Policy Brief n° 12/2020.

[79] ETUC, "Commission delays action on collective bargaining for self-employed", ETUC Website, 30 June 2020, https://www.etuc.org/en/pressrelease/commission-delays-action-collective-bargaining-self-employed.

As the world of work is changing, collective labour law should too. Restricting the scope of the right to collective bargaining to traditional employees in an employment relationship does not fit the needs of the new ways of work and the digital age. With the criteria offered by the ECSR—namely, regarding an imbalance of power between the providers and engagers of labour—possibly also supported by indicators such as having several clients, having the authority to hire staff and having the authority to make important strategic decisions about how to run the business, a distinction should be made between economically dependent workers and genuine self-employed workers. Only by excluding the latter group of workers can free competition be safeguarded while giving the first category the chance to collectively stand up for their interests and rights and to protect or improve the terms and conditions of their employment.

CHAPTER 3

The European Court of Justice and Trade Union Power in Europe

Lorenzo Cecchetti

1 Introduction

With the entry into force of the Lisbon Treaty in 2009, the Charter of Fundamental Rights of the European Union (CFR)[1] acquired 'the same legal value as the Treaties'.[2] The CFR, at the same time, elevated numerous economic and social rights relating to the employment relationship to the primary law level,[3] which were now labelled as 'fundamental',

---

[1] The CFR was proclaimed on 7 December 2000 by the three political institutions of the Union, the European Parliament, the Commission and the Council, which issued an institutional declaration affirming that their actions would respect the CFR. This latter has been subsequently adapted at Strasbourg, on 12 December 2007.

[2] Article 6(1) of the Treaty on the European Union (TEU).

[3] To put it in a nutshell, primary law comprises the Treaties as well as the Annexes and the Protocols attached to that, and the CFR (and sometimes general principles). Generally speaking, general principles of law (where not considered to be primary law), customary international law and international agreements entered into by the EU are subjected to primary law, yet they take precedence over secondary law (which comprises regulations, directives, decisions, recommendations and opinions).

L. Cecchetti (✉)
Department of Law, LUISS University, Rome, Italy
e-mail: lcecchetti@luiss.it

© The Author(s), under exclusive license to Springer Nature Switzerland AG 2022
B. Colfer (ed.), *European Trade Unions in the 21st Century*, St Antony's Series, https://doi.org/10.1007/978-3-030-88285-3_3

and which had previously either mainly or only enshrined in secondary EU law. This has important consequences for the hierarchy of norms, the judicial review of EU legislation and national legislation—to the extent that national provisions fall within the scope of the application of the CFR—and for workers' and trade unions' possibility of invoking fundamental social rights guaranteed by the EU legal order, including with respect to so-called horizontal disputes (i.e. disputes between private parties, such as those between employees and private employers).[4] Indeed, the major part of the social *acquis* of the EU legal order resides in secondary law and, as far as employment relations are concerned, primarily in directives (most of which provide for minimum harmonisation). According to the settled case law of the CJEU, directives 'cannot of itself impose obligations on an individual and cannot therefore be relied upon as such against an individual'[5] (such as private employers). On the contrary, even when not specifically addressed to individuals, primary law provisions, including fundamental (social) rights enshrined therein, can have direct effect in horizontal disputes too.[6] I will come back on this concept in Sect. 3.

Against the backdrop of the well-known *encadrement* of the labour relations collective dimension (and, consequently, of trade unions power) by the EU's internal market law (Sect. 2, where the concept of *encadrement* is defined), the chapter examines the CJEU's post-Lisbon case law with a specific focus on two aspects: first, recourse to EU social law by unions to challenge national legislation and acts; and, second, the CJEU's approach to preliminary ruling proceedings concerning fundamental social rights enshrined in both the CFR and EU secondary law (both analysed in Sect. 3). During the period under consideration here, these litigation strategies involving recourse to EU law before courts by trade unions have been employed throughout the EU, leading to

---

[4] Please note that the primary law status acquired by the CFR is deemed to have far-reaching implications for the protection of the social fundamental rights within the scope of the Union action (see e.g. the European Parliament's resolution of 12 February 2019 on the implementation of the Charter, and the commitment, enshrined in the European Pillar of Social Rights, to take into consideration the fundamental economic and social rights within the context of the economic governance). These aspects are considered to fall beyond the scope of this analysis.

[5] See e.g., Case 152/84, *Marshall*, Para. 48, and Case 91/92, *Faccini Dori*, Para. 20.

[6] See e.g., Case 43/75, *Defrenne II*.

compelling results. Special attention will be devoted to the recent *CCOO* case,[7] which provides an outstanding example of the potential for unions to pursue such litigation strategies by bringing about a significant rise in the level of protection of workers in both the public and private sectors (Sect. 4). Finally, some conclusions are drawn regarding the impact of the CJEU's case law regarding union power in Europe (Sect. 5).

The litigation strategies just mentioned are deemed to be a mode of judicial enforcement of EU labour law (Bercusson 2009, p. 497 and ff.), and an expression of the fundamental right to take collective action and to have access to effective judicial protection (now enshrined in Articles 28 and 47 of the CFR respectively). Indeed, the recourse to EU law by unions before national and EU courts ('judicialization') has been conceived as an excellent instrument to conduct social struggles (Roman 2012, p. 12; McCann 1994; see also Peraro 2020). In more general terms, it has been argued that the preliminary ruling procedure shall be also understood as a sort of system of 'private enforcement of EU law' in the hands of individuals, which is strictly linked to the direct effect doctrine (Gallo 2018, p 65 ff.; see also Sciarra 2001, p. 241 ff., and Craig and de Búrca, 2020, p. 218 ff.). Nonetheless, it has been highlighted that the use of the preliminary ruling procedure to challenge national legal acts systematically may bring about significant drawbacks in the long term (Simitis 1996).

2 The *Encadrement* of the Collective Dimension of Labour Relations by EU Law

In the early 2000s, the rules governing the internal market (namely, as far as they are concerned in this contribution, the freedom of establishment[8] and the freedom to provide services[9]) have been considered to clash with national labour law provisions. In other words, the traditional distinction between the European integration through the internal market and the national labour and social law, which informed the structure of the Treaty of Rome and echoed the respect for the Member States'

---

[7] Case C-55/18, *CCOO*.

[8] Case C-341/05, *Laval*; Case C-346/06, *Rüffert*; and Case C-319/06, *Commission v Luxemburg*.

[9] Case C-438/05, *Viking*; and Case C-201/15, *AGET Iraklis*.

welfare systems (Cancilla 2009, pp. 39 ff.) and consequently led the CJEU to conduct 'a relatively relaxed proportionality review, upholding most [national] measures as justified' (see Garben 2017, p. 33) was called into question. The major issues arose in relation to the traditional collective dimension of labour law, which permits combining subordination relationships and contractual freedom (Supiot 2015, p. 124 and ff.) (i.e. freedom of association, collective bargaining rights, and collective action) and led to some well-known cases before the CJEU.[10] It seems necessary to clarify that EU law literature usually refers to this kind of case law by using the French term '*encadrement*' to highlight the possibility for (some general principles of) EU law to bind (*encadrer*) national law and private actions beyond the scope of normative competences conferred upon the Union. Indeed, under Article 153(5) TFEU, the Union has not normative competences in relation to 'the right of association, the right to strike or the right to impose lock-outs'.[11]

The primary lessons that can be drawn from the CJEU's judgements in the *Laval, Rüffert, Commission v Luxembourg* (concerning the free movement of services) and *Viking* (regarding the freedom of establishment) cases, which have been extensively commented upon by legal scholars who have highlighted both sides of the argument, can be summed up as follows.

First, the said fundamental freedoms can apply to the exercise of fundamental social rights, and specifically to the rights to undertake

---

[10] Please note that the said clash occurred in cases where there was a link with the European Union law. Generally speaking, the said link can consist in the presence of either a cross-border element or a national law implementing EU law. As for the cross-border situation, it is noteworthy to mention the paradigm shift occurred in the principles underpinning the internal market over time, which moved from the principle of discrimination on the basis of nationality to a more intrusive 'market access' test (see e.g. Case C-76/90, *Säger*), along with further developments of paramount importance in the European integration process, namely the enlargement of the Union as well as its evolution process from the embedded liberalism to neoliberalism (see Giubboni 2017, pp. 55–119; Moreau 2018; Azoulai 2020). This distinct expansion of the Union's economic constitution over national (not-only-labour) law and national regulatory prerogatives led to several preliminary ruling proceedings being referred to the CJEU and was able to essentially 'put on the back-foot' any national law capable of hindering the four freedoms (Barnard 2008, p. 486).

[11] The same remains true for other competences retained by the Member States which fall outside the scope of this chapter.

collective bargaining (now enshrined in Art. 12 of the CFR) and collective action (Art. 28 of the CFR, and to the former intrinsically linked),[12] Article 153(5) TFEU notwithstanding.[13] The misalignment between the proclamation of fundamental rights and the deficiency of normative competences is highly significant (on the ambiguities behind this structure, see Ryan 2003, p. 84) and has not been modified by the entry into force of the Lisbon Treaty.[14] Thus, the notable carve-out of collective bargaining rights from the EU treaties' competition law provisions[15] (see also Pecinovsky 2021, in this volume) was considered inapplicable to the four freedoms.[16] In this way, the collective dimension of labour relations has been *encadré* or 'framed' (Mengozzi and Morviducci 2018, pp. 92–96) by EU law (more precisely by the CJEU's case law), as happened to other branches of national law falling within Member States' retained competences.[17]

Second, the freedom of establishment and the freedom to provide services can apply to trade unions.[18]

Third, the right to take collective action, including the right to strike, is recognised as a fundamental right which forms an integral part of the general principles of Union, thus it can constitute a restriction on the freedoms under analysis.[19]

---

[12] Case C-438/05, *Viking*, Para. 58–60; Case C-341/05, *Laval*, Para. 30 and ff.

[13] Case C-341/05, *Laval*, Para. 44; Case C-438/05, *Viking*, Para. 44.

[14] Indeed, pursuant to Article 51(1) CFR: 'The Charter does not extend the field of application of Union law beyond the powers of the Union or establish any new power or task for the Union, or modify powers and tasks as defined in the Treaties'. Similarly, see Article 6(1) (2) of the TEU.

[15] Case C-67/96, *Albany*, Para. 52–70.

[16] Case C-438/05, *Viking*, Para. 48–54.

[17] Case C-341/05, *Laval*, Para. 87; Case C-438/05, *Viking*, Para. 40.

[18] Case C-341/05, *Laval*, Para. 98; Case C-438/05, *Viking*, Para. 56–66. This statement is far from evident since the free movement provisions impose obligations primarily upon the Member States, and it involves one of the major conundrums of EU law, namely the issue of horizontal direct effect—as regards the scope of this analysis—of primary law provisions. Moreover, differently from what occurs in relation to the horizontal effects of the free movement of workers' provisions, the horizontal effect of the freedom to provide services denies the fundamental principle of territorial application of (national) labour law (see Giubboni 2017, pp. 70–71).

[19] Case C-341/05, *Laval*, Para. 99–100; Case C-438/05, *Viking*, Para. 72–74.

Fourth, the CJEU held that the said 'restrictions' may be justified if they are deemed to pursue an overriding reason of public interest, such as the protection of workers,[20] and collective action is the last— still effective and proportionate—resort.[21] In other words, this is the first acknowledgement in the CJEU's jurisprudence of the right to strike as a fundamental right[22] within the EU's legal order, although the exercise of this right is strictly constrained in accordance with the prevailing neoliberal paradigm in the EU (Barnard 2008, pp. 486 and 490). Moreover, the more balanced approach adopted by the Court in the *Commission v Germany* case[23] has found no follow-up in the CJEU's case law.[24]

On the contrary, the more recent *AGET Iraklis*[25] and *Alemo-Herron*[26] cases seem able to exacerbate the already questionable balancing test adopted in the *Laval-quartet* and seem to strengthen the free movement provisions on the basis of the proclamation in the CFR of the freedom to

---

[20] Case C-341/05, *Laval*, Para. 103; Case C-438/05, *Viking*, Para. 81 ff.

[21] Case C-438/05, *Viking*, Para. 87.

[22] Case C-341/05, *Laval*, Para. 90–91 and ff.; Case C-438/05, Para. 43–44 and ff.

[23] Case C-271/08, *Commission v Germany*, Para. 49, and 51–65 and, more precisely, Para. 51–52 (where the CJEU referred by analogy to Case C-112/00, *Schmidberger*, Para. 81–82).

[24] Among these judgements see Case C-201/15, *AGET Iraklis*, and the judgement mentioned in footnote no. 62 below.

[25] Case C-201/15, *AGET Iraklis*, which concerned the compatibility with EU law of the Greek national legislation conferring upon an administrative authority the power to oppose collective redundancies after assessing the conditions in the labour market, the situation of the undertaking and the interests of the national economy. While the said national legislation was considered, in principle, not precluded by directive 98/59/EC on the approximation of the laws of the Member States relating to collective redundancies, the CJEU held that such a measure did not comply with the principle of proportionality and thus was in breach of the freedom of establishment (now enshrined in Article 49 TFEU) and consequently Article 16 CFR.

[26] Case C-426/11, *Alemo-Herron*, which dealt with the applicability of a collective agreement entered into by the transferor to the transferee under Article 3 of directive 2001/23/EC on the approximation of the laws of the Member States relating to the safeguarding of employees' rights in the event of transfers of undertakings, businesses or parts of undertakings or businesses. The CJEU held that the interpretation of the said Article must comply with the fundamental right enshrined in Article of the 16 CFR. The *effet utile* of directive 2001/23 was immolated to the name of transferee's contractual freedom (see Para. 35).

conduct a business,[27] this being the one major drawback for the unions of the primary law character acquired by the CFR.

The principles affirmed in these rulings raised significant challenges to the traditional role and functioning of trade unions in the EU (Sciarra 2008). Nevertheless, the case law briefly recalled does cover the interplay between union power and EU law fully. In this regard, the entry into force of the Lisbon Treaty and the interplay between the CFR and the rights provided in EU secondary law opened new litigation possibilities for unions, which are described in the following section.

3 The CJEU's Post-Lisbon Treaty Case Law on the EU Social Rights: The Trade Unions' Litigation Strategy and the Judicialisation of the CFR

The recent CJEU case law on fundamental social rights in the EU will be briefly analysed in this section from two different, albeit linked, perspectives. Firstly, as mentioned above, the *encadrement* of the collective dimension of labour relations under EU law does not cover the link between EU law and unions' power fully. Indeed, trade unions have frequently utilised secondary EU law to challenge national legislation and to judicially enforce EU labour and social law (Bercusson 2009, p. 497 and ff.), mainly through the preliminary ruling procedure (as detailed below in this section). In this respect, the primary law character acquired by CFR has significant consequences since it entails modifications to the European Union's hierarchy of norms and augments the possibilities for judicial review of EU legislation and national legislation (Bercusson 2009, pp. 9–11; on the implications of the entry into force of the Lisbon Treaty for the action for annulment under Article 263 TFEU see Albors-Llorens 2012, p. 517 and ff.), to the extent that this latter falls within the scope of application of the CFR.[28] Indeed, on the one hand, even before the

---

[27] Pursuant to Article 16, entitled 'Freedom to conduct a business': 'The freedom to conduct a business *in accordance with Union law and national laws and practices* is recognised'. (emphasis added).

[28] Pursuant to Article 51(1) CFR: 'The provisions of [the] Charter are addressed to the institutions, bodies, offices and agencies of the Union with due regard for the principle of subsidiarity *and to the Member States only when they are implementing Union law*' (emphasis added).

entry into force of the Lisbon Treaty, EU legislation was required to comply with the fundamental rights protected by the CJEU. Yet, the possibility to interpret an EU act in light of fundamental social rights or to challenge its validity under Article 263 of the TFEU alleging a violation of the said fundamental social rights was confined to only a handful Treaty provisions and to the general principles of EU law as acknowledged by the CJEU. On the other hand, as pointed out in the introductory section, the elevation to the status of primary law of a significant number of economic and social rights relating to the employment relationship, which were previously either mainly or only enshrined in EU secondary law, can have important consequences for strategic employment litigation. Indeed, primary law provisions, in addition to enjoying primacy, are capable of having direct effect even in so-called horizontal disputes (despite not being specifically addressed to individuals).[29]

In short, an EU law provision can have 'direct effect' 'whenever its characteristics are such that it is capable of judicial adjudication' (Pescatore 2015, p. 151 ff. spec. p. 153), this being understood as the capacity of being interpreted and applied by the Courts (O'Leary 2005, p. 50 ff.). In general, university textbooks state that the traditional direct effect test consists in a threefold test: it is generally said the EU law provision shall be 'clear', 'sufficiently precise' (to provide national courts with 'workable indications'), and 'unconditional' (no need for implementing measures implying some discretion) (Pescatore 2015; See further on the direct effect doctrine Gallo 2018; Schütze 2018). Yet, to determine whether an EU law provision enjoys direct effect does not entail a mere technical assessment. Indeed, since the inception of the direct effect doctrine, CJEU's policy-related choices have played a significant role: as it has been underscored by Pescatore, in the reasoning of the CJEU in the well-known *Van Gend and Loos* case[30] it was decisive the specific idea of Europe shared by judges rather than the arguments based on legal technicalities on the matter (see again Pescatore 2015, p. 137 and p. 153). What's more, it has been argued that direct effect is a 'glimmering' and 'evolving' doctrine (Gallo 2018, p. 163 ff.) that varies in its intensity, 'dimension' and structure on the basis, inter alia, of the piece of EU law

---

[29] In addition to the abovementioned Cases 43/75, *Defrenne II*, C-438/05, *Viking*, and C-341/05, *Laval*, it suffices to recall Case C-415/93, *Bosman*, Case C-281/98, *Angonese*, and, albeit with some differences, Case C-171/11, *Fra.bo SpA*.

[30] Case 26/62, *Van Gend and Loos*.

at issue, the specific characteristics of the national situation and disputes (Pescatore 2015; Gallo 2018; and Gallo 2019). Other elements play a role in the CJEU's assessment, such as the allocation of competences between EU and Member States, the 'trajectory' of a certain right in the European integration, and, albeit indirectly and without jeopardising the principle of autonomy of EU law, the commitments imposed upon Member protection by international law.[31] Put simply, and to conclude on this doctrine, suffice it to say that when an EU law provision has direct effect individuals (thus unions too) will be able to rely upon it, inter alia, before national judges to challenge national provisions which fall within the scope of EU law and which do not comply with the latter.

As for the principle of primacy (or supremacy), according to this principle EU law shall have precedence over incompatible national law, entailing a duty of consistent interpretation upon national judges (and public administrations) and leading to, as the case may be, the disapplication by the national body of the incompatible national law (in cases where the EU law provision enjoys direct effect[32] and consistent interpretation reveals impossible) and/or to damages actions against the Member State.[33]

With regard to the employment relationship, the so-called horizontal (direct) effect often occurs by invoking the secondary law provisions in combination with the fundamental rights (normally enshrined in the CFR).[34] In general, as highlighted, the foregoing is a consequence of preliminary ruling questions referred to the CJEU pursuant to Article 267 of TFEU by a national judge before which a dispute linked to the EU legal order has been brought.[35]

---

[31] The recent case law on the fundamental right to paid annual leave (now enshrined in Article 31(2) of the CFR), which will be briefly recalled below in this section, upholds this viewpoint. I have further elaborated upon this aspect in my doctoral thesis.

[32] Case C-573/17, *Popławski II*, Para. 62–63.

[33] See Joined Cases C-6/90 and C-9/90, *Francovich*, and the following CJEU's case law.

[34] See the well-known Case C-144/04, *Mangold*, and the following CJEU's case law (which it is generally referred to as the 'Mangold doctrine').

[35] Either by invoking a right provided for by EU law or by alleging an incompatibility of the national legislation with EU law.

With regard to this first aspect, over the last ten years[36] trade unions have brought cases before national courts alleging an incompatibility of a national act with EU law and resulting in preliminary ruling proceedings referred to the CJEU on several occasions (being directly involved in the proceeding in more than twenty cases as of December 2019). In approximately half of these cases, the CJEU has ruled on the interpretation of secondary EU law provisions according to trade unions' perspectives on the interpretation of EU law (although, in preliminary ruling procedures, the CJEU merely rules on either the interpretation or the validity of EU law, in non-technical language this means 'in favour of' the unions), such as in the *Federación de Servicios Públicos de la UGT*,[37] *Ingeniørforeningen i Danmark*,[38] *FNV Bondgenoten*,[39] *HK Danmark*,[40] *TSN and YTN*,[41] *Mascolo*,[42] and *Unionen*[43] cases. In other cases, the CJEU's ruling on the interpretation of EU law has not followed the unions' perspectives ('not in their favour' in this case, the aforementioned remarks apply),[44] though this did not automatically result in any diminished legal protection

---

[36] The time period analyzed coincides with that after the entry into force of the Lisbon Treaty, regardless of the applicability *ratione temporis* of this latter. The analysis of the CJEU's case law is updated to December 2019.

[37] Case C-151/09, *Federación de Servicios Públicos de la UGT*.

[38] Case C-499/08, *Ingeniørforeningen i Danmark*.

[39] Case C-242/09, *Albron*.

[40] Joined Cases C-335/11 and C-337/11, *HK Danmark*.

[41] Joined Cases C-512/11 and C-513/11, *TSN and YTN*.

[42] Joined Cases C-22/13, C-61/13 to C-63/13 and C-418/13, *Mascolo*.

[43] Case C-336/15, *Unionen*.

[44] Case C-354/13, *FOA*; Case C-533/13, *AKT*; Case C-80/14, *USDAW*; Case C-64/16, *Associação Sindical dos Juízes Portugueses*; Case C-147/17, *Sindicatul Familia Constanța*.

for labour rights as the *Guisado*[45] and *Syndicat des cadres de la sécurité intérieure*[46] cases show.

In almost all cases mentioned here,[47] EU law and the preliminary ruling procedure have served the unions as a tool to challenge national legislation before national courts, including regarding even collective agreements entered into by the very same unions,[48] in order to, as the case may be, render inapplicable these provisions (where possible),[49] or to seek a more protective interpretation of EU social law (resulting in the fostering of the effectiveness of rights conferred upon individuals by EU law).[50]

The second perspective from which the recent CJEU rulings can be analysed concerns the interplay between primary and secondary EU law in horizontal disputes between a worker and his/her private employer. More precisely, in these cases, the worker (sometimes assisted by trade unions) has invoked both the directive provisions and the fundamental labour

---

[45] Case C-103/16, *Guisado*, which deserves to be outlined. The case can be summed up as follows: a request for preliminary ruling concerning the interpretation of Article 10(1) and (2) of directive 92/85/EEC and Article 1(1)(a) of directive 98/59/EC made in a horizontal dispute between, on the one hand, the worker dismissed, in the context of a collective redundancy, while she was pregnant (Jessica Porras Guisado), and, on the other hand, the employer (Bankia SA), various Trade Union branches, and the Spanish Wages Guarantee Fund. Most notably, the request for preliminary ruling addressed the transposition into Spanish legislation of Article 10 of directive 92/85 which prohibits, except in exceptional cases, the dismissal of pregnant workers in order to determine whether it constituted a correct transposition. The CJEU held, inter alia, that Article 10(1) of directive 92/85 must be interpreted as precluding national legislation which does not prohibit, in principle, the dismissal of a worker who is pregnant, has recently given birth or is breastfeeding as a preventative measure, but which provides, by way of reparation, only for that dismissal to be declared void when it is unlawful. At the same time, though, the Court specified that Article 10(1) does not require to grant priority status in relation to being either retained or redeployed within collective redundancies to the said categories of workers, without prejudice to the right of Member States to provide for a higher level of protection for such workers).

[46] Case C-254/18, *Syndicat des cadres de la sécurité intérieure*.

[47] The only exception being the Case C-103/16, *Guisado*, where Trade Union branches sided with the employer and the Wages Guarantee Fund, see footnote no. 45 above.

[48] Case C-512/11, *TSN and YTN*.

[49] And/or (in cases in which EU law cannot lead to disapplication) to seek compensation for damages in accordance with the CJEU's case law on the principle of Member State liability for breach of EU law.

[50] See for instance the Case C-335/11, *HK Danmark*, questions 1 and 2.

rights enshrined in CFR, namely the general principles of equal treatment and non-discrimination in employment (now enshrined in Article 21(1) CFR), the workers' right to information and consultation within the undertaking (now enshrined in Article 27 of the CFR), and the fundamental rights to working conditions which respect the worker's health, safety and dignity, to a limitation of the maximum working hours, to daily and weekly rest periods, and to an annual period of paid leave (now enshrined in Article 31 CFR). In this regard, it is noteworthy to briefly recall the rulings in the *Dansk Industri*,[51] the *AMS*,[52] and the *Bauer* and *Max-Planck*[53] cases.[54] In the *Dansk Industri* case, the CJEU ruled that the general principle prohibiting discrimination on the grounds of age, now enshrined in Article 21(1) CFR, and given concrete expression by directive 2000/78/EC, precludes, including in disputes between private persons, national legislation such as that at issue in the proceedings before the referring court (in this case, the Danish Supreme Court).[55] The duty to disapply national provisions follows from several logical steps.[56] The

---

[51] Case C-441/14, *Dansk Industri*.

[52] Case C-176/12, *Association de médiation sociale* (reference for a preliminary ruling concerning the consequences of the incompatibility between the French legislation—excluding a specific category of workers from the calculation of staff numbers within the meaning of Article 3(1) of directive 2002/14/EC—and EU law for private employers).

[53] Joined Cases C-569/16 and C-570/16, *Bauer*; and Case C-684/16, *Max-Planck-Gesellschaft* (references for a preliminary ruling concerning the compatibility of German legislation—preventing the payment of an allowance to the worker of his/her legal heirs, as the case may be, in lieu of paid annual leave not taken by him/her—with the—now labelled—'essential principle of EU social law' consisting in the right to paid annual leave enshrined in Article 31(2) of the CFR, and the consequences of the breach of this fundamental right (also) for private employers). See also Case C-385/17, *Hein*.

[54] All the cases concerned horizontal disputes where fundamental social rights came to the fore and which are deemed to be the conceptual basis of the recent judgement in the *CCOO* case. In the *Dansk Industri* and *AMS* cases unions played a major role in invoking EU law before national judges, thus these cases do not differentiate from those recalled in the first part of this section.

[55] On the basis of the so-called *Mangold* doctrine.

[56] *I.e.*, the statement about the non-compliance of the national law or act with EU law (which is based on the directive's provisions), the proclamation of the direct effect of the said general principle (which permits the disapplication to occur even in horizontal disputes), the overlapping between the scope of application of the latter and that of the directive (Case C-441/14, *Dansk Industri*, Para. 25–26), and the impossibility to strike a balance between that general principle and the principles of legal certainty and the protection of legitimate expectations in favour of the latter (Case C-441/14, *Dansk*

same reasoning was not possible in the *AMS* case mainly due to the fact that Article 27 CFR makes reference to *'the cases and [...] the conditions provided for by Union law and national laws and practices'*. Indeed, this provision, according to the CJEU, is not able to pass the above-mentioned direct effect test.[57] Nonetheless, the over-formal approach to the dividing line between general principles/primary law provisions which can have direct effect and those which cannot seems far from convincing (Murphy 2014, p. 170 ff.). Indeed, should the said test be strictly applied, as done in the *AMS* case, this will recant the very beginning of the direct effect doctrine in EU law. Indeed, as pointed out, this latter cannot be conceived as an assessment merely based on the legal technicalities of the matter (see again Pescatore 2015, p. 137 and p. 153).

This is evident from the recent line of jurisprudence regarding the fundamental rights enshrined in Article 31 CFR,[58] and most notably from the *CCOO* case, which lies at the crossroad between duty of consistent interpretation and direct effect (in a broad sense) and which is characterised by the de facto joint use of primary and secondary law provisions by the CJEU both when scrutinising of the compatibility between the national legal order and EU law and when determining the consequences of the incompatibility in horizontal disputes.[59] A second aspect that characterises (many of) these cases is the reference to the worker's position of

---

Industri, Para. 43). It is important to note that this judgement, by combining together primary and secondary law, maximized the effectiveness of the EU social law in horizontal situations provoked the strong response of the Danish Supreme Court in its ruling of 6 December 2016.

[57] Case C-176/12, *Association de médiation sociale*, Para. 45–49.

[58] Pursuant to Article 31 CFR: '1. Every worker has the right to working conditions which respect his or her health, safety and dignity. 2. Every worker has the right to limitation of maximum working hours, to daily and weekly rest periods and to an annual period of paid leave'. Indeed, this Article, albeit making no reference to 'the cases and [...] the conditions provided for by Union law and national laws and practices', requires EU or national law 'to specify the exact duration of annual leave and, where appropriate, certain conditions for the exercise of that right' (Joined Cases C-569/16 and C-570/16, *Bauer*, Para. 85, Case C-684/16, *Max-Planck*, Para. 17, and Case C-55/18, *CCOO*, Para. 74). The distinction between the two circumstances in substantive terms is far from clear.

[59] See Case C-55/18, *CCOO*, Para. 72; Cf. Joined Cases C-569/16 and C-570/16, *Bauer*, Para. 93, and Case C-684/16, *Max-Planck*, Para. 82.

weakness in the employment relationship,[60] which seems to be linked to the need to guarantee the effectiveness of the rights conferred upon the workers by the directives which give concrete expression to the fundamental rights enshrined in Article 31(2) CFR, irrespective of the nature of the employer which was a private entity. Nevertheless, it seems possible, on the one hand, to invoke other directive provisions in combination with the said fundamental rights,[61] and, on the other hand, to invoke other provisions of CFR to enhance trades unions' power *vis-à-vis* Member State's legislation, as the *Ammattiliitto* case shows.[62]

4 The Recent *CCOO* Case on the Right to a Limitation of Maximum Working Hours and to Daily and Weekly Rest Periods

The two dimensions of the CJEU's case law examined in Sect. 3 (namely: the trade unions' litigation strategy involving the use of EU social law before national courts, and the judicialisation of the CFR in this respect, triggering the consequent interplay between primary and secondary law in horizontal disputes), came together in the recent *CCOO* case (for a first comment on this judgement see on this judgement see Marcelle and Van den Haute 2019).

The judgement rendered by the Court of Justice's Grand Chamber on 14 May 2019 concerns the fundamental rights governing the limitation of the maximum working hours and of the right to daily and weekly rest periods at work, both of which are enshrined in Article 31(2) CFR. More precisely, the point at issue was whether Deutsche Bank, a private employer, was under an obligation to set up a system to record the time worked by each member of staff each day. The case was brought

---

[60] See Case C-684/16, *Max-Planck*, Para. 41, and Case C-55/18, *CCOO*, Para. 44, 45 and 55.

[61] For instance, under recital no. 1 of directive 2008/104/EC (on temporary agency work),that directive 'is designed to ensure full compliance with Article 31 of the Charter'. We might hence wonder whether a worker of a privately owned temporary-work agency and user undertaking can invoke against these subjects the principle of equal treatment laid down in Article 5 of the directive (and/or other rights provided for in the directives) in combination with Article 31 CFR, where there is a breach of those rights. See also Para. 5.

[62] Case C-396/13, *Ammattiliitto*.

before the Spanish High Court (*Audencia National*) by a trade union, the *Federación de Servicios de Comisiones Obreras (CCOO)* (English: Federation of the service workers' unions), arguing that this obligation was necessary to verify compliance with both the working times agreed upon[63] and the obligation to provide union representatives with information on the amount of overtime worked each month.[64] According to CCOO, this obligation derived from Articles 34 and 35[65] of the Spanish Workers' Statute (*Estatudo de los Trabajadores*) as interpreted in light of Article 31(2) CFR, Articles 3, 5, 6 and 22 of EU directive 2003/88 (concerning the organisation of working time), and ILO Convention nos. 1 and 30.[66] Conversely, the employer referred to judgements no. 246/2017 of 23 March 2017 (REC 81/2016) and no. 338/2017 of 20 April 2017 (REC 116/2016) of the Spanish Supreme Court (*Tribunal Supremo*), which held that Spanish law did lay down such an obligation of general application.[67] In this context, the referring court had doubts as to whether the interpretation of Article 35(5) of the Workers' Statute that had been adopted by the Supreme Court was consistent with the obligations provided for by directives 2003/88 and 89/391 (regarding health and safety at work).[68]

---

[63] Rules on working time are laid down in several national sectoral collective conventions and company collective agreements (Case C-55/18, *CCOO*, Para. 22).

[64] Case C-55/18, *CCOO*, Para. 19.

[65] Pursuant to Article 35 entitled 'Overtime': '(…) 5. For the purpose of calculating overtime, every worker's working time shall be recorded on a daily basis and the total calculated at the time fixed for payment of remuneration. Workers shall be given a copy of the summary with the corresponding payslip'.

[66] Respectively, Convention Limiting the Hours of Work in Industrial Undertakings to Eight in the Day and Forty-eight in the Week adopted in Washington on 28th November 1919, and Convention concerning the Regulation of Hours of Work in Commerce and Offices adopted in Geneva on 28th June 1930.

[67] According to the Supreme Court's case law, in short, on all occasions when Spanish law intended to required time worked to be recorded, it provided for that specifically as it has been done in Article 35 of the Workers' Statute; this was considered to be consistent with Article 22 of directive 2003/88 (Case C-55/18, *CCOO*, Para. 25).

[68] The national judge observed inter alia that a 2016 survey of the work force in Spain revealed that 53.7% of overtime worked had not been recorded (Case C-55/18, *CCOO*, Para. 26), and asked the CJEU, in essence, whether the Articles of the directive mentioned above read in conjunction with Article 31(2) CFR, must be interpreted as precluding a law of a Member State that, according to the interpretation given to it by

Following the path set out by Advocate General Pitruzzella,[69] the CJEU first laid down some general considerations regarding Article 31(2) CFR and directive 2003/88. This approach differs from that adopted in the Court of Justice's line of jurisprudence regarding the interplay between primary law (or general principles) and secondary law in horizontal disputes mentioned previously and seems to enhance the fundamental character of these rights in the legal discourse. Indeed, according to the CJEU, the directive, which intends to improve the living and working conditions of workers through the approximation of national provisions concerning, in particular, the duration of working time, must be interpreted having regard to the importance of the fundamental right of every worker to a limitation on the maximum number of working hours and to daily and weekly rest periods.[70] It follows that Member States must ensure that directive 2003/88 is fully effective, and, thus, that the minimum rest periods laid down in the directive are observed and they must actively prevent the maximum weekly working time—as set out in Article 6(b) of directive 2003/88—from being exceeded.[71]

Following this, the Grand Chamber examines whether, and to what extent, it is necessary to set up a system that enables the duration of time worked each day by each worker to be measured,[72] and concludes that the Member States must require employers to set up an objective, reliable and accessible system to enable such a measurement to take place.[73] It follows that EU law must be interpreted as precluding a law of a Member

---

national case law, does not require employers to set up a system enabling the duration of time worked each day by each worker to be measured (Para. 29).

[69] Opinion delivered by Advocate General Pitruzzella in Case C-55/18, *CCOO*, Para. 33–88.

[70] Case C-55/18, *CCOO*, Para. 32–33.

[71] Case C-55/18, *CCOO*, Para. 40. In other terms, despite the discretion enjoyed by the Member States, the implementation measures of the said directive must not be liable to render the rights enshrined in Article 31(2) CFR and Articles 3, 5 and 6(b) of that directive meaningless.

[72] Case C-55/18, *CCOO*, Para. 46–57, where the CJEU analyses the relevant substantive and procedural provisions of the Spanish legal order.

[73] This being aimed at ensuring the effectiveness of those rights provided for in directive 2003/88 and of the fundamental right enshrined in Article 31(2) CFR (Case C-55/18, *CCOO*, Para. 60). In this regard, Member States have discretion over 'the specific arrangements for implementing such a system, in particular the form that it must take, having regard, as necessary, to the particular characteristics of each sector of activity concerned, or

State that, according to the interpretation given to it in national case law, does not require the said system.[74] This principle is not called into question by the costs that setting up such a system may involve for employers since, as recital no. 4 of directive 2003/88 states, the effective protection of the health and safety of workers should not be subordinated to purely economic considerations.[75] The Court did not explicitly carry out the direct effect test, stressing instead the duty of consistent interpretation upon national courts.[76] Consequently, the referring court, disregarding the *Tribunal Supremo*'s case law mentioned above,[77] is required, also in horizontal disputes, to interpret national law in order to guarantee the effectiveness of the fundamental right in Article 31(2) CFR, to which directive 2003/88 gives specific form. To this end, the national courts, not only will have to disregard the said national case law, but they will also have to protect the fundamental rights at issue by acknowledging a legal obligation, not explicitly laid down in the national law, upon (even private) employers. In so doing, as mentioned, the judgement may be seen as being at the outer limits of the duty of consistent interpretation. This is clearly reflected in the CJEU's formula for assessing the non-compliance with EU law, which consists in the fact that the national law '*does not require* employers to set up a system enabling the duration of time worked each day by each worker to be measured'.[78]

---

the specific characteristics of certain undertakings concerning, inter alia, their size' (Para. 63).

[74] Case C-55/18, *CCOO*, Para. 71.

[75] Case C-55/18, *CCOO*, Para. 66. Nor is it called into question by the fact that certain specific provisions of EU law provide explicitly for such an obligation (Para. 64–65).

[76] Case C-55/18, *CCOO*, Para. 68–71.

[77] Indeed, according to the CJEU's settled case law, the requirement to interpret national law in a manner that is consistent with EU law includes the obligation for national courts to change their established case slaw, where necessary, if it is based on an interpretation of national law that is incompatible with the objectives of a directive (Para. 70).

[78] Case C-55/18, *CCOO*, Para. 71 (emphasis added).

5 Concluding Remarks

By primarily analysing the CJEU's post-Lisbon case law, this chapter has pointed to two major considerations regarding the protection of workers' rights in Europe today. First, the *Laval-quartet* and subsequent case law (recalled in Sect. 2) do not fully cover the interplay between trade union power and EU law, since unions have relied to a significant extent on EU law to challenge national law before national courts (primarily raising questions to be referred to the CJEU under Article 267 TFEU), as discussed in Sect. 3. Second, the entry into force of the Lisbon Treaty and the interplay between the CFR and the rights provided in EU secondary law opened new potentialities in litigation as several cases show (examined in Sects. 3 and 4), which can ultimately result in the increased protection of social rights *vis-à-vis* the national level. In this respect, the possibility for unions to invoke the social rights granted by the EU legal order before national judges has proven to be an effective judicial enforcement mechanism of EU labour law, and, in this way, helps to assure its effectiveness (in French, its '*effet utile*') also in horizontal disputes.

Without disregarding the fact that, as of today, the character of primary law acquired by the CFR has not had any appreciable impact on the balance between fundamental economic freedoms and fundamental social rights (conversely, it could be argued that the CFR has shown its 'dark side' in this regard),[79] several issues deserve further clarifications by the CJEU. Among these, suffice it to recall the direct effects of fundamental rights in horizontal situations (see Leczykiewicz 2013, p. 492, where the Author proposed a pathway similar to that adopted by the CJEU; see generally on this issue Frantziou 2019), the scope of application of the CFR (see Lazzerini 2018), and the interplay mechanisms between primary and secondary law in horizontal disputes, mentioned in Sects. 3 and 4 (on this interplay between primary and secondary law see Rossi 2019, and the recent judgement in the *TSN* case[80]).

---

[79] *I.e.* the use of Article 16 of the CFR to enhance the four freedoms and beyond their scope of application, see further Para. 2 above. Generally, on the interplay between the former and the fundamental rights enshrined in the CFR, see the recent opinion delivered by Advocate General Campos Sánchez-Bordona in Case C-78/18, *Commission v Hungary*, Para. 93–113.

[80] Joined Cases C-609/17 and C-610/17, *TSN*, where the CJEU stated that such fundamental rights do not apply to provisions of national legislation and collective agreements more favourable to the protection of the safety and health of workers which have

However, the recent Court of Justice case law shows the potentialities of the CFR to be used, in combination with EU secondary law provisions, in strategic employment litigation throughout the EU, despite some far-reaching consequences of this case law have been pointed out. These concerning, inter alia, the allocation of competences between the EU and Member States (Prechal 2010), the legitimacy of the CJEU (see Simitis 1996), the relationship between the latter and national judges (O'Leary 2002, p. 289 ff.).[81]

With regard to the potentialities, it may be recalled that, within the context of the European Pillar of Social Rights (EPSR), proclaimed in 2017,[82] several pieces of secondary EU law that give concrete expression to fundamental social rights as enshrined in the CFR have recently been passed. Among these are directive 2019/1158 (on the work-life balance for parents and carers), whose recital no. 3 refers to the fundamental rights enshrined in Article 33 CFR,[83] and directive 2019/1152 (on transparent and predictable working conditions), whose recital no. 1 refers to the fundamental rights enshrined in Article 31 CFR. In this light, we might wonder whether there is a sufficient link between the fundamental social rights laid down in the Charter and (some of) these secondary law provisions[84] capable of allowing, upon the expiry of the transposition period for these two directives (in August 2022) and provided that Member States have not implemented them correctly, their 'joint use' by national courts. Moreover, new significant measures under the

---

been adopted under Article 15 of directive 2003/88). See further on this issue the recent opinion of Advocate General Kokott in the Joined Cases C-119/19 P and C-126/19 P, *Francisco Carreras Sequeros* et al.

[81] See footnote no. 56 above.

[82] The EPSR is a non-binding soft law instrument which expresses 20 key principles 'essential for fair and well-functioning labour markets and welfare systems in twenty-first century Europe' and foresees the enactment of several legislative and policy proposals.

[83] Pursuant to Article 33 of the CFR, entitled 'Family and professional life': '1. The family shall enjoy legal, economic and social protection. 2. To reconcile family and professional life, everyone shall have the right to protection from dismissal for a reason connected with maternity and the right to paid maternity leave and to parental leave following the birth or adoption of a child'. (Please note that this provision does not make any reference to national law and practices and that, as stated in the Explanations relating to the Charter of Fundamental Rights, Article 33 contains both elements of a right and of a principle in the meaning of Article 52 (5) CFR, see 'Explanation on Article 52—Scope and interpretation of rights and principles').

[84] Cf. Opinion delivered by Advocate General Cruz Villalón in Case C-176/72, *AMS*.

umbrella of the EPSR are expected to be enacted in the years to come (as announced in Commission President von der Leyen's Political Guidelines and in the Commission Working Programme 2021),[85] in relation to which trades unions are called upon to play a key role both *ex ante* (e.g. through involvement in social dialogue, as the case of fair minimum wages shows)[86] and, where appropriate, *ex post* (e.g. through litigation strategies involving EU law, that has been partly reviewed in this chapter).

In conclusion, it has been argued in this chapter that it would be shortsighted to consider the Court of Justice's case law as a mean to merely uphold the economic freedoms to the detriment of trade unions. It seems, on the contrary, that the Court strives to ensure the effectiveness of EU law *acquis* as a whole. Where it is called to interpret the EU social law this 'effectiveness paradigm' applies too thanks to 'characteristics arising from the very nature of EU law', such as the primacy enjoyed by EU law over the laws of the Member States and the direct effect of a whole series of provisions which are applicable to both individuals and Member States.[87] The possibility to enforce these social rights before national courts has augmented with the entry into force of the Lisbon Treaty, since primary law provisions, as pointed out above, can have direct effects even in the so-called horizontal relationships, and, consequently, this shall be true for the fundamental social rights now enshrined in the Charter (cf. Lenaerts 2020). This is why, without disregarding the importance of the open issues surrounding the CFR mentioned above in this section, the enactment of new pieces of EU law legislation providing for social rights protected by the CFR would probably result in the expansion of the employment strategic litigation possibilities enjoyed by trade unions, and thus in strengthening the methods through which they promote solidarity—in the form of fundamental rights—within the EU.

---

[85] See respectively von der Leyen U., 'A Union that strives for more. My agenda for Europe: political guidelines for the next European Commission 2019–2024', 2019, spec. pp. 9–10, and Commission's Work Programme 2021, spec. pp. 4–5.

[86] See the 2020 Commission's Second phase consultation of Social Partners under Article 154 TFEU working document concerning fair minimum wages. In this regard, please note that in October 2020, the Commission submitted to the EU legislators a proposal for a directive on an adequate minimum wage.

[87] Opinion 2/13, Para. 161 ff.

Bibliography

Albors-Llorens A., 'Remedies Against the EU Institutions After Lisbon: An Era of Opportunity?', in *Cambridge Law Journal*, 2012, pp. 507–536.

Azoulai L., 'Le sens des libertés de circulation dans le droit de l'Union européenne', in Bergé J.-S., Giorgini C. (eds), *Le sens des libertés économiques de circulation*, Bruylant, Bruxelles, 2020, pp. 103–111.

Barnard C., 'Viking and Laval: An Introduction', in Barnard C. (eds), *The Cambridge Yearbook of European Legal Studies, Vol. 10 (2007–2008)*, 2008, Hart, Oxford and Portland, pp. 463–492.

Bercusson B., *European Labour Law*, Cambridge University Press, Cambridge, 2nd Ed., 2009.

Cancilla F.A., *Servizi del welfare e diritti sociali nella prospettiva dell'integrazione europea*, Giuffrè, Milan, 2009.

Craig P. & de Búrca G., *EU Law. Text, Cases, and Materials*, Oxford University Press, Oxford, 7th Ed., 2020.

Frantziou E., *The Horizontal Effect of Fundamental Rights in the European Union: A Constitutional Analysis*, Oxford University Press, Oxford, 2019.

Gallo D., *L'efficacia diretta del diritto dell'Unione europea negli ordinamenti nazionali. Evoluzione di una dottrina ancora controversa*, Giuffrè, Milan, 2018.

Gallo D., 'Effetto diretto del diritto dell'Unione europea e disapplicazione, oggi', in Osservatorio sulle fonti, No. 3, 2019, pp. 1–42.

Garben S., 'The Constitutional (Im)balance between 'the Market' and 'the Social' in the European Union', in *European Constitutional Law Review*, 2017, vol. 13, pp. 23–61.

Giubboni S., *Diritto del lavoro europeo. Una introduzione critica*, CEDAM, Padua, 2017.

Lazzerini N., *La Carta dei Diritti Fondamentali dell'Unione Europea. I limiti di applicazione*, Franco Angeli Editore, Milan, 2018.

Leczykiewicz D., 'Horizontal Application of the of Fundamental Rights', in *European Law Review*, 2013, p. 479 and ff.

Lenaerts K., 'The Horizontal Application of the Charter', in *Quaderni costituzionali*, 2020, pp. 633–636.

Marcelle V. & Van den Haute B., 'Arrêt « CCOO »: l'obligation de mesurer le temps de travail', In *Journal de droit européen*, 2019, p. 366 and ff.

McCann M., *Rights at Work, Pay Equity Reform and the Politics of Legal Mobilization*, Chicago University Press, Chicago, 1994.

Mengozzi P. & Morviducci C., *Istituzioni di Diritto dell'Unione europea*, CEDAM, Padua, 2nd Ed., 2018.

Moreau M.-A., 'Regards croisés sur l'exercice des compétences sociales dans l'Union européen', in Barbou des Places S., Pataut E., and Rodière P. (eds),

Les frontiers de l'Europe sociale, Éditions Pedone, Paris, Collection Cahiers Européens (No. 11), 2018, pp. 39–49.

Murphy C., 'Using the EU Charter of Fundamental Rights Against Private Parties after Association De Médiation Sociale', in *European Human Rights Law Review*, 2014, p. 170 and ff.

O'Leary S., *Employment Law at the European Court of Justice: Judicial Structures, Policies and Processes*, Hart, Oxford, 2002, p. 289 ff.

O'Leary S., 'Solidarity and Citizenship Rights in the Charter of Fundamental Rights of the European Union', in de Búrca G. (eds), *EU Law and the Welfare State: In Search of Solidarity*, Oxford University Press, Oxford, 2005, p. 50 ff.

Pecinovsky P., *The Right to Collective Bargaining for Economically Dependent Workers with a Self-employed Status*, this volume, 2021.

Peraro C., *Diritti fondamentali sociali e tutela collettiva nell'Unione europea*, Edizioni Scientifiche Italiane, Naples, 2020.

Pescatore P., 'The Doctrine of "Direct Effect": An Infant Disease of Community Law', in *European Law Review*, 2015, Vol. 2, pp. 135–153.

Prechal S., 'Competence Creep and General Principles of Law', in *Review of European Administrative Law*, 2010, Vol. 3, No. 1, pp. 5–22.

Roman D., 'Introduction. Les droits sociaux, «droits des pauvres» ou droits de l'Homme?', in Roman D. (eds), *Les droits sociaux, entre droits de l'Homme et politiques sociales. Quels titulaires pour quells droits?* Paris, 2012, pp. 1–24.

Rossi L.S., 'The Relationship between the EU Charter of Fundamental Rights and Directives in Horizontal Situations', in *EU Law Analysis Blog*, 25th February 2019.

Ryan B., 'The Charter and Collective Labour Law', in Hervey T. K. & Kenner J. (eds), *Economic and Social Rights under the EU Charter of Fundamental Rights—A Legal Perspective*, Hart, Oxford & Portland, 2003, pp. 67–90.

Schütze R., Direct Effects and Indirect Effects of Union Law, in Schütze R. and Tridimas T. (eds), *Oxford Principles of European Union Law—Volume I: The European Union Legal Order*, Oxford University Press, Oxford, 2018, pp. 265–299.

Sciarra S., 'Job Centre: An Illustrative Example of Strategic Litigation', in Sciarra S. (eds), *Labour Law in the Courts. National Judges and the European Court of Justice*, Hart, Oxford, 2001, p. 241 ff.

Sciarra S., 'Viking and Laval: Collective Labour Rights and Market Freedoms in the Enlarged EU', in Barnard C. (eds), 2008, pp. 559–580.

Simitis S., 'Dismantling or Strengthening Labour Law: The Case of the European Court of Justice', in *European Law Journal*, 1996, pp. 156–176.

Supiot A., *Critique du droit du travail*, PUF, Quadrige, 2015.

EU Legal Acts

Directive (EU) 2019/1158 of the European Parliament and of the Council of 20 June 2019 on work-life balance for parents and carers and repealing Council Directive 2010/18/EU.

Directive (EU) 2019/1152 of the European Parliament and of the Council of 20 June 2019 on transparent and predictable working conditions in the European Union.

Directive 2008/104/EC of the European Parliament and of the Council of 19 November 2008 on temporary agency work.

Directive 2003/88/EC of the European Parliament and of the Council of 4 November 2003 concerning certain aspects of the organisation of working time.

Directive 2002/14/EC of the European Parliament and of the Council of 11 March 2002 establishing a general framework for informing and consulting employees in the European Community.

Directive 2001/23/EC of the Council of 12 March 2001 on the approximation of the laws of the Member States relating to the safeguarding of employees' rights in the event of transfers of undertakings, businesses or parts of undertakings or businesses.

Directive 98/59/EC of the Council of 20 July 1998 on the approximation of the laws of the Member States relating to collective redundancies.

Directive 92/85/EEC of the Council of 19 October 1992 on the introduction of measures to encourage improvements in the safety and health at work of pregnant workers and workers who have recently given birth or are breastfeeding.

European Commission, Proposal for a directive of the European Parliament and of the Council on adequate minimum wages in the European Union, COM/2020/682 final.

European Commission, Commission Work Programme 2021 - A Union of vitality in a world of fragility, COM(2020) 690 final.

European Commission, Second phase consultation of Social Partners under Article 154 TFEU on a possible action addressing the challenges related to fair minimum wages {SWD (2020) 105 final}, C(2020) 3570 final.

European Parliament, Resolution of 12 February 2019 on the implementation of the Charter of Fundamental Rights of the European Union in the EU institutional framework (2017/2089(INI).

European Parliament, Council, European Commission, Interinstitutional Proclamation on the European Pillar of Social Rights (2017/C 428/09).

CJEU's Case Law and Advocate General's Opinions

Judgement of 19 November 2019, Joined Cases C-609/17 and C-610/17, *TSN*.

Judgement of 24 June 2019, Case C-573/17, *Popławski II*.

Judgement of 14 May 2019, Case C-55/18, *Federación de Servicios de Comisiones Obreras (CCOO) v Deutsche Bank SAE*.

Judgement of 11 April 2019, Case C-254/18, *Syndicat des cadres de la sécurité intérieure*.

Judgement of 20 November 2018, Case C-147/17, *Sindicatul Familia Constanţa*.

Judgement of 13 December 2018, Case C-385/17, *Hein*.

Judgement of 6 November 2018, Joined Cases C-569/16 and C-570/16, *Bauer*.

Judgement of 6 November 2018, Case C-684/16, *Max-Planck-Gesellschaft*.

Judgement of the Court of 27 February 2018, Case C-64/16, *Associação Sindical dos Juízes Portugueses v Tribunal de Contas*.

Judgement of 22 February 2018, Case C-103/16, *Guisado*.

Judgement of 6 April 2017, Case C-336/15, *Unionen*.

Judgement of 21 December 2016, Case C-201/15, *AGET Iraklis*.

Judgement of 19 April 2016, Case C-441/14, *Dansk Industri (DI), acting on behalf of Ajos A/S*.

Judgement of 30 April 2015, Case C-80/14, *Union of Shop, Distributive and Allied Workers (USDAW)*.

Judgement of 17 March 2015, Case C-533/13, *Auto- ja Kuljetusalan Työntekijäliitto AKT ry*.

Judgement of 12 February 2015, Case C-396/13, *Sähköalojen ammattiliitto ry*.

Judgement of 18 December 2014, Case C-354/13, *Fag og Arbejde (FOA)*.

Judgement of 26 November 2014, Joined Cases C-22/13, C-61/13 to C-63/13 and C-418/13, *Mascolo and Others*.

Judgement of 13 February 2014, Joined Cases C-512/11 and C-513/11, *Terveys- ja sosiaalialan neuvottelujärjestö (TSN) ry v Terveyspalvelualan Liitto ry and Ylemmät Toimihenkilöt (YTN)*.

Judgement of 15 January 2014, Case C-176/12, *Association de médiation sociale v Union locale des syndicats CGT and Others*.

Judgement of 18 July 2013, Case C-426/11, *Alemo-Herron*.

Judgement of 11 April 2013, Joined Cases C-335/11 and C-337/11, *HK Danmark*.

Judgement of 12 July 2012, Case C-171/11, *Fra.bo SpA*.

Judgement of 21 October 2010, Case C-242/09, *Albron v FNV Bondgenoten*.

Judgement of 12 October 2010, case C-499/08, *Ingeniørforeningen i Danmark*.

Judgement of 29 July 2010, Case C-151/09, *Federación de Servicios Públicos de la UGT*.

Judgement of 15 July 2010, Case C-271/08, *European Commission v Federal Republic of Germany.*
Judgement of 19 June 2008, Case C-319/06, *Commission v Luxemburg.*
Judgement of 3 April 2008, Case C-346/06, *Rüffert.*
Judgement of 18 December 2007, Case C-341/05, *Laval.*
Judgement of 11 December 2007, Case C-438/05, *Viking.*
Judgement of 22 November 2005, Case C-144/04, *Mangold.*
Judgement of 12 June 2003, Case C-112/00, *Schmidberger.*
Judgement of 6 June 2000, Case C-281/98, *Angonese.*
Judgement of 21 September 1999, Case C-67/96, *Albany International BV v Stichting Bedrijfspensioenfonds Textielindustrie.*
Judgement of 15 December 1995, C-415/93, *Bosman.*
Judgement of 14 July 1994, Case 91/92, *Paola Faccini Dori v Recreb Srl.*
Judgement of the Court of 19 November 1991, Joined Cases C-6/90 and C-9/90, *Andrea Francovich and Danila Bonifaci and others v Italian Republic.*
Judgement of 25 July 1991, Case C-76/90, *Säger.*
Judgement of the Court of 26 February 1986, Case 152/84, *M. H. Marshall v Southampton and South-West Hampshire Area Health Authority.*
Judgement of 8 April 1976, Case 43/75, *Gabrielle Defrenne v Société anonyme belge de navigation aérienne Sabena* (so-called *Defrenne II*).
Judgement of 5 February 1963, Case 26/62, *NV Algemene Transport- en Expeditie Onderneming van Gend & Loos v Netherlands Inland Revenue Administration.*
Opinion of the Court (Full Court) of 18 December 2014, Opinion 2/13 on the Accession of the European Union to the European Convention for the Protection of Human Rights and Fundamental Freedoms.
Opinion of Advocate General Kokott delivered on 26 March 2020, Joined Cases C-119/19 P and C-126/19 P, *Francisco Carreras Sequeros et at.*
Opinion of Advocate General Campos Sánchez-Bordona delivered on 14 January 2020, Case C-78/18, *European Commission v Hungary.*
Opinion of Advocate General Pitruzzella delivered on 31 January 2019, Case C-55/18, *Federación de Servicios de Comisiones Obreras (CCOO) v Deutsche Bank SAE.*
Opinion of Advocate General Cruz Villalón delivered on 18 July 2013, Case C-176/72, *Association de médiation sociale v Union locale des syndicats CGT and Others.*

CHAPTER 4

Trade Unions and Migration in Europe

Rolle Alho

1 Introduction

The power of trade unions in Europe in the twentieth and twenty-first centuries has been fundamentally intertwined with the framework of the nation state. For unions, the puzzle of how to relate to 'migration' is in practice linked to national borders and the nation state because there is typically no direct means to regulate migration *within* nation states—even if internal migration may sometimes be a significant issue within national public discourse.[1]

Migration raises a fundamental question of solidarity for unions regarding 'who are unions for?'. Historically, unions have often been torn,

[1] We should note that many migrants are granted residency status for reasons that are not work-related, therefore, a good deal of migration takes place outside of the context of work and is therefore not managed within policies related to 'labour migration' specifically, such as regarding asylum, refugees and family reunification. While this chapter focuses on the influence of migration on labour markets and trade unions, we will consider migration policy in broad terms.

R. Alho (✉)
University of Helsinki, Helsinki, Finland
e-mail: rolle.alho@helsinki.fi

on the one hand, between ideas of universalistic, transnational solidarity between workers, and on the other, between, protectionist views that can regard immigration as a threat to the labour market position of 'native' workers (see Penninx & Roosblad 2000).

The positions and strategies that unions adopt with regards to migration are important for unions' future, for example, as regards whether they succeed in representing a workforce that is increasingly diverse. The inclusion of migrants as union members, activists and staff has been identified as an opportunity that can strengthen unions' power resources—that have been weakened in most countries in the last decades (e.g. Alho 2015; Marino et al. 2017). Unions can—in addition to the inclusion of migrants—lobby for the introduction of legislation that promotes the position of migrants in the labour market and thine wider society. The focus in this chapter, however, is on unions' recourse to law in terms of their preferences and goals regarding state-level labour migration policy.

National labour migration policy has potential effects on the labour markets, including the outlook for unions. Consequently, what labour migration policies national governments adopt is de facto a trade union issue. This chapter examines the relationship between unions and migration by focusing on European unions' responses to labour migration in the 2000s and 2010s specifically.

Perhaps surprisingly, union responses to migration have gained increased interest among scholars since the start of the 2000s despite the decrease of the general role and influence of unions in most countries during this period. The increased scholarly interest is exemplified by two book anthologies that focus on union responses in a number of European countries, namely: Penninx and Roosblad (2000) and Marino et al. (2017). In addition, a number of PhD theses focusing on unions' responses to migration and migrant workers in various countries have been published in recent years, including: Alho (2015) on Finland and Estonia, Berntsen (2015) and Roosblad (2002) (on the Netherlands), Ristikari (2013) on Finland, Marino 2015; Krings 2009a (on Austria, Germany, Ireland and the UK) and Munakamwe (2018) on South Africa. This increased interest is probably explained at least in part by the increased salience of migration in public discourse in many European countries during this time, and also by the fact that many unions and scholars alike see the integration of migrant workers within the unions as a potential strategy for union renewal.

Moreover, an increasing number of studies that fall into the 'trade union renewal' genre have focused on the relationship between unions and migrant workers. Within the literature that focuses on the prospects for trade union renewal, the inclusion of migrants in unions is seen as an important question, including for Milkman (2010) who consider the United States and Ford (2019) who focuses on a number of Asian countries. Furthermore, many studies in the European context have looked at short-term labour migration, which is particularly visible in the construction and the agricultural sectors (including Lillie & Sippola; Alho 2015; Wagner 2018).

According to Penninx and Roosblad (2000, pp. 4–6) a key question is whether unions should resist or agree to employer demands '*for the recruitment of workers from abroad to fill vacancies*'. Historically, 'local' workers have often feared that immigrants would threaten their jobs and their wellbeing, and that they could disrupt the social order in a negative way (e.g. Guerin-Gonzales & Strikwerda 1993, p. 3). For these reasons—despite their legacy of international solidarity—immigration has often been a sensitive and difficult issue for unions to deal with (see Castles & Kosack 1973; Penninx & Roosblad 2000, p. 9).

The study by Penninx and Roosblad (2000) was based on responses from trade unionists in seven Western European countries between 1960–1993, during an era characterised by the guest worker system in many West and North European countries and migration that was precipitated by the processes of decolonisation. This study showed that unions often supported employer demands for the liberalisation of migration policy, but in countries where unions were involved in national decision-making (e.g. Sweden and Austria), they could also effectually seek to influence the circumstances under which such immigration occurred.

Meanwhile, the study of Marino et al. (2017), which was based on responses from trade unionists in eleven European countries between the 2000s and the mid-2010s, concludes that unions' chances of influencing national labour migration policies has diminished over the last decades. Specifically, union influence within corporatist, national decision-making bodies has deteriorated, which has weakened their influence over national labour migration policy too. Secondly, the enlargement of the European Union (EU) has diminished the possibilities for unions to influence labour migration and mobility within the EU due to the freedom of movement guaranteed under EU-law (ibid., p. 372).

On the other hand, studies conducted in the Nordic countries (see Alho 2015 for Finland; Bucken-Knapp 2009 for Sweden) point towards the fact that unions in those countries have maintained much of their political clout and continue to exert influence over national migration policies as regards non-EU countries, as EU Member States have the right to determine how many third-country (i.e. non-EU) nationals may enter their labour market (see Article 79(5) of the Treaty on the Functioning of the EU).

In addition, even if trade unions (according to Marino et al. 2017) have less influence over state migration policies and have fewer possibilities to influence who has the right to enter the labour markets from abroad, they still have a role in regulating migration because they have the potential to influence under which conditions migrants are employed and, for example, what residence rights they might have.

The rest of the chapter is organised as follows: first, I describe why labour migration is an important issue for trade unions. Following this, I discuss how the migration and labour market context has changed in Europe since the 2000s, which is important for understanding union responses to the phenomenon. After this I discuss how we might make sense of unions' responses to labour migration. Penultimately I present empirical examples of union stances vis-à-vis migration. The final section concludes.

2 Theoretical Considerations: Why Is Labour Migration an Important Issue for Trade Unions?

National migration policies have consequences for labour markets—from the macro-level employment relations to the workplace level. On a broader societal level, migration policy has the potential to constrain—or enable—the integration of migrants into societies. Labour migration is also related to union power resources. Migration policies that facilitate migrants' integration to the labour market on an equal basis with settled workers in terms of rights and working conditions does not by default threaten unions' power resources—and in the case that migrants join trade unions, immigration can strengthen the position of the unions (Alho 2015; Milkman 2010).

On the other hand, if inward migration occurs in a fashion in which migrants perform the same jobs with lower wages as settled workers, and become union members to a lesser degree than locals do, inward migration may have negative consequences for unions, including as regards wages and working conditions (Alho 2015; Finseraas et al. 2020). The attempt by some employers to take full advantage of labour migration by bypassing national legislation, collective agreements and/or minimum wages by underpaying migrants ultimately can also work against the interests of other employers who adhere to formal regulation (e.g. Refslund 2016, p. 613). In such a situation, the only clear winners are those employers in whose interest it is to cut standards in pay and working conditions (Watts 2002, p. 73).

In contrast, if national migration policy has the effect of securing migrants' rights (for example, with the introduction of relatively secure residence rights) migrant workers will be better integrated and unions will find it easier to reach out and organise them. However, migration policies can also render migrant workers in a vulnerable position especially in cases when their right to reside in a country is tied to a certain occupation or workplace. In such cases losing one's job may mean losing one's right to reside (Guerin-Gonzales & Strikwerda 1993, pp. 155–174), which weakens migrants' bargaining position vis-à-vis their employer. This hinders the possibility for unions to defend their working conditions and undermines their capacity to organise migrants as union members, which may ultimately have a negative impact on unions' bargaining position (Alho 2015). Those migrants who are marginalised due to migration policies may also be reluctant to contact or join trade unions for fear of drawing attention to themselves.

These aspects render state-level migration policy a critical issue for the unions, and unions can seek to influence its formation—depending on the unions' political clout—directly by lobbying (Alho 2015; Greer et al. 2013; Haus 2002; Krings 2009a; Marino et al. 2017; Penninx & Roosblad 2000), or indirectly, by trying to influence the public debate and public perceptions of inward migration in a way that serves the unions' interests (Alho 2015).

These starting points lead us to the question of what types of strategies unions have developed in terms of inward migration. Do unions perceive that restrictive—or open-migration policies serve their interests? As will be shown below, there has been great variety across Europe, and union strategies have differed across countries and time. Before that, let us briefly describe the context in which labour migration in Europe takes place.

3 Changing Migration and Labour Market Setting in Europe

Since the 2000s, trade unions have endured a period of substantial changes in their operating environments, which pose existential challenges for the labour movement. Some of these issues should be highlighted in order to contextualise the ways in which unions respond to migration. Specifically, this includes the increased precaritisation of the labour markets; the diversification of migration; the politicisation of immigration and increase of short-term migration, each of which is dealt with below.

3.1 The Precarisation of the Labour Market

As is summarised in brief in the introduction to this volume, unions have been challenged over recent decades by the processes of globalisation and de-industrialisation, the growth of the service sector, neoliberal state policies and the growth in precarious work (see Doellgast et al. 2018). Thus, inward migration in Europe takes place in a context that poses many challenges for unions, as migrants enter a labour market that is generally less regulated than was the case in the heyday of industrialisation, in the decades following the Second World War.

3.2 The Diversification of Migration

Migration has grown in recent decades and many countries that had traditionally been countries of emigration have become countries of immigration (e.g. Ireland, Italy, Finland and Portugal). In addition, there has been a qualitative shift in the migration patterns compared to previous decades, with increased migration between countries with no history of notable economic or colonial ties (e.g. with post-2004 migration Polish migration to Ireland as an example). Notably, as migration has become a more diverse phenomenon, collective action can become more difficult if unions fail to communicate with migrant workers in a situation of increasing linguistic, ethnic, religious and cultural diversity. Many sociological accounts have emphasised a potentially negative effect of ethnic diversity on collective action (e.g. Putnam 2000) and such accounts can be found already in the writings of Karl Marx and Friedrich Engels on the effect of Irish Catholic workers on the organisation of the British working class. However, empirical studies on union organisation show that diversity does not necessarily impede the capacity of unions to organise migrant workers if unions manage to build links to and communicate effectively with migrant workers (Milkman 2010; Holgate 2005; Doellgast et al. 2018). On the other hand, increasing diversity caused by inward migration can require more linguistic and cultural competence and sensitivities for unions.

3.3 *The Politicisation of Immigration*

Migration has become an increasingly contentious issue in many European countries. As a consequence, whatever position unions take on immigration, they risk alienating part of their extant and potential members and supporters.

3.4 *The Increase of Short-Term Migration*

Today here are increased possibilities for workers to work on a short-term basis in other EU/EEA (European Economic Area) countries than heretofore, given the reduction in travel costs and the increasing tendency of employers to 'post' workers that are based in one EU/EEA country to work in another. Temporary migration poses difficulties for unions to reach out to migrant workers and to oversee their working conditions (Alho 2015; Berntsen 2015; Wagner 2018).

The next section presents an analysis of union responses to labour migration across Europe.

4 Trade Unions' Responses to Labour Migration

Despite the historical all-embracing efforts to unite 'all workers' (see Hyman 1971), trade unions have, in practice, tended to develop around defending the interests of workers that share a more or less similar set of skills and/or position in a certain industry, workplace or occupation (Hyman 2001, pp. 6–16; Virdee 2000, p. 547; Webb & Webb 1894/2003). As noted, the history of trade unions is linked intrinsically to the nation state (e.g. Erne 2008, p. 3). As unions in Europe have been embedded in the institutions and decision-making bodies of particular nation states, unions' understanding of who belongs to 'us' and 'them' has also revolved around the division between 'native' and 'migrant' workers. This is a division that by no means is a natural one, but rather one that is caused by the real and imagined boundaries that the nation state inevitably produces. National borders can be regarded as institutions themselves that govern the extent of inclusion and exclusion between a territorial or membership group or groups of workers (Cassarino 2006). Union positions vis-à-vis the nation state can strengthen—or weaken—this division, which can contribute to the hierarchical categories and divisions between 'us' and 'them'.

Some unions have traditionally feared that admitting large numbers of migrants could exert downward pressure on wages and working conditions and could undermine their bargaining position (McGovern 2007). The extent to which this fear is based on an accurate analysis of the evidence is not the question here, but clearly such perceptions have guided union responses to migration.

In many Western European countries (e.g. Austria, Germany, the Netherlands and Switzerland) where so-called guest worker programmes were introduced after the Second World War until the 1970s, unions consented to labour migration but demanded that guest workers should only be given short-term work permits, which could be renewed only if there was a demand for labour. Such policies were clearly designed to defend the interests of native workers and excluded guest workers from the possibility of becoming integrated in society, which placed them in an unequal position in relation to native workers (Penninx & Roosblad 2000). This stance is well illustrated by the following quote:

> In order to protect German employees, all legal possibilities must be utilised to send home foreign workers who are no longer needed. If they do not go voluntarily, regulations which permit their expulsion will just have to be applied more stringently.—Edmund Duda, representative of the peak-level DGB (Deutscher Gewerkschaftsbund/German trade union confederation DGB) in 1973. Quoted in Guerin-Gonzales and Strikwerda (1993, pp. 287–288)

Nowadays, it would be unlikely to hear such an outspoken stance as was presented by Edmund Duda among the official stances of European trade unions, who tend to promote a discourse of solidarity and equal rights irrespective of the county of origin of any worker (see, e.g. Marino et al. 2017, pp. 361–362; ETUC 2019). In Germany, for example, DGB has accepted that migrant workers are there to stay; Tapia and Holgate (2018,

p. 193) argue that since the beginning of the 1970s the increased presence of migrants, and pressure from 'black and white rank-and-file union members' (in the UK at least) has led to a shift in the migration policy of British, French and German unions from '*a more restrictive to a more inclusive and solidaristic approach*'.

However, the change in European unions' position vis-à-vis migration does not mean that unions would favour totally unrestricted labour migration: from the unions' perspective, the state should regulate migration in a manner that does not allow for social dumping (referring here to a practice of employers to use migrant workers with the purpose of undermining existing wages and working conditions in order to make profit) that allows for the exploitation of migrant workers (Alho 2015). Unions have understood that labour migration could weaken their bargaining position if it occurs in a fashion that they have no way of controlling (see Alho 2015; Penninx & Roosblad 2000; Wagner 2018). On the other hand, unions in many countries have assessed that very restrictive migration policies are not in the interests of the unions nor of migrant workers because such policies tend to render migrants vulnerable and feed the underground economy (Bengtsson 2013; Haus 2002; Krings 2009a; Watts 2002).

The actors who most prominently advocate for the liberalisation of national migration policies are employer organisations for whom labour migration presents a welcome increase in the supply of labour (e.g. Alho 2015). In addition, many governments in the ageing European welfare states embrace labour migration as a solution to labour shortages and to the demographical challenges associated with ageing populations (Menz & Caviedes 2010). Pro-migrant rights and human rights organisations also often advocate for more liberal migration policies based on humanitarian concerns.

Drawing this together, scholars point to a multitude of explanatory variables as regards unions' preferences as regards labour immigration, including: the institutional position of the unions in the receiving country; the employment situation in the receiving country: and the specific national legacies relating to migration, which we discuss in turn below.

4.1 The Institutional Position of the Unions in the Receiving Country

In countries where unions are strongly embedded in the state's decision-making processes, including through strong ties with governing political parties and through social dialogue arrangements, unions can seek to directly influence the national regulatory framework as regards labour migration policy (see Marino et al. 2017, p. 382; Penninx & Roosblad 2000). Specific examples of such countries include: Austria, Denmark (see Refslund 2016), Finland (see Alho 2015), Germany, the Netherlands and Sweden (see Lundh 1995). In contrast, the possibilities for unions to influence migration policy is weaker where unions are not formally embedded in the state's decision-making processes, for example in Ireland and the UK (e.g. Marino et al. 2017, p. 382).

Unions who are relatively well-embedded in national decision-making bodies have often accepted the removal of restrictions on labour migration where governments take measures to curb the 'risks' associated with it, for example, by taking actions to guarantee equal wages between native and migrant workers (Alho 2015; Penninx & Roosblad 2000, p. 187). Access for unions to the national decision-making bodies does not, however, predetermine unions' positions in terms of openness or restrictiveness towards migration. The Swedish trade union movement, for example, has been more open to migration than its Austrian counterpart has, even though unions in both countries are strongly embedded in the state's decision-making processes (see Neergaard & Woolfson 2017; Gächter 2017). However, in Europe, unions with a relatively weak embeddedness in national institutional decision-making bodies seem to be more likely to take steps to promote the judicial rights of the most vulnerable migrants, such as through the regularisation of undocumented migrants (Penninx & Roosblad 2000). For examples of this type of 'progressive' union positions see Rinaldini and Marino (2017) for Italy, Miguel Martínez Lucio (2017, p. 294) for Spain, Kolarova & Peixoto (2009, pp. 65–77) for Portugal, and Connolly and Sellers (2017) for the UK. In such cases, unions' have operated as an oppositional force towards state policies that put migrants in a vulnerable position due to their residency entitlements.

4.2 The Employment Situation in the Receiving Country

When the availability of jobs is relatively high and unemployment is low, unions are in a more favourable position as regards accepting a more 'open' labour migration policy than they might otherwise be (Penninx & Roosblad 2000; Krings 2009a). The Irish and British unions' relatively open stances towards inward migration form the EU accession countries following enlargement in 2004 has partly been explained by the good employment situation in those countries, which included exceptionally low levels of unemployment in the UK at the beginning of the 2000s (Krings 2009a, p. 58). The employment situation does not, however, predetermine unions' views on migration as Austrian unions, for example, have supported restrictive positions on labour immigration, despite relatively low levels of employment in that country (ibid., p. 60).

4.3 National Legacies of Migration

Trade unions are embedded within national contexts that help to shape how labour migration is framed and perceived (Ford 2019, p. 155; Marino et al. 2017, p. 369; Penninx & Roosblad 2000, p. 206), and dominant discourses and perceptions of immigration within the national context—whether positive or negative—have been shown to shape unions' positions on labour immigration (e.g. Krings 2009a).

Although these factors do not provide a comprehensive framework that can explain how unions in a given country may react to labour migration, they can be helpful for understanding the choices that unions make (cf. Marino et al. 2017, p. 369). In the following section, we take a closer look at some of the key developments in union responses to migration over the last two decades in a sample of European countries.

5 National Level Commonalities and Variances in Union Positions vis-à-vis Labour Migration

5.1 Commonalities

There have been many documented commonalities in union positions towards inward migration in the EU since the 2000s. Simply put, across many European countries, the unions' primary goal has been to guarantee that national migration policies do not undermine working standards in the receiving country (see Eldring et al. 2012; Krings 2009a; Marino et al. 2017; Refslund 2016). In the EU-context, the question is also related to how unions can influence EU-level policies that are related to labour migration, a typical example being the much-debated Posted Workers Directive, which many employers have relied upon to avoid host country regulations (e.g. Lillie & Greer 2007; Meardi 2012).

Migrants—as a category—are disproportionately represented in precarious and low-wage work and tend to cluster in certain low-skilled sectors and occupations (Piore 1979; Wills et al. 2010). The task of protecting the working conditions of migrants and of organising this cohort as union members has been difficult especially for those unions that represent labour intensive sectors where the prospect of overseeing and influencing the nature of working conditions is generally challenging for unions, for example in the construction, hospitality and agriculture sectors and, more recently, in the platform economy (Berntsen 2015; Doellgast et al. 2018; Wagner 2018). This is still the case, even if national legislation typically guarantees equal wages and working conditions for citizens as well as non-citizens. Across countries, unions have demanded more resources and more effective enforcement by national labour inspectorates to oversee migrants' working conditions (Alho 2015; Golden 2015, p. 272). In many countries, however, the labour inspectors are required to inform the police if they encounter undocumented migrant workers, which can be problematic both from an individual standpoint and from the perspective of protecting working conditions more generally.

Notably, a further commonality is that there are no major studies that show that unions across Europe would have advocated positions regarding inward migration that would radically diverge in terms of openness or restrictiveness from the position taken by the national governments (see, Marino et al. 2017 for a comparative study of trade union responses to migration in eleven EU-countries and Alho 2015 for a review of the Finnish and Estonian cases). There are, for example, at least no major signs of unions actively propagating a widespread opening of the EU/EEA labour markets for third-country nationals who in many cases need work permits to take on employment, which in many sectors are dependent on government officials' assessment of whether 'labour market demand' exists (and which consequently segment workers' according to citizenship). That being said, there have been cases in Spain, Italy and France where union leaders have lobbied for legislation that facilitates legal migration pathways and that hence improves the situation for migrant workers (Haus 2002, pp. 141–149; Watts 2002, p. 3).

Questions related to residence permits are particularly problematic for migrants in those cases when the right to reside and work is tied to a particular employer. A critical interpretation of this is that such legislation preserves the notion of 'fortress Europe' that perpetuates global inequalities by curbing the legal pathways into European labour markets from outside of the EU/EEA (see Alho 2015). Paananen (1999) has also critically remarked that unions have at times associated themselves with the exploitation of migrants' discourse in order to defend restrictions on inward migration as it gives a more humanitarian impression, but merely disguises a desire for protectionism.

That being said, there are no signs of unions supporting populist and far-right-wing demands to radically curb inward migration either, although some trade union members are attracted by these ideas (ETUI 2019). However, those parts of the European population, NGOs and civil society actors that would like to see radically either more 'open' or 'closed' national borders are, for the time being at least, not likely to find many allies in trade unions who rather advocate what could be called 'managed labour migration', a concept that is often embraced by the European Trade Union Confederation (ETUC)[2] (see ETUC's Action Plan for Migration 2013).

When advocating for restrictions on inward migration, unions tend to emphasise the fact that they are not 'against' migrants—or immigration as such— but typically argue that restrictions on various types of labour migration are needed because employers can and do in many sectors exert downward pressure on wages and working conditions by 'exploiting' migrants (Alho 2015; Krings 2009a; Canek 2017).

However, across countries, the prospects for unions to 'manage' migration have gradually decreased due the increased options for workers to be highly mobile within the EU and EEA[3] framework of free movement. This means that labour migration policy in these countries nowadays in practice mostly refers to policies related to 'third country-nationals' or 'TCN's (i.e. non-EU or EEA country nationals) who work in the EU/EEA, or who seek to move to move to the EU/EEA territory for the purposes of work. In addition, the control of a large part of inward migration from third countries takes place beyond the scope of labour migration policies specifically (e.g. humanitarian migration) e.g. (e.g. Menz & Caviedes 2010, p. 1). Irrespective of these administrative categories, migrants who primarily move for purposes other than work (e.g. asylum seekers, refugees or persons who move due to family reunification) will often also enter the labour market (Alho 2021; Galgóczi 2021). At the time of writing, it remains to be seen how British trade

---

[2] The umbrella organisation representing European trade union confederations.

[3] EEA membership includes the extension of the rules and responsibilities of the EU's single market—including the free movement of persons—to the non-EU member states in the bloc.

unions may manage to influence UK labour immigration policy after that country's withdrawal from the EU.

Despite the aforementioned developments that decrease the possibilities for unions to control inward migration, the enlargement of the EU since 2004 have shown that national trade union organisations in the EU-15 counties did have some influence (albeit to varying degrees) over the shape of inward labour migration flows from the new EU-countries (see e.g. Alho 2015; Krings 2009a).

Haus (2002) and Watts (2002) have claimed, on the basis of studies focusing on Spain, Italy, France, the UK and the US, that union responses have converged since the 1990s to support more open migration policies than before because they see restrictive policies neither as desirable nor as fulfilling their purpose of 'protecting' national labour markets. On the other hand, the recent EU enlargement rounds point to enduring cross-country variances as regards union stances towards migration in especially the 'older' EU member states, which we turn to in the next section.

5.2 Variances

The EU enlargement s 2004 was the largest and most profound enlargement of the EU to date, and was followed by subsequent rounds in 2007 (with enlargement to Bulgaria and Romania) and 2013 (with Croatia). The continuing EU-15 member states had the possibility to impose so-called 'transitional arrangements' to temporarily restrict the free movement of workers from those countries that joined the EU since 2004. The imposition of restrictions was defended by many governments with the rationale that they would ease EU enlargement by avoiding labour market 'disruptions' in the receiving countries by deterring an 'excessively' large influx of workers from the new accession countries to the 'old' EU-countries where wages were (and remain) substantially higher (Marino et al. 2017, p. 357).

The EU-15 states opted to impose such restrictions beginning from May 2004 for periods of varying lengths with the exception of Ireland, Sweden and the UK, and access to social benefits was also restricted for migrants from the new EU-countries to Ireland and the UK (Doyle et al. 2006, p. 9). Notably, the trade union movement in the three countries that did not impose restrictions did not advocate for transitional arrangements either and, thus, did not depart from the respective governments' positions on the matter.

While the trade unions in the EU have by and large endorsed European integration and the principle of free movement within the EU, the transitional arrangements (from 2004 onwards) found backing from unions in many of the EU-15 countries (e.g. Krings 2009a; Marino et al. 2017; Refslund 2016, p. 612). This meant that workers from the new member states were required (with some exceptions) to apply (and pay) for work permits in order to be allowed to work in their host countries. How should we best explain the divergent stances of trade unions across different countries vis-à-vis labour the restrictions on migration from the new EU-countries? Let us first look at the 'liberal' labour migration stances of the British, Irish and Swedish unions.

In Ireland, Sweden and the UK, the immediate opening up of the labour markets to the citizens of the new EU-countries in 2004 was enhanced by low unemployment figures in all three countries (Connolly & Sellers 2017, p. 232). This might help to explain why the union confederations in each country were not opposed to the absence of transitional arrangements, as has been discussed. However, there were other factors that help explain the relatively liberal stance of the unions in these countries. The Irish unions concluded that labour market disturbances could be avoided without the imposition of restrictions (Doyle et al. 2006, p. 22). On the other hand, the Irish unions were not directly consulted by the Irish government on the matter (Hyland 2017, p. 255) but in any case, they did not oppose the opening up of the Irish labour market to workers from the new EU-countries from 2004. Ultimately, many in the Irish trade union movement believed that the opening up of the labour market could undermine the exploitation of EU migrant workers as it would reduce the number of migrants working under a work permit scheme (and in so doing strengthen their bargaining position vis-à-vis employers) (Doyle et al. 2006). In the Swedish case, the influential LO (*Landsorganisationen i Sverige*) national confederation, concluded that, as the EU Accession Treaty only allowed transitional arrangements for persons arriving as 'employees' and did not pose restrictions on persons arriving as 'self-employed', the transitional arrangements would be a flawed option. The Swedish unions' rationale was that any transitional restrictions would only lead to job-seeking migrants from the new EU member states entering the Swedish labour market as bogus self-employed workers, whose working conditions the Swedish unions would find it difficult to influence (Bengtsson 2013; Bucken-Knapp 2009, pp. 119–120). The British unions meanwhile assessed that employment standards should be protected by the enforcement of rights, and not by placing restrictions on the cross-national mobility of workers (Krings 2009a), and, in addition, by actively organising migrant workers into trade unions (Connolly & Sellers 2017, p. 233).

In sum, the British, Irish, and Swedish unions concluded that imposing restrictive migration policies for workers from the new EU-countries—albeit even of a limited nature—would not effectively defend the terms and conditions of employment. The openness of the British and Irish unions has in addition been explained in part by ideological positions of the two countries' union movements, which both favoured the principle of free movement of workers per se (Krings 2009a). The Irish unions, however, later changed their position and supported the Irish government's decision to impose restrictions on the entry of Romanian and Bulgarian workers when these countries joined the EU in 2007 (Hughes 2011, p.26). The change in position was due in part to numerous incidents where migrant workers from the new EU-member states had not been paid according to Irish standards as a consequence of the lack of any effective enforcement of labour standards (Golden 2015).

Trade unions in many other EU-15 countries, however, took opposing stances compared to the liberal approach of the British, Irish and Swedish unions. Despite some internal divisions within national level unions, unions in Austria, France, Germany, Italy, the Netherlands and Spain aligned with their national governments' decisions to restrict labour mobility through the imposition of transitional arrangements regarding workers from the new EU-countries after the post-2004 enlargement rounds (Marino et al. 2017, p. 357). In Finland, the Central Organisation of Finnish Trade Unions (SAK-Suomen Ammattiliittojen Keskusjärjestö) lobbied actively for the imposition of transitional arrangements (Alho 2015). In Germany and Austria, the trade union movement was also active in lobbying for restrictions on free movement for citizens from the post-2004 EU accession countries (Krings 2009b). In some countries, including Finland, blue collar unions have opposed the liberalisation of national migration policy for jobseekers coming from outside of the EU/EEA with the argument that increased inward migration would be detrimental to the chances of unemployed Finns (and settled immigrants) finding employment (Alho 2015).

Only few studies on union responses to migration in the Central and Eastern European (CEE) countries have been conducted (see Alho 2015 for Estonia; Canek 2017 for Czech Republic; Kubisa 2015 for Poland).

These studies show that labour migration from other EU-countries has not been a major concern for at least the unions in the Czech Republic, Estonia, and Poland due—at least in part—to the small number of EU-migrants arriving in those countries. In contrast, the question of inward migration from non-EU/EEA countries is a major concern for unions, which they frame within the discourse of social dumping.

Migration has had profoundly dissimilar effects in different labour markets and across different sectors, both because of the difference in the numbers of migrants entering each sector and due to the impact that migration has on employment relations in different sectors. From this perspective, it is not surprising that there are—in addition to cross-country variances—also intra-country variances in union positions vis-à-vis migration. Unions representing different sectors *within* countries have given different weight to migration policy depending on how the arrival of migrant workers might affect their sector (see Alho 2015; Bengtsson 2013; Hyland 2017). In the Finnish case, for example, unions in sectors that experience the entry of migrants have often lobbied for more restrictive migration policies than unions representing more 'protected' sectors (Alho 2015).

The scholarship on the effects of migration on unions and union policy has mostly concentrated on sectors where unions have encountered challenges in protecting the conditions of migrants, such as in the construction and services sectors. On the other hand, despite the diverging effects of inward migration on various unions *within* countries, it is generally the national level union confederations that draft the unions' positions on what type of migration policy they wish to see governments implementing (Alho 2015; Marino et al. 2015). Therefore, the positions of the national level unions regarding migration policy tend to reflect compromises reached between the member unions or are primarily formed by those unions with the most political clout and interest in the migration question.

6 Summary and Discussion

While migrating for work to Europe—and within Europe—has certainly improved the living and working standards of many and has contributed to national economies, the developments we have witnessed since the 2000s have led to an increased vulnerability of migrants' position in such sectors of work where employment has in general become less secure. Trade unions across Europe have often been faced with the problematic side of labour migration, including cases of exploitation of migrant workers and employers who, at times, employ migrant workers on terms and conditions that undercut national labour standards. During this time many unions have sought to obtain the classic goal of the labour movement—that of equal pay for equal work.

For unions, a key question for unions is whether restrictive or open migration policy can best guarantee that migration for work occurs in a fashion that is socially sustainable. As has been described in this chapter, despite many similarities, union positions have differed markedly across national contexts—and in some cases, within countries. There have also cases where unions have changed their positions over time.

The primary drawbacks of a restrictive state migration policy regime are that it often renders the individual migrants vulnerable by, for example, making the right to live in a country dependent on having a certain employment contract, which weakens their bargaining position vis-à-vis their employer. From this perspective, national migration regulations produce hierarchies and vulnerabilities. Currently the possibility for EU/EEA governments and unions to curb migration is, however, limited to regulating non-EU/EEA citizens' right to work and reside in a given national context. In addition, a growing number of migrants in the European labour market have entered Europe via other channels than those related to labour migration, including those who arrive in Europe as refugees, which the unions cannot—at least directly—influence. Despite these changes, unions still have some possibilities to lobby for policy changes that are related to intra-EU and extra-EU migration and mobility. Consequently, in practice, the question is not simply whether unions are for or against migration. Instead, unions have to assess which specific dimensions of migration policy is relevant for them, and whether they have any realistic means to influence it.

The transition periods that some EU/EEA countries' trade union movements supported in the context of the enlargement of the EU since 2004 resulted in unwanted effects as regards labour standards partly because new EU-migrants were often dependent on work permits to secure employment, and because companies had the possibility to legally 'post' workers cross-nationally, which reduced the national unions' and state authorities capacity to oversee and manage their working conditions (Wagner 2018). On the other hand, problems in overseeing the working conditions new EU-migrants' were not avoided in Ireland and in the UK either, despite both countries having taken a open approach to inward migration from the new EU member states in 2004.

Unions across Europe are well aware of the problems related to the working and living conditions of undocumented migrant workers and unions in a number of countries have actively lobbied for their regularisation. The defence and promotion of migrant workers' rights are intertwined with the broader struggle against precarisation of the labour market because migrants are disproportionally represented in precarious employment (Doellgast et al. 2018).

In order for unions to counter the many challenges relating to migration, including how migrants and ethnic minorities can be included as members, activists, and decision-makers within the union movement, the labour movement must decide how to relate to questions of migration policy in an increasingly diversified labour market. The literature to date points to a number of union strategies for organising migrants into unions, which unions have applied with varying degrees of effort and success (see Alho 2015; Connolly & Sellers 2017, pp. 234–239; Doellgast et al. 2018; Holgate 2005; Hyland 2017; Marino et al. 2017; Wagner 2018). These strategies include, for example, the building of new coalitions with NGOs, community groups and faith-based organisations.

Another important strategy for unions to deal with cross-national labour migration is to co-operate transnationally in order to protect the working conditions of migrants, which is a strategy for which there are also successful—as well as less successful—examples (see Berntsen 2015; Greer et al. 2013). These strategies require linguistic and cultural resources and competences from trade union activists. Ultimately, unions need to carefully assess what type of policies can best facilitate migrants' inclusion in the workplace, within unions and in society at large. This raises fundamental questions for unions regarding what they are for and how they should organise and deploy their (often diminishing) resources.

BIBLIOGRAPHY

Alho, R. (2015). *Inclusion or exclusion: Trade union strategies and labor migration?*. PhD thesis, University of Turku: Institute of Migration.

Alho, R. (2021). Finland: Integration of asylum seekers and refugees in a tightened policy framework. In Bela Galgóczi (ed.) *Betwixt and between: Integrating refugees into the EU labour market*, Brussels, European Trade Union Institute ETUI.

Bengtsson, E. (2013). Swedish trade unions and European Union migrant workers. *Journal of Industrial Relations*, 55(2), 174–189.

Berntsen, L. E. (2015). Agency of labour in a flexible pan-European labour market: A qualitative study of migrant practices and trade union strategies in the Netherlands. *Jyväskylä Studies in Education, Psychology and Social Research* (526).

Bucken-Knapp, G. (2009). *Defending the Swedish model: Social Democrats, trade unions, and labor migration policy reform*. Lanham, MD: Lexington Books.

Canek, M. (2017). Trade unions and migration in the Czech Republic, 2004–15. In S. Marino, J. Roosblad, & R. Penninx (Eds.), *Trade unions, immigration and immigrants in Europe in the 21th century: New approaches under changed conditions*. Cheltenham: Edward Elgar Publishing.

Cassarino, J. P. (2006). *Approaching Borders and Frontiers: Notions and Implications'*. CARIM Research Reports. Florence: European University Institute.

Castles, S., & Kosack, G. (1973). *Immigrant workers and class structure in Western Europe*. London: Institute of Race Relations.

Connolly, H., & Sellers, B. (2017). *Trade unions and migrant workers in the UK: Organising in a cold climate*. In S. Marino, J. Roosblad, & R, Penninx (Ed.), *Trade Unions and Migrant Workers*, pp. 224–243. Edward Elgar Publishing.

Doellgast, V. L., Lillie, N., & Pulignano, V. (Eds.). (2018). *Reconstructing solidarity: Labour unions, precarious work, and the politics of institutional change in Europe*. Oxford University Press.

Doyle, N., Hughes, G., & Wadensjö, E. (2006). *Freedom of movement for workers from central and eastern Europe*. Stockholm: Swedish Institute for European Policy Studies (SIEPS).

Eldring, L., Fitzgerald, I., & Arnholtz, J. (2012). Post-accession migration in construction and trade union responses in Denmark, Norway and the UK. *European Journal of Industrial Relations*, 18(1), 21–36.

Erne, R. (2008) *European Unions Labor's Quest for a Transnational Democracy*. Ithaca, NY: Cornell University Press.

ETUC. Action Plan for Migration 2013. https://www.etuc.org/en/document/action-plan-migration (accessed 31 December 2019).

ETUI. (2019). European Trade Union Institute (ETUI) Conference *"Trade unions and the threat of populism and the far right: how to win back the workers' vote"*, Brussels 29 January 2019.

Finseraas, H., Røed, M., & Schøne, P. (2020). Labour immigration and union strength. *European Union Politics*, 21(1), 3–23.

Ford, M. (2019). *From Migrant to Worker: Global Unions and Temporary Labor Migration in Asia*. New York: Cornell University Press.

Gächter, A. (2017). Trade unions and migration in Austria, 1993–2015. In S. Marino, J. Roosblad, & R. Penninx (Eds.), *Trade unions, immigration and immigrants in Europe in the 21th century: New approaches under changed conditions*. Cheltenham: Edward Elgar Publishing.

Galgóczi B. (Ed.). (2021). *Betwixt and between: integrating refugees into the EU labour market*. Brussels, ETUI.

Golden, D. (2015). *Challenging the Pro-European Consensus: Explaining the Uneven Trajectory of Euroscepticism in Irish and Italian Unions across time*. PhD thesis. University College Dublin.

Greer, I., Ciupijus, Z., & Lillie, N. (2013). The European Migrant Workers Union and the barriers to transnational industrial citizenship. *European Journal of Industrial Relations, 19*(1), 5–20.

Guerin-Gonzales, C., & Strikwerda, C. (1993). Labor, migration, and politics. *The politics of immigrant workers: Labor activism and migration in the world economy since 1830*. New York: Holmes and Meier.

Haus, L. (2002). *Unions, Immigration, and Internationalization: New Challenges and Changing Coalitions in the United States and France*. New York: Palgrave MacMillan.

Holgate, J. (2005). Organizing migrant workers: A case study of working conditions and unionization in a London sandwich factory. *Work, employment and society, 19*(3), 463–480.

Hughes, G. (2011). Free movement in the EU. *The case of Ireland*. Berlin: Friedrich Ebert Stiftung.

Hyland, M. (2017). Trade unions and migrant workers in Ireland: New organisational opportunities under changed circumstances. In S. Marino, J. Roosblad, & R. Penninx (Eds.), *Trade unions and migrant workers* (pp. 266–286). Cheltenham: Edward Elgar Publishing.

Hyman, R. (1971). *The Workers' Union*. Clarendon Press.

Hyman, R. (2001). *Understanding European trade unionism: Between market, class and society*. Sage.

Kolarova, M., & Peixoto, J. (2009). *Sindicatos e imigração em Portugal* (Vol. 34). Observatório da Imigração, ACIDI, IP.

Krings, T. (2009a). A race to the bottom? Trade unions, EU enlargement and the free movement of labour. *European Journal of Industrial Relations, 15*(1), 49–69.

Krings, T. (2009b). *Organised labour and migration in the global age: A comparative analysis of trade union responses to migrant labour in Austria, Germany, Ireland and the UK*. PhD Dissertation, School of Law and Government, Dublin City University.

Kubisa, J. (2017). Trade unions and migrant workers in Poland: First stage of a work in progress. *Trade Unions and Migrant Workers: New Contexts and Challenges in Europe, 330*.

Lillie, N., & Greer, I. (2007). Industrial relations, migration, and neoliberal politics: The case of the European construction sector. *Politics & Society, 35*(4), 551–581.

Lucio, M. M. (2017). Trade unions and immigration in Spain: The politics and framing of social inclusion within industrial relations. In S. Marino, J. Roosblad, & R. Penninx (Eds.), *Trade unions, immigration and immigrants in Europe in the 21th century: New approaches under changed conditions*. Cheltenham: Edward Elgar Publishing.

Lundh, C. (1995). Invandrarna i den svenska modellen. In P. Kettunen & T. Rissanen (Eds.), *Arbete och nordisk samhällsmodell* (pp. 151–184). Tammerfors: Tammerfors universitet.

Marino, S., Penninx, R., & Roosblad, J. (2017). Introduction: How to study trade union action towards immigration and migrant workers? In *Trade unions and migrant workers: New contexts and challenges in Europe*. Cheltenham: Edward Elgar Publishing.

Marino, S., Roosblad, J., & Penninx, R. (Eds.). (2017). *Trade unions and migrant workers: New contexts and challenges in Europe*. Cheltenham: Edward Elgar Publishing.

McGovern, P. (2007). Immigration, labour markets and employment relations: Problems and prospects. *British Journal of industrial relations*, 45(2), 217–235.

Meardi, G. (2012). Union immobility? Trade unions and the freedoms of movement in the enlarged EU. *British Journal of Industrial Relations*, 50(1), 99–120.

Menz, G., & Caviedes, A. (2010). Introduction: Patterns, trends, and (ir)regularities in the politics and economics of labour migration in Europe. In *Labour migration in Europe* (pp. 1–22). London: Palgrave Macmillan.

Milkman, R. (2010). Introduction. In R. Milkman, J. Bloom, & J. Narro (Eds.), *Working for justice: The LA model of organizing and advocacy* (pp. 1–19). Ithaca: Cornell University Press.

Munakamwe, J. (2018). *Emerging political subjectivities in a post migrant labour regime: Mobilisation, participation and representation of foreign workers in South Africa (1980–2013)*. PhD thesis, Johannesburg: University of Witstwaterstand.

Neergaard, A., & Woolfson, C. (2017). Sweden: A model in dissolution? In S. Marino, J. Roosblad, & R. Penninx (Eds.), *Trade unions, immigration and immigrants in Europe in the 21th century: New approaches under changed conditions*. Cheltenham: Edward Elgar Publishing.

Paananen, S. (1999). *Suomalaisuuden armoilla: Ulkomaalaisten työnhakijoiden luokittelu*. Ph.D. diss., University of Helsinki.

Penninx, R., & Roosblad, P. (Eds.). (2000). *Trade Unions, Immigration, and Immigration in Europe 1960–1993*. New York: Berghahn Books.

Piore, M. J. (1979). *Birds of passage: Migrant labour and industrial societies*. Cambridge: Cambridge University Press.

Putnam, R. D. (2000). *Bowling alone: The collapse and revival of American community.* Simon and schuster.

Refslund, B. (2016). Intra-European labour migration and deteriorating employment relations in Danish cleaning and agriculture: Industrial relations under pressure from EU8/2 labour inflows? *Economic and Industrial Democracy, 37*(4), 597–621.

Ristikari, T. (2013). *Finnish trade unions and immigrant labour.* PhD thesis, University of Tampere.

Rinaldini, M., & Marino, S. (2017). Trade unions and migrant workers in Italy: Between labour and social rights. In S. Marino, J. Roosblad, & R. Penninx (Eds.), *Trade unions, immigration and immigrants in Europe in the 21th century: New approaches under changed conditions.* Cheltenham: Edward Elgar Publishing.

Roosblad, J. (2002). *Vakbonden en immigranten in Nederland (1960–1997).* Amsterdam: Aksant.

Tapia, M., & Holgate, J. (2018). Fighting precariousness: Union strategies toward migrant workers in the UK, France and Germany. In V. Doellgast, N. Lillie, & V. Pulignano (Eds.), *Reconstructing solidarity: Labour unions, precarious work, and the politics of institutional change in Europe.* Oxford University Press.

Virdee, S. (2000). A Marxist critique of black radical theories of trade-union racism. *Sociology, 34*(3), 545–565.

Wagner, I. (2018). *Workers without borders: Posted work and precarity in the EU.* ILR Press.

Watts, J. R. (2002). *Immigration policy and the challenge of globalisation.* New York: Cornell University Press.

Webb, S., & Webb, B. (1894/2003). *History of trade unionism.* Barnes & Noble Digital.

Wills, J., Datta, K., Evans, Y., Herbert, J., May, J., & McIlwaine, C. (2010). *Global cities at work: New migrant divisions of labour.* Pluto Press.

CHAPTER 5

Confronting a Moral Abyss: Unions and the Role of Law in the France Télécom Case

Julia López López

Global capitalism has in recent decades intensified the tendency to liberalise markets to an ever greater degree with important negative consequences for workers' rights. Due to their capacity to move internationally, multinational firms especially have tended to escape from the limits put in place by national labour protections, thereby, inducing the de facto destruction of labour rights. The historically changing role of multinationals, in setting the conditions of work across the globe, has in effect intensified the commoditisation of labour; various developments such as the privatisation of firms, the "uberisation" of many sectors of the economy and attacks on both unions and collective workers' representation have shaped the evolution of contemporary labour law. In making

J. L. López (✉)
Labor Law and Social Security Law, University Pompeu Fabra, Barcelona, Spain
e-mail: julia.lopez@upf.edu

© The Author(s), under exclusive license to Springer Nature Switzerland AG 2022
B. Colfer (ed.), *European Trade Unions in the 21st Century*, St Antony's Series, https://doi.org/10.1007/978-3-030-88285-3_5

decisions regarding the location of their business and manufacturing activities, enterprises are sensitive to regulations at the level of individual countries (Lyon–Caen 2018).

In the European Union (EU), the pressure of financial markets has tended to generate a decline in labour rights especially through the implementation of legal labour market reforms at the national level. These typically neoliberal reforms have promoted flexibility and precarity with differing intensity among the EU's member states, while failing to resolve the problem of massive and persistent unemployment in the bloc, "It is clear that the European Union is encouraging the erosion of nationally based employment protections and provoking a growing divergence of outcomes. However, the trends are contradictory and uneven".

The neoliberal model of industrial relations has required a massive process of downsizing of firms and of collective dismissals with important negative consequences in various rights such as those involving health and safety at work[1]. This decline in rights has very real human consequences, as the France Télécom case attests. Between 5 and 10% of the EU's workforce affirms having suffered bullying in the workplace (European Parliament 2018, p. 8)[2].

Theorising such tendencies, Baccaro and Howell maintain that the evolution of industrial relations has crystallised into a neoliberal model that has involved attacks on collective bargaining and on the role of unions in the workplace. In their comparative analysis of France, UK, Germany and Italy for the period 1974–2005, they find that all countries have moved in a neoliberal direction (Baccaro & Howell 2012)[3]. A goal of neoliberalism has been to diminish union structure and to question their legitimacy of to represent workers. Unions have been challenged by harsh critiques that often focus on the nature representation itself and on

---

[1] In the likes of Greece, Spain, and Portugal the adoption of strict fiscal austerity caused the economies to recede and thus placed more strain on national health services. Suicides and outbreaks of infectious diseases are becoming more common in these countries, and budget cuts have restricted access to health care. See the report on collective dismissals, ILO 2016. N. Countouris, S. Deakin, M. Freedland, A. Koukiadaki and J. Prassl.

[2] Bullying and sexual harassment at the workplace, in public spaces and political life in the EU, European Parliament, Policy Department for Citizens' Rights and Constitutional Affairs, March, 2018, Pag. 8.

[3] Baccaro, L. & Howell, C. (2012) A common neoliberal trajectory: the transformation of industrial relations in advanced capitalism, *Politics and Society* 39(4), 521–563.

internal union democracy among others[4]. Partly in response to this, the need to find space for the participation of worker voice has been posed as of central importance in the current multilevel scenario of industrial relations (Bogg & Novizt 2014).

In this context, the case of France Télécom[5] has occupied numerous front pages in the news media (see ETUI 2019). The trial of the company's CEOs has placed the process of downsizing in the firm under legal scrutiny and highlighted the shocking deaths by suicide of more than 35 workers in the context of that plan. The landmark trial at the Paris Tribunal de Grande Instance (the Paris High Court) was triggered by a complaint filed with the Paris public prosecutor by the SUD PTT (Fédération des activités postales et des Télécommunications/federation of postal and communication workers) union[6], accusing France Télécom and its senior executives of *"moral harassment"* and of *"endangering others"*. On 20 December 2019 the Court found France Télécom and the managers guilty of the crime of systematic moral harassment. Orange (the successor company to France Télécom, will not appeal the sentence, and several managers have been condemned with prison sentences and fines.

---

[4] Unions have taken responsibility to increase internal democracy as the TUC Equality Audit 2018 has shown. Here, the TUC considers the steps that UK unions are taking to promote equality within their memberships, structures and processes, and to ensure they reflect the diversity of their membership.

[5] Here ETUI describes the process in France Télécom from the point of view of unions, stating *"... In practice, the policy used to ensure this downsizing of staff was particularly brutal and destabilising. Managers, in order to get rid of surplus staff, applied tactics aimed at humiliating employees or shunting them around from one location or position to another, ignoring the many warnings issued by both occupational health doctors and members of the company's health & safety committee. The disastrous result: a spate of suicides among France Télécom staff"*.

[6] The main trade union confederations with membership across the entire economy maintained their representativeness. The CFDT had 30.32% of the votes, slightly ahead of the CGT with 28.57%. The CGT-FO came third, with 17.93%, followed by CFE-CGC at 12.27% and the CFTC at 9.49%. The recently created UNSA (Union of autonomous trade unions) and SUD (Solidarity, Unity, Democracy) unions achieved less support, with 5.35% and 3.46% respectively. According to the second assessment of trade unions' representativeness in the public sector based on the results of the workplace elections held from 29 November to 6 December 2018, CGT remains the leading trade union organisation in the civil service as a whole (across the state, local government and hospital sectors) with 21.8% of the votes (a drop of 1.3 percentage points compared to 2014), followed by the CFDT (with 19%, a drop of 0.3 points).In 2018, CFDT has become, the leading French trade union in the public and private sectors combined, see https://www.eurofound.europe.eu/country/france/actors-and-institutions.

This case is a very emblematic one due to its strong relevance for some central themes of contemporary labour law, namely the privatisation of firms, the individualisation of labour conditions and the commodification of labour. The reaction of unions defending workers is also an important example of the significance of countervailing actors responding against managerial strategies that violate labour rights; the role played by unions in this case has been crucial. France Télécom, now known globally by its trademark "Orange", began a process of downsizing the number of workers in France as the multinational firm moved part of its production overseas. The management decided to implement this process without a formalised collective dismissal process, trying to avoid negotiatiing with the workers' representatives and using instead a strategy of moral harassment against workers, pressing them to terminate their labour contracts. During the period of transformation of the firm, the multinational and its management violated the right to dignity of workers in matters of health and safety, providing us with a shocking case of moral abyss in the evolution of industrial relations systems.

A combination of relevant dates can help us understand different patterns across countries and concerning both equality policies and cultural behaviour. One crucial factor of differentiation between countries involves the legislation enacted to address violence and harassment. Such legislation varies across the EU, reflecting cultural, social, legal and administrative differences between member states especially in terms of health and safety at work (Picierno 2018).

In the case of France, even though this country has approved important norms on equality and non-discrimination, such as the 2019 Decree on the Gender Pay Gap (Decree no. 2019–15 Égalité salariale femmes/hommes) in effect as of 01 January 2019 for companies with more than 250 workers and from 01 March 2020 for those between 50 and 250 workers)[7], comparative data on moral harassment and violations of Article 3 of the European Convention of Human Rigths (ECHR) contextualises the case of France Télécom within a broader frame. As the data in shows Graph 1, France, in comparison with other EU member states, presents a high prevalence of bullying and harassment at work. The country also presents a moderately high percentage of violations of Article 3 ECHR as reported in Graph 2.

---

[7] France, Law in. 2019–15, of 8 January 2019.

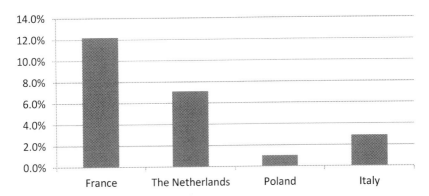

Graph 1 Prevalence of bullying and harassment at work by country (*Source* Own elaboration from data of European Work Conditions Survey [2015] cited in European Parliament's Policy Department for Citizens' Rights and Constitutional Affairs [2018] *Bullying and sexual harassment at the workplace, in public spaces, and in political life in the EU*, available at: http://www.europarl.europa.eu/RegData/etudes/STUD/2018/604 949/IPOL_STU(2018)604949_EN.pdf. Percentage of persons in national surveys who report having suffered harassment at the workplace)

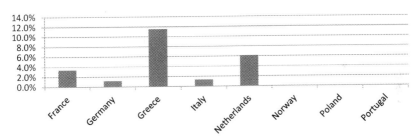

Graph 2 Percentage of violations of Article 3 ECHR (Inhuman or degrading treatment) of total number of judgments and by state (1959–2018) (*Source* Own elaboration from data of Statistics on ECHR: Violations by Article and by State 1959–2018 [see: https://www.echr.coe.int/Pages/home.aspx?p=reports& c] This table has been generated using the metadata for each judgement contained in HUDOC, the Court's online case-law database)

1 FORMALISING THE PARTICIPATION OF UNIONS AS THE BASIS FOR THE JUDICIAL CASE AGAINST FRANCE TÉLÉCOM: REGULATION IN DOWNSIZING PROCESSES

The judicial decision in the France Télécom case used multilevel legal references to justify the finding of institutional harassment by the firm during the process of collective dismissal. It is important to underline the complex legal framework which connects workers' rights to dignity with the model of industrial relations that is rooted in the workplace.

The role of regulation in collective dismissals has been constructed in a multilevel dynamic that has clearly understood such processes as collective ones. In this sense, the EU Council Directive on collective dismissal 98/59/EC of 20 July 1998 on the approximation of the laws of the member states relating to collective redundancies[8] guarantees the participation of workers' representation and the administrative authority when the collective terminations of contracts occur, thereby, imposing certain regulatory limits on firms' power to dismiss collectively. In the EU Directive, collective dismissals refer to dismissals that are brought about by an employer for one or more reasons not related to the individual workers concerned where the number of redundancies in a period of time is collective, as defined by each member state. In these cases of termination of contract, the directive imposes a process of consultation and information on employers and labour representatives in an effort to reach an agreement. The information that the firm has to share with workers representatives is specified in detail in the directive[9], along with the procedural requirement for participation not only of workers representatives but also of public authorities[10]. Thus, EU law offers certain guarantees to protect the general interest of workers in cases of collective dismissal.

As in EU Law, at the national level member states—in this case France—also have national regulations for collective dismissals that oblige firms to provide engage with worker representatives to provide information and to engage in consultation. In the French case, under Article 1233–3 of the Labour Code, a collective dismissal on economic grounds is the dismissal by the employer for one or more reasons which are not

---

[8] *Official Journal L 225, 12/08/1998 P. 0016–0021.*

[9] Article 2 EU Council Directive on collective dismissal 98/59/EC.

[10] Article 3 and 4 EU Council Directive on collective dismissal 98/59/EC.

inherent to the employee and derive from the transformation of employment or from the modification of the employment contract that has been rejected by the employee. There are circumstances that allow the employer to dismiss employees on economic grounds, namely: economic difficulties, as manifested either by a sustained trend in at least one prescribed economic indicator or by any other factor capable of justifying these difficulties. A collective dismissal requires the employer to inform and consult the social partners and to adopt an Employment Safeguard Plan, which is relevant to guarantee employment stability for workers, (De le Court & Canalda 2012) when the company has a workforce of at least 50 employees and it plans the redundancy of 10 employees or more over a 30-day period. In all other cases, the employer needs only to inform and consult the works council on the restructuring plan[11]. The legal order guarantee participation of workers representants in the collective dismissal processes.

Therefore, the participation of unions or worker's representation and of administrative authorities are specified in both EU legislation and in the French Labour Code in order to safeguard not only stability in employment but also other fundamental rights. France Télécom, in the case analysed here, has been accused not only of failing to adhere to these elements of the Labour Code but also of committing a crime. The legal references guarantee a process of negotiation in the collective dismissal which was violated by the firm.

[11] According to article L. 1233–26, a company is subject to restructuring legislation for any new dismissal on economic grounds for the subsequent three months, if it has a workforce of at least 50 employees and if 10 or more employees are dismissed in the preceding three months without dismissing 10 employees or more over a 30-day period. According to article L. 1233–27, a company is subject to restructuring legislation for any new dismissal on economic grounds for the three months after the end of the calendar year, if it carries out more than 18 dismissals from 01 January to 31 December without presenting a job protection plan. In companies with a workforce of fewer than 10 employees, there is a shorter redundancy procedure (six weeks) and there is no requirement for an Employment Safeguard Plan. Employee representatives have to be consulted and their opinion is conveyed to the labour inspectorate.

2 THE FUNDAMENTAL RIGHT OF DIGNITY AND LEGAL PROTECTION AGAINST MORAL HARASSMENT AND INSTITUTIONAL HARASSMENT IN THE INDIVIDUAL AND COLLECTIVE DISMENSIONS

The right to dignity stands as a pillar in the constitutional principles set out by the Charter of Fundamentals Rights of the European Union. According to Article 1 of the Charter, human dignity is inviolable. It must be respected and protected; Article 2.1. stipulates that everyone has the right to life; Article 3.1 guarantees the right to the integrity of the person in terms of his or her physical and mental integrity. These rights provide the regulatory context for our analysis of the France Télécom case—and the charge that the company was guilty of moral harassment— because, in applying EU regulations, member states have to respect these fundamental rights.

The protection against moral harassment is built on multilevel references. The main reference at the European level is the "Framework Directive" 89/391 of 12 June 1989[12] and the Framework Agreement on Harassment and Violence at Work[13], in the context of the European Strategy on Health and Safety (2007–2013).

The Directive 89/391 defines "work environment" using the framework provided by ILO Convention 155 and the prevention principle. These bases for the directive concern health and safety, specifying rules for hazard identification, and for worker participation that are meant to introduce adequate measures to eliminate risk. Health and safety considerations are incorporated within general management processes in this approach to regulation.

The aim of the Framework Agreement is to increase the awareness and understanding among employers, workers and their representatives of workplace harassment and violence, and to provide employers, workers

---

[12] Council Directive of 12 June 1989 on the introduction of measures to encourage improvements in the safety and health of workers at work (89/391/EEC), Consolidated version as per 3/2008, OJ L 391.

[13] In 2007 the European Trade Union Confederation (ETUC/CES), the Confederation of European Business (BUSINESSEUROPE), the European Association of Craft Small and Medium-sized Enterprises (UEAPME—since 2018, rebranded as SMEunited) as well as the European Centre of Enterprises with Public Participation and of Enterprises of General Economic Interest (CEEP) signed the framework agreement on harassment and violence at work.

and their representatives at all levels with an action-oriented framework to identify, prevent and manage problems of harassment and violence at work.

On the other hand, the European Parliament Resolution of 11 September 2018 on measures to prevent and combat mobbing and sexual harassment in the workplace, in public spaces, and in political life in the EU (2018/2055(INI)[14] is the most recent in a long series of hard and soft regulations that are designed to protect health and safety at work.

In the case of France Télécom, the managers set out a strategy for dismissing people in a way that undermined their dignity. As has been underlined, *Leaders, feeling helpless to intervene, may reinforce the culture*

---

[14] The main references at the EU level regarding health and safety are Articles 2 and 3 of the Treaty on European Union (TEU) and Articles 8, 10, 19 and 157 of the Treaty on the Functioning of the European Union (TFEU), the Charter of Fundamental Rights of the European Union, which entered into force following the adoption of the Treaty of Lisbon in December 2009, particularly Articles 1, 20, 21, 23 and 31, Directive 2006/54/EC of the European Parliament and of the Council of 5 July 2006 on the implementation of the principle of equal opportunities and equal treatment of men and women in matters of employment and occupation, Council Directive 2004/113/EC of 13 December 2004 implementing the principle of equal treatment between men and women in the access to and supply of goods and services, which defines and condemns harassment and sexual harassment, the United Nations legal instruments in the field of human rights and notably of women's rights, including the United Nations Charter, the Universal Declaration of Human Rights, the International Covenants on Civil and Political Rights and on Economic, Social and Cultural Rights, the Convention on the Elimination of All Forms of Discrimination Against Women (CEDAW) and its Protocol, and the Convention against Torture and Other Cruel, Inhuman or Degrading Treatment or Punishment, Directive 2012/29/EU of the European Parliament and of the Council of 25 October 2012 establishing minimum standards on the rights, support and protection of victims of crime, and replacing Council Framework Decision 2001/220/JHA, the Framework Agreement on Harassment and Violence at Work of 26 April 2007 between ETUC/CES, BUSINESSEUROPE, UEAPME and CEEP. Other important resolutions include that of 20 September 2001 on harassment at the workplace, of 26 November 2009 on the elimination of violence against women, of 5 April 2011 on priorities and outline of a new EU policy framework to fight violence against women, of 15 December 2011 on the midterm review of the European strategy 2007–2012 on health and safety at work, of 25 February 2014 with recommendations to the Commission on combating Violence Against Women and the accompanying European Added Value Assessment of November 2013, of 24 November 2016 on the EU accession to the Istanbul Convention on preventing and combating violence against women, and of 26 October 2017 on combating sexual harassment and abuse in the EU, and Pillinger, J, the European Trade Union Confederation report entitled "Safe at home, safe at work—Trade union strategies to prevent, manage and eliminate work-place harassment and violence against women". https://www.etuc.org/sites/default/files/document/files/en_-_brochure_-_safe_at_home_1.pdf

of abuse. This phenomenon is a complex one that can only be addressed through systemic response and change in organizational culture (Sloan et al. 2010, p. 95). This managerial abuse of power is recognised in the judicial sentence that found institutional harassment with an impact not only in individual cases but also in the collective dimension.

Even though France has not ratified ILO Convention 155 on Health and Safety, there is extensive legislation protecting this right at the national level. In France, the fundamental rights of dignity and health and safety are legally protected, and moral harassment is a crime. As specified in article 222-33-2 of Sect. 3 of the French Criminal Code[15], moral harassment is defined repetitive behaviour that implies a deterioration of labour conditions which violate dignity and that produce an impact on the mental health of workers and that compromise their professional life. The judgement also applied Article 222-33-2-2 which specifies the notion of moral harassment as being present in institutional behaviour where managerial power uses disproportionate and unjustified measures[16]. The case of France Télécom was resolved with a finding of responsibility not only of the managers but also of the firm for developing an institutional culture of systemic harassment with collective consequences, which in this case resulted in mass suicide.

In summary, the legal order has created a multilevel basis for the protection of workers against moral harassment that rests on the rights to dignity and to a healthy and safe workplace. This protection is of crucial importance. As the Télécom case clearly shows, brutal forms of violation of workers' dignity—and health and safety—take place not only in countries with weak labour rights but also in countries such as France where the legal order at least nominally protects fundamental rights very strongly.

---

[15] Law no. 2014-873 of August 4, 2014, Article. 40. Penal Code—last modified 01 January 2020.

[16] page 98. See the Judgement of 20 December 2019 at the Tribunal de Grande Instance of Paris (the Paris High Court), 31st Chamber, 2nd section No. 0935790257.

2.1 Labour is not a Commodity: The Role of Unions and Workers' Representatives

The global economy and multinational firms have created a dynamic in the industrial relations systems in which fundamental rights are routinely violated. This trend is present not only in countries without formal regulatory structures of labour law but also in countries where the constitutional and infra-constitutional legal order clearly affirms fundamental labour rights. This negative trend can be attributed in part to multinationals' spillover strategies that are designed to promote the evaporation of labour rights at the national level. From fires in Bangladesh to the France Télécom suicides, there is a tragic element in common across many contexts, involving violations of workers' dignity and employer indifference to their health and safety. Industrial relations systems that lack robust protections of these basic rights in effect treat labour as only a commodity and treat the lives of people as only numbers in the calculation of total dismissals. How can we reconstruct all of this in ways that reassert the principle of de-commodified labour? The dynamic of solidarity and of the joint responsibility of firms has been defended as integral to the construction of democracy in the workplace (Supiot 2018)[17]. In this and in other ways, the role of law is essential to achieve successful and fair societies (Hall & Lamont 2018)[18]. The role of law must be understood in a complex perspective including geographically—incorporating into our understanding the interrelations between international, supranational, national and local levels—and taking account also the integration of both hard and soft law. ILO Conventions, EU norms and national norms together create a complex multilevel framework of regulation which recognises labour rights and reinforces de-commodification strategies. In the Social Justice Declaration for a Fair Globalization (2008), the ILO builds on the Declaration of Philadelphia and the Declaration of Fundamental Principles and Rights at work with a "human -centered agenda". More recently in 2015, the ILO established a new Decent Work Agenda (ILO, 2015) seeking to promote employment, social protection,

---

[17] Face à l'irresponsabilité: la dynamique de la solidarité, Conférences du Collège de France, 2018. Edited by Alain SUPIOT. Paris, Collège de France, 2018.182 pp. ISBN 978-2-7226-0475-9.

[18] Hall, PA and Lamont, M. Successful Societies. (2009). How institutions and culture affect health.Cambrigde, 2009.

social dialogue and tripartism, as fundamental principles and rights at work.

France Télécom violated not only French national law but also international labour norms on dignity and health and safety. However, the law standing alone would have been insufficient in the defence of the company's victims. French unions have played a crucial role in the entire process of defending workers rigths. It was unions that judicialised the case—providing us a clear example of how judicialisation is increasing being used by organised labour as a form of protest against violations of worker rights (Lopez Lopez 2019) and as an instrument that is crucial to guaranteeing labour agency in a multilevel perspective (Lopez Lopez 2014) Dignity and solidarity are the main references in the de-construction of the new commodification of labour put in place in recent decades by the intensified pressure of markets. Law is a fundamental pillar for those seeking a response to such pressures. The article 31 of the Charter of Fundamentals Rights declares, as part of Title IV *"Solidarity"* regarding *"Fair and Just Working Conditions"* that every worker has the right to working conditions which respect his or her health, safety and dignity. As the principles underpinning important legal texts assert, workers are not simply a number in a collective dismissal. This basic principle was forgotten by France Télécom, which led to a shocking succession of suicides in its workforce. The response to this moral abyss has come from the law, unions and judges who have succeeded in re-establishing in this case that labour is not a commodity.

Bibliography

Bogg, A. and Novizt, T. eds. (2014). Voices at work continuity and change in the common law world, Introduction, (edit) Oxford University Press, pag. 31

Declaration of Social Justice and Fair Globalization, ILO, Ninety. seventh session, Geneva, 10 june 2008.

De le Court, A. and Canalda Criado, S. (2012) 'Empleabilidad, plan de acompañamiento social y plan de recolocación. Una perspectiva comparada', *Justicia laboral: revista de Derecho del Trabajo y de la Seguridad Social,* 51, p. 35–62.

Hatzfeld, N. (2016). Une lutte syndicale exemplaire chez Peugeot-Sochaux (1995–2000).La remise en cause d'un système discriminatoireDans 'un système discrimitoireretutional harasment zation permitted the unions to obtain e Travail et emploi 2016/1 (n° 145), pages 173 à 196.

Lyon-Caen, A. (2018). Sustainable development, social rights and international trade, in Perulli, A. and Treu, T. Sustaninable development, global trade and social rights, (edit.) Wolters Kluwer, pag. 33.

Lopez Lopez, J. (2019). Modes of collective action. judicialization as form of protest in J.Lopez (ed) Collective bargaining and collective action. labour agency and governance in the 21st century, Hart Publishing.

Lopez Lopez, J. (2014). Solidarity and the re-socialization of risk: Analyzing ETUC strategies to face the crisis in Contouris, N. and Freedland, M. Resocializing Europe in times of crisis, (edits) Cambridge University Press, 2014.

Report Pina Picierno, on Measures to prevent and combat mobbing and sexual harassment at the workplace, in public spaces and political life in the EU, Committee on women's rights and gender equality, 18 of July 2018, (2018/2055 INI).

2030 Agenda for Sustainable Development, UN General Assembly, September 2015.

CHAPTER 6

The Renewal of Trade Unionism in France?

Dominique Andolfatto and Dominique Labbé

Since the middle of the nineteenth century, across all industrialised countries, unions have been primarily involved with defending the occupational interests of their members.[1] Somewhat later, trade unionism spread to Southern Europe, where it has constituted, as was the case in the North, as a vector for the recognition of individual and collective workers' rights but also, more broadly, as a vector for the democratisation of society. Following the classic trade union approach of Freeman and Medoff (1984), we propose to study trade unions firstly as professional organisations, but also as organisations that contribute meaningfully to

---

[1] The authors thank David Palmer for his careful proofreading of this chapter, his helpful remarks and his assistance for the translation into English.

D. Andolfatto (✉)
Credespo (Law and Political Science Centre), Université de Bourgogne Franche-Comté, Dijon, France
e-mail: dominique.andolfatto@u-bourgogne.fr

D. Labbé
Pacte (Social Sciences Laboratory), Université de Grenoble-Alpes, Grenoble, France
e-mail: Dominique.labbe@univ-grenoble-alpes.fr

© The Author(s), under exclusive license to Springer Nature Switzerland AG 2022
B. Colfer (ed.), *European Trade Unions in the 21st Century*, St Antony's Series, https://doi.org/10.1007/978-3-030-88285-3_6

the political and democratic system (Gumbrell-McCormick and Hyman, 2013).

However, since the end of the twentieth century, trade unions have experienced a dramatic decline in membership in many countries while their economic and social functions—including collective bargaining activities, involvement in employee representative committees, and participation in various public and social dialogue institutions—have paradoxically tended to increase at all levels, from the level of the workplace right up to the European and international level and, of course, at the level of the nation state. French trade union organisations have been particularly affected by this change, but the contributions in this volume show that these changes are not particular to France. The first part of this chapter will review the processes of unionisation and de-unionisation in France. This will include a presentation of the main union organisations in France, and the forces and events that conditioned their development. The second part discusses the various opportunities and possibilities for renewal that exist today (what we dub the prospects for 're-unionisation').

1   Unionisation and De-unionisation in France

Among the major industrialised countries, the situation of trade unions in France is quite unusual. We begin by describing this French context before presenting its main explanations.

1.1   Unionisation in France

According to respected surveys (see Visser, 2006 and 2015; for France: Andolfatto and Labbé 2007), France is the industrialised country with the lowest proportion of union members in the workplace, as only about 7 out of every 100 French workers are members of a trade union. This rate falls to only 1 in 20 in the private sector, which is the lowest recorded rate in the OECD. However, France is also one of the countries where trade unions are most fragmented, as many union organisations are in direct competition with each other for members, resources and influence (see Table 1 below).

According to these same sources, France scores another trade union record, as the country where the number of union members has fallen most sharply since the late 1970s, given the 70% reduction in the rate of unionisation rate over the past four decades (see Table 2 below).

Table 1 Unionisation in France in 2018

Organisations	Members (in thousands, approx.)
– *Confédération Générale du Travail* (CGT)	500
– *Confédération Française Démocratique du Travail* (CFDT)	500
– *Force Ouvrière* (FO)	300
– *Union Nationale des Syndicats Autonomes* (UNSA)	120
– *Fédération Syndicale Unitaire* (FSU)	120
– *Confédération Française des Travailleurs Chrétiens* (CFTC)	120
– *Confédération Générale des Cadres* (CGC)	120
– *Union Syndicale Solidaires* (USS)	80

Source Andolfatto and Labbé 2007 (estimates for 2004–2016 are based on shop floor elections). This data includes pensioners who remain union members in some instances. The membership of small union organisations that are specific to a few civil servant bodies, such as the FGAF (*Fédération générale autonome des fonctionnaires* / Autonomous Federation of Civil Servants) or to certain professions, such as the SNPL (*Syndicat national des pilotes de ligne* / National Airline Pilots' Union) are not taken into account.

Regarding the main union organisations, CGT was founded in 1895 and was dominated by communists between 1945 and 2001. In 1948, anti-communists factions within CGT founded FO. UNSA and FSU, founded in the 1990s, have been historically composed of civil servants. The CFTC, founded in 1919, finds its roots in the Catholic social teaching and Christian democratic traditions. In 1964, the majority of the CFTC left Catholicism behind and founded the CFDT. The CGC is only for professionals, and USS is an extreme left-wing off-shoot of the CFDT.

Between the 1950s and 1978, union membership varied between 24–30%. Notably, the loyalty of union members was also quite high, and membership on average lasted about ten years. This rate was lower still than that of other countries, including the United Kingdom, Germany and the Scandinavian countries, but it was higher than, for example, the United States or Italy. Ultimately, what is clear is that unionisation has not always been low in France. In addition, during these decades, the absolute number of workers has increased rapidly (from 10 to 17 million), and the working class has been rejuvenated, feminised, and the average levels of education among workers has increased significantly. Finally, employment in the services sector has become much more prevalent, as it has in many comparable European economies. During this period, unions were well-placed to gain members and were also capable of adapting to changes in the French economy as they occurred.

Table 2 The rate of unionisation in France (1949–2015)

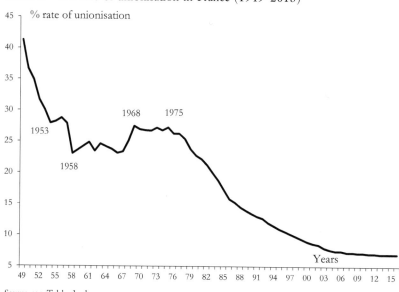

Source see Table 1 above

On the other hand, since 1979, the unionisation rate has fallen dramatically from 30 to 7%. The trade union arena has also changed significantly during this time. After the Second World War, nine out of ten union members belonged to the CGT with the remaining members spread between the only two other extant confederations (i.e. CFTC and CGC). Today, this compares with one out of four union members belonging to CGT, and with at least eight confederations and other bodies competing for members and influence, as the French trade union landscape has fragmented dramatically.

To explain the defection of French workers from trade unions, explanations (one exogenous and one endogenous) are typically put forward. These form part of the general framework of the challenges facing trade unions which are outlined in the introduction to this book. The first—and more common—explanation focuses on cultural, economic and social changes that are typically seen as exogenous to trade unions, that we explore in the next section.

1.2 Exogenous Factors that Contribute to the Decline in Trade Union Membership in France

The analysis of the decline of French trade unions' membership most often focuses on the negative consequences of changes in the productive system. It is logical for a union to lose members if the number of employees decreases in the companies where it is established. This has occurred in France in the textile, steel, mining, shipbuilding and automotive industries to name only a few. However, as discussed, while unemployment has increased steadily in France since 1974, the employed population, which is subject to unionisation, has also increased. Yet, the proportion of union members has steadily fallen. So, explaining this decline by pointing to unemployment alone is insufficient. In some European countries, including Sweden, Belgium and even Germany, Italy and the United Kingdom, unionisation has been much more resilient, despite economic circumstances that are comparable to those in France (Andolfatto and Contrepois, 2016). Of course, redundancies, company closures, the rise in precarious work, the stagnation in purchasing power and the growth in poverty levels (Todd, 2020) have all helped to nurture a negative climate for unionisation even where employment in many sectors has been maintained or increased. In these circumstances, paying union dues becomes more difficult, collective action becomes more uncertain and potentially rewarding, and 'free-riding' (i.e. benefiting from union representation and action without maintaining membership) becomes more attractive.

Secondly, discrimination against trade unions, and anti-union sentiment, is also regularly cited as an explanation for de-unionisation in France. Some 15,000 protected employees (including staff representatives, elected works council members and trade union delegates) are dismissed every year, amounting to approximately one elected representative out of forty (DARES, 2017b; Guillaume et. al., 2018). The most frequently cited reasons for these dismissals are the company's economic situation and serious professional negligence. But these official reasons often mask the true desire of employers to get rid of bothersome union activists. Naturally, especially during periods of unemployment, the threat of dismissal or intimidation by employers is a major deterrence for union membership. In other words, the cost of collective and union action can be high.

Promoting activists to managerial positions is another form of anti-union action that is less well-known but quite frequent. By promoting an activist, the employer can simultaneously weaken the union position, through the loss of an activist, while also potentially benefiting from gaining access to the activist's experience. In recent years, this practice has spread especially with the growth of company-level collective bargaining.

Thirdly, cultural changes are often cited to explain union decline in France. Particular focus is placed on the rise of individualism, which prioritises personal fulfilment and devalues collective action (Ion, 1997; Andolfatto, 2002). Trade unions, like political parties or other large *'omnibus'* organisations, have fallen victim to this shift. In this context, new types of (often post-materialist) activism has emerged, workplace demands and commitments are often more specific and tailored to individual needs (Inglehart, 1977; Ion, 1997). This trend is reinforced by the extension of compulsory education and increased uptake of university education which delays the entry into the workforce and makes it difficult to transmit the values and traditions on which trade unionism is based. Similar difficulties can also be observed within the trade unions themselves, which partly explains the ageing union membership—with fewer young people under the age of 30 and more and more in their fifties—and the challenges facing unions in their attempts at renewal (DARES, 2017a, Siblot, 2009; Olivesi, 2013).

Following the same line of thought, the transformation and virtual disappearance of the traditional blue collar working population which has traditionally given the unions many of their members and leaders and, above all, its community bonds, values and ways of acting collectively, also partly explains the decline of the labour movement as it has been known, and has hindered the prospects for union renewal.

Changes in the organisation of companies, with the elimination of hierarchical levels of management, and the increased importance of community-based managers at the workplace level, have also undermined the role of trade unions as the intermediary between employees and managers. Today, a more direct dialogue has developed between the various stakeholders, which also goes some way to explaining the decline of trade union representatives at the workplace.

Lastly, the changes that have occurred in the dynamics of capitalism itself should also be mentioned. Trade unions played an important role in the Fordist system that marked the rapid economic growth after 1945, which saw sustained increases in the average size of companies, productivity gains and wages. Trade unions have also played an important role in the creation and development of the welfare state; in France, for examples, unions participate in the management and delivery of the social security system. From the 1970s onwards, these favourable factors began to be removed amid inflation, the slowdown in productivity gains, wage cuts, job insecurity and an overall reduction in the size of the welfare state. Within the neoliberal ideology, which has gained much ground especially since the 1980s, trade unions are often seen as obstacles to the efficient functioning of markets and as presenting unwelcome limitations on individual freedoms, which justified their removal from decision-making, which also partly explains their loss of political influence (Jefferys, 2007).

All these explanations shed light on the problems facing unions in France, but it can be argued that these changes have occurred in all (or at least most) developed countries. We have also seen that France is the developed country where the decline in unionisation has been the most stark, and we must therefore consider the causes that may be more specific to trade unions in France to better understand their decline and current condition.

1.3 *Endogenous Factors that Contribute to the Decline of Trade Union Membership in France*

The adaptation of trade unions to the new economic and social environment has led some of them to lose interest in their members. Four main characteristics reflect this attitude in France.

Firstly, the weakening results from the gradual extinction of basic teams—union members and workplace-level reps—and the ambience they had created in many companies. Until the 1970s, the trade union officer or delegate was somewhat comparable to the British shop-steward, as an employee among others, with a set amount of hours set aside so that he (and only occasionally she) could help to solve his colleagues' individual and collective grievances. Since the union depended mainly on members' dues for financial resources, the union leadership could not risk losing interest in them. However, the union delegate's role was a difficult one, and there was typically rapid turnover of grassroots union officers. However, as the pool of available was relatively, finding replacements was easy.

Secondly, regardless of the current low rates of union membership, an apparent vitality of French trade unionism can be seen in the high rates of strikes, demonstrations and other forms of mobilisation that union members partake in and organise, while many trade union officers typically dedicate much time to participating in various workplace and welfare state committees and seeking to influence public policymaking. To explain this apparent vitality, the concept of '*virtual unionism*' has been coined (Milner and Mathers, 2013). Indeed, more and more trade unionists have become full-time trade union representatives. Most of these officers are paid by their companies and no longer through membership dues, severing the ties between union officers and the grassroots. According to Rosanvallon (1988), these officers have become '*welfare state civil servants*'. In companies, branches, and at the inter-branch level, many officers believe they have a general right to decide on behalf of all employees, without having to consult them. Officers' time is mainly spent in meetings and they rarely meet workers outside the campaigns for shop-floor elections. This has further distanced trade unionists from workers and increased the feelings of mistrust that many members feel for union leadership (Ubbiali, 2002; Dufour and Hege, 2002; Machu, 2019; Béroud, 2020).

Thirdly, the effects of this transformation have been combined with structural changes within the French trade union movement. At the same time that membership has been decreasing, trade union superstructures have been extended. For example, CGT confederal staff have increased fivefold since 1974 while the number of its members has been reduced by more than two thirds (from 1.8 million to 500 000). This has also contributed to keeping trade union leaders at a distance from the workforce and making them less sensitive to the changes that have taken place at the coalface.

In addition, all trade union confederations have adopted a dual organisation model, becoming both federal and general, and both highly centralised and standardised. The resulting bureaucracy typically consumes a lot of time and resources and has simultaneously failed to answer requests regarding internal debate and democracy within the unions. This has also contributed to the great difficulties that unions have faced integrating professionals, nurses, social workers and, more generally, the service sector employees within their ranks.

As a consequence of these shifts, far from mobilising the largest number of people possible, trade unions have seen their grassroots diminish, and instead of transcending corporatism, unions in France only resist in a few strongholds. What's more, who, for many in the general public, the strong occupational identity and special working conditions for workers in many of these strongholds, such as for railway workers, postal workers, electricians and local authority employees, have become symbolic of the malaise and contradictions within the French labour movement.

Lastly, politicisation and competition between unions are a further reason for the weakening of union membership (Andolfatto and Labbé, 2011). We have previously highlighted the extreme fragmentation among the French trade unions. Moreover, over the past thirty years, public disputes and power struggles between unions have continued, in particular, with regard to the control of the welfare state bodies and works councils (*comités d'entreprise*) of large companies, and as a result, many workers have become suspicious of trade unions, which has made relations between union officials, members and workers even more difficult.

In short, French trade unionists today form a sort of '*cartel*' in the sense of the '*cartel party*' thesis of Katz and Mair (2002). Such organisations jockey for power among themselves, from the shop floor to the national welfare state bodies and beyond, but increasingly conspire to share important institutional and financial resources, both from the state and from employers, between themselves. Thus, despite the quintessentially French environment of trade union pluralism, this 'cartel' manages to stymie the emergence of new challenger union organisations.

Given these challenging circumstances, can the decline in union membership be reversed, and under what conditions might trade unions in France be revitalised? These questions are tackled in the next section.

2   Re-Unionisation?

Apart from the relatively small CGC (which primarily organises professionals), which published a small increase in the number of dues received at its 2019 Congress, all the other confederations have acknowledged that the number of their members is stagnating or is continuing to decline. This is particularly the case for the CGT and the CFDT, which, taken together, amount to more than half of all union members in France.

It should be noted first of all that, since at least part of the reason for the dramatic loss of union members over recent decades comes from exogenous (macro-sociological) factors, the disappearance of these factors or their mitigation, should logically facilitate some re-unionisation, or at least a stabilisation of membership. According to studies by the French Ministry of Labour, trade union involvement is still difficult and union members are often less active than in the past but participate more in company elections and strikes (DARES, 2016, 2017a). Nevertheless, these studies do not indicate a revival in unionisation but at best some degree of stabilisation, as we have noted.

However, if we examine the endogenous factors described above, one may wonder how trade unions can effectively stop the decline and see increased rates of membership. This question is discussed by various authors (Frege and Kelly 2013; Phelan, 2007b; Gumbrell-McCormick and Hyman, 2013). It is a question of trade unions using alternative strategies to those that have been traditionally implemented. According to the studies mentioned, four answers appear to dominate.

2.1 Four Main Implications for Re-Unionisation in France

Firstly, re-unionisation implies the '*organization of the unorganized*' (Phelan, 2007b). Across all industrial countries, the economic sectors where trade unions have traditionally been strong have declined. Trade unions must therefore turn to new sectors and categories or of workers (including women, migrants and temporary workers but also higher education graduates) and to non-unionised companies, particularly in the services and trading sectors. Enlarging unionisation rates can be facilitated in part by unions forming new relations with political parties and social movement organisations that campaign on such issues (Milkman, 2000; Dupuis and Rioux, 2016) and by engaging in what Gumbrell-McCormick and Hyman call '*the battle of ideas*' (2013).

Secondly, unionisation campaigns require resources and '*organisers*'. Mergers between trade unions can allow saving to be made by pooling resources and through the development of synergies (Gumbrell-McCormick and Hyman, 2013; Oesch, 2008). However, for the time being, clear results are limited (Voss and Sherman, 2000; Behrens et al., 2006; Piotet, 2009). One of the main difficulties seems to relate to the '*iron law of oligarchy*' as expressed by Robert Michels more than a century ago (Michels, 1915). For American trade unions—which were among the first to experience reorganisations on a large scale—there has been resistance from traditional organisations and in particular from trade union leaders where bureaucratic routines are often deeply rooted. As Lipset

(1960) argued, everything regarding the organisation of trade unions implies giving leaders a prominent position and establishing '*an authoritarian and oligarchic regime*'. Therefore, reorganisation can only succeed on a local basis and might benefit from the introduction of new people into leadership positions with experience of social movements outside of the trade union movement, and with the support of federations and confederations (Voss and Sherman, 2000).

Thirdly, the decentralisation of collective bargaining could bring trade union activity closer to potential members which may help to strengthen and develop internal democracy (Gumbrell-McCormick and Hyman, 2013). In addition, there is broad consensus that strengthening trade union involvement in formalised social dialogue not only improves working conditions but also economic competitiveness (Freeman and Medoff 1984; Doucouliagos and Laroche, 2003; Ferracci and Guyot 2019).

In the French case, this has led to an important shift over the past twenty years with the rapid development of collective bargaining at company level, while collective bargaining at the national and branch levels has remained stable (Table 3 below). This is worth emphasising

Table 3 Scope and themes covered by collective bargaining in France about here-

Levels		1983	1990	1999	2010	2018	2019
National	All sectors	47	48	30	25	26	54
National and regional	Branches	901	905	765	1, 36	1,262	785
Firms	Total	1 955	6,479	30.965	33,826	39,034	36,540
	Working hours (%)		38	80	25	24	20
	Wages (%)		58	36	33	32	32
	Employment (%)		3	4	12	6	5
	Subsidies to unions (%)		10	6	9	15	22
	Profit sharing, retirement savings (%)		–	3	24	25	22

Source French Ministry of Labour (*Bilans annuels de la négociation collective/Annual Statement of Collective Bargaining 1983–2020*)

because the decentralisation of collective bargaining is often seen as something purely negative for trade unions and workplace democracy. However, it is clear that there are also potential benefits in terms of workplace democracy.

The wages and working hours of a large number of workers in the private sector now depend on collective agreements that are negotiated at company level, including in the French automotive sector (Reaney and Culinane, 2019). This represents an important change in industrial relations practices that has taken place gradually since the late 1980s, as France has moved away from a model where the main issues were dealt with via national negotiations which were often tripartite in nature, involving unions, employers and the state (Supiot, 1989; Enjolras, 2019). The new flexible system allows employers to adjust wages and working conditions to the prevailing economic conditions and to the needs of their businesses, although crucially, such moderations must obtain union endorsement.

This approach affords more importance to workplace-level union officers who negotiate directly with employers, although they are also paid by them. However, the strengthening of this negotiating role has not led to a notable stream of new members. Many explanations are possible for, particularly that of the aforementioned '*free rider*' phenomenon (Olson, 1965), since, in France, collective contracts are extended to all employees, whether they are union members or not. In addition, many employees have become suspicious of these contracts, which are often defensive in nature and tend to secure no major improvements in the terms and conditions of employment. Lastly, many trade unionists no longer give priority to recruiting new members. An explanation for this can be found in the large number of contracts that include references to the subsidies and resources allocated to trade unions (set out in the second-to-last line in table 3), in addition to those already provided by law. As a result, membership dues, in order to sustain the functioning of the trade union organisation, become less necessary. At workplace level, the employer provides a union office and all the necessary means for the organisation's day-to-day functioning (e.g. material means, communication, paid time to prepare meetings...), and many companies provide a large endowment (e. g. time off for meeting, material means, travel expenses...). On the other hand, given the intimate relations that can form, it may be difficult for these trade unionists to refuse employers' demands. For example, in 2018, CFDT trade unionists signed 93% of the agreements they negotiated and CGT signed 84%. In addition, employer funding has strengthened the institutionalisation and bureaucratisation of trade union organisations. Employers need fair trade union representatives to deal with them in order to adapt labour law to companies as best as possible, in a context of decentralisation in the making of this law.

Fourthly, international action is sometimes seen as a possible way for unions to effectively respond to globalisation (Gumbrell-McCormick and Hyman, 2013). However, the results of this to date have been mixed. Lillie and Martinez-Lucio (2006) give the example of the unionisation of seafarers and dockers, focusing on the international collective action of that has been undertaken by dockers on the west coast of the United States (pp. 167–170) which they contrast with the seeming impossibility of overcoming national differences and specificities when trying to coordinate international collective action within multinational automobile companies (*ibid.*, pp. 170–172).

This raises the question of the role of international institutions, including the International Labour Office (ILO) (Anner, 2007; Louis, 2011; Maupain, 2013), the International Trade Union Confederation (ITUC) and the European Trade Union Confederation (ETUC), which has received relatively limited academic study given its potential significance (Gobin, 1999; Degryse and Tilly 2013; Andolfatto and Basson 2013; Dufresne and Gobin, 2016; Colfer, 2019). A new type of trade unionism—more Europeanised or globalised in nature—has been developing in these organisations for decades, but it has proven difficult to measure its particular impact in terms of unionisation rates. Moreover, once again, the transnational or international-level movements tend to promote the professionalisation and bureaucratisation of trade union officers, rather than the recruitment or retention of members.

Finally, this review suggests that a grassroots approach to the study of unionisation is required.

2.2   *A Grassroots Analysis of Unionisation*

This raises the question of why employees join a trade union in the first place and how can unions create the most favourable conditions for recruitment. Of course, in the '*closed shop*' or '*union shop*' systems, the question makes little sense as membership is essentially mandatory, although such contexts are increasingly rare. In the French case, the former only concerns a few sectors (including technicians of the

Parisian media sector, in the entertainment industry and for some longshoremen) and it is indeed tending to disappear. In some countries, access to certain benefits is conditional on having union membership (e.g. regarding unemployment benefit in the so-called Ghent system in Belgium, Denmark and Sweden). However, in France, primarily for ideological reasons, trade unions have been opposed to private insurance schemes, and the republican tradition condemns discrimination regarding the provision of this type of service. Consequently, except in the rare cases outlined above, union membership tends to be a voluntary act. Clearly, to promote re-unionisation in France, it is important for unions to understand what people's motivations are for joining a union.

Arguably, there are three primary motivations for obtaining union membership (Andolfatto and Labbé, 2011). For most members, these can be cumulative, and it is sometimes difficult to determine which is the primary motivation for membership, if one exists.

Firstly, the '*intro-determined*' membership is essentially motivated by the values and personality of the member themselves. Here, one joins a union because one believes it is one's duty, and the member identifies with the trade union's values. The worker spontaneously makes contact with union representatives, and sometimes the member even sets up their own local branch if one does not yet exist. Until the early 1980s in France, three out of ten new members were motivated by such feelings. Many of these new members had previously been members of youth associations or political organisations, with members of the Communist Party (Parti communiste français/PCF) gravitating towards CGT and Catholics towards CFTC and CFDT. However, at the beginning of the twenty-first century, only about one tenth of new members can be described as '*intro-determined*'.

Secondly, there is a form of '*extro-determined*' membership. For nearly half of new members, unionisation occurs after having been approached by a union officer or from having experienced encouragement (or pressure) from work colleagues to join. Simply put, many union members join because they are asked to do so. However, this pressure is not usually felt as coercive or constraining as it was combined with the encouragement from the local branch members and can be considered as '*sympathetic*', being facilitated by positive feelings regarding the union's image in the workplace. This type of membership has also declined in the past decades, although less starkly than the *intro-determined*' type (discussed above), and a majority of new members today, in one way or another, have been solicited by the union in the workplace.

Thirdly, utilitarian membership sees members join to obtain information, to be protected from one's superiors, or to improve one's working conditions and salary. In the 2000s, in France, this was the primary motivation for nearly half of all union members. A survey from 2011 shows similar results in the United Kingdom (Charlwood & Forth, 2011). When a worker has a full-time shop-steward in their workplace, they often expect to gain help in the event of sanctions (81%), to negotiate a rise in salary (77%), or to obtain an improvement in working conditions (50%). In addition, some new members can be explicitly motivated by having interest in a '*union career*' by seeing membership as a stepping stone towards becoming a paid union officer.

Even in the apparently more centralised systems, such as in Scandinavia, Kjellberg notes that '*the existence of a union workplace organisation is extremely important in promoting union membership*' and that the '*decision to join a union is highly influenced by the workers' immediate environment at the workplace ([i.e.]colleagues and union representatives), while the dominant reasons for maintaining one's membership are related to the ability of the union to achieve satisfactory results and afford protection in unanticipated situations*'. Furthermore, the author contends that a trade union presence at the workplace level also plays a major role in promoting unionisation in the United Kingdom, North America and Japan: '*The British case illustrates how one-sided decentralisation, by the almost complete disappearance of support to shop-stewards from industry-wide agreements, also weakens unions considerably at the workplace level*' (Kjellberg, 2007, p. 267).

The historic peak in unionisation in the late 1970s in France, Italy and the United Kingdom corresponded to maximum presence of unions at the workplace (Cox, 1981; Revelli, 1981; Labbé, 1996). In the United Kingdom, for example, shop-stewards elected by all employees conducted negotiations with employers and imposed closed shops in most large establishments. The workers supported these shop-stewards largely because of the daily services and supports that they provided for union members at the workplace (Cox, 1981).

Lastly, and importantly, French trade unions are still focused on the pre-digital world. Their websites tend to be dull, often containing out-of-date information, and they still struggle to coordinate and promote collective action via social networks, inability undoubtedly worsens their capacity to reach especially younger workers.

3 Conclusion

Until the end of the twentieth century, the weakening of trade unions in France through membership loss did not pose an existential threat for the French labour movement, as unions benefited from protective laws that regulated dismissals, wages and working conditions. Today, this is no longer the case because, in the name of flexibility and corporate performance, these laws can frequently be bypassed through, for example, the decentralisation of collective bargaining to the workplace level. This situation has reinforced the professionalisation of trade union representatives and has contributed to the gap that has grown between union officials and grassroots union members and employees. It has also changed the image of trade unions among workers, who increasingly perceive them as external actors who are still often too close to management.

This situation is clearly not favourable to any process of re-unionisation. Although French trade unions remain fairly well established in some large companies, their existence now depends to a large degree on government and employer subsidies and on a wage tax as a result of some major reforms such as the *'renovation de la démocratie sociale'* (renewal of social democracy) Act (2008) and the *'vocational training, employment and social democracy'* Act (2014).

Under these circumstances, union renewal through an increase in membership remains a challenge for French unions. This lack of renewal fuels a crisis of representation and latent social discontent that is often expressed in wildcat strikes and demonstrations that periodically grind the country to a halt. In 2018–19, the *'gilets jaunes'* (yellow vest) movement and the railways strikes at the SNCF national transport company once again illustrated what is often seen as a quasi-permanent state of deadlock in France (see Colfer & Bazin, this volume). Does this movement foreshadow the emergence of a more fluid form of organisation that could help to regenerate trade unionism in France? While it is clearly a symptom of a crisis of representation, this movement has remained specific and has not succeeded in challenging trade union organisations in companies—at least not yet. This is likely to remain the case in France as long as the state provides strong legal protects for trade unions, making them difficult for employers to avoid.

Bibliography

ANDOLFATTO (Dominique), 2002, 'Syndicalisme et individualisme', Projet, 271, pp. 81–98.

ANDOLFATTO (Dominique), BASSON (Jean-Charles), 2013, 'Vers une européanisation du syndicalisme français?', in ANDOLFATTO (Dominique), ed., *Les syndicats en France*, Paris: La documentation française (3rd edition).

ANDOLFATTO (Dominique), CONTREPOIS (Sylvie), eds, 2016, *Syndicats et dialogues social. Les modèles occidentaux à l'épreuve*, Bruxelles: Peter Lang.

ANDOLFATTO (Dominique), LABBÉ (Dominique), 2007, *Les syndiqués en France*, Rueil-Malmaison: Editions Liaisons.

ANDOLFATTO (Dominique), LABBE (Dominique), 2011, *Histoire des syndicats (1906–2010)*, Paris: Seuil.

ANNER (Mark), 2007, 'The Paradox of Labour Transnationalism: Trade Union Campaigns for Labour Standards in International Institutions', in PHELAN (Graig), ed., 2007a, *The Future of Organised Labour*, Bruxelles: Peter Lang, pp. 63–90.

BEHRENS (Matthew), HURD (Richard), WADDINGTON (Jeremy), 2006, 'How does Retructuring Contribute to Union Revitalization?', in FREGE (Carola), KELLY (John), eds, *Varieties of Unionism. Strategies for Union Revitalization in a Globalizing Economy.* Oxford: Oxford University Press, pp. 117–136.

BÉROUD (Sophie), 2020, 'De quoi la réforme de la représentativité syndicale est-elle le nom?', in GROUX (Guy), ROBERT (Richard), FOUCAULT (Martial), eds, *Le social et le politique*, Paris: CNRS Editions, pp. 129–139.

CHARLWOOD (Andy), FORTH (John), 2011, 'Les mutations de la représentation des salariés en Grande-Bretagne', *La Revue de l'Ires*, 68(1), pp. 43–73.

COLFER (Barry), 2019, 'The European trade union confederation under austerity' *Social Science Review*, vol. 9, SI7, p. 9–27.

COX (Andrew), 1981, 'Le mouvement syndical britannique et la récession économique des années soixante-dix', in ARMINGEON (Klaus) *et al.*, *Les syndicats européens et la crise*, Grenoble: Presses Universitaires de Grenoble, pp. 61–99.

DARES, 2016, 'La syndicalisation en France', *Dares Analyse*, 25, May.

DARES, 2017a, 'De l'adhérent au responsable syndical', *DARES Analyse*, 15, March.

DARES, 2017b, 'Les licenciements et les ruptures conventionnelles des contrats des salariés protégés, principaux indicateurs', *DARES résultats*, 18, March.

DEGRYSE (Christophe), TILLY (Pierre), 2013, *1973–2013: 40 ans d'histoire de la Confédération européenne des syndicats*, Bruxelles: ETUI.

DOUCOULIAGOS (Christos), LAROCHE (Patrice), 2003, 'What do unions do to productivity? A meta-analysis', *Industrial Relations*, 42-4, pp. 650–691.

DUFOUR (Christian), HEGE (Adelheid), 2002, *L'Europe syndicale au quotidien. La représentation des salariés en France, Allemagne, Grande-Bretagne et Italie*, Bruxelles: PIE-Peter Lang.

DUFRESNE (Anne), GOBIN (Corinne), 2016, 'Le dialogue social européen ou la déconstruction du droit social et la transformation des relations professionnelles', in LAPOINTE (Paul-André), ed., *Dialogue social, relations du travail et syndicalisme*, Québec: Presses de l'Université Laval, pp. 23–63.

DUPUIS (Mathicu), RIOUX (Claude), 2016, 'Etats-Unis: crise du syndicalisme et de la négociation collective', in ANDOLFATTO (Dominique), CONTREPOIS (Sylvie), *op. cit.*, pp. 123–138.

ENJOLRAS (Laurriane), 2019, 'Les syndicats face aux mutations du travail', in DUBET (François), ed, *Les mutations du travail*, Paris: La découverte, pp. 179–193.

FERRACCI (Marc), GUYOT (Florian), 2019, *Dialogue social et performance économique*, Paris: Presses de Sciences-po.

FREGE (Carola), KELLY (John), eds., 2013. *Comparative Employment Relations in the Global Economy*. Londres: Routledge.

FREEMAN (Richard), MEDOFF (James), 1984, *What Do Unions Do?* New York: Basic Books.

GOBIN (Corinne), 1999, *L'Europe syndicale entre désir et réalité: essai sur le syndicalisme et la construction européenne à l'aube du XXIème siècle*, Bruxelles: Editions Labor.

GUILLAUME, (Cécile), POCHIC, (Sophie), CHAPPE (Vincent-Arnaud), 2018, 'The promises and pitfalls of collective bargaining for ending the victimization of trade union activists: Lessons from France'. *Economic and Industrial Democracy*, 39-3, pp. 536–557

Gumbrell-McCormik (Rebecca), HYMAN (Richard), 2013, *Trade Unions in Western Europe. Hard Times, Hard Choices*, Oxford: Oxford University Press.

HAIVEN (Larry), LÉVESQUE (Christian), ROBY (Nicolas), 2006, 'Pistes de renouveau syndical: défis et enjeux', *Relations industrielles*, 61-4, pp. 567–588.

ION (Jacques), 1997, *La fin des militants?*, Paris: Editions de l'Atelier.

INGLEHART (Ronald), 1977, *The Silent Revolution*. Princeton: Princeton University Press.

JEFFERYS (Steve), 2007), 'Forward to the Past? Ideology and Trade Unions in France and Britain', in PHELAN (Graig), ed., 2007a, *The Future of Organised Labor*. Bruxelles: Peter Lang, pp. 209–241.

KJELLBERG (Anders), 2007, 'The Swedish Trade Union System in Transition: High but Falling Union Density', in PHELAN (Graig), ed., 2007b, *Trade Union Revitalisation*, Bruxelles: Peter Lang, pp. 260–285.

LILLIE (Nathan), MARTINEZ-LUCIO (Miguel), 2006, 'International Trade Union Revitalization; the Role of National Union Approaches', in FREGE (Carola),

KELLY (John), eds., *Varieties of Unionism. Strategies for Union Revitalization in a Globalizing Economy*, Oxford: Oxford University Press, pp. 159-180.

KATZ (Richard), MAIR (Peter), 2002, 'The Ascendancy of the Party in Public Office: Party Organization Change in Twentieh-Century Democracies', in GUNTHER (Richard), MONTERO (Jose Ramon), LINZ (Juan), dir., *Political Parties. Old Concepts and New Challenges*, Oxford: Oxford University Press, pp. 113-135.

LABBÉ (Dominique), 1996, *Syndicats et syndiqués en France depuis 1945*, Paris: L'Harmattan.

LOUIS (Marieke), 2011, *L'Organisation international du travail et le travail décent. Un agenda social pour le multilatéralisme*, Paris: L'Harmattan.

LIPSET (Seymour), 1960, *Political Man. The Social Basis of Politics*, New York: Doubleday.

MACHU (Laure), 2019, 'Représenter et négocier', in DREYFUS (Michel), PIGENET (Michel), eds, *La CGT en question(s). Regards croisés sur 125 années d'un syndicalisme de transformation sociale*, Dijon, EUD, pp. 93-109.

MAUPAIN (Francis), 2013, *The Future of the International Labour Organization in the Global Economy*, Oxford/Portland: Hart Publishing.

MICHELS (Robert), 1915, *Political Parties. A Sociological Study of the Oligarchical Tendencies of Modern Democracy*, New York: Heart's International Library Co.

MILKMAN (Ruth), ed., 2000, *Immigrants and Union Organizing*, Ithaca: Cornell University Press.

MILNER (Susan), MATHERS (Andrew), 2013, 'Membership, influence and voice: a discussion of trade union renewal in the French context', *Industrial Relations Journal*, 44-2, pp. 112-138.

MINISTÈRE DU TRAVAIL [Ministry of Labour], 2020, 2019, 2011, 1991, 1984, *Bilan annuel de la négociation collective*, Paris: rapports officiels.

OESCH (Daniel), 2008, *Les syndicats de Suisse de 1990 à 2006: stratégies, fusions et évolution de leurs effectifs*, Berne: Union syndicale suisse.

OLIVESI (Stéphane), 2013, *La communication syndicale*, Rennes: Presses universitaires de Rennes.

OLSON (Mancur), 1965, *The Logic of Collective Action: Public Goods and Theory of Groups*, Cambridge: Harvard University Press.

PHELAN (Graig), ed., 2007a, *The Future of Organised Labour*, Bruxelles: Peter Lang.

PHELAN (Graig), ed., 2007b, *Trade Union Revitalisation*, Bruxelles: Peter Lang.

PIOTET (Françoise), ed., 2009, *La CGT et la recomposition syndicale*, Paris: Presses universitaires de France.

REANEY (Ruth), CULINANE Niall (2019), 'Competitiveness Bargaining in France: A study of multiple action in the automotive industry', To be published in *Economic and Industrial democracy*.

REVELLI (Marco), 1981, 'La bureaucratie syndicale et les militants de base en Italie', in ARMINGEON (Klaus) et al., *Les syndicats européens et la crise*, Grenoble: Presses Universitaires de Grenoble, pp. 105-131.

ROSANVALLON (Pierre), 1988, *La question syndicale*, Paris: Fondation Saint-Simon/Calmann-Lévy.

SIBLOT (Yasmine), 2009, 'La difficile transmission d'un syndicalisme 'à statut', in PIOTET (Françoise), ed, *La CGT et la recomposition syndicale*, Paris: PUF, pp. 95-121.

SUPIOT (Alain), 1989, 'Déréglementation des relations du travail et autoréglementation de l'entreprise', *Droit social*, 3, pp. 195-205.

TODD (Emmanuel), 2020, *Les luttes des classes en France au XXIe siècle*, Paris: Seuil.

UBBIALI (Georges), 2002, 'Qu'est-ce qu'un professionnel du syndicalisme?', in LABBÉ (Dominique), COURTOIS (Stéphane), eds, *Regards sur la crise du syndicalisme*, Paris: L'Harmattan, pp. 81-95.

VISSER (Jelle), 2006, 'Union membership statistics in 24 countries', *Monthly Labor Review*, 129 (1), pp. 38-49.

VISSER (Jelle), 2015, *ICTWSS Data base*, Amsterdam, Amsterdam Institute for Advanced Labour Studies AIAS.

VOSS (Kim), SHERMAN (Rachel), 2000, 'Breaking the Iron Law of Oligarchy: Union. Revitalization in the American Labor Movement', *American Journal of Sociology*, 106-2, pp. 303-349.

CHAPTER 7

France: Macron's Orders and Trade Union Power in the Field of Health at Work

Sylvie Contrepois

In spite of massive popular opposition, French president, Emmanuel Macron, introduced a raft of major reforms to the French Labour Code during the last months of 2017 (Quijoux, Gourgues, 2018). Among other things, the reforms aimed in particular to reorganise the different levels of collective bargaining that exist in France, to reduce the resources available to staff representative institutions, to overhaul the occupational health system, to reform the regulation of redundancies and to reform the organisation of certain forms of work, including telework (i.e. remote working).

These ordinances elicited much public opposition, not only because they undermine employee rights but also because they seek to disrupt the dynamic of collective action in France. Until the turn of the 2000s, the French industrial relations system was characterised by the high level

S. Contrepois (✉)
Centre de Recherches sociologiques et politiques de Paris (CNRS), Paris, France

Institut régional du travail d'Occitanie, Université de Toulouse - Jean Jaurès, Toulouse, France

© The Author(s), under exclusive license to Springer Nature Switzerland AG 2022
B. Colfer (ed.), *European Trade Unions in the 21st Century*, St Antony's Series, https://doi.org/10.1007/978-3-030-88285-3_7

of protection it granted to workers and their representatives thanks in particular to extensive labour rights (Herrera, 2009).[1] The 2017 reforms make legal action by unions much more complex to initiate and much more uncertain from the point of view of the results that can be expected (Serverin, 2019; Lyon Caen, 2017; Moussy, 2018).[2]

However, over the past thirty years, a more systematically legal approach, which could go as far as to bring employers to court, had already been adopted by many trade unions as an effective strategy for driving actions towards a positive outcome (Pélisse, 2009). Especially, in the light of declining union membership, such an approach has proven to be an important tool in the unions' armoury (see Andolfatto, this volume). Several emblematic struggles led by unions have taken place in the fields of discrimination at work (Hatzfeld, 2016), the protection of employment (Depoorter, Frigul, 2014), and health and safety at work (Beynel, 2020).

Notably, President Macron's orders will undermine one of the key pillars of trade union strategies in France—namely, recourse to the law. They will do so directly through the reorganisation of the Conseil de Prud'hommes (the French Labour Court) and by reforming the process of abusive dismissals. The reforms will also undermine this pillar of union strength indirectly through a drastic cut in the resources granted to employee representatives in the workplace. Indeed, effective recourse to the law had traditionally been based on the important (but time-consuming) outreach work done by employee representatives in the workplace (Bouchareb, 2011; Cristoffalo, 2014).

This chapter will explore the indirect effects of President Macron's labour reforms. It will do so by focusing more particularly on the field of health and safety at work, where employee representatives traditionally enjoyed extensive powers through CHSCT (Comité d'hygiène, de sécurité et des conditions de travail/hygiene, safety and working conditions committees), first established in 1982 under the Auroux laws. Indeed, trade unions had gradually invested in this specific institution and came

---

[1] The website http://fr.worker-participation.eu/ compares the different European industrial relations systems. It shows in particular that France is the country where collective bargaining coverage - 98% - is the highest.

[2] https://www.publicsenat.fr/article/politique/ordonnances-une-brutale-devaluation-du-cout-du-travail-analyse-le-juriste-antoine.

to exercise one of their most effective forms of power over management at the level of the company (Henry, 2012; Goussard, Tiffon, 2017).

It is very likely that the reduction in the resources allocated to staff representative institutions and the replacement of the CHSCTs by the CSSCT (Commissions santé, sécurité et conditions de travail / Health, Safety and Working Conditions Commission), which have far fewer powers that their predecessor committees, will have major negative repercussions for the effectiveness of employee representation and, more broadly, on trade unions' ability to resort to the law to establish a more favourable balance of power between employees and employers, and to mobilise influence over public policy. What's more, outreach work, hitherto made possible by the relatively extensive coverage of employee representative institutions, will be particularly hampered by these developments.

Companies had two years, until 1 January 2020, to merge their employee representative institutions, and it is still too early to make a precise diagnosis of the medium- and long-term impact of these reforms on unions and workplaces. This chapter aims to shed light on the scope of these changes. We will analyse their effects in detail, on the scale of two sectors that were previously relatively well-endowed in terms of staff representation, namely the electricity and gas industries. This chapter aims to shed light on how the power and influence of the unions active in these sectors will be affected by the implementation of these reforms.

To do this, we will rely on data drawn from official statistics, which we have supplemented with research into the activities of the employee and employer organisations that are active in the electricity and gas industries. The online part of this research enabled us to access the texts of collective agreements, written analyses from the social partners that were made at the various stages of negotiations, as well as various other contextual data.

The first and second sections of this chapter are dedicated, respectively, to a brief presentation of the overhaul of employee representative institutions under President Macron's labour reforms, and a review of the specific cases of the electricity and gas industries. The third section is devoted to an analysis of projections made from the results of the 2016 workplace elections as well as of the agreements relating to the establishment of workers representative institutions and union rights. The fourth section looks at the progress of the negotiations and the texts of the CSE (Comité social et économique/Social and economic committee) implementation agreements that were eventually signed in autumn 2019.

Finally, a concluding section seeks to put our analysis into its wider context.

1 Content and Scope of President Macron's Labour Reforms

Until 2018, the various aspects of employee representation were carried out through the auspices of works councils (CE—Comités d'entreprises), staff representatives (DP—Délégués du personnel) and hygiene, safety and working conditions committees (CHSCT—Comités d'hygiène, de sécurité et des conditions de travail). Each of these joint bodies were composed of members elected by company staff and each had the legal personality to take legal action. President Macron's labour reforms, which passed into law in December 2017, profoundly modified this system. They did so primarily by replacing these three institutions with a single entity.

Previously, works councils (CE) could be set up in workplaces and companies with at least 50 employees, and had the dual mission of managing social work and issuing advisory opinions on the economic and social policy of a workplace. Staff representatives (DP) were elected in workplaces and companies with at least 10 employees and were responsible for handling individual and collective grievance from employees and ensuring compliance with labour regulations.

Hygiene, safety and working conditions committees (CHSCT), set up in workplaces with at least 50 employees, were responsible for ensuring the improvement of working conditions and the respect for employee safety. The CHSCT offered important prerogatives in terms of staff representation, both in terms of preventing accidents and occupational diseases and by obtaining financial repair. The CHSCTs were notably empowered to carry out periodic inspections and investigations in the event of accidents or illness at work. They also needed to be consulted by employers when new working practices were to be implemented and when companies were being restructured. The opinions issued by CHSCTs had legal value and could be referred to in the context of legal proceedings which more and more frequently pitted employees against their employers. Intervening as close as possible to the work units, CHSCTs constituted an essential support for the outreach work by union officers at workplace level, and consequently for the effectiveness of union representation.

With President Macron's reforms, these three institutions were merged into a single entity through the establishment of Economic and Social Committees (CSE) (Ministère du travail, 2018). This merger, which was to be carried out in all French companies by 1 January 2020, would be accompanied by a reduction in the resources provided for staff representatives, both in terms of the number of elected officials and the number of hours to be dedicated to staff representation. It therefore has resulted in a significant change in the conditions of workplace representation. Thus, for example, in the new arrangement, the elected and deputy elected officials lose the right to sit together, which hinders their ability to coordinate their activities.

But above all, the merging of these institutions has very important consequences in terms of representing the interests of employees in the fields of health and safety at work. In fact, while the new Health, Safety and Working Conditions Committees (CSSCT) can be set up without staffing conditions in any company, they only become compulsory in a workplace of over 300 employees (as opposed to the threshold of 50 employees for the previous CHSCTs).

Crucially, unlike their predecessors, CSSCT have no legal personality. Under the terms of Article L. 2315–38 of the Labour Code, these bodies are entrusted, by delegation from the CSE, with all or part of the latter's powers relating to health, safety and working conditions, except regarding the use of experts in cases of "immanent danger" or "important restructuring" and regarding the advisory powers of the committee. They can therefore neither take legal action nor issue any opinion, and only the CSE (on which the CSSCTs depend) has this power. In terms of composition, the representatives of these committees are appointed from among the elected members of the CSEs, unless a collective agreement states otherwise.

The CSSCT may, however, take charge of the analysis of occupational risks and can propose preventive actions. If the CSSCT does not have the possibility of having recourse to expertise, it can however make expert proposals to the CSE and can prepare consultations on matters relating to health and safety.

The impact that this overhaul of the employee representative institutions will have on the ability of trade unions to effectively represent the interests of their members are not yet fully clear. The transition to the CSE system took place only gradually between the end of 2017 and the start of January 2020. After the first nine months of the reform there were only 9,000 CSEs, representing about 6% of workplaces of more than 10 employees.

In the following section, we take a look at how these reforms have played out within companies in the electricity and gas Industries. Until the implementation of President Macron's labour reforms, employees in this sector benefited from one of the largest employee representative organisations networks in France, as well as from the most extensive trade union rights. Thus, the way that these reforms have played out in this sector may serve as a bellwether for other sectors and industries across France.

2 Case Studies—the Electricity and Gas Sectors

The electrical and gas industries (IEG—Industries électriques et gazières) group together all the companies in France that are engaged in the production, transport and distribution of electricity and gas. It resulted from the restructuring of the two major national monopolies that operated in the energy sector until the early 2000s, namely: Electricité de France (EDF) and Gaz de France (GDF).

As of 31 December 2018, this organisation had 158 member companies with various legal statuses, including: public limited companies, mixed economy companies (with up to 85% public capital), Régies (Company managed by officials of a public authority) and Societies of Collective Agricultural Interest in Electricity (private electricity distributors operating in a limited geographical area). Taken together, nearly 138,000 people are employed across these companies, more than 90% of whom work in companies that resulted directly from the restructuring of the two aforementioned erstwhile national monopolies, namely: EDF SA (Electricité de France—80% of the workforce), ENEDIS, RTE (Réseau de transport de l'électricité), ENGIE SA, GRDF (Gaz Réseau Distribution France), GRTgaz (Gestionnaire du reseau de transport de Gaz), STORENGY (underground gas storage) and ELENGY. The remaining 10% are distributed across some 144 other gas or electricity production or distribution companies, state-owned companies, cooperatives, most of which (117) have fewer than 50 employees.

The culture of the social actors involved in this sector is marked by the concept of joint management which was inherited from the programme of the Conseil National de la Résistance—National Council of the Resistance. The organisation of professional relations within EDF and GDF was also shaped by the process of nationalisation of various companies involved in the production, transport and distribution of electricity which took place in 1946 (Tixier & Duclos, 2000: 69). From this date and for more than sixty years following, social dialogue was centralised at the level of the general management of both EDF and GDF (Parmantier, 2011). In the absence of sectoral agreements, the Ministry of Industry extended all or part of the decisions taken within the two national monopolies to Non-Nationalized Enterprises (ENN—Entreprises non nationalisées). The CGT union occupied a central place in the social dialogue process, with company management and public authorities making very few decisions on social policy without the union's approval.

The nature and context of relations between the social partners changed during the 1990s with the introduction of new provisions that were intended to decentralise collective bargaining (Tixier & Duclos, 2000: 73). This was followed in the early 2000s with yet more radical reforms, with the implementation of the 10 February 2000 law relating to the modernisation and development of the public electricity service. This law, adopted in line with European directives and aiming at the deregulation of the markets dominated by monopolies, laid the foundations for the opening up of the French energy market to competition and set up new frameworks that were designed to change the employment statute. The law specifies in particular (in article 45) that *"professional agreements can supplement, [...] the statutory provisions or determine the modalities of application within the limits fixed in the statute"*.

Following this, the public authorities gradually withdraw from the social dialogue processes in the sector. Two employers' organisations were created with a view to developing branch-level negotiations, namely: the Union Française de l'Electricité (UFE) and the Union Nationale des Employeurs des Industries Gazières (UNEmIG). The new branch agreements are automatically applied to member companies of UFE and UNEmIG and were then extended to other companies after passing through the Commission Nationale de la négociation collective (National Collective bargaining Commission).

In the wake of the modernisation law, in 2007, the French government adopted two decrees aimed at aligning the system of employee representation for companies in the sector with the provisions of the national Labour Code. The former Joint Production Committees (CMP—Comités mixtes à la production) and high consultative committee of the CMP (Comité supérieur consultatif des CMP) have therefore been replaced by local works councils (Comités d'établissements) and central works councils

(Comité central d'entreprise). Likewise, the secondary and higher Staff Commissions—which were dealing with individual staff issues—have been partially replaced by staff representatives (*Délégués du Personnel*). The first staff elections were held in October 2007, and the new staff representative bodies were installed by 31 December 2007.

During this period, another event occurred which radically altered the landscape of social relations in the sector, with the merger between GDF and Suez, a French utilities company, which occurred on 22 July 2008. The new GDF SUEZ group now has 106,000 employees across France, of which only 29,000 work in the energy sector, with the remaining employees working in the service to companies in the energy (41,000) and environmental (33,000) sectors. As a result of this merger, the companies within the GDF SUEZ group apply several different collective agreements. However, while they are a minority within the group, IEG employees are strongly represented among union leaders at the group.

As soon as President Macron's reforms were signed into law, some companies in the electricity and gas industries rapidly negotiated CSE implementation agreements and installed the new institutions. However, most companies in the sector have gone through a more protracted negotiation process.[3]

In the following sections, we analyse the transition processes that led to the establishment of the new CSE bodies in this sector. First, we show the effects that could be expected from a "mechanical" implementation of the CSE, that is to say without any negotiation and by the strict application of legal provisions. We then explore the progress of the negotiations and the content of the agreements that were eventually signed.

3 Negotiating CSE Agreements: A Very Unfavourable Situation

As soon as the negotiations regarding the establishment of CSEs began, the social partners made various projections in order to assess the different possible scenarios that might emerge and their potential consequences in terms of resources for staff representation. In the light of these projections, and after a few months of negotiations, the various representative unions were extremely worried. Thus, on 11 November 2018, the inter-union alliance within the electrical and gas industries called on employees

---

[3] https://ufictfnme.fr/representativite-dans-la-branche-des-ieg/, May 11, 2018.

in the following terms: "*The first feedback from the ongoing negotiations confirms a "undermining work"orchestrated at the branch level and common to all companies in IEG. Faced with this significant change in employee representation in companies in our professional branch of the electricity and gas industries, the federations FNME-CGT, CFE-CGC energies, FCE-CFDT and FNEM-FO denounce the irresponsible attitude of employers in the industry and require real resources to accomplish their mission and alert employees. If the employers' proposals are maintained, the staff representatives will no longer be able to ensure the collective and individual defense of the interests of employees at branch level, in companies and as close as possible to employees (...) The unions stress that in the event accident, penalty, sexism, discrimination, claim or simply for a claim or information on your individual rights, IEG employees would no longer have local contacts*".[4] We ourselves made similar projections based on an assessment of the nine companies representing the largest share of the workforce in the electricity and gas industries.

We previously carried out an inventory of representative institutions and trade union rights in these companies, by analysing the data contained in the minutes of the professional elections of 2013 and 2016, which are made public by the Ministry of Labour. We were able to add to this data, in particular with regard to the CHSCTs, thanks to the information available regarding company agreements and social reports posted online by company management or union organisations, as well as across the union press and employer announcements. Finally, article R. 2314–1 of the French labour code stipulates the number of seats provided for regular delegates according to the scope (i.e. number of employees) covered by the CSE, as well as the number of hours employee representatives can dedicate to their representative work.

The projections that we carried out were based on the assumption that CSEs would have the same scope than the works councils that were in existence on the date of the entry into force of the new orders. For each works council, we counted the number of employee representatives and the number of CHCSTs, as well as the number of seats for each of these bodies. We then projected the number of seats for the future CSE on the basis of the workforce declared by each company on 24 November 2016, the date of the first round of the last works council elections.

[4] https://www.miroirsocial.com/mise-en-place-du-cse-l-intersyndicale-des-ieg-met-en-garde.

Table 1 summarises the main developments that could have resulted from a strict application of the law, assuming that the scope of the new CSEs closely matches that of the old works councils.

Table 1 Projection: the consequences of setting up CSEs

Company	Number of seat of full reps in each institution	Share of seats in the CHSCT	Projections CSE Share of spared seats
EDF (78 198 employees)	56 CE, 418 Seats 96 DP, 825 Seats 127 CHSCT, 806 Seats TOTAL = 2101 Seats	CE 22%, CHSCT 39%, DP 40%	56 CSE, 977 Seats 46,5 %
CNR (1 401 employees)	5 CE, 31 Seats 5 DP, 29 Seats 5 CHSCT, 33 Seats TOTAL = 93 Seats	CE 33%, CHSCT 36%, DP 31%	5 CSE, 43 Seats 46,2 %
Enedis (30 800 employees)	26 CE, 194 Seats 28 DP, 305 Seats 70 CHSCT, 530 Seats TOTAL = 1029 Seats	CE 19%, CHSCT 51%, DP 30%	26 CSE, 443 Seats 43,1 %
ENGIE (5 758 employees)	4 CE, 34 Seats 9 DP, 77 Seats 9 CHSCT, 77 Seats TOTAL = 188 Seats	CE 14%, CHSCT 43%, DP 43%	4 CSE, 69 Seats 33,7 %
GRT Gaz (3 226 employees)	4 CE, 29 Seats 7 DP, 54 Seats 9 CHSCT, 98 Seats TOTAL = 181 Seats	CE 16%, CHSCT 54%, DP 30%	4 CSE, 60 Seats 33,1 %
GRDF (9 359 employees)	9 CE, 66 Seats 27 DP, 181 Seats 43 CHSCT, 266 Seats TOTAL : 513 Seats	CE 13%, CHSCT 52%, DP 35%	9 CSE, 147 Seats 28,7 %
GRDF/Enedis (3 738 employees)	4 CE, 31 Seats 11 DP, 77 Seats 13 CHSCT, 115 Seats TOTAL = 233 Seats	CE 14%, CHSCT 52%, DP 34%	4 CSE, 60 Seats 26,9 %
RTE (8 846 employees)	4 CE, 37 Seats 10 DP, 91 Seats 41 CHSCT, 241 Seats TOTAL = 369 Seats	CE 10%, CHSCT 65%, DP 25%	4 CSE, 82 Seats 22,2 %
Storengy (893 employees)	1 CE, 8 Seats 6 DP, 29 Seats 7 CHSCT, 38 Seats TOTAL = 75 Seats	CE 11%, CHSCT 51%, DP 38%	1 CSE, 15 Seats 20 %

- Seats are for regular delegates, and each regular delegate has an Alternate.
- **How to read this table:** RTE has 4 works councils, 10 staff representative (DP) institutions and 41 CHSCTs. The total number of full delegate positions is 369, of which 65% are allocated to the CHSCT. If 4 CSEs had been created on the basis of the shape of the former works councils and on the basis of the legal provisions in terms of number of seats, the total number of seats of full delegates would have been 82, i.e. a decline of 77.8%.

This table shows that setting up the CSEs on the strict basis of legal texts and within the scope of the former works councils, would lead to a reduction in the number of seats of permanent delegates ranging between 53.5% and just below 80%. This decrease would be more noticeable in companies where industrial relations have been built on a requirement of proximity with the workers and of extensive coverage in terms of staff representatives and CHSCTs. It is thus in companies where the seats of representatives to the CHSCT constituted more than 50% of the seats of elected officials that the resources dedicated to employee representation are most likely to be greatly reduced.

This reading is confirmed by a more in-depth analysis of the situation within each company. It appears, in fact, that in units where the number of CHSCTs had been extended by collective agreement, due to the dangerous nature of the tasks carried out, that the strict application of the legal provisions would have the effect of considerably weakening the resources available to staff representation in the fields of health, safety and working conditions. The following table presents the situation at RTE as an example.

Table 2 clearly shows how a strict application of the legal provisions on the evolution of the configuration of industrial relations would look like. It is indeed in units where the staffing of the bodies had been calculated so as to ensure the greatest proximity between staff representatives and their constituents—maintenance department in the case of RTE—that the resources of staff representation risk being reduced to the greatest extent. The ratio between the number of staff representative seats and employees would drop from 1 in 20 to 1 in 160 in the maintenance department. This same ratio would experience a much less significant decrease at the headquarters, but still a notable one, since it would drop from 1 in 53 to 1 in 108. This reduction in resources is taking place to the detriment

Table 2 Projected situation at RTE

Units	Number of seats of full reps in each institution	Share of CHSCT's seats	Projections CSE Share of spare seats
Fonctions centrales (2 496 employees)	1 CE, 10 seats 1 DP, 16 seats 3 CHSCT, 21 seats TOTAL = 47 seats	CE 21% DP 34% CHSCT 45%	1 CSE, 23 seats 48,94 %
Développement & ingénierie (1 345)	1 CE, 9 seats 1 DP, 11 seats 7 CHSCT, 42 seats TOTAL = 62 seats	CE 15% DP 18% CHSCT 68%	1 CSE, 18 seats 29,03 %
Exploitation (834 employees)	1 CE, 7 titulaires 1 DP, 9 seats 8 CHSCT, 40 seats TOTAL = 56 seats	CE 13% DP 16% CHSCT 71%	1 CSE, 15 seats 26,79 %
Maintenance (4 171 employees)	1 CE, 11 seats 7 DP, 55 seats 23 CHSCT, 138 seats TOTAL = 204 seats	CE 5% DP 27% CHSCT 68%	1 CSE, 26 seats 12,75 %
TOTAL 8846 employees	4 CE, 37 seats 10 DP, 91 seats 41 CHSCT, 241 seats TOTAL = 369 seats	CE 10% DP 25% CHSCT 65%	4 CSE, 82 seats 22,22 %

of the bodies that intervene in the field of health, safety and working conditions, since only a small part of the new representatives on the CSE will be entrusted with responsibility in these fields. This observation applies to all the companies for which we have made projections. In the case of EDF, it was the potential development of staff representation in nuclear power plants that appeared to be the most problematic issue. These establishments were in fact covered by numerous CHSCTs.

The consequences of the implementation of President Macron's labour reforms were therefore not designed to be different only according to the configuration of industrial relations in each company, and according to the specific provisions that existed in the area of trade union rights and staff representation within them. They also promised to be more or less severe depending on the size of the staff representation that had been set up to deal with the specific challenges posed by the different types of jobs in terms of health, safety and working conditions.

We should point out that our projections only relate to the three joint institutions and thus do not include the resources granted by collective agreements that were dedicated to trade union rights, namely: local union representatives, central union representatives, union representatives on the works council (RS CE—Représentant syndical au comité d'entreprise) and on the Health, Safety and Working conditions committee (RS CHSCT—représentant syndical au CHSCT). In general, the disappearance of institutions should thus automatically remove representatives that have been mandated by union organisations.

In this context, the EDF CGT union believed that *"The major issue of these negotiations on the CSE is therefore to preserve union representation as close as possible to the daily lives of agents to defend local claims, statutory rights and jobs "*, and that the union *"must fight against the bureaucratisation of union activity"*.[5]

In the light of these projections, we can now examine the progress of the negotiations as well as the agreements which have ultimately been signed within the companies under consideration here.

4 The Difficult Maintenance of the Union Balance of Power

In the year following the promulgation of President Macron's labour reforms, collective agreements were negotiated by the social partners in most companies across the electricity and gas sector, in order to define the frameworks within which negotiations could take place regarding the merger of employee representative bodies and, possibly, on the right for unions to organise. These agreements were most often signed in the third quarter of 2018 and have precipitated discussions about how the new CSEs should function.

In some cases, these discussions were part of the larger framework of multi-annual programmes known as "renewal of social dialogue" (Rénovation du dialogue social). For example, EDF launched such a programme in 2016 and developed it, from October 2018, through the "Social Dialogue 2020" (Dialogue social 2020) project, that was specifically dedicated to the establishment of CSEs.[6]

---

[5] https://cgt-edf-recherche.fr/mise-en-oeuvre-du-comite-social-et-economique/

[6] https://cgt-edf-recherche.fr/mise-en-oeuvre-du-comite-social-et-econo...

A first fact to note is that the negotiations which preceded these collective agreements were generally fractious and adversarial. From mid-December 2018, the IEG inter-union negotiating body (*intersyndicale des Industries Électriques et Gazières*) threatened employers in the following terms: "*Employers must review their first copies today, otherwise they would take the risk of being alone at the negotiating table and then distraught in the face of out of control protest movements*".[7]

However, no social movement punctuated the negotiations on the establishment of CSEs in the sector. At most, some of the negotiation sessions were subject to organised boycotts, as happened at GRDF as we will see below. Among the disagreements, there were three sticking points in particular that arose between the social partners.

The first point concerned the number of employees that would be covered by the new CSEs and, possibly, the geographic area they had to cover when units were distributed throughout the country. In several companies, the establishment of CSEs coincided with the reorganisation of departments, units or directorates. In such cases, employers systematically took advantage of these reorganisations to increase the number of employees that would be covered by the CSEs than was the case for the former works councils. By contrast, the trade unions tried to keep the numbers as close as possible to those of the former works councils, or to even see them reduced, so as to maintain the greatest possible proximity between employee representatives and employees.

At EDF, for example, at the start of negotiations, management proposed a drastic reduction in the number of institutions. Its initial proposal was to replace the 56 existing works councils with 41 CSEs.[8] This proposed reduction would target some areas than others, and would involve the replacement of 5 works councils of the engineering centres as well as the 9 CHSCTs which were attached to them by a single CSE, which would be provided with a single health and safety commission. Also, for the Research and Development unit, which had to be covered by a CSE, management proposed only one CSSCT in place of the three CHSCTs that had existed before, despite the fact that staff in these sectors are exposed to chemical, radiological, biological and electrical risks.

---

[7] https://www.miroirsocial.com/mise-en-place-du-cse-l-intersyndicale-des-ieg-met-en-garde.

[8] https://www.scecfdtcvdl.fr/CSE-EDF-SA-DIPNN-Quel-dialogue-social-demain#.XiXfjRfjJN0.

Needless to say, these decisions have been severely criticised by the trade unions. In its publication *Le Fil Électrique*, the EDF CGT union took a stand on 02 April 2019, stating: "*The current proposals by EDF management constitute a step backwards for staff representation in the CSEs, and for employees. The CGT denounces this will to keep representatives away from workers and proposes a map respecting this essential proximity between elected reps and workers. (…) It requires that members and alternates sit together. (…) A CSE will be implemented at the R&D perimeter, but the management offers a single CSSCT instead of the 3 current CHSCTs. This choice implies a decrease in the number of elected staff and the number of hours dedicated to occupational safety and health issues. In fact, these elected officials will have little knowledge of the risks and specificities of each of the 3 R&D sites (…). How to ensure equivalent treatment of the different situations identified with a single CSSCT for all EDF R&D?*".[9]

A second stumbling block in the negotiations concerned the number of, and resources that would be available to, the health, safety and working conditions committees (CSSCTs). In most companies, the trade unions have emphasised the importance of these committees and have made the outcome of the negotiations conditional on a specific allocation of resources that go beyond the legal minimal provisions.

In the same spirit, the third stumbling block in the negotiations concerned the role of the alternate delegates. In most cases, unions have tried to obtain more favourable provisions than those prescribed by the law to mobilise these representatives, so as to better take charge of the operation of the various committees of the CSE and, in particular, the CSSCTs.

Certain negotiation situations have become particularly tense. For example, at GRDF, management had started the talks by indicating that it planned to reduce the resources dedicated to employee representative bodies and trade unions rights by 35%. The four largest union organisations then joined forces to boycott the negotiations. On 23 January 2019, the unions declared that they were ceasing any dialogue with management, from the local to the national levels inclusive, until further notice. After three months of this boycott, CFDT, FO and CFE-CGC finally

---

[9] https://cgt-edf-recherche.fr/mise-en-oeuvre-du-comite-social-et-economique/

signed the agreements for the establishment of the CSE and on trade union rights; only CGT did not sign these agreements.

On these three points, our observations confirm those which were also noted by ORSEU in a report delivered to the Ministry of Labour on 23 September 2019. This Institute noted, in fact, that *"The possibility of reviewing the perimeters of staff representation has been heavily used by company management (…). The defensive strategy of the unions has been to limit the cut in resources. One of the goals is notably to counteract the centralization imposed by employers by maintaining the means for elected officials to stay in contact with the field"* (Farvaque, 2019).

Our analysis of the agreements that were signed shows that the trade unions have only very marginally succeeded in negotiating more favourable provisions than what was provided by the law, and that there is wide variation across different companies.

Thus, at GRDF, the number of representative bodies has been reduced by a third with 6 Social and Economic Committees set up as opposed to the 9 that previously existed. As a result of this agreement, the number of seats for full representatives has been reduced by 60%, while the number of hours allocated to representation has been reduced by 30% compared to the situation that existed in 2016. It is anticipated that this new situation will significantly reduce the outreach work that was carried out by the staff representatives within the staff representative bodies and, above all, the CHSCTs.

To take another example, negotiations at EDF finally led to the establishment of 52 CSEs at the end of June 2019—compared to 56 works councils that had existed previously—each strictly endowed with the number of seats of regular representatives provided for by the text of the new legal orders.[10]

The organisation of these CSEs partially resembles that of the former works councils, some of which have a stronger network of local institutions than others. In spite of everything, these local institutions are much less numerous today: only 69 CSSCTs have been set up while there previously existed 127 CHSCTs predominantly focused in the work units where the most dangerous activities took place. In addition to this, and in accordance with the orders, the 96 representative bodies of employee representatives at EDF have now completely disappeared, and only a few

---

[10] L'accord collectif relatif à la mise en place de ces CSE du 28/06/2019.

units have local representatives (*"Représentants de proximité"*), with 173 such representatives spread across 19 workplaces.

In total, the number of seats for regular staff representatives has been cut in half, and will barely reach a thousand today for a company with nearly 155,000 employees, amounting to a ratio of one representative for each 155 employees. About 50% of these seats will be allocated to the CSSCTs. The collective agreement provides, however, that alternate representatives may be mobilised and should have an active role and should receive agendas, associated documents and minutes of all CSE meetings. The collective agreement further stipulates that in order to *"promote the professionalisation of alternate members of the CSEs"*, it is intended that the alternates may participate in the preparatory meetings of the CSE on the credit of hours allocated to holders of the CSE. In addition, alternate representatives can also be members of the Health, Safety and Working Conditions Commission (CSSCT) and other CSE committees. The collective agreement also recommends that they be designated as secretaries in such committees.

With regard to representation time, more favourable provisions than the law provides have also been obtained. The collective agreement notably provides for a 30% increase in CSE units comprising at least one "basic nuclear installation" (INB—Installation nucléaire de base). In addition, CSE secretaries benefit from credits of an additional 10 to 40 h per month depending on the CSE.

If, according to the data disseminated during the first months of negotiations by the CGT energy federation, it appeared that on average the loss of the number of staff representatives could have been limited to only 30%,[11] after a fuller assessment of the evidence, it now appears doubtful, that these losses could have been so limited. However, in most of the companies where an agreement has already been signed, the union organisations have succeeded in emphasising the need for more delegate positions on the CSSCTs. The argument on which the unions typically relied is that of the essential role played by these delegates, thanks to their proximity to employees, in terms of the promotion of health and safety. However, even if slightly increased in comparison with the prescriptions set down in the orders, this number of health and safety delegates will not be sufficient to subsume the full role of the CSSCTs. A four-year

---

[11] https://ufictfnme.fr/representativite-dans-la-branche-des-ieg/

review following the installation of the CSEs would be useful to assess this coverage.

5 Conclusion

President Macron's labour reforms paved the way for a drastic reduction in the resources allocated to staff representation in French companies. At the end of the two-year period that was devoted to the negotiation of the establishment of new social and economic committees (CSEs), it is indeed clear that such a reduction in resources has taken place.

Across the electrical and gas industries, where employee representation and union rights have traditionally been very favourable to employees, union organisations have failed to bring the negotiations to a successful conclusion. While they have been able to limit the loss of resources, they have rarely succeeded in obtaining provisions that are more favourable than those prescribed in law.

For their part, employers have taken fully advantage of the room for manoeuvre left to them by the new legal provisions to redefine the shape and geographical scope of the workplace units that the new CSE are designed to cover. This redefinition notably took place at the expense of the strong representation network that the CHSCTs had previously provided. The representation of employees in the field of health safety and working conditions has therefore clearly been weakened.

In the final analysis, we can therefore predict, in keeping with Nicolas Farvaque's team (see Farvaque et al., 2019), a high risk of intensification of work for elected officials, due in part to the much larger scope of the new CES, and concomitantly, the drying up of local unionism. In these conditions, recourse to the law will become much more difficult to use as a strategic pillar to defend and promote trade union action.

Bibliography

Beynel Eric, *La raison des plus forts, Chroniques du procès France Télécom*. Illustré par Claire Robert. Editions de l'Atelier, 2020.

Bouchareb Rachid, «L'action syndicale face aux discriminations ethno-raciales», *Sociologie Pratique*, Presses de Sciences Po, 2011/2 n° 23, pages 69 à 81.

Cristoffalo Paula, «Négocier l'égalité professionnelle: De quelques obstacles à la prise en charge syndicale de la thématique», *Nouvelle revue de psychologie*, ERES, 2014/2 n° 18, pages 133 à 146.

Depoorter Pascal, Nathalie Frigul, «De quoi les Conti sont-ils le nom? Radicalisation des luttes sociales et restructurations financières», *Travail et Emploi*, 2014/1 n° 137, pages 51 à 68.

Farvaque Nicolas (et al.), *Appropriation et mise en œuvre des ordonnances du 22 septembre 2017 réformant le droit du travail, Etude de terrain qualitative*, Rapport pour la DARES, ministère du travail à la demande du Comité d'évaluation des ordonnances, 23/09/2019.

Goussard Lucie, Tiffon Guillaume, *Syndicalisme et santé au travail*, Editions du Croquant, 2017

Guillonneau Maud, Evelyne Serverin, «Les affaires prud'homales dans la chaîne judiciaire de 2004 à 2018, Baisse des demandes, concentration des litiges, juridictionnalisation de leur traitement», Rapport pour le ministère de la Justice, Juillet 2019. En ligne: http://www.justice.gouv.fr/art_pix/Le_contentieux_Prud-homal_valid_19.09.2019.pdf

Hatzfeld Nicolas, «Une lutte syndicale exemplaire chez Peugeot-Sochaux (1995–2000), La remise en cause d'un système discriminatoire», *Travail et Emploi* n°145, janvier-mars 2016, p. 173–196

Henry Odile, «Introduction. Expertise, syndicalisme et conditions de travail», *La Revue de l'Ires*, vol. 74, no. 3, 2012, pp. 63–74.

Herera Carlos Miguel, *Les droits sociaux*, Presses universitaires de France, collection Que-sais-je, 2009.

Lyon Caen Antoine, *Ordonnances Macron, commentaires pratiques et nouvelles dispositions du Code du travail*, Dalloz-Sirey, 2017.

Ministère du travail, 2018, Comité économique et social, 100 questions-réponses. https://travail-emploi.gouv.fr/IMG/pdf/qr_comite_social_et_eco nomique.pdf

Moussy Pascal, «Les ordonnances Macron tentent de sanctuariser la répression du travailleur refusant d'adhérer aux sacrifices voulus par la célébration consensuelle des «nécessités du fonctionnement de l'entreprise»», *Chronique ouvrière*, 10 janvier 2018, En Ligne: https://www.chronique-ouvriere.fr/spip.php?article956

Parmantier Bernard. Le secteur des industries électriques et gazières en France: Évolution des relations sociales de la nationalisation à la privatisation. In: Relations sociales dans les services d'intérêt général : Une comparaison France-Allemagne [en ligne]. Cergy-Pontoise : IFAEE, 2011 (généré le 04 janvier 2020). Disponible sur Internet: http://books.openedition.org/cirac/472. ISBN: 9782905518644. https://doi.org/10.4000/books.cirac.472.

Pélisse Jérôme, «Juridicisation ou judiciarisation? Usages et réappropriations du droit dans les conflits du travail.» *Politix*, 2009/2, n°86, pages 73 à 96.

Quijoux Maxime, Gourgues Jérôme, 2018, «Syndicalisme et gilets jaunes», *La vie des idées*, https://laviedesidees.fr/IMG/pdf/20181219_giletsyndic.pdf

Tixier Pierre-Eric, Duclos Laurent, "La transformation du système de relations professionnelles de l'entreprise" in Tixier Pierre-Eric, Mauchamp Nelly, *EDF-GDF. Une entreprise publique en mutation*. La Découverte, « Recherches », 2000, https://www.cairn.info/--.htm

CHAPTER 8

Organised Labour and Fluid Organisations: Insights from the Gilets Jaunes Movement

Barry Colfer and Yoann Bazin

1 Introduction

On 17 November 2018, nearly 300,000 people marched in Paris and other cities across France. Many did so specifically to protest against a new petrol tax that was being proposed by the French government. Many others sought to express a range of other grievances in the light of the agenda of economic and social liberalisation that had been pursued by President Emmanuel Macron's since his election to the Élysée Palace[1] in May 2017.

---

[1] The official residence of the President of the French Republic.

B. Colfer (✉)
Department of Politics and International Studies, University of Cambridge, Cambridge, UK
e-mail: bc348@cam.ac.uk

Y. Bazin
Human Resource Management, EM Normandie, Oxford, UK
e-mail: ybazin@em-normandie.co.uk

© The Author(s), under exclusive license to Springer Nature Switzerland AG 2022
B. Colfer (ed.), *European Trade Unions in the 21st Century*, St Antony's Series, https://doi.org/10.1007/978-3-030-88285-3_8

Over the following months, coordinated largely via social media, thousands of people occupied roundabouts, intermittently blocked roads and gathered in city centres, especially on Saturdays, seeking to oppose and undermine the president's proposed reforms. The movement took its name from the distinctive yellow "high-vis" vests ("Gilets Jaunes" in French) worn by activists which car users in France are obliged by law to carry in their vehicles. While the movement spread to other countries and continued into 2021 (the time of writing), the movement was at its peak in France between this first mass event in November 2018 and the end of 2019, the period which will be the focus on this chapter. The arrival of the Gilets Jaunes raises important questions regarding the nature of social movement activism, and regarding the place of traditional social movement actors, such as the trade union movement.

Such a series of mobilisations could be seen as unremarkable in a country known for its tradition of demonstrations and strikes. However, there were important features of the Gilets Jaunes that sets it apart from any number of anti-establishment social movements in France that went before, such as "ATTAC"[2] in the late 1990s, which called for reforms in the financial sector, the "bonnets rouges" (red caps) who opposed the introduction of new taxes on truck transport in Brittany in 2013, or the "Nuit Debout[3]" protests in Paris in 2016 against proposed labour reforms. Notably, the Gilets Jaunes emerged rapidly, and on a national scale, without any apparent centralised structures or leadership, and without the support, and beyond the structures, of any trade union, political party or civil society organisation.[4] Despite this, the movement continued to grow over the initial months, and extracted important concessions from government, as we shall see.

Notably, many Gilets Jaunes who came forward to speak as representatives of the movement, or even to voice specific concerns, were

[2] Association pour la Taxation des Transactions financières et pour l'Action Citoyenne/Association for the Taxation of financial Transactions and Citizen's Action.

[3] As a protest against a reform of labour legislation in 2016, thousands of people occupied main squares and other public spaces to debate political issues and to tentatively organise a convergence between anti-capitalist struggles. More intense in bigger cities (especially, in central Paris and the surrounding region) the gatherings slowly decreased after a few months.

[4] While Gilets Jaunes-inspired movements emerged elsewhere across the globe, including most notably in Belgium, Germany and Italy, this contribution focuses exclusively on the French Gilets Jaunes movement.

met with scepticism, rejection and even threats of violence from other activists. Meanwhile, many Gilets Jaunes wanted to express and vent their grievances with President Macron's agenda, but were reluctant to engage in conventional politics at the local or national levels, as seen, for example, with the movement eschewing coordinated involvement in the May 2019 European elections and March 2020 local elections in France. This is partly explained by the fact that the movement has attracted supporters and activists from across the political spectrum and can be seen as a broad coalition that opposes President Macron's government from a range of angles and starting points.

The aim of this chapter is firstly to try to understand how this phenomenon emerged, and how it challenges key elements of social movement organisation theory. We build on Zygmunt Bauman's analysis according to which "fluidity" would be "the leading metaphor for the present stage of the modern era" (Bauman, 2000, p. 2). His expression "liquid modernity" describes the result of decades of neo-liberal deregulation and flexibilisation that is aimed at removing all obstacles, rigidities and limitations on individual (and corporate) freedom. As a result, we live in societies in which social institutions "can lo longer (and are not expected) to keep their shape for long, because they decompose and melt faster than the time it takes to cast them" (Bauman, 2014, p. 1). A growing body of work has sought to extend this approach to what is called "fluid organisations". In this contribution, we will show how movements such as the Gilets Jaunes challenge the traditional understanding of leadership and purpose within social movement organisations including trade unions, and how this might present new ways to view distributed leadership in complex, fluid organisations more generally.

Secondly, this contribution will consider the implications that the Gilets Jaunes may have for the French labour movement specifically, given that the unions and Gilets Jaunes share many of the same goals, tactics, and indeed, activists and supporters. Taking a specific example, we will show how the high-profile series of strikes organised by the CGT[5] trade union and others at the SNCF[6] national transport company throughout 2018, while only partly successful in themselves, prepared the ground for

---

[5] Confédération Générale du Travail/ General Confederation of Labour/General Confederation of Labour.

[6] Société nationale des chemins de fer français/the French National Railway Company.

the Gilets Jaunes. We will consider how the looser, leaderless structure of the Gilets Jaunes allowed for the emergence of an effective but potentially unsustainable movement that engaged with a broad cross-section of society, in opposition to similar issues and grievances as the unions had opposed at SNCF.

The clearest difference between the two movements is seen in the highly structured, hierarchical and organised nature of the CGT, and the decentralised, non-hierarchical street movement that makes up the Gilets Jaunes. Comparing these two scenarios, we will ask if there are lessons that French unions can learn from the Gilets Jaunes—and vice-versa.

Following this short introduction, section two reviews the structure and nature of the French labour movement in recent years, with a focus on the 2018 strikes at SNCF. Section three examines the emergence and nature of the Gilets Jaunes movement. Section four considers what an examination of these two movements tell us about organisation theory—by reviewing the solidity of organised labour and the fluidity of social movement organisations such as the Gilets Jaunes. The final section concludes.

2 The French Industrial Relations Landscape and The 2018 SNCF Strike

2.1 French Trade Unions

The French industrial relations system has traditionally been pluralist, with extensive intervention by government in labour relations. French trade unions are often seen as powerful, given their ability to mobilise workers and to strike. However, their power is not in their paid-up members, as less than 8% of employees in France belong to a trade union, a figure that has collapsed from a high of about 30% in the 1950s. Starkly, French unions have lost two-thirds of their members since the 1970s (Andolfatto & Labbé, 2007, p. 233). This figure is below the likes of the UK, Germany, Sweden and even the USA (see Table 1). In the private sector, the unionisation rate is even lower at just 5%, and stands at 14% among civil servants.

While France has among the lowest rates of union membership in the European Union (EU), it is also among the most fragmented. There are five recognised national union confederations, and many smaller ones. By comparison, there is only one in each of Germany and the UK, for example (see Table 2).

Table 1 Trade union membership in France, Germany, Sweden, UK, and USA

	Trade Union Density[a] 1970	Trade Union Density 2018
France	22.2	8.8
Germany	32	16.5
Sweden	67.7	64.9
United Kingdom	44.8	23.4
United States	27.4	10.1

[a]Trade Union density is the proportion of the labour force that belong to a trade union
Source OECD (2021)

Table 2 French trade union confederations

Name	Orientation	Founded	Members
CFDT—*Confédération française démocratique du travail*/ French Democratic Confederation of Labour	Reformist/moderate, Christian democratic background	1964	875,000
CGT—*Confédération Générale du Travail*/ General Confederation of Labour	Former communist, radical	1895	710,000
FO—*Force Ouvrière*/ Workers' Force	Broke away from CGT, radical	1948	300,000
CFTC—*Confédération française des travailleurs chrétiens*/ The French Confederation of Christian Workers	Reformist/moderate, Christian democratic background	1964	160,000
CFE—CGC French Confederation of Management—General Confederation of Executives/*Confédération française de l'encadrement—Confédération générale des cadres*	Moderate, organising management and executive positions	1944	14,000

CFDT is the biggest confederation, coming from a reformist, Christian democratic and moderate background. Next in size is CGT which formerly had close links with the French Communist Party and is generally more radical in its tactics. FO broke away from CGT in 1948 in opposition to its communist associations. These three confederations account for 80% of union members. CFTC is Christian democratic in orientation but smaller, while CFE-CGC primarily represents managers and executives.

CFDT advocates a conciliatory approach to employers and government, traditionally positioning themselves as a social partner, while CGT and FO are more prone to strikes and direct action. The CGT dominates in traditional sectors such as the railways and power generation, while CFDT dominates among delivery employees and office workers. The five recognised unions retain the right to compete in workplace elections and to participate in a network of statutory and workplace representative bodies. It is within these structures that unions maintain much of their relevance and strength.

France has always been an outlier in Europe regarding relations between unions and political parties, given the semi-sacred nature of the 1906 Charter of Amiens, one of the founding documents of European trade unionism. This declaration by CGT sees French unions eschew entanglements with political parties by asserting their political independence. This lack of formal ties with political parties makes French unions almost unique in Europe, but the truth is somewhat more complicated, with the development of close relations between CGT and the French Communist Party (Parti Communiste Français/PCF), and looser ones between CFDT and the French Socialist Party (Parti socialiste/PS). Nonetheless, there has never been the same organic links between unions and parties in France as there have been in many countries, including in the likes of Germany, Sweden or the UK (Upchurch et al., 2009).

Despite the relatively low rates of formal unionisation, workers in France lie second only to Cyprus in terms of the number of days not worked due to strikes between 2010–2018, at 120 days per annum per thousand workers (behind Cyprus' remarkable 289 days) (ETUI, 2020). Compared to comparable economies such as Germany, Poland, Spain and the UK during this same period, it is clear that French workers remain among those most inclined to strike (see Table 3) and notably, many workers who strike are not paid-up members of any union.

As is often the case in Europe, low rates of unionisation in France can be explained in part by the fact that unionised and non-unionised employees alike benefit from the fruits of union negotiations, as close to 98% of workers are covered by the terms of collective agreements that result from negotiations between unions and employers.

Table 3 Number of days not worked due to strikes, Europe selected countries 2010–2018

	Number of days not worked due to strikes per 1000 workers between 2010 and 2018
France	120
Germany	18
Poland	2
Spain	49
United Kingdom	19

Thus, instead of French unions enjoying strength in numbers through large memberships, a primary source of union influence in France lies in the statutory powers that unions maintain through mechanisms of joint regulation. Under French law, elected union delegates represent all employees in firms of over 50 staff on works councils and health-and-safety committees. These bodies must be consulted regularly on a range of managerial decisions, giving unions a daily say in the running of companies across the private sector. French union clout is also bolstered by a long tradition of public sympathy for their cause.

Thus, the unions' day-to-day work is increasingly undertaken by cadres of semi-professional union officials, with a limited role played by rank-and-file members beyond their participation in elections to these bodies. This can lead to feelings of alienation among French employees, and what can sometimes be characterised as an out-of-touch union élite (Levy, 2008). What's more, French unions' power in the workplace has been challenged and undermined by President Macron's reform agenda since his election in 2017.

2.2 Macron's Reform Agenda

In September 2017, in his first year in office, President Macron signed a controversial set of executive orders that would make sweeping changes to France's complex system of labour laws at a highly stage-managed ceremony at the Élysée Palace, the official residence of the French President. These reforms are part of a wider programme of state-led liberalisations which seek to shift the balance of power away from unions and workers and towards employers.

Among other things, Macron's reforms make it easier for companies to hire and fire by putting a cap on damages that workers can seek from employers after being dismissed. The reforms also undermine collective bargaining power by enabling managers and employees to negotiate workplace rules on a company-by-company basis and by reducing the number of workplace representative bodies from three to one. This is in keeping with a Europe-wide trend towards the decentralisation of collective bargaining (see Leonardi & Pedersini, 2018; Contrepois, 2021). Crucially, the reforms also sought to liberalise the county's pension system and to raise the pension age.

According to the Élysée palace, President Macron's reforms were motivated by the view that *"French labour law no longer fully responds to the economic realities associated with globalisation, company and sector diversity, new technologies and employees' expectations. It creates rigidities and inequalities that constitute obstacles to initiative and recruitment"* (Government of France, 2020[7]).

Defeating presidential reforms was always going to be difficult during this presidential term (2017–2022) given that President Macron's *La République En Marche* (LREM) party and its allies hold a comfortable majority in the National Assembly. In reality, the best hope for opponents to cause this government to change course is through a combination of protest and the precipitation of negative public opinion. This was seen when the President faced a sustained period of resistance from unions in response to his proposed labour reforms throughout 2018, as we shall see, when the government ultimately prevailed. This episode present a clear test case of union power in modern France, and a notable prelude to the arrival of the Gilets Jaunes.

2.2.1 Trade Union Responses to President Macron's Reforms

In late 2017, the CGT, FO and teaching unions staged strikes and demonstrations against President Macron's raft of proposed labour reforms and sought to draw allied unions into the fray. Deep splits soon emerged between those unions that were determined to fight the reforms and those that were prepared to compromise. Unlike CGT and its allies, the larger CFDT was reluctant to strike, instead putting in place training sessions for their activists on how to apply the reforms in the workplace.

---

[7] https://www.gouvernement.fr/en/labour-law-reform.

The first sustained conflict that President Macron encountered in this regard was at SNCF, the state-owned railway company.

2.2.2 SNCF Strike

Employees at SNCF have traditionally had "for life" contracts and could request the right to retire at the relatively early age of 55. As a perk of employment, immediate family members could receive free rail travel. Under proposed reforms, new employees would not receive these benefits, while continuing employees would maintain them. However, unions at SNCF feared the government's reforms were only the first steps towards a British-style privatisation drive of the national railway.

The four major rail unions called for a series of rolling strikes, starting on 22 March 2018, lasting until 28 June, which resulted in widespread disruption and cancellations across the network, which, at its peak, cost SNCF €21 million a day (Le Monde, 2018[8]). Sensing an opportunity to link their struggle to a broader defence of public services, CGT and SUD-Rail (a sectoral level union)—called for demonstrations in Paris in solidarity with public-sector workers. Following some initial success, such alliances proved unsustainable, as civil servants did not engage in sustained sympathetic actions, and as students were unable to draw on the memory of 1968 to sustain their opposition beyond the summer exam period.

Left-wing parties tried to inject energy into the movement. Filmmaker François Ruffin, an MP for the left-wing La France Insoumise (FI) party, organised a 'party' in Paris to ironically celebrate President Macron's first year in office, to which 40,000 revellers attended. In a rare case of unified action between unions and political parties, on 26 May 2018, 30,000 activists from FI, CGT and groups protesting against police violence demonstrated in Paris (Mestre, 2018[9]). However, despite these moments of success, the strikes and protests at SNCF petered out by the autumn.

2.2.3 How Did SNCF Strike End?

The strikes at SNCF ended when solidarity between civil servants and train drivers was exhausted, having run between April–November 2018. The strikes ultimately cost SNCF more than €1 billion and secured

---

[8] https://www.lemonde.fr/entreprises/article/2018/07/20/la-greve-aurait-coute-790-millions-d-euros-a-la-sncf_5334099_1656994.html.

[9] https://www.lemonde.fr/politique/article/2018/05/24/manifestation-du-26-mai-le-comite-adama-s-invite-dans-le-cortege-de-tete_5304112_823448.html.

important concessions, including a commitment of €3.6 billion in government investment in network infrastructure over the next decade and with the state agreeing to take on a sizeable portion of SNCF's debt. However, the unions failed to prevent the changes to the terms and conditions for new workers, and, in the absence of sustained solidarity, the conflict was essentially over by midsummer. Indeed, by mid-June, the Senate had approved the reform package by a vote of 245-82, authorising the changes to take effect from January 2020 (Béziat, 2018[10]).

Put simply, organised labour could not mobilise effective resistance against the reforms by themselves. It became clear that rail workers could not win this battle alone, and only with support from unions in other sectors, political parties and activists, could they realistically think of turning their strike into a larger struggle against President Macron's planned programme of liberalisation. However, the rounds of protests and strikes throughout 2018 made it clear that the ingredients for a more sustained movement against his government were present. The next section considers how these ingredients contributed to the emergence of the Gilets Jaunes movement in late 2018.

3 THE GILETS JAUNES MOVEMENT

3.1 The Yellow Vest as a Symbol of Frustration

The Gilets Jaunes movement originates in its grassroots. On 16 January 2018, a 32-year-old mason created a Facebook group entitled "Colère 24"[11] to protest against the introduction of new speed limits on minor French roads, an increase in highway fees, the rising cost of living and various other austerity and privatisation measures,[12] all of which were perceived as an attack on lower-income people who lived in the hinterlands of France's major cities. This new group called for demonstrations to take place on roundabouts and in town centres throughout the region on 17 February (see Image 1).

---

[10] https://www.lemonde.fr/economie/article/2018/06/15/sncf-les-enjeux-de-la-negociation-sur-la-convention-collective_5315490_3234.html.

[11] This translates as 'Anger 24' - 24 being the national administrative code for the Dordogne region.

[12] 'Franceinfo, Jan. 26 2018. Colère 24: qui se cache derrière ce groupe'.

Protesters in neighbouring regions quickly adopted similar names, formats and modes of organisation (e.g. "Colère 33", "Colère 17", "Colère 19", for the Gironde, Charente-Maritime and Corrèze regions, respectively) to organise on the same day. In local television news coverage of the protests, one can see people wearing high-visibility yellow vests, some emblazoned with anti-Macron slogans.

While the "Colère 24" mobilisations remained mainly local and relatively small, another activist group under the banner of "Les Gilets Jaunes" picked up the wearable symbol in the weeks following. On 29 March, protesters resisting the construction of a high-speed train near Le Mans in the northwest of the country also wore yellow vests.[13] Hereinafter, a pattern emerges, with locally coordinated mobilisations and street demonstrations being organised primarily online around a wide range of anti-Macron frustrations, and with the *gilets jaunes* as a shared symbol.[14]

Following these initial events, what would become the wider Gilets Jaunes movement rapidly took shape, despite its fragmented nature, and its lack of central leadership.

3.2 What Sparked the Movement?

On 29 May 2018, Priscillia Ludoski, who would go on to become a prominent figure within the movement, created a *Change.org* online petition calling for a decrease in petrol prices that quickly gathered more than 1.2 million signatures.[15] On 10 October, two truck-drivers, Eric Drouet and Bruno Lefevre, launched a Facebook page calling for a national blockade against the planned petrol tax. The page also called for a protest event to take place on 17 November.

On 09 November, in the city of Albert in Northern France, protesters against President Macron wore yellow vests, with similar scenes in Neubourg in Normandy the following day. On 14 November, President Macron reaffirmed that the taxes would stay, and cast doubt on the

---

[13] Franceinfo, March 29 2018. Sarthe: le bruit et l'horreur.

[14] On October 24, in the lead-up toward the first big mobilisation, Ghislain Coutard will encourage all people supporting the movement to place their yellow vest visibly on their windshield: https://www.facebook.com/ghislain.coutard/videos/10216601170797079/.

[15] Change.org, May 29 2018. Pour une Baisse des Prix du Carburant à la Pompe!

legitimacy of the movement by saying: "*They have the right to demonstrate...[but] I say beware, there are many people trying to inflitrate the movement*". Such accusations of the movement being hijacked or directed by opponents of President Macron and by political extremists become common. Meanwhile, Prime Minister Édouard Philippe adopted a more assertive tone, declaring "*If someone says 'I will blockade', he knows that, by doing so, he takes a risk*".[16]

On 17 November, some 282,000 Gilets Jaunes demonstrated by occupying roundabouts, roads and highways all across France, in what would become the first "act" of the movement (Mulholland, 2018).[17] By early December 2018, less than a month after the first major mobilisation had taken place, the proposed petrol tax was abandoned while an increase in the minimum wage was introduced alongside several tax cuts. Taken together, this was seen as a major victory for the movement. Thus, this may beg the question, while the SNCF strike was in vain, why did the Gilet Jaunes succeed, in this narrow sense at least?

3.3 Forms and Tactics of the Movement

As the movement developed, mobilisations saw hundreds of thousands of people in high-visibility vests occupying roundabouts, blocking roads and gathering in towns and city centres. All this happened without any formal structure or backing of traditional social movement organisations including labour unions and political parties, and without any centralised coordinating individual or group.

The nature of protest differed between, and sometimes within, localities. Many protests took the form of groups, and event temporary structures, often in the middle of roundabouts, aimed at creating visibility among passing motorists. Other protests involved blockading traffic, with widely differing levels of duration and frequency. While it is impossible to generalise from such disparate events, the authors' local observations recorded many discussions around which strategies to pursue, along with strong judgements (positive as well as negative) of what other groups in neighbouring areas were doing.

---

[16] Les Echos, Nov. 14th 2018. Gilets jaunes: le rappel à la loi d'Edouard Philippe.

[17] https://www.telegraph.co.uk/news/2018/11/17/one-killed-16-injured-yellow-jackets-protests-rising-fuel-prices/.

The more visible, and, more importantly for politicians and journalists, more "countable" events occurred primarily on Saturdays, when the most intense blockades and demonstrations took place. While participation decreased quickly after the initial 282,000 demonstrators, there were still some 136,000 participants reported during the first half of December 2018 and after a series of smaller mobilisations in late 2018, the movement returned with 85,000 demonstrators in January 2019, with a slow but steady decrease over the following months (See Fig. 1).

Notably, thousands of people remained on roundabouts and on the streets for weekly protests throughout even the winter months, despite the French government having backed down by mid-December. Clearly the Gilets Jaunes had tapped into a willingness for disparate groups of people throughout the country to protest in solidarity, something that notably the CGT and its allies had struggled to sustain the previous summer.

3.4 Reactions of the Unions

On 12 November, as the Gilets Jaunes mobilisations were gaining momentum, but before the first major "act" of the movement, CFDT leader, Laurent Berger declared that his union "*do not support these blockades*", suspecting them of being "*manipulated*" and "*politically infiltrated by the far-right*", echoing the words of President Macron (De Comarond, 2018[18]). Meanwhile, CGT, published a memo stating that: "*The call launched on a Saturday, without any real ambition to block the economy, comes from a legitimate anger but of which underlying motivations are obscure and for which solutions to find a way out of the mechanisms are unclear, if not dangerous for the interests of labour*". In the same vein as CFDT, the memo also claims that "*several far-right political parties seem to be 'instrumentalising' the movement*" (CGT, 2018[19]).

For their part, FO's Yves Veyrier stated that "*We are not surprised by the anger (…) The Gilets Jaunes movement is not the failure of labor unions, it is the failure of those who don't listen to the unions (…) FO hasn't waited

---

[18] Les Echos, Nov. 14th 2018. Les syndicats bousculés par le phénomène des "gilets jaunes".

[19] CGT, Nov. 17th 2018. 17 novembre: entre exaspération et instrumentalisation.

Image 1 'Colere 24' flyer calling for action on 17 February 2018

Fig. 1 Number of reported demonstrators November 2017–February 2018 (*Source* Ministère de l'Intérieur)

for the Gilets Jaunes to worry about the consequences of the rise of petrol prices for employees" (Mediapart, 2018).[20]

Thus, the union leadership took note of the Gilets Jaunes from the start, but drew attention to the threat of infiltration by the far-right, and of the disparate and multifarious nature of the movement's demands. It took a few months of sustained and successful protests for French unions to reluctantly support, or at least to stop rejecting, the Gilets Jaunes, as we shall see.

For their part, around the first "act" in November 2018, the Gilets Jaunes spokespersons, and the general tone of the movement, was often deeply hostile towards the unions, which were portrayed as staid and part of a corrupt, self-serving elite—in short, part of the problem that the movement was seeking to attack. However, at a national meeting of activists on November 2019, dubbed "an assembly of assemblies", a full year on from the high watermark of the movement, Gilets Jaunes from across France passed a resolution calling for participation in a national strike to be held on December 5 that year (Quijoux & Gourgues, 2020).[21]

From 05 December 2019 until the onset of the COVID-19 pandemic in the first months of 2020, a new wave of strikes gripped France. These strikes saw unions calling for a broad set of demands around the cost of living, salaries, unemployment and precarity which echo

---

[20] Mediapart, Nov. 27th 2018. Syndicalistes contre la vie chères: agir maintenant!

[21] https://www.jacobinmag.com/2020/01/france-strikes-trade-unions-gilets-jaunes.

many of the multifarious demands and tone of the Gilets Jaunes. In December, the CGT mobilised visibly at Gilets Jaunes demonstration in Paris and Toulouse, where rail workers—many of them veterans of the 2018 SNCF strikes—were prominent. Here, the movements crossed paths, without fully converging, but there was a distinct softening in rhetoric at least on the union side, with CGT confederal secretary Fabrice Angéï declaring, regarding the Gilets Jaunes, that *"the movement doesn't come from nowhere. The unions' recent actions…nourished the movement"* (Haynes & Knaebel, 2019).[22]

3.5 Negotiations and Results

Negotiating with (and studying) a social movement as fluid as the Gilets Jaunes is, by its very nature, complicated. Although reluctant to engage initially, the French government attempted to organise meetings with the Gilets Jaunes, but somewhat comically struggled to identify who to invite to talks. On the movement's side, many supporters wanted to clarify the movement's demands in order to start negotiating, but no clear list of demands emerged from the diverse collection of groups and online pages that made up and sustained the movement, and what did emerge was so wide-ranging to make any meaningful negotiation impossible.

Around 26 November 2018, news began to circulate that eight spokespersons would meet Prime Minister Édouard Philippe. As active, visible figures within the movement, their identities were already widely known, namely: Mathieu Blavier, Marine Charrette-Labadie, Eric Drouet, Jason Herbert, Priscillia Ludosky, Thomas Miralles, Maxime Nicolle and Julien Terrier. These individuals were highly cautious and assertive in their status as mere spokespersons[23] and not representatives, with the stated aim of articulating the demands and frustrations of the movement, rather than negotiating on its behalf. However, their status almost instantly triggered fierce reactions from other Gilets Jaunes, ranging from scepticism and vocal disagreement, through to threats of physical violence and death.

In the end, some of the spokespersons declined to meet the Prime Minister given that they did not consider themselves as representatives,

---

[22] https://notesfrombelow.org/article/gilets-jaunes-and-unions-convergence-over-what.

[23] "Porte-paroles" in French.

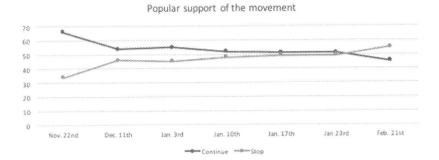

Fig. 2 Public support for the Gilets Jaunes 2018–2019

while others declined given the negative reactions they had received. In the end, only two showed up, one of whom (Jason Herbert) left because the meeting was not being streamed live, and ultimately the meeting was cancelled (Liabot, 2018).[24] While similar attempts were made over subsequent weeks, they each faced similar stumbling blocks, and ultimately failed to materialise.

Facing these difficulties would be disastrous for most traditional social movement organisations, including union. Such actors would simply be dismissed as disorganised and unrepresentative, and thus illegitimate to make any claims on behalf of anyone. However, despite its fluidity, the Gilets Jaunes secured major concessions and the movement enjoyed the support of a majority of the French population overall several months, only dipping below 50% towards the end of January, weeks after the government's initial concessions (Fig. 2, Odaxa, 2019).[25]

4 Solid Organized Labour and Fluid Social Movement Organizations

4.1 A "Strange" Movement

By its very nature, the Gilets Jaunes movement differs in at least three important ways from many other social movements organisations,

---

[24] https://www.lejdd.fr/Politique/gilets-jaunes-pourquoi-la-rencontre-avec-edouard-philippe-a-tourne-court-3811340.

[25] Odaxa by France Inter.

including labour unions. First, we have seen that the movement proceeds without recognised leaders or representatives, and its power is decentralised and distributed amongst its participants. Second, the movement is not aligned with any traditional political organisations and draws support from across the political spectrum. Third, the movement has no consistent coordinating structure and has proceeded through a series of decentralised events and initiatives. This leads Jeanpierre (2019, p. 20) to claim that, with respect to the Gilets Jaunes, *"formally speaking, its 'methods' have not resembled the traditional image of what social movements are in France"*.

Positions and affiliations of the Gilets Jaunes differed from region to region, from roundabout to roundabout, and even from member to member. As Ingrid Levavasseur, a prominent figure within the movement, described, with a little condescension: *"The Gilets Jaunes don't have the codes, they don't adopt those of union leaders with their little unspontaneous walks around…They reject the rules of those who they consider to be from the system of the old institutional world"* (Levavasseur, 2018, p. 100). As a result, decisions to continue actions, to gather for demonstrations or to present demands were typically debated and negotiated locally, and the form this took varied considerably from place to place.

4.2 Solid versus Liquid Organisations

As we have seen, the CGT-led strikes at SNCF in 2018, and the emergence of the Gilets Jaunes a few months later, differ markedly regarding the structure of the two movements, and regarding their ultimate levels of success. As Jeanpierre (2019, p. 7) notes, *"in just a few months, the movement* [the Gilets Jaunes] *has obtained more than the union or citizen movements of the last ten years, and more than what most professional politicians or commentators would have thought possible in today's context"*. While many movements shared some of the characteristics of the Gilets Jaunes, few were able to reach their levels of visibility and capacity to disrupt, which can be considered among the major achievements of the movement.

The decentralised characteristics of the Gilets Jaunes, the fact that it remains decoupled from existing political structures, and its lack of formal structures, are akin to the features of "fluid organisations". Organisations are said to be fluid *"in the sense that membership is contested or unclear and their boundaries are open or permeable"* (Dobusch & Schoeneborn,

2015, p. 1006). Thus, although challenging for traditional conceptual frameworks, such movements—including the Gilets Jaunes—remain organisations nonetheless (King et al., 2010). For fluid organisations themselves, being "constantly unfrozen" (Schreyögg & Sydow, 2010) can be a strength as well as a curse, as these cases show.

One of the primary challenges for fluid organisations has to do with boundaries. Aldrich (1971) considers organisations to be *"boundary-maintaining systems"* and Schreyögg & Sydow (2010, p. 1253) contend that *"organizations cannot exist without boundaries"*. Clearly, the Gilets Jaunes movement maintained an open approach to its activities, and anyone could get involved. However, once involved, many shared practices went beyond wearing a yellow vest, and as a result, membership was a constant negotiation. In keeping with Dobusch & Schoeneborn (2015, pp. 1005–1006), such organisations *"tend to be 'fluid' in the sense that membership is contested or unclear and their boundaries are open or permeable"*.

These fluid characteristics made the Gilets Jaunes characteristically different from traditional social movement organisations and from organised labour in particular. In this regard, while the Gilets Jaunes can be seen as highly fluid, unions can be see as their opposite—as rather solid, non-fluid organisations (see Table 4).

In keeping with this, to be conceptually considered "organized", the Gilets Jaunes would need to meet three criteria. First to have interconnected instances of decision-making. Second, to see its actions attributed to a collective entity or actor. Third, for its collective identity to be accomplished through "speech acts" (Dobusch & Schoeneborn, 2015). One

Table 4 The characteristics of solid and liquid organisations

Fluid/liquid organizations	Solid organizations
Fluid post-structural shapes	Fixed hierarchical structures
Minimal government regulation	Highly regulated by government
Shifting identities	Fixed identities
Loose partnerships & unstable relationships	Close partnerships & stable relationships
Short-term fluid goals & commitments	Long-term solid goals & commitments
Shifting responsibilities	Clear attribution of responsibilities

Adapted from Steele and Dredge (2017)

can see that the Gilets Jaunes does not satisfy these criteria, at least not entirely. And yet, the movement managed to achieve more than the traditional solid modes of organizing deployed by the established unions only months previously.

4.3 A Movement, a Moment or a Riot: Representative of a Wider Trend?

Unions in Europe today maintain less structural, associational and institutional power than heretofore (Gumbrell-McCormick & Hyman, 2013). Meanwhile, the Gilets Jaunes and other "street movements" over the past decade, such as Occupy Wall Street (hereinafter "Occupy"),[26] Extinction Rebellion, the Gezi Park protests in Turkey, and the movement for democracy in Hong Kong, show that social movements and street protests are alive and well. A clear issue relates to the challenges that such movements face in being sustainable in the long term, especially when compared with unions, which tend to be durable, despite having lost members and influence over recent decades.

That said, the Gilets Jaunes have faced a similar critique as Occupy, regarding their ability to harness political force to achieve tangible results. According to Calhoun (2013, p. 26), "*movements are relatively long-term collective engagements in producing or guiding social change*". As we have shown, the Gilets Jaunes extracted an impressive list of concessions, but a key question remains—is this aggregation of disparate grievances and individuals a "movement" in the traditional sense? In the case of Occupy, Gitlin (2013, p. 3) claims that the lack of fit between the core activists of the movement and those supporters who participated only intermittently "*blocked transformation into an enduring structure capable of winning substantial reforms over time*". Similar limitations can be identified with the Gilets Jaunes, and while we do regard it as a "movement", we acknowledge that there are conceptual difficulties in doing so. Indeed, as Calhoun (2013, p. 26) reminds us, "*there is no shame in being more moment than movement*".

Many commentators referred to this violence as a sign that the Gilets Jaunes demonstrations were more "*émeutes*" than anything else.

---

[26] While the Occupy Wall Street movement originated in the United States, it gave rise to similar, sometimes loosely linked, Occupy movements elsewhere in the world, with similar anti-establishment rhetoric and goals.

According to Joshua Clover, the French word *émeutes* translates into English as "riots", *which are often "understood to have no politics at all, a spasmodic eruption to be read symptomatically"* (Clover, 2019, p. 4). Clover links what he sees as a *"new era of riots"* with the changing nature of capital in contemporary capitalism. Talking about the 2014 riots in St Louis in the United States, Clover's account bares resemblance to the Gilets Jaunes: *"The matching scenes from around the nation convey an uncanny sense of coordination, of organization without organization"* (Clover, 2019, p. 182–183).

As a result of this comparison between the Gilets Jaunes, the trade union movement, and indeed, other social movements such as those outlined above, we are tempted to paradoxically consider the Gilets Jaunes as a movement, precisely because it was a moment. This moment was repeated through multiple "acts", thus echoing with Occupy and other movements. At the same time, the movement resembles a riot in its true political sense, reflecting a political insurrection that cannot be understood without acknowledging other forms of physical and symbolic violence. The Gilets Jaunes therefore amounts to a movement because these moments and riots are only a small fraction of a wider organisation—although not structured in the classic sense—and are embedded in a political context that give the movement meaning and purpose, although one that is constantly in flux. We further argue that it is this lack of structure that presents the greatest limitation for the Gilets Jaunes in achieving any longer term goals.

5 Conclusion

Here we have looked at two stories that unfolded in France around the same time. Both involve social movement activities that are grievance-based, both of which were designed to thwart planned government actions. With the strikes at SNCF in 2018, we see how the enormous mobilisation of effort and traditional means of withdrawing labour was of relatively limited effect in the face of a determined President. With the Gilets Jaunes, we see a new phenomenon where the old strategies and methods of mobilisation no longer apply. Without any coordinated centre of structuration, the movement exacted some notable victories, and attracted massive attention and popular involvement.

However, while the Gilets Jaunes attract passionate activists from a broad range of backgrounds, the movement's demands are often disparate and multifarious and prove difficult to sustain. Meanwhile, French unions have impressive institutional power and clear influence over public discourse, but are often characterised as representing the narrow interests of already protected workers, and the work of unions is increasingly undertaken by a professional cadre of technocrats, with limited input and involvement from rank-and-file members.

Therefore, given the many shared interests between these two movements—focused as they each are on social justice, economic distribution and equality—we cautiously argue that the Gilets Jaunes and the unions can learn from one another. In this case, CGT can learn from the tactics, spontaneity, horizontal coordination and grassroots nature of the Gilets Jaunes, while the Gilets Jaunes can learn from the institutional capacity of the unions in their search for structuration.

The SNCF strikes and the arrival of the Gilets Jaunes, both in 2018, suggests that the ingredients exist for a more sustained movement against President Macron's reforms. Thus, as we said at the outset, whether the CGT should be seen as having failed, or as having helped set the foundations for the biggest street movement seen in Europe in decades, remains open to debate.

In conclusion, we argue here not that unions are irrelevant, nor that looser networks of mobilisation are the future, but rather that there are clearly ways for new forms of social movements and trade unions to interact and to learn from each other in order to gain traction and to achieve tangible results. Notably, a tentative convergence around the Gilets Jaunes manifestations in 2019, culminating in the 05 December strikes, show how opportunities for cooperation exist between the unions and this newer sort of movement. Ultimately, while the Gilets Jaunes succeeded in the short term, as the tax that was their initial target was removed, the movement risks falling apart given its lack of structure. They also risk reinventing the wheel, by mirroring the creation of the trade union movement at the end of the nineteenth Century!

Bibliography

Aldrich, H. E. 1971. Organizational boundaries and inter-organizational conflict. *Human Relations*, 24(4), pp. 279–293.

Andolfatto, D. & Labbé, D. 2007, *Les syndiqués en France*, Rueil-Malmaison: Editions Liaisons.

Bauman, Z. 2000. *Liquid Modernity*, Cambridge: Polity Press.

Béziat, E. 2018. SNCF: les enjeux de la négociation sur la convention collective, Le Monde, 15 June 2018, available at: https://www.lemonde.fr/economie/article/2018/06/15/sncf-les-enjeux-de-la-negociation-sur-la-convention-collective_5315490_3234.html.

Calhoun, C. 2013. Occupy wall street in perspective. *British Journal of Sociology*, 64(1), pp. 26–38.

CGT. 2018. Entre exaspération et instrumentalisation, CGT news, 17 November 2018, avaialble at: http://www.ud37.cgt.fr/2018/10/17-novembre-entre-exasperation-et-instrumentalisation/.

Clover, J. 2019. Riot. Strike. Riot: The new era of uprisings. Verso.

De Comarond, L. 2018. Les syndicats bousculés par le phénomène des "gilets jaunes". Les Echos, Nov. 14th 2018, available at: https://www.lesechos.fr/economie-france/social/les-syndicats-boulcules-par-le-phenomene-des-gilets-jaunes-147328.

Dobusch, L. & Schoeneborn, D. 2015. Fluidity, identity, and organizationality: The communicative constitution of Anonymous. *Journal of Management Studies*, 52(8), pp. 1005–1035.

ETUI. 2021. Average annual number of days not worked due to strikes per 1000 workers, *ETUI Strikes Map of Europe* available at: https://www.etui.org/Services/Strikes-Map-of-Europe.

Gitlin, T. 2013. Occupy's predicament: The moment and the prospects for the movement. *The British Journal of Sociology*, 64(1), pp. 3–25.

Gumbrell-McCormick, R. & Hyman, R. 2013. *Trade Unions in Western Europe; Hard Times, Hard Choices*, Oxford: OUP.

Hayns, J. & Knaebel, R. 2018. The Gilets Jaunes and the Unions: A convergence over what?, *Notes from Below,* available at: https://notesfrombelow.org/article/gilets-jaunes-and-unions-convergence-over-what.

Jeanpierre, L. (2019). *In girum: les leçons politiques des ronds-points*. La Découverte.

Le Monde. 2018. La grève aurait coûté 790 millions d'euros à la SNCF, *Le Monde*, 20 July 2018, available at: https://www.lemonde.fr/entreprises/article/2018/07/20/la-greve-aurait-coute-790-millions-d-euros-a-la-sncf_5334099_1656994.html.

Leonardi, S. & Pederisini, R. 2018. *Multi-employer bargaining under pressure: decentralisation trends in five European countries*, ETUI: Brussels.

Levavasseur, I. 2018. Rester Digne. Paris: Editions Flammarion.

Levy, J.D. 2008. From the Dirigiste state to the social anaesthesia state: French economic policy in the Longue Durée, *Modern & Contemporary France*, 16(4), pp. 417–435, https://doi.org/10.1080/09639480802413371.

Liabot, T. 2018. Gilets jaunes: pourquoi la rencontre avec Edouard Philippe a tourné court, *Le Journal Du Dimanche*, 30 November, available at: https://www.lejdd.fr/Politique/gilets-jaunes-pourquoi-la-rencontre-avec-edouard-philippe-a-tourne-court-3811340.

Mediapart. 2018. Syndicalistes contre la vie chères: agir maintenant! *Mediapart*, 27 November 2018. Available at: https://blogs.mediapart.fr/les-invites-de-mediapart/blog/271118/syndicalistes-contre-la-vie-chere-agir-maintenant.

Mestre, A. 2018. Manifestation du 26 mai: le comité Adama s'invite dans le cortège, Le Monde, 24 May 2018, available at: https://www.lemonde.fr/politique/article/2018/05/24/manifestation-du-26-mai-le-comite-adama-s-invite-dans-le-cortege-de-tete_5304112_823448.html.

Mulholland, R. 2018. One killed, hundreds injured in 'yellow jackets' protests over fuel prices in France, *The Telegraph*, 17 November 2018, available at: https://www.telegraph.co.uk/news/2018/11/17/one-killed-16-injured-yellow-jackets-protests-rising-fuel-prices/.

OECD. 2021. Trade Union Membership statistics, *OECD.Stat*, available at: https://stats.oecd.org/Index.aspx?DataSetCode=TUD.

Quijoux, M. & Gourgues, G. 2020. France's strikes show the unions are alive, Jacobin, 01 August 2018, available at: https://www.jacobinmag.com/2020/01/france-strikes-trade-unions-gilets-jaunes.

Schreyögg, G. & Sydow, J. 2010. Crossroads—Organizing for fluidity? Dilemmas of new organizational forms. *Organization Science*, 21(6), pp. 1251–1262.

Steele, J. & Dredge, D. 2017. The liquid organization of volunteer tourism: Implications for responsibility. *International Journal of Tourism Research*, 19(6), pp. 715–726.

Upchurch, M., Taylor, G. & Mathers, A. 2009. *The crisis of social democratic trade unionism in Western Europe: The search for alternatives*, Aldershot: Ashgate.

CHAPTER 9

The Decline of the Czech Trade Union Movement

Martin Štefko

1 Introduction

By the end of the 1980s, ČMKOS (*Českomoravská konfederace odborových svazů*/Bohemian-Moravian Confederation of Trade Unions), the dominant union confederation in the Czech Republic, had almost the same number of members as the entire United Kingdom trade union movement in 2006, despite the UK being some six times larger. However, the fall of the totalitarian communist regime caused a decline in trade union

---

[1] Living and Working in the Czech Republic: Working life in the Czech Republic by Renata Kyzlinkova, Stepanka Lehmann, Petr Pojer and Sona Veverkova, Eurofound, 2018 https://www.eurofound.europa.eu/country/czech-republic#actors-and-institutions (Accessed 18.1.2021). Further data are mentioned here https://www.worker-participation.eu/National-Industrial-Relations/Countries/Czech-Republic/Trade-Unions (Accessed 18.1.2021).

M. Štefko (✉)
Faculty of Law, Charles University, Prague, Czech Republic
e-mail: stefkom@prf.cuni.cz

membership, as happened similarly to other ex-communist countries in Central and Eastern Europe. According to Eurostat data,[1] trade union density in the Czech Republic was around 80% in 1993[2] but experienced a sharp decline to around 21% in 2006, and falling to 17% by 2009. Since then, none of the relevant Czech agencies or trade unions have published any reliable data on this subject. Nowadays, experts surmise that only around 10% of the workforce in the country is currently unionised.[3] The primary reason for this stark decline in unionisation rates since 1993 is often put down in large part to a loss of credibility and power on the part of the official communistic trade union organisation. The now defunct Communist Party of Czechoslovakia (1921–1992) and the official trade union organisation had been closely tied, and trade unions executed a number of state functions and were involved with the distribution of a number of government benefits (or sanctions) to their members, whose membership was not entirely voluntary during the communist regime.

The exodus of union members was unavoidable. New alternative democratic trade unions needed to distinguished themselves form the state bureaucracy and from political life in order to gain the workers' confidence. However, respective regulations have not changed significantly as we will discuss in Sect. 2 of this contribution.

It is clear that trade unions must reverse this negative trend in membership in order to survive and to remain politically relevant. Primarily, unions must regain credibility and must fight to obtain new members. New members would mean an increase in power for respective trade union organisations in labour relations. Simply put, Czech unions also would benefit from increased income streams. In reality, many trade unions have had to exist with very limited financial resources (despite some notable exceptions), as we will describe in Sect. 3.

Section 4 analyses two strategies that created an alternative to the blood, toil and tears way in the labour movement; two strategies intended to earn new members at the expense of other contestants. These two strategies demonstrate how some unions can become not only a real obstacle to the freedom of association, but they also illustrate the current nature and status of the Czech labour movement. The final section concludes.

---

[2] Czechoslovakia was formally dissolved on 01 January 1993 bringing the modern states of the Czech Republic and Slovakia into existence.

[3] There are no official statistics for the entire country. The most recent nationwide statistics published by trade unions in 2009 put union density at 17 per cent.

2 Legal Framework of Employees' Representatives

Czech employees are represented on both a statutory and contractual basis. The latter applies to a national social dialogue that is performed by a special body named the Council of Economic and Social Agreement (in Czech Rada hospodářské a sociální dohody, in English hereinafter the "RHSD"). Since its creation, the RHSD has been based on an informal tripartite agreement concluded between the government and the strongest trade union confederations and employers' associations. The initial agreement from 1990 has never been replaced put on a statutory footing.

All remaining representative organisations can be formed only on a statutory basis and their status is governed by the Czech constitution and legal statute. Respective rules are considered to be within the scope of public law and can be found in the Charter of Fundamental Rights and Freedoms,[4] Labour Code, collective bargaining legislation and the national civil code. Czech law recognises four types of representative organisations, namely: trade unions, works councils,[5] representatives concerned with occupational safety[6] and European Works Councils.

An employer is required to create the conditions for employee representatives to enable them to perform their duties, in particular to provide them, in accordance with operational means and in appropriate extent, with reasonably equipped rooms, to cover the costs of maintenance and to provide them with relevant background documents and information that are necessary for employee representatives to execute their responsibilities.[7] Furthermore, employee representatives are entitled to time off work to undertake union duties; all representatives are entitled to undertake such activities during working hours and to be compensated for any loss of wages, if they occur. However, only trade union officials enjoy the

---

[4] The Charter is considered to be a formal part of the Czech Constitution.

[5] Works councils can mediate in relations between employers and employees and are called upon to enforce employees' information and consultation rights.

[6] These rules enabled the Czech Republic to ratify the ILO Workers' Representatives Convention (1971, No. 135), in October 2000.

[7] In spite of this, there are cases where certain employers try to exert influence over trade union bodies, including by means of offering certain benefits to trade union representatives.

highest protection against dismissal for trade union activities. Section 61 of the Labour Code states that a dismissal of a trade union official is to be regarded as automatically void and invalid, unless the employer has valid grounds for the dismissal and provided a court considers the further employment of the trade union official as unjust.[8] Other representatives of employees are covered by substantially weaker protection, including those representatives that are members of European Works Councils.[9]

2.1 Council of Economic and Social Agreement

RHSD, that was established in the early 1990s, represents the only state platform for social dialogue between employers, trade unions and the government in the Czech Republic. Even in 2019, representatives of the largest employer associations (Czech Confederation of Industry and Transport of the Czech Republic, in Czech Svaz průmyslu a dopravy České republiky; and Confederation of Employers' and Enterpeuners' Unions of the Czech Republic, in Czech Konfederace zaměstnavatelských a podnikatelských svazů České republiky) and trade unions' associations, including ČMKOS and the smaller ASO ČR (Asociace samostatných odborů České republiky/the Association of Independent Trade Unions of the Czech Republic), meet to discuss crucial proposals of law or political affairs. Notably, the government ceased to negotiate a full-scale agreement in 1995 and since then, no new agreement has been reached.

The outcomes of social dialogue can still be formalised in higher-rank collective agreements. Year by year, trade union federations or confederations and employer associations conclude around twenty higher-rank collective agreements in various sectors across the Czech economy. However, those agreements are typically limited in scope and tend to be confined to general terms and conditions usual in specific branch of economy.

---

[8] This is a unique protection guaranteed under Czech Labour Code; no other employee enjoys the same level of legal protection against dismissal.

[9] As derived by Supreme Court decision docket file No. 21 Cdo 398/2016.

2.2 Trade Unions

Employees, including managerial personnel, are granted the right to join trade union organisations of their own choosing, without interference from employers or from state authorities. Trade unions are also granted the right to independently establish their own constitutions and rules, to organise their internal administration and to elect their representatives.[10]

Czech law does not recognise shop stewards, and employees are represented directly by trade unions. From a legal perspective, Czech law recognises one legal status of trade union organisation regardless of its scope of operation. A large national trade union federation with thousands of members and a trade union organisation operating at a single facility with three employees have the same legal status under private law. In accordance with the law, three employees can establish a trade union organisation or employer organisation and the relevant legislation does not set forth any criteria for association relating to the minimum required density that a union (or employer) organisation must achieve in the workplace.

The Czech civil code spells out that a trade union is a society (in Czech "spolek"), but many trade unions oppose this classification due to its legal implications. The main reason given for their level of contempt for the regulation of societies is the significant restrictions that it places on the unions' room for manoeuvre, which some unions even consider to be a violation of respective ILO conventions.[11] In fact, the civil code and relevant supplementary legislation have introduced many obligations for societies, but the relevant provisions apply only/and to the extent when/under which appropriate under the terms of the Czech Republic's international obligations.

A trade union is an incorporated association, which means it is a separate entity from its members. The union rule book, like the articles of association of a company, provides for the institutions that govern the union. Trade unions are also voluntary associations, and can come into being as a creature of law following a formal procedure. The registrar shall not scrutinise an application to establish a trade union organisation

---

[10] ILO Convention No. 87, supra note 7, art. 2.
[11] Especially Freedom of Association and Protection of the Right to Organise Convention, ILO Convention No. 87.

that is lodged at a regional court, and a trade union organisation can be established the day an application is delivered.

In accordance with Czech law, trade unions are the only legitimate representative bodies for employees that have the right to collective bargaining. Trade unions represent all employees in labour relations, including those who are not union members. The Labour Code of 2006 gives trade unions the right to participate in decision-making,[12] the right to engage in co-determination, and the right to consult and gain information in matters relating to employees' interests. Furthermore, trade unions enjoy a significant right of control over the observance of labour law by the employer and the right to perform assessments regarding occupational safety. Trade unions had been deemed by the legislator as the sole representative of employees since 1945. During the communist era (1948–1989), the independent trade unions that had existed were effectively incorporated into state mechanisms and no other representatives were allowed to be created. Despite the Velvet Revolution in 1989, which precipitated the fall of the communist regime, trade unions remain to keep control over Czech workforce and have been able to resist any attempts to water down their (limited) prerogatives. The trade unions' supremacy over other employee representative organisations represents one the most prominent examples of the country's mixed administrative, legal and political legacy, that includes elements from the erstwhile totalitarian era and the modern Czech state.

2.3 Other Representatives

Works councils (in Czech Rada zaměstnanců) and representatives (in Czech zástupce pro oblast bezpečnosti a ochrany zdraví při práci) concerned with occupational safety (hereinafter "safety representatives") are relatively rare in the Czech Republic for two main reasons: firstly, the supremacy of trade unions and secondly, the weak legal status afforded to them under Czech law. Firstly, a particular trade union organisation can function on a plant or even sub-plant level. All trade union confederations establish subsidiary organisations for this purpose their (which are considered to be of the same legal status as their parent trade union organisations). However, the law has not conferred the status of a juridical

---

[12] Section 320 of the Labour Code envisions giving trade unions the right to prior consultations on proposals of labour legislation.

person on "safety representatives" and they therefore cannot negotiate on behalf of all employees with legal effect and they cannot conclude collective agreements. Similarly, works councils have no legal authority to call strikes. Meanwhile, trade union organisation enjoy legal personality and can operate on a much larger scope than a works council or a "safety representative" can. It appears that, mainly for these reasons, trade unions are able to seize and sustain momentum wherever they exist. Although Czech law allows for trade unions, works councils and other representatives to co-exist within the same workplace, in reality, the establishment of works councils is mostly conceived as an alternative solution for those very strange situations where employees' interests cannot be defended by a trade union. Such rare cases can exist, when employees are reluctant to be active to protect their rights.

Those few works councils that have been created can mediate when it comes to relations between employers and employees and are called upon to enforce employees' information and consultation rights. They must have at least three members and at most fifteen. Works council members are elected by the employees of the entire workforce in a particular workplace. Oddly enough, neither council member must be employees of the respective employer. The Labour Code does not regulate any smaller units in this regard. One "safety representative" can be elected for every ten employees. Both members of works councils and "safety representatives" are elected by all employees at a particular workplace every three years.

The Czech Labour Code also contains provisions for the implementation of the European Works Council Directive (Directive 94/45/EC). A European Works Council enables employees of multinational companies, meeting certain conditions, to have access to information regarding the company and to discuss it with the employer. So far only one business has established a European Works Council under Czech law, while other European Works Councils have been created on the basis of foreign law.

3   Miners' Merits

The Public Pension insurance scheme (in Czech důchodové pojištění) is based on a sophisticated calculus that is difficult to outsmart. A simple truth is that those who managed to retire earlier and live longer can obtain accumulative old-age pension payments that far exceed what they paid-in. When the Czech Republic gained independence in 1993, it resurrected its public pension insurance scheme. The new united[13] and universal[14] pension insurance scheme initiated in 1995 was re-conceived in order to be more just and sustainable. In this context, a "just" system was understood to mean one where the rigid implementation of equality was adhered to, and where all those who are insured have their old-age benefits calculated under the same formula without any preference afforded for previous loyalty to any political regime or party, and where all occupations are treated the same.

Notably, miners are the only group that managed to maintain the advantageous regulations under the equalised pension insurance scheme of the democratic Czech Republic that they had enjoyed under the communist regime. The last relevant reform that was enacted by Act No. 213/2016, known as the Employment Category Preservation Act of 2016 (hereinafter "Reform of 2016").[15]

The miners' unions (in Czech Odborový svaz pracovníků hornictví, geologie a naftového průmyslu) have been able to put three subsequent Czech governments under severe pressure and extracted tangible results for their members in the process. Specifically, they were able to rally their members who feared losing their jobs in the case of the Paskov mine closure in 2013. To a certain degree, trade unions were able to build ties and to cooperate with local management, which helped to intensify the frustration of the endangered workers.[16]

The miners' unions applied a mixture of threats and good PR policy. The miners' representatives stated several times that they were able to transport their members to the seat of government and to "take things

---

[13] This covers the whole economically active population, including wage-earners, groups of people performing work or analogous activities and the self-employed.

[14] There is one mandatory scheme for the whole Czech population.

[15] In Czech zákon č. 213/2016 Sb. kterým se mění zákon č. 155/1995 Sb., o důchodovém pojištění, ve znění pozdějších předpisů, a zákon č. 582/1991 Sb., o organizaci a provádění sociálního zabezpečení, ve znění pozdějších předpisů.

[16] Cf. management speech delivered on 15 May 2015 in its essence highlighted: "... *Miners in this country in comparison with their colleagues abroad can feel that they are left alone. The Czech Republic does not honour their work*". The speech can be found in SIBRT, Marek. Jurášek: "We work on, negotiations are not easy" (available in Czech na změně v důchodech dále pracujeme. Jednání jsou náročná). *Horník* [online], 2015, Vol. 45, No. 18, p. 4, accessible at http://www.ihornik.cz/archiv/hornik-2015-18.pdf, citation 28 November 2019.

into their own hands", i.e. to storm the Parliament. To survive constitutional scrutiny, the legislature had re-written the explanatory report of the Reform of 2016 several times. The final version justified miners' early retirement with a recourse to *"the special and unique trait of mining"*, and in particular the negative implications that it has for the health of mineworkers. The explanatory report provided two specific justifications for the special status that was afforded to miners, namely: the shortened life expectancy of miners and the high rate of occupational injuries. Regarding the former, the legislature states: *"Miners' early retirement has a long legal tradition (...) is backed up by 5-year difference in miners' life expectancy compared to the rest of the population"* (Docket file No. ODOK 2016, p. 9).[17] Regarding the latter, the legislation states that: *"Miners are eligible for occupational injury remedies six times more often than other occupations. Technological progress is eliminated because business owners have to undertake mining in deeper destinations. Therefore, there are not one but mostly health hazards to miners' health. The combination of these circumstances and demands [justifies] the affirmative action towards miners"*.[18]

The legislature intended to compensate miners for the harm they suffered over the course of their work. It was inspired by a set of arguments stemming from a Constitutional Court case where the court supported the principle of the exceptional circumstances that miners find themselves in, because of the arduous physical work and extreme working conditions they endure.[19] However, this decision also upheld the concept of occupational invalidity mainly because it was not intended and applied to miners only. Hence, the legislator misinterpreted said decision in the Reform of 2016.

The government justified the Reform of 2016 with reference to a trade union statement that miners lived on average 5,8 years less in 1995 than the national average,[20] and the national parliament passed introduced a retirement age that was seven years lower than the national standard

---

[17] Explanatory paper regarding the new retirement age for miners, page 9, available at https://apps.odok.cz/veklep-detail?pid=KORN9PHKLSFX.

[18] Explanatory paper regarding the new retirement age for miners, page 10, available at https://apps.odok.cz/veklep-detail?pid=KORN9PHKLSFX.

[19] Cf. file No. Pl. US 15/02.

[20] Cf. http://www.osphgn.cz/clanky/aktuality/nektere-zdravotni-duvody-pro-drivejsi-odchod-horniku-do-starobniho-duchodu.html (Citation 31 January 2018).

under the 2016 reforms. In addition, the Reform of 2016 created an old-age pension system specifically for miners,[21] which allowed mineworkers to apply for a retirement an additional three years earlier. The total length of early retirement for miners can therefore be a total of 10 years below the standard retirement age in the Czech Republic. Evidence from official statistics on mortality and occupational injuries does not justify this 10-year reduction. As such, based on the available mortality data, a 55-year-old man is expected to live to 78,93 years; thus, if he retires at 65, he would spend 13,93 years in retirement, whereas a miner of the same age who retires at age 55 could be expected to spend 23,93 years in retirement.[22]

The second reason that was mobilised to justify the Reform of 2016 relates to health hazards. The legislature of 2015 stated that miners' shorter lives are caused by mortal accidents and other injuries. Statistical data on the number of occupational injuries (that are considered by law to be different from occupational diseases) prove that miners were affected by the highest rate of injury only in 1996 (760 injured men from a total 1563 injured), in year 2011 (186 injured men), 2012 (179 injured men), 2013 (167 injured men) and 2014 (238 injured men). Other workers suffered injuries more often in the period from 1997 to 2010, as well as in 2015 and 2016, while all other workers keep to the higher retirement age of 65 (i.e. they remain in work longer than miners do on average). Health workers suffered the highest number of occupational injuries in 2009 (212), 2010 (180) and 2016 (194). Workers in the automotive industry were affected most in 2015 (173) and workers in mechanical engineering (i.e. workers in factories producing food, beverages, tobacco, textile, etc.) accounted for the highest rates in 1997, 1998, 1999, 2000, 2001, 2002,

---

[21] As Švehláková, a state official at the Czech Social Security Administration, calculated that miners with life-cycle monthly income from CZK 8720 to 22,690 have the same pension of 16,674 CZK. Cf. ŠVEHLÁKOVÁ, S.: Závěrečná práce—Zvýhodněná kategorie pojištěnců v systému DP—hornické důchody, Prague: PF UK, 2016, p. 11. Jahoda, R.; Malý, I.; Sirovátka, T.: ESPN Thematic Report on Retirement regimes for workers in arduous or hazardous jobs Czech Republic 2016, p. 6.

[22] According to statistical data, men aged 52 have life expectancy of 26,5 years on average, men of 55 have life expectancy of an additional 23,93 years and so on. Mortality data collected by the Czech Statistical Unit are available at https://www.czso.cz/csu/czso/umrtnostni-tabulky-za-cr-regiony-soudrznosti-a-kraje-2015-2016.

2003, 2004, 2005, 2006, 2007 and 2008 (200).[23] The highest number of occupational accidents was experienced by lumberjacks in 2016, and machine operators had the highest number of occupational diseases in 2015.[24] For example, locksmiths reported 26 times the rate of occupational carpal tunnel syndrome compared to miners.[25] Based on health hazards and the number of occupational injuries experienced, miners had the highest rate of injury only in 5 of the 21 years between 1996 and 2017 for which such data were collected.

4   Trade Unions under Pressure

Nowadays, trade unions in the Czech Republic are generally organised along industrial lines, but not according to any one pattern with one union per industry and one industry per union. First of all, local trade unions and their organisations at the regional or national levels are, from a legal perspective, afforded the same legal status. Employees can be represented by more than one local trade unions at the same workplace. While the existence of more than one union within an enterprise has never been prohibited by law, under the previous totalitarian regime, it was the will of the Communist Party and so it was followed by all citizens obediently.

Several preconditions can be identified that can lead to interunion conflict and to the emergence of a "shadow" trade union organisations (i.e. fake trade union organisation). This includes the country's aforementioned legal traditions, the absence of any exclusivity rule (i.e. the multiplicity of trade unions at a particular employer), and the desire for consensus. In addition, there is no independence test that trade unions are not controlled by the employer set forth in the law. Hence, even a "house union" that is controlled by middle management or by senior executives is regarded as a trade union under Czech law. Notably, Czech courts have derived a rather loose test that checks if the trade union in

---

[23] All reports were prepared by the State Public Health Agency and are available at http://www.szu.cz/publikace/data/nemoci-z-povolani-a-ohrozeni-nemoci-z-povolani-v-ceske-republice?lang=1.

[24] Research done by the State Health Agency, available at http://www.szu.cz/uploads/NZP/Hlaseni_a_odhlaseni_2015.pdf. Citation 31 January 2018.

[25] Research done by the State Health Agency, available at http://www.szu.cz/uploads/NZP/Hlaseni_a_odhlaseni_2015.pdf. Citation 31 January 2018.

question protects employees' interests, which most "house unions" can pass easily.[26]

There are no obstacles for the cloning of local trade union organisations, without any respect for the specific characteristics of certain branches of the Czech economy. Incentives for such strange behaviour are connected with the distinctly mixed legacy of Czech labour law. Once rich and sophisticated, the Czech collective labour law was profoundly changed both during the Nazi and (primarily) the communist eras, where the role assigned to collective agreements was diminished to a set of soft plans that merely implemented the directives of the State. After the country's return to democracy, it is obvious that Czechs had to adopt not only new democratic regulations but they also needed to re-build the relevant informal structures that are still lacking today.

Notably, not only is the existence of more than one union not prohibited under Czech law, it is in fact facilitated by the law, as no legal mechanisms are offered to overcome the no-cooperation policy executed by any trade union organisation at a particular employer. The Labour Code forces all trade unions to agree upon both matters of procedure and substance. Other trade unions can only apply pressure on a trade union organisation with limited membership to impose a trade union consensus in decision-making. Employers are prohibited under the Constitution to enforce so-called yellow dog contracts, i.e. employers shall not oblige employees to not enter, establish or associate any trade union organisation. Any employer who informs their employees that their businesses are *"trade-union-free, and they want it to stay this way"* would commit an administrative tort. Finally, due to the doctrine that nobody can be forced to join a union, which was established before the Second World War, the closed shop had long been rejected in the Czech Republic, and this remains so today.

4.1 Raids on Trade Union Members

The strongest trade union organisations are associated with ČMKOS— the Czech-Moravian Confederation of Trade Unions whose members share agreed upon rules for defending employees' rights and interests. Under ČMKOS rules, each member union confederation or federation

---

[26] Cf. Supreme Court decision docket file No. 21 Cdo 1037/2009.

shall establish a local union organisation to represent the employees of a particular employer. Nowadays, the biggest trade union organisation OS KOVO (Odborový svaz KOVO/Czech Metalworkers' Trade Union) has deviated from this aforementioned best practice and has started to intrude into establishments that lie beyond their traditional scope. OS KOVO has created regional organisations which collect union dues, represent local workers and help them to communicate directly with their employers.

The law distinguishes between the establishment of a trade union organisation and its capacity to interact with an employer. This distinction is connected with the minimum threshold requirement, namely that a trade union organisation must bring together at least three employees in the same workplace to be formed.[27] ILO Convention No. 87 makes it unlawful for any national legislation to require prior authorisation before a trade union organisation can be established. From the day it has unionised three employees, a union organisation can notify the employer that it has started to operate at its facility. From that moment the employer has to fulfil its duty to accommodate at least one employee representative associated with the union.

However, collective bargaining at the branch level is the exception and not the rule. Firstly, and as discussed, both local trade unions and their federations and confederations are trade unions from a legal perspective. Secondly, employees can be represented by more than one local trade unions at the same employer, because Czech law does not provide for any formal method to choose one trade union organisation at any given employer, and there are employers with dozens of local trade unions in the Czech Republic.[28] Furthermore, and as also discussed, Czech law does not recognise shop stewards, as employees are represented directly by trade unions.

As is the case in many European countries, trade union members in the Czech Republic are getting older, and trade unions had to get to grips with moving online in order to reach new generations and to maximise the opportunities associated with the network society. Unfortunately, many of the older and more established trade unions have never

---

[27] Czech law recognises other subsidiary employment relationships which do not equip an employee with full legal protection. Employees in subsidiary employment relationships do not count for the purposes of meeting the minimum threshold requirement for the formation of a trade union.

[28] One example is ČEZ a.s. (the Czech Electricity Corporation) with 36 trade unions.

fully committed to maintaining a meaningful online presence for many reasons (e.g. low income, ageing leaders, other priorities). However, in 2018 a new trade union confederation (in Czech Zaměstnanecké forum) was established with a total of some fifteen local organisations based in various subsidiaries of foreign companies based in the Czech Republic. Supported by a team of three, including a skilled auditor, a lawyer and an active politician, the confederation covered a gap in the market that the traditional trade union organisations had been unable to accommodate. However, each employer that entered into formal relations with the online trade union was left without serious help from the employer organisations. Some employers have claimed to be subject to featherbedding when the new trade union confederation demanded financial contributions and threatened that it will go to court, and respective trade union officials have remained silent regarding the new union.

Despite the apparent weakness of the union movement in the Czech Republic, corporations located in the country have borne witness to unusual developments in the Czech labour movement by European standards—in particular when few employees or sometimes even one employee[29] are able to establish a local trade union organisation. From legal perspective, trade union officials are well protected and trade unions enjoy strong legal status.

5 Conclusion

In the Czech Republic, trade unions can influence the promulgation of new law at the RHSD, have greater potential for strike readiness or strikes,[30] and their presidents and senior officers often obtain senior posts in national political organs, such as in the national parliament. The traditional trade unions, which have been experiencing a decline in membership, are becoming weaker and their traditional territory can

---

[29] The employer is forbidden to scrutinise real members of a local trade union organisation. It suffices that the respective trade union organisation declares that it has met the threshold of three employees.

[30] There are not any official statistic data on strikes in the Czech Republic. However, trade unions sometimes make public their strikes if they were successful. Some data can be derived from case law as well. Based on said sources, it can be concluded that every year they are a few strikes.

be exploited by other similar non-governmental organisations and movements, such as the online union. Clearly, members are indispensable for every trade union organisation, and this weakness is something that the traditional unions must tackle in order to survive. A constant flow of new members does not only bring with it economic resources but this can also increase a trade union's representativeness and its power on both the local and levels. At its highest point, the strongest trade union organisations can achieve national recognition to participate on the RHSD, which directly influences the formation of national laws.

This chapter has described two basic stories that are central to the current state of the Czech trade union movement. The successful campaign by the miners' trade unions which ensured the provision of early retirement on a full old-age pension for their members is an example of union effectiveness in straightened times. Officials from the miners' unions were able to persuade the government that miners tended to live shorter lives as a result of their dangerous (but essential) work and the legislator established a special pension scheme for these workers.

The other story relates to OS KOVO and their seeking new members beyond the scope of their traditional sphere of influence, which breached a long-standing informal agreements and which in any case, at least in some cases, has not yet been able to provide significant improvements for new members. Some trade union federations went so fat as to undertake legal steps to deter OS KOVO from "poaching" members. Cases like this allow us to pause and rethink the ultimate purpose of trade unions. Clearly the defence of workers' interests should be the primary reason why any trade union exists and enjoys the protection of ILO conventions, national constitution and statutes. The protection granted by ILO Convention No. 87 especially covers the goal of "*furthering and defending the interests of workers*". Workers' organisations are thus protected to the extent to which they are organised for this purpose. In line with ILO principles, the same protection is enjoyed only by "*persons who genuinely represent the interests of employees*".[31] *Genuine Czech trade unions have to do two things in order to survive. They have to go online for many sectors of Czech economy accommodated new virtual economy. The second step became obvious in connection with COVID time. Trade unions must increase rally efforts to unite workers on country level and bargain*

---

[31] ILO, Freedom of Association: Digest, supra note 10, ¶ 260.

on their behalf in these challenging times. Their low profile during COVID time left other movements space to gather and lead unsatisfied people to argue for change of COVID protective measures.

BIBLIOGRAPHY

Becker, U., Pieters, D., Ross, F. & Schoukens, P. 2010. *Security: A general principle of social security law in Europe*, Groningen: Europa Law Publishing.
Pichrt, J. & Štefko, M. 2015. *Labour law and industrial relations—Czech Republic* (2nd ed.), The Netherlands: IEL, Kluwer Law International.
SÍBRT, Marek. 2015. Jurášek: 'We work on, negotiations are not easy' (available in Czech na změně v důchodech dále pracujeme. Jednání jsou náročná). *Horník* [online], Vol. 45, No. 18, p. 4.
Living and Working in the Czech Republic: Working life in the Czech Republic by Renata Kyzlinkova, Stepanka Lehmann, Petr Pojer and Sona Veverkova, Eurofound, 2018 https://www.eurofound.europa.eu/country/czech-republic#actors-and-institutions (Accessed 18 Jan 2021).
Šimečková, E. 2000. Employment Law in Ius Regale Montanorum by Wenceslas II. ('Pracovněprávní ustanovení horního zákoníku Václava II.' *Právník*, No. 3, pp. 294–309.
Cited reports provided by the State Public Health Agency are available at http://www.szu.cz/publikace/data/nemoci-z-povolani-a-ohrozeni-nemoci-z-povolani-v-ceske-republice.

CASE LAW

Supreme Court decision on 6 March 2017, docket file No. 21 Cdo 398/2016
Supreme Court decision on 16 December 2010, docket file No. 21 Cdo 1037/2009

CHAPTER 10

Trade Union Participation and New Forms of Collective Action: Pension Reform in Spain as a Case Study

Eusebi Colàs-Neila

1 On the (Alleged) Decline of Trade Unions and Their Adaptation to Challenges: Pension Reform in Spain as a Case Study

Trade unions play a central role in promoting and protecting democracy not only in the workplace but also beyond in the broader sociopolitical arena. Spain is a powerful example of this in its recent past. Along with other actors, trade unions have been active agents in the country's democratic transition following four decades of dictatorship between 1939 and 1975 (Fishman, 1990). The adoption of the 1978 constitution saw the establishment of a democratic model of industrial relations based on the principle of political and social pluralism that affords a preeminent position to trade unions at the heart of the country's constitutional order.

E. Colàs-Neila (✉)
Faculty of Law, Univ. Pompeu Fabra, Barcelona, Spain
e-mail: eusebi.colas@upf.edu

© The Author(s), under exclusive license to Springer Nature Switzerland AG 2022
B. Colfer (ed.), *European Trade Unions in the 21st Century*, St Antony's Series, https://doi.org/10.1007/978-3-030-88285-3_10

The Spanish Constitution indeed identifies unions and employers' associations as key actors in the political, social and economic arenas (Section 7),[1] at the same level as political parties (Section 6).[2] According to the Constitutional Court, '*(t)he Constitution has enshrined (...) [trade unions] as a key element in shaping our state as a "social and democratic state governed by the rule of law"*' under Article 1.1.[3] This means that, beyond being an instrument of defence, protection and promotion of workers' collective interests, trade unions are also '*key institutions of the political system*',[4] '*social organisations with constitutional relevance*'[5] and, ultimately, an '*essential institution of the Spanish constitutional system*'.[6]

This prominent role given to trade unions by the Spanish Constitution contrasts with the process of erosion of their power to act that have been introduced by various legal reforms, especially those implemented over the past decade, '*serving the objectives of flexibility first and deregulation later*' (Chacartegui, 2016). A very clear example of this regarding collective bargaining can be found that follows a similar pattern to many European countries. In fact, the European Union (EU) maintained a strong position in encouraging legal reforms deregulating collective labour rights, especially domestic collective bargaining systems (Bogg & Ewing, 2017; Pecinovsky, 2019).

But legal reforms are not the only challenge that trade unions must face. A fundamental transformation of the production regime that impacts labour laws is underway, and union practices that were useful in the past are less so today (Stone, 2004). There are several other factors, including the decline in union membership, a new highly digitalised

---

[1] Section 7: '*Trade unions and employers' associations contribute to the defence and promotion of the economic and social interests which they represent. Their creation and the exercise of their activities shall be free in so far as they respect the Constitution and the law. Their internal structure and their functioning must be democratic*'.

[2] Section 6: '*Political parties are the expression of political pluralism, they contribute to the formation and expression of the will of the people and are an essential instrument for political participation. Their creation and the exercise of their activities are free in so far as they respect the Constitution and the law. Their internal structure and their functioning must be democratic*'.

[3] Judgement 8/2015, 22 January 2015 (ECLI:ES:TC2015:8).

[4] Judgement 11/1981, 8 April 1981 (ECLI: ES: TC: 1981:11).

[5] Judgement 18/1984, 7 February 1984 (ECLI:ES:TC:1984:18).

[6] Judgement 101/1996, 11 June 1996 (ECLI:ES:TC:1996:101).

productive context, a massive decline in standard employment contracts and a corresponding increase in atypical forms of employment and 'precarious jobs', that together lead to the weakening of union influence and their traditional position as relevant political and socio-economic actors.[7]

However, it is also important to note their efforts to adapt to this new context, by exploring and implementing new strategies and instruments and creating structures of solidarity and resistance that differ from those traditionally used and by maximising the possibilities offered by the network society. This contribution attempts to highlight this from the perspective of trade unions' 'political voice' (Ewing, 2014) by examining the democratic mechanisms of participation in regulatory processes that are used by trade unions and how they have adapted their approaches and tools of collective action to continue to exert influence in this field. For this purpose, the role that trade unions have played in the reforms of Spain's public pension system will be analysed as a case study, using a diachronic perspective as it helps to combine tradition and innovation as regards the actors involved and instruments used.

The contribution considers the following points. First, trade union participation in pension reform in Spain through traditional industrial relations mechanisms (i.e. tripartite agreements) will be analysed. The Spanish case presents the peculiarity of the existence of a complex mechanism involving the participation of political parties, on the one hand, and social partners, on the other, with the aim of maximising the degree of consensus and support for the reforms. Second, the chapter focuses on how trade unions have formed new alliances with NGOs and other associations for a socio-economic purpose, through the use of information and communication technologies (ICTs), through which they have explored collectively various alternative legislative procedures, such as the popular legislative initiative. And finally, it deals with the rise of new grassroots movements, such as 'Marea Pensionista',[8] a pensioners' platform that arose in response to the discontent generated by recent pension reforms, including some reforms that had been negotiated with the most representative trade unions in this field and others that had been introduced unilaterally. The most striking aspect, from the perspective of the actions

---

[7] The first references to 'precarious jobs' can be found in Rodgers & Rodgers (1989). On these developments, see Pulignano, Köhler & Stewart (2016).

[8] This translates as 'the pensioner tide' in English.

undertaken and instruments adopted during this alliance, is the combination of traditional (rallies and demonstrations) and innovative instruments (judicialisation) as a means of influencing regulatory changes.

2 The Toledo Pact as a Mechanism of Trade Union Participation in Pension Reform

The Spanish social security system belongs to the social insurance model (Bonoli, 2003).

Roughly speaking, this is a public system, under constitutional mandate (Article 41), and it includes two levels of protection. On the one hand, there is a pay-as-you-go pension scheme, that is financed by contributions from employers and workers, which guarantees a range of benefits to workers and their families, based on their qualifying periods and contribution record. At the same time, there is a non-contributory or universal pension scheme, based on means-testing, aimed at protecting those citizens who have not contributed enough to qualify for a contributory pension.[9] As will be noted, different reforms have taken place over the last three decades, mainly regarding the contributory level. The latest reforms, as has occurred in many other European countries, have been based on a set of circumstances, including an ageing population, the economic crisis and the spread of austerity policies, which have been designed to ensure the sustainability of the pension system, and that are regarded by many (including the trade unions) as regressive in nature.[10]

The national parliament is exclusively responsible for regulating the pension system under the Spanish Constitution. Despite this, the participatory role of trade unions has been a relatively major and consistent feature within the framework of the so-called Toledo Pact.[11] This is a sort of national agreement reached in 1995, whose objective is to achieve the greatest possible consensus among political parties prior to undertaking any reform on an issue that is of great concern to Spanish society. The idea was to defuse the potentially most contentious areas of public

---

[9] A comprehensive summary of the essential aspects of the social security system in Spain can be found at OECD (2019).

[10] A more detailed description of these changes can be found at Natali & Stamati (2013) and Suárez-Corujo (2014).

[11] For an analysis of the Toledo Pact, see Panizo Robles (2011); a analysis focusing on the participation of the social partners see Colàs-Neila (2018).

policy and to avoid them becoming the subject of electoral confrontation. However, from a broader perspective, the Toledo Pact process represents a 'consensual method of reform' (Tortuero Plaza et al., 2010), a complex mechanism enabling political and socio-economic participation in which legislative, executive powers and social partners participate.

From a procedural point of view, it is possible to identify three main stages in the development of the Toledo Pact. The first took place in parliament. In fact, strictly speaking, the Toledo Pact is the name commonly given to a parliamentary commission within the Parliamentary Committee on Budgetary Affairs [*Comisión de Presupuestos del Congreso de los Diputados*], where all parliamentary groups are represented. At this commission, discussions on possible reforms in the field of social security are debated. Notably, public hearings take place here, where specialists from various fields are invited at the proposal of the parliamentary groups, either because of their technical knowledge (e.g. jurists, economists, demographers) or because they belong to institutions with a particular relevance to the matter at hand (e.g. trade unions, NGOs, public institutions). As a result of the work conducted by the commission, proposed recommendations can be agreed which are then submitted to parliament to be adopted at a plenary session. It is at the second stage when the participation of social partners occurs. Once parliament adopts the proposed recommendations, the government then calls on the most representative trade unions and employers' association at the national level to begin a bargaining process. Finally, based on this tripartite agreement, the government submits a proposal for a law to be approved by both houses of parliament, according to the usual legislative process applicable in this field.

Four major reforms have been passed through the Toledo Pact system since 1995. The schematic sequence of recommendations approved by parliament (first stage), tripartite agreements (second stage) and the enactment of subsequent laws approved by parliament (third stage) is as follows:

1. The original version of the Toledo Pact (1995) resulted in two tripartite agreements and two corresponding regulations:

   > The agreement on consolidating and rationalising the social security system (09 October 1996) and subsequent Act

24/1997, of 15 July, on consolidating and rationalising the social security system.

The agreement on improving and developing the social protection system (09 April 2001) and subsequent Act 35/2002, of 12 July, establishing measures for a gradual, flexible retirement system.

2. The renewal of the Toledo Pact (2003) led to one result:

The agreement on social security measures (02 June 2006) and subsequent Act 40/2007, of 04 December, on measures within the field of social security.

3. The follow-up of the Toledo Pact (2003–2008) and the Report of the Toledo Pact (2011) were the bases of the most recently passed agreement, namely:

The social and economic agreement for growth, employment and pension guarantee (02 February 2011) and subsequent Act 27/2011 of 01 August, on adapting and modernising the social security system.

Within the framework of this contribution, it is important to highlight a point directly linked to the participation of the social partners. The stakeholders involved from the trade union and employers' side participated only in the last two agreements (2006 and 2011, signed with the Socialist government of President Zapatero). The first was signed only by the government, then led by the centre-right Partido Popular (PP) and the two most representative trade unions, namely the Comisiones Obreras/Workers' Commissions (CCOO) and the Unión General de Trabajadores/the General Workers' Union (UGT), in 1996. With the second pact, passed in 2001, the UGT ultimately did not sign up to the agreement, despite the participation of the two most representative employers' associations, the Confederación Española de Organizaciones Empresariales/Spanish Confederation of Employers' Associations (CEOE) and the Confederación Española de la Pequeña y Mediana Empresa/Spanish Confederation of Small and Medium-Sized Firms (CEPYME) as well as the other most representative trade union, CCOO.

From a diachronic perspective, major pension reforms during Spain's democratic period have also included unilateral amendments imposed by the government. Moreover, this has been a practice that both the major political parties have followed, namely: the centre-left Partido Socialista Obrero Español (PSOE) in 1985 and more recently the PP in 2013, following the implementation of the Toledo Pact, the second of which broke the consensus in using this mechanism. Notably, both of these cases share points in common, including: their dire economic crisis context, the regressive orientation of the reforms, the majority support obtained in parliament led by the governing party and the strong social contestation which resulted from it.

The implementation of the Toledo Pact reveals its strengths and weaknesses. A clear positive outcome is that this process provides legitimacy for reforms (Tortuero Plaza et al., 2010), especially regarding specific types of amendments that have proved to be so controversial in the past that they led to a general strike in 1985. However, a number of vulnerabilities are also laid bare. First, the process primarily depends on the will of all the stakeholders at play in order to work, insofar as there is no legal basis that enforces its use. This dependence is predictable mainly from the side of the political parties, as the last unilateral reform demonstrates, but this also applies to the social partners, as shown by the fact that only half of the reforms were agreed by all of them. Second, bargaining power is attributed *erga omnes* to the most representative trade unions at a national level, regardless of their number of members. The remaining trade unions, including those considered most representative at the level of the autonomous communities, participate in only a limited manner during the parliamentary commission hearings. The general strike called by some major trade unions in some autonomous communities against the 2011 pension reform (Galicia, Basque Country, Navarre and Catalonia), and the emergence of the aforementioned 'Marea Pensionista' pensioner campaign is a good example of this. Thirdly, trade union participation does not adequately maximise the effectiveness of social rights. One of the core recommendations of the Toledo Pact in 1995 was regarding the separation of funding sources of pensions, thereby implying that contributory benefits can only be funded by workers and employers' contributions. The classic cyclical problems associated with a pay-as-you-go pension system are primarily related to periods of high unemployment. Consequently, funds to pay benefits decrease and this is used by political and economic forces as an excuse to deepen reforms that are aimed at reducing public benefits and promoting private pension systems.

Facing the clear limitations and instability of this method of participation in the policy-making process, unions have developed new forms of collective action in order to influence social protection standards in Spain, which we explore in the following section.

3 New Strategies Followed by Unions: New Alliances and the Use of Popular Legislative Initiatives as Instruments of Change

As noted, the participatory role played by unions in the national tripartite social agreements has been irregular and have been conditioned by the political will of the government. This has led unions to develop new strategies using non-traditional instruments to further influence regulatory changes in the field of social protection. This includes the formation of alliances and collaborations with other agents, such as civil society organisations and NGOs at the local and regional levels and the use of popular legislative initiatives as a new form of collective action (Colàs-Neila & Fargas, 2019). A good example of this is the 2017 Guaranteed Minimum Income Act of Catalonia.[12]

Alongside the national social security system, the autonomous communities in Spain can develop and maintain social assistance systems. Within this framework, many of the communities recognise an active insertion income (*renta activa de inserción*), which is an economic benefit aimed at people without adequate economic resources who are at risk of social exclusion; involvement in the 'renta activa' is conditioned by the fact that the beneficiary follows an insertion itinerary. One of the main achievements of what amounts to a guaranteed minimum income, in comparison with those benefits, is that it is not subject to the follow-up of an insertion itinerary. This is intended to provide something that is closer to a basic income scheme, by recognising a guarantee minimum income as a universal right to avoid citizens falling below the poverty line. However, beyond its importance in terms of its content and underlying aims, the mechanism through which the scheme was developed is worth exploring.

---

[12] Catalan Parliament Act No. 14/2017, of 20 July. An analysis of the content of the Act, as conducted by members of the relevant committee, can be seen at Arcarons, Garganté & Toledano (2013).

The popular legislative initiative is an instrument of direct democracy provided for in the legal system of Spain and various autonomous communities (Cabello Fernández, 2017). In the Catalan case, it is regulated by Act No. 1/2006, of 16 February.[13] The Act's statement of reasons defines the initiative as a non-governmental bill proposed by subjects who do not have any decision-making power and which helps to create political debate on some issues that have yet to be raised by political parties despite the interest they have for a sector of the population. Arguably the most important features of this norm refer to the issues upon which the legislative initiative can be implemented, the subjects that have legal standing, the mechanism to be used and the relevant parliamentary procedure.

It is only possible to present a popular legislative initiative for matters that are within the competence of the Catalan Parliament by Spanish or European citizens with legal residence in Spain who do not have their political rights suspended. There is a formalised procedure consisting of two stages. First, the application process implies the need to present a bill (proposal) to the parliament's bureau that has the support of 50,000 persons, whose signatures and personal data can be verified. A promoting committee of the legislative initiative must be created, comprising a minimum of three persons and that must include the proposers of the bill. Second, after it is declared admissible, the usual parliamentary legislative procedure is applied with some small differences to allow for the involvement of the promoting committee.

It follows from the above that this mechanism of legislative participation is intended for use by natural persons and not by associations or legal persons. It is not, therefore, a specific mechanism for trade union participation in the elaboration or promulgation of legal regulations. However, there are extra-legal mechanisms that can allow associations, including unions, to support and engage in their development as member entities, mainly through the collection of signatures. This implication of various types of civic associations, included unions, was one of the reasons the initiative has succeeded.

In the specific case under analysis, the promoting committee presented 121,191 signatures to the Parliament of Catalonia on 20 December 2013, which amounted to more than double the minimum required. There are material and formal reasons explaining this broad support. On the

---

[13] The current consolidated version can be retrieved from https://portaljuridic.gencat.cat/eli/es-ct/l/2006/02/16/1 (Accessed: 15 January 2021).

one hand, this reflects the deep concern in broad sectors of Catalan society regarding the increased rates of poverty within the context of harsh austerity that many citizens had endured in the wake of the post-2008 financial crisis and the associated reduction in public services. On the other hand, as has been suggested, the involvement of various associations—including the unions—was crucial for the collection of so many signatures. The organisational structure of the associations and their coordinated actions allowed the initiative to spread and gain the support of citizens.

This participation was developed at two consecutive levels from a temporal point of view. First, an informal law-making process took place to agree on the contents of the non-governmental bill that was to be proposed, and second, was the formal popular legislative initiative process according to the applicable regulation as noted earlier. In this second stage, the promoting committee was composed of a large number of persons, most of whom represented various civic associations, including the general secretaries of the trade unions that were involved.[14] Moreover, these civic associations appear as member entities, giving public support to the initiative. A total of 73 members that included a diverse variety of associations, among which official associations (*Col·legi d'Educadores i Educadors Socials de Catalunya/Association of Social Educators of Catalonia, Col·legi Oficial de Treball Social de Catalunya/Official Association of Social Work of Catalonia*), neighbourhood associations (*Confederació d'Associacions Veïnals de Catalunya/Confederation of Catalonian Residents' Associations, Federació d'Associació de Veïnes i Veïns de Barcelona/Barcelona Federation of Residents' Associations, Federació de Veïns de Santa Coloma de Gramenet/Federation of Santa Coloma de Gramanet Residents*), political parties (*Candidatura d'Unitat Popular/Popular Unity Candidacy, Esquerra Republicana de Catalunya/Catalan Republican Left, Iniciativa per Catalunya Verds/Initiative for Catalonia—the Green Party*), social movements (*Dempeus per la Salut Pública/Standing for Public Health, Marea Pensionista de Catalunya/Pensioner Tide of Catalonia, Moviment 15 M/15 M Movement*) and trade unions (*Sindicat de Comissions de Base, Comissions Obreres/Workers' Commission of Catalonia, Unió General de Treballadors/the General Workers' Union of Catalonia* and *Unió*

---

[14] The members of the promoting committee can be see here: https://www.rendagarantidaciutadana.net/index.php/ca/membres-comisio (Accessed: 15 January 2021).

Sindical Obrera de Catalunya/Workers' Trade Unionist Confederation of Catalonia).[15]

Beyond the specific instrument used, it is also important to note the diverse stakeholders with whom trade unions are involved with through this strategy, which often differ from those that they traditionally relate to (i.e. business associations and government). These collective actions consist essentially of occasional collaborations with other associations at the local or regional levels in order to achieve a specific goal through their legalisation by means of a legal instrument that is recognised in the legal system. These strategies are not uncommon in comparative law, as Stone and Cummings (2011) show in detail in the case of Los Angeles.[16] As they note, these alliances between trade unions and other community organisations have succeeded in influencing labour conditions through mechanisms other than those usually applied. In this case, the instrument used involves community benefit agreements that were achieved among local government, companies and other actors, such as neighbourhood associations and trade unions.

To conclude this section, it should be noted that there are other examples in Spain at the national level of popular legislative initiatives being supported and developed by various civic associations acting together, including trade unions. This is the case of the popular legislative initiative aimed at introducing changes in mortgage legislation, including the introduction of giving in payment (*datio in solutum*) in mortgage legislation, led by one of the strongest and most renowned social movements created over the past decade: Plataforma de Afectados por la Hipoteca (the Platform for those in mortgage distress).[17]

As Gumbrell-McCormick and Hyman (2013) have pointed out, trade unions must face a process of constant reinvention in order to be effective. This experience of collaboration with other associations by Spanish unions to promote popular legislative initiatives can be seen as a good example of this (often slow) process of adaptation or reinvention.

---

[15] The members supporting the initiative are listed here: https://www.rendagarantidaciutadana.net/index.php/ca/membres-comisio (Accessed: 15 January 2021).

[16] Other relevant examples relating to other American and Canadian cities can be found in Galley (2015).

[17] Information about the various activities developed by them at different levels can be retrieved from https://afectadosporlahipoteca.com/ (Accessed: 15 January 2021).

4 The Emergence of New Actors in the Face of Austerity Policies and Discontent with the Role of Trade Unions within the Toledo Pact: The Case of *Marea Pensionista* and The Combination of Innovative and More Traditional Strategies

Despite the strengths noted with respect to the Toledo Pact, mainly regarding the maximisation of support for new reforms and hence their legitimacy, the fact remains that some sectors of unionism and the wider citizenry have shown their discontent, as discussed above. Moreover, the latest reforms that have been introduced unilaterally have contributed to the emergence of new actors that disagree with the unambiguously regressive orientation and content of these reforms with respect to pension in terms of rights, the main consequence of which is a reduction in the amount of pension. This is the case with the pensioner platforms that have appeared throughout Spain under the name *Marea Pensionista* over recent years.

The Marea Pensionista is a clear example of the various anti-austerity social movements that have emerged in Spain over the past decade. Using a common title of Marea (in English, tide), these movements have drawn together different civil society associations, including trade unions, that have exerted pressure on the national and regional governments to reverse regulations that reduced the budgets of certain public services. These movements have focused their actions on particular areas of public services, using a distinctive colour added to their common name, with 'Marea Blanca' (white tide) for health care, 'Marea Verde' (green tide) for public education and 'Marea Naranja' (orange wave) for social services.[18] However, as noted previously, there is strong discontent within the pensioner movement regarding the actions of the most representative unions at a national level in the agreed social security reforms within the context of the Toledo Pact which complicates the relations between some elements of the trade union movement with the prominent Marea Pensionista.

---

[18] Regarding these social movements, including the methods of the 15 M movement and their relations with the trade union movement, see Luque Balbona & González Begega (2016).

As López López (2015) has noted, Spanish trade unions have combined litigation, as an innovative mode of protest, alongside more traditional mechanisms. And this 'hybridisation' has been reproduced in this social movement strategy. Traditional methods and forms of action including rallies, demonstrations and informative meetings on the consequences of legal reforms have been combined with the pursuit of legal proceedings.

These platforms are organised locally and have achieved national coordination through the 'Coordinadora Estatal para la Defensa del Sistema Público de Pensiones' (the State Coordinator for the Defense of the Public Pension System).[19] This multilevel territorial area of tireless action and the multiplicity of traditional instruments used have meant that more and more citizens become aware of the consequences of the proposed pension reforms, even if they were not yet directly affected by them. Two examples of this are the weekly rallies held in town and city squares throughout the country which began in Bilbao and spread to other cities such as Barcelona or Valencia, that continued almost uninterrupted for more than two years, and more recently with a coordinated march to Madrid, in 2019, where a massive demonstration was held, bringing together thousands of pensioners from different parts of Spain.[20] The conjunction of various political, economic and social circumstances, including the pressure exerted by these groups using such traditional instruments, succeeded in paralysing some of the government's initiatives, including two specific legal interventions, namely: the 2018 State Budget Act and subsequent different exceptional pension revaluations that had been passed by the government.

The 2018 Stage Budget Act had been passed in the middle of that year, after many months of paralysis and difficulties in reaching an agreement between the PP—who were in government at the time—and other parliamentary forces. The Partido Nacionalista Vasco/ Euzko Alderdi Jeltzalea (PNV/EAJ—Basque Nationalist Party) finally voted in favour following a number of amendments, including some important changes in the field of social security that they had pushed for. This position of the PNV/EAJ

---

[19] More information can be accessed here: https://www.facebook.com/COESPE/ and https://twitter.com/pensionazo_no?lang=ca (Accessed: 15 January 2021).

[20] Regarding the march to Madrid and subsequent demonstration, see https://elpais.com/economia/2019/10/15/actualidad/1571167586_016091.html (Accessed: 15 January 2021).

regarding this field can be explained by the demonstrations led by the group of pensioners in the Basque Country (Nagusiak, Asociación de Pensionistas de Bizkaia/Bizkaia Pensioners' Association),[21] which were especially large, and the fact that the pensioner collective has a major presence in the main electoral bases of the party. As a consequence, their voice was taken into consideration in the position adopted by the party within the Spanish parliament. The aspects introduced in the budget law as a result of this were not minor, and included several far-reaching measures.

This included a gradual increase of bereavement allowances over the next two years, from 56 per cent to 60 per cent of the regulatory basis of calculation (This is an amount expressing the average amount of contributions made over a period of time that the lawmaker uses to calculate the pension.). The significant gender impact of this measure should be noted, given that 92% of beneficiaries are women (Secretaría de Estado de Seguridad Social, 2019). The other two major changes are related to Act 23/2013, one important piece of the last unilateral reform that had been introduced by the PP government, which introduced a sustainability factor and a new revaluation index of social security pensions. The 2018 Stage Budget Act delayed the entry into force of the sustainability factor from 2019 to 2023. The sustainability factor is a new index measurement resulted from a complex formula that links the calculation of the pension to life expectancy at the moment the benefit is obtained, and it is aimed at guaranteeing the financial sustainability of the public system of social security. However, the new index would have very negative consequences in terms of social sustainability; according to Zuribi (2016), there will be a reduction of the benefit which is estimated to be in the order of 35% lower for new pensioners in 2050. Regarding the revaluation index for pensions, it was increased beyond the legal parameters fixed unilaterally by the PP. While the formula implemented by Act 23/2013 only guaranteed a minimum increase of 0.25% per annum, which was applicable from 2014 to 2017, the 2018 State Budget Act amounting to an exceptional increase of 1.6% for 2018.

The pressure exerted by pensioner platforms achieved some other minor but important outcomes as regards this last point following the 2018 Budget Act, which has also had an important influence on the sociopolitical context in Spain. The associated political context has been

---

[21] Information on this association can be retrieved from https://sites.google.com/view/nagusiak/berriak-noticias-news?authuser=0 (Accessed: 15 January 2021).

characterised by strong tensions. Almost simultaneously to the approval of the budget, a vote of no confidence was held against the PP government that allowed PSOE to assume government. Two general elections took place during 2019 but parliament has been unable to elect a new president until the beginning of 2020. The almost continuous election campaign experienced during this time possibly helped the government to become more sensitive to the demands of the vocal and well-organised pensioner platforms, especially when we consider that pensioners represent a significant number of votes (and a cohort that tends to vote in high numbers). As a consequence, the application of the regulation in this field has remained temporarily suspended and exceptional specific revaluations have been passed, namely: 1.6% for 2018 and 2019 and 0.9% for 2020. However, despite their relative success, the pensioners did not achieve their ultimate goal, namely, the repeal of the 2013 reform and the return to the previous indexation system, which was based on the consumer price index, so as to protect purchasing power.

On the other hand, resort to judicial proceedings has been another instrument that some unions have pursued to try to reverse regressive legal changes. Simply put, this approach involves the ultimate pursuit of solutions being externalised to the judiciary (López López, 2019). This approach has also been emulated by the aforementioned platforms, including *Marea Pensionista* in Barcelona with support from the *Col·lectiu Ronda*, a lawyers' cooperative, through the submission of various lawsuits against the Social Security General Fund [*Tesorería General de la Seguridad Social*], whereby a number of pensioners set out reasons for why the constitutional interpretation of the regressive reforms should be overturned.

Before the aforementioned Act 23/2013 was passed, a piece of legislation was enacted, through the Decree Law 28/2012, that suspended the legal criteria to revaluate pensions linked to the consumer price index, which would have implied an increase of 2.9% instead of that fixed at 1 per cent. The claims initially were based on the constitutionality of the norm. However, before the hearings, the Constitutional Court declared that the measure was fully in accordance with the constitution,[22] following an

---

[22] Judgement 49/2015, of 05 March 2015 (ECLI:ES:TC:2015:49) found that the constitutional principle of non-retroactivity was not breached by the measure, and that citizens did not have a vested right to a pension indexation according to the consumer price index, but a mere expectation.

opposite trend to that of other European constitutional courts in substantially the same situations.[23] Facing this, the lawsuits increased reference other international standards, including the European Charter of Socials Rights and the case law of the European Committee of Social Rights, especially in the cases submitted by Greek trade unions against austerity measures.[24] As a consequence, various judgements of the Social Courts of Barcelona were issued, albeit only on one occasion did they uphold the pensioners' claims.[25] Despite its very limited effects, this strategy helped to trigger a modest debate within the judiciary, expressed in some decisions regarding the direct application of international standards to the Spanish pension system. Such precedents are usually rarely cited used in this field, although they have revealed themselves to be an important way for unions and other social movements to cope with regressive legal reforms that were introduced under austerity.

5 Some Tentative Conclusions

The Toledo Pact is a mechanism that provides for the involvement of diverse interests of political and social actors in the promulgation of reforms relating to matters of a politically highly sensitive nature—such as public pension provision. It could be said that this is a manifestation of the will of the constituent to give equal weight to a wide range of voices in the democratic shaping of the rules that govern society, including the recognition of the trade unions as relevant actors in the sociopolitical arena. As

---

[23] Significantly in Portugal (Judgement 862/12, of 19 December 2012, declaring the reduction of pensions contrary to the legitimate expectations of the beneficiaries) and in Italy (Judgment 70/2015, of 10 March 2015, according to which the measure was not proportional nor reasonable and was against the legitimate expectations of employees).

[24] *Federation of pensioners (IKA-ETAM) v Greece* (Complaint No. 76/2012), *Panhellenic Federation of Public Service Pensioners v Greece*, (Complaint No. 77/2012), *Pensioners' Union of the Athens-Piraeus Electric Railways (ISAP) v Greece* (Complaint No. 78/2012), *Panhellenic Federation of Pensioners of the Public Electricity Corporation (POS-DEI) v Greece* (Complaint No. 79/2012), and *Pensioner's Union of the Agricultural Bank of Greece (ATE) v Greece* (Complaint No. 80/2012).

[25] The plaintiffs' grounds were upheld by Judgement of the Social Court No. 12 of Barcelona, of 04 September 2015 (ECLI: ES:JSO:2015:60), despite the High Court of Catalonia reversing it. On the other hand, Judgement of the Social Court No. 10 of Barcelona, of 12 June 2015, and Judgement of the Social Court No. 31 of Barcelona, of 08 June 2015, while considering the European Charter of Social Rights to be directly applicable, deemed that the regulations were not contravened.

a result, regulatory outcomes can be seen as an expression of the widest possible majority from across the political and social spheres. Despite the fact that the Toledo Pact has once again been activated, after the 2013 unilateral reforms, its main weaknesses have led to the search for alternative ways for unions and other social movement organisations to try to further influence the legislative process.

On the one hand, the pact's subjection to political will, which can also be a barrier to union participation, led trade unions to explore new strategies. The alliances with other stakeholders for a specific purpose through their involvement with popular legislative initiative are an encouraging example that demonstrates the unions' ability to adapt and strive to further develop their functions and scope. The Catalan case demonstrates the potential for unions to influence the introduction of legislative changes that improve the protection of the most vulnerable. Trade unions are living organisations that are adapting to all manner of changes taking place around them, albeit very slowly most of the time. This experience can be presented as a manifestation of how the opportunities to promote solidarity associated with the network society can be maximised. Thus, traditional and formalised instruments (such as the popular legislative initiative) can be combined with the support of digital technology, bringing different stakeholders together, including trade unions.

On the other hand, the social discontent in the wake of some government reforms suggest that perhaps even more perspectives should be taken into account for the effective functioning of the Toledo Pact, and in order to maximise its democratic representativeness. Meanwhile, most representative trade unions should try to forge alliances with different organisations and citizen platforms and should actively integrate as wide a range of perspectives as possible, so as to defend and bolster their position in the tripartite bargaining process. Pensioner platforms have demonstrated their ability to indirectly influence legal reforms by combining innovative methods with more traditional instruments, the latter of which have proven to still be effective in many scenarios. Ultimately, the views of pensioners and other cohorts in society should be taken into account by trade unions to make their organisations more open and relevant to the widest socio-economic spectrum and to be as representative and relevant as possible.

References

Arcarons, J., Garganté, S., & Toledano, D. (2013). *Rescatem les persones : preguntes i respostes sobre la iniciativa legislativa popular per la renda garantida de ciutadania*. Barcelona: Icaria.

Bogg, A., & Ewing, K. D. (2017). The Continuing Evolution of European Labour Law and the Changing Context for Trade Union Organizing. *Comp. Lab. L. & Pol'y J.*, *38*, 211 232.

Bonoli, G. (2003). Two Worlds of Pension Reform in Western Europe. *Comparative Politics*, 35 (4).

Cabello Fernández, M. D. (2017). *Democracia directa e iniciativa legislativa popular*. Valencia : Tirant lo Blanch.

Chacartegui, C. (2016). Introducción. In C. Chacartegui (Ed.), *Negociación colectiva y gobernanza de las relaciones laborales: una lectura de la jurisprudencia tras la reforma laboral* (pp. 7–12). Albacete: Bomarzo.

Colàs-Neila, E. (2018). Pension reforms and participation in Spain. *Studia z Zakresu Prawa Pracy i Polityki Społecznej*, *25*(4), 415–428.

Colàs-Neila, E., & Fargas, J. (2019). Guaranteed Minimum Income: New Spaces for Trade Union Action. *Oñati Socio-Legal Series*, 109–127.

Ewing, K. D. (2014). The Importance of Trade Union Political Voice. Labour Law Meets Constitutional Law. In A. Bogg & T. Novitz (Eds.), *Voices at Work. Continuiny and Change in the Common Law Work* (pp. 277–299). Oxford: Oxford University Press.

Fishman, R. M. (1990). *Working-class organization and the return to democracy in Spain*. Ithaca [N.Y.]: Cornell University Press.

Galley, A. (2015). Community Benefits Agreements. *Mowat Research*, (110).

Gumbrell-McCormick, R., & Hyman, R. (2013). *Trade Unions in Western Europe. Hard Times, Hard Choices*. Oxford: Oxford University Press.

López López, J. (2015). Anti-austerity Activism Strategies: Combining Protest and Litigation in Spain. In A. Blackett & A. Trebilcock (Eds.), *Research Handbook on Transnational Labour Law* (pp. 164–180). Cheltenham: Edward Elgar.

López López, J. (2019). Modes of Collective Action: Judicialisation as a Form of Protest. In J. López López (Ed.), *Collective Bargaining and Collective Action. Labour Agency and Governance in the 21st Century?* (pp. 41–56). Hart Publishing.

Luque Balbona, D., & González Begega, S. (2016). Crisis económica y coaliciones anti-austeridad en España (2010-2014). Viejos y nuevos repertorios de protesta. *Sociología Del Trabajo*, (87), 45–67.

Natali, D., & Stamati, F. (2013). Reforming pensions in Europe: a comparative country analysis (ETUI Working Papers No. 2013.08). Brussels.

OECD. (2019). Pensions at a Glance 2019. Country Profile: Spain. Retrieved from https://www.oecd.org/els/public-pensions/PAG2019-country-profile-Spain.pdf

Panizo Robles, J. A. (2011). Dos décadas de reformas de la Seguridad Social: Del Pacto de Toledo de 1995 al Acuerdo Social y Económico de 2011. *Revista de Trabajo y Seguridad Social*.

Pecinovsky, P. (2019). EU Economic governance and the right to collective bargaining: Part 2. From imposed restrictions of the right by EU Member States towards a social economic governance. *European Labour Law Journal*, (1), 43–68.

Pulignano, V., Köhler, H.-D., & Stewart, P. (ed.) (2016). *Employment relations in an era of change. Multi-level challenges and responses in Europe*. Brussels: ETUI.

Rodgers, G., & Rodgers, J. (1989). *Precarious Jobs in Labour Market Regulation: The Growth of Atypical Employment in Western Europe*. Brussels: ILO.

Secretaría de Estado de Seguridad Social. (2019). *Pensiones de la Seguridad Social (Enero 2019)*. Madrid. Retrieved from https://revista.seg-social.es/wp-content/uploads/2018/11/Datos-pensiones-noviembre-2018.pdf.

Stone, K. V. W. (2004). *From Widgets to Digits. Employement Regulation for the Changing Workplace*. Cambridge: Cambridge University Press.

Stone, K. V. W., & Cummings, S. (2011). Labor Activism in Local Politics: From CBAs to "CBAs." In G. Davidov & B. Langille (Eds.), *The Idea of Labour Law*. Oxford: Oxford University Press.

Suárez-Corujo, B. (2014). *El sistema público de pensiones: crisis, reforma y sostenibilidad*. Valladolid: Lex Nova - Thomson Reuters.

Tortuero Plaza, J. L., del Aguila Cazorla, O., Martín Jiménez, E., & Moreno Romero, F. (2010). *La reforma de la jubilacion: Políticas de pensiones y políticas de empleo* (Premios FIPROS - Fondo para el Fomento de la Investigación de la Protección Social). Retrieved from http://www.seg-social.es/prdi00/groups/public/documents/binario/143941.pdf

Zuribi, I. (2016). Las pensiones en España: situación y alternativas de reforma. *Papeles de Economía Española*, (147), 167–187.

CHAPTER 11

Danish Trade Unions and Young People: Using Media in the Battle for Hearts and Minds

Torsten Geelan

1 Introduction

Denmark has often been considered the industrial relations (IR) model par excellence with high levels of union membership, density and collective bargaining[1]. Over the last decade, however, the institutional context has transformed considerably.[2] One of the most worrying trends is the decline in union membership, after many years as one of the few

---

[1] A 2010 study using material from the Danish statistical office and the employers' federation DA found that 71% of those employed in the private sector and 100% of those in the public sector were covered by collective bargaining in 2007. This produces an average level of coverage of 80% (LO 2010a).

[2] For an overview of these institutional changes, which include cuts to unemployment benefits and union exclusion from the labour market policy process, see Jørgensen and Schulze (2012).

T. Geelan (✉)
Department of Sociology, University of Copenhagen, Copenhagen, Denmark
e-mail: tg@soc.ku.dk

advanced European economies in which union membership remained steady (Blanchflower 2007). The decline has been most severe for the Danish Confederation of Trade Unions and its affiliates (LO)[3]; between 2000 and 2014, LO unions lost approximately a third of all their members, a drop from 1,208,000 to 867,000. One of the drivers is structural change in the composition of the workforce that has caused natural membership of LO unions to drop, and other sectors of the labour force to grow (see Table 2 in the Appendix).

The other important factor has been the Conservative-Liberal Coalition Government's liberalisation of unemployment insurance in 2002, which successfully weakened the Ghent system[4] of union administered unemployment insurance that acts as an effective recruitment mechanism (see Lind 2009 for a detailed discussion). This labour market reform and subsequent ones (e.g. lowering the percentage of union membership that is tax deductible) has allowed competing organisations that do not engage in collective bargaining—referred to as the 'ideological alternative unions'—to compete for members with their offer of cheap unemployment insurance.

Particularly worrisome for the LO labour movement has been the ideological alternative union's successful recruitment of young workers, a target group which these organisations dedicate large resources to recruiting using cutting edge marketing strategies and new media. Since the turn of the century, union density among young[5] people between the ages has fallen from 67.5% in 1994 to 51.1% in 2008 (LO 2010b) and the adult-youth gap in density has doubled. The popularity of the ideological alternative unions among young people has continued unabated during

---

[3] The peak organization has 17 member unions whose membership comprises all categories of manual workers (skilled, semi-skilled and unskilled) and a little less than half of salaried employees, including groups such as office clerks, shop assistants and technical assistants.

[4] The Ghent system of union administered unemployment insurance has been the most influential explanation of union membership stability, providing a strong incentive for workers to join unions to protect themselves from the ebbs and flows of the business cycle (Ebbinghaus and Visser 1999). Others have pointed to the low degree of competition over members among Danish unions (Scheuer 2007: 234). Both of which have now changed in a fundamental way.

[5] There is no agreed upon age range for the category 'young people'. For this paper the age range is 15–39 due to the classifications used in the survey data. Other research in this area sets the cut-off point slightly lower at 35 (Cheung et al. 2012: 303).

the economic recession as LO unions struggle to recruit new labour market entrants. Young people are prime candidates for recruitment because they have little experience of the labour market and workplace-related issues and are therefore unlikely to have understood the important difference between a union that engages in collective bargaining and one that does not, free riding and undermining collective organisation in the labour market.

The decline in union membership poses a serious threat to the power resources of the LO and its affiliated federate unions. As we know, membership provides unions with the fundamental basis from which to exert power within the labour market and the political arena. Including material and human resources, strength and legitimacy in collective bargaining with employers and in negotiations with Governments, and the ability to engage in collective action. In this way, union membership cuts across other forms of union power, which explains its pervasive use in the literature as a crude indicator of the vitality of labour movements.[6] In the long term, the decline in Danish union membership and density also threatens the Danish tradition of voluntarism, in which the social partners self-regulate wages and working conditions through collective bargaining, assuming that high union density is a prerequisite for this form of wage regulation.

In an effort to establish how best to tackle the decline in union membership, the LO initiated a Gallup survey in 2011 to investigate the public's understanding of the role of trade unions in the labour market, with a view to determining why an increasing number of workers were choosing the ideological alternative unions. It revealed that almost 70% of the public thought that wages and conditions were agreed at the Parliamentary level and not by trade unions, a finding that was even higher for young people. Thus there was little understanding of the benefits of choosing to become a member of a LO union, which is more expensive than an ideological alternative union. The survey findings were presented at the LO Congress in 2011, and to address the publics limited understanding LO affiliates agreed to commit financial and human resources

---

[6] Although what exactly union membership is a measurement of has been shown to vary considerably with the cultural, geographical and temporal specificities in which it is embedded (Sullivan 2010). A high level of union membership can mask a low level of membership engagement and capacity for mobilisation, and vice versa as in the case of France.

over the next four years of the congress period to develop and launch a campaign (LO 2011)—marking a clear shift in strategy from political mobilisations to union organising following the election of a Social Democratic-led coalition Government just months earlier.

This paper presents a case study of the 'Are you OK?' campaign launched in 2012 by the LO and the Confederation of Professionals in Denmark (FTF). Together these two organisations represent almost 100 affiliated unions and 30,000 shop stewards. The campaigns aim is to increase knowledge of collective bargaining and collective organisation among the public, particularly among 20- to 40-year-olds, and for this knowledge to provide the foundation for more union members, thereby strengthening collective bargaining and collective organisation, and increasing its legitimacy. The campaign uses a variety of communication forms to reach existing and potential union members and is the largest of its kind in the history of the Danish labour movement. The central research questions it addresses are:

- What is the campaign's message?
- What forms of communication are used?
- How effective has the campaign been in reaching and informing young people?

2   Trade Unions, Young People and the Media

Changing the image of trade unions is a central aspect of union attempts to organise young workers and for good reason. An analysis of the European Social Survey (Schnabel and Wagner 2007) found that attitudinal variables (being positive towards union influence at work and in society) play an important role in the determining the likelihood of union membership.[7] Similarly, a recent cross-national study (Scheuer 2011) found that employees indicating high or very high support for unions have a four out of ten density (38 and 42%), while those less supportive have densities ranging from 23 to 35%. Knowledge of how the labour market functions is also shown to play an important role; the perceived

---

[7] In Denmark, a recent Gallup poll conducted on May Day 2014 found that 69% of the public felt that the LO labour movement has an important function in society. Accessed at: http://www.lo.dk/English%20version/News/may%20day.aspx.

presence of a collective agreement triples the likelihood of union membership. This finding is especially pertinent for the study at hand, in which the Danish public is unaware of who engages in collective bargaining, and hence, one would assume also unaware of whether they are covered by such agreements. The take home message is that while the likelihood of unionisation is determined by institutional and compositional factors such as those highlighted earlier, changing public attitudes towards unions and their understanding of the role trade unions play in the labour market is one area where unions can make a difference.

Efforts to influence the attitudes of young workers towards trade unions and collective organisation are directed towards two spheres of influence: the educational system and the mass media.

2.1 Education

The formative experience of education shapes young people's values, their understanding of work and the labour market, and how they interpret their later transition into it. Education also provides the interpretive framework through which young people process the mediated discourses they are exposed to. By influencing the curriculum one can help ensure that it reflects the realities of work and highlights the importance of collective organisation, providing " a more solid background for the reception of media messages on trade unions" (Walsh 1988: 215). In the light of this it can be plausibly argued, "the greatest weapon for unions might lie in education at school, so that those youngsters with core characteristics become members when joining the workforce, regardless of union presence or power at any particular workplace" (Cregan and Johnson 1990: 101).

From this perspective, the public's limited knowledge of the Danish labour market and the collective bargaining system is a failure both of the educational system to properly inform its citizenry and a failure of union engagement. To influence the curriculum, unions have initiated projects that aim to provide teachers at all levels with information about unions and their contribution to workers and society, and sent speakers to schools to answer student's questions. When the LO-initiated Gallup survey mentioned earlier was made public in 2011, it stimulated a political discussion among unions and the political parties about the need for reforming the school curriculum to include a more comprehensive treatment of the labour market. What the content should be, and how this could be achieved, was subject to heated political debate—a reminder of the deeply politicised nature of education. At the moment of writing, the LO's youth consultant and their network of federate youth consultants and student groups (see Geelan 2013a: 405) are focusing their efforts on developing new educational materials in collaboration with the centre-left think tank CEVEA. Exploring new ways of getting teachers to adopt them, given the logistical difficulty and limited efficacy of sending speakers out to schools with very diverse audiences.[8]

2.2 Media

The mass media is the other sphere that unions engage in to influence the attitudes of young people, and the one that this study predominantly focuses on. This external dimension to union communication refers to union engagement through different types of communication channels (McCormick and Hyman 2013: 153). Numerous studies in the Anglophone countries have shown a consistent negative news media bias towards trade unions and industrial conflict (e.g. O'Neil 2007). The image portrayed is often one of scrupulous bureaucratic organisations that are against any form of modernisation and deplore any form of individuality.[9] As Hodder (2014: 163) rightly points out, "the impact the media plays in the public perception of trade unions cannot be understated". This persisting media bias can partly be attributed to the decline of the industrial correspondent declining union resources, which have made it more difficult for unions to produce news in-house and keep up with the latest trends in journalism.

The LO provides one example of how unions can attempt to address this imbalance. Since 2011, the LO youth consultant has spearheaded an effort to increase the media coverage of young workers by training young union activists to be influence the scope of public debate. The potential to reach young people through the Internet and social media (e.g. Facebook, YouTube and Twitter) has also received considerable attention in recent years (e.g. Bryson et al. 2010), as this demographic spends

---

[8] In the UK, the TUC and PCS have been involved in this type of work for some time, an emphasis that has also continued since the onset of the great recession of 2008 (Hodder 2014: 163).

[9] For a detailed discussion of this see the DPhil thesis of Thomas (2012) on trade unions and newspaper tabloids in the UK between 2001 and 2010.

more time on them than any other segment of the workforce. While existing research has explored the types of media employed by unions (Panagiotopoulos and Barnett 2014) and highlighted the importance of considering the audience (Panagiotopoulos 2012), there is little empirical work on how the Internet and social media is used in practice to organise or campaign. My own research has only begun to scratch the surface (Geelan 2013a, b). Moreover, the overwhelming attention these new forms of communication have received neglects the continued importance of traditional forms of mass media that are still very much in use by unions such as radio, television and union magazines. This appears to be an unfortunate case of throwing out the baby with the bathwater. These other mediums deserve just as much, if not more attention; television, for example, is still the most powerful medium for shaping the opinions and concerns of the mass audience as argued by Walsh (1988). Thus, to overcome this gap in our understanding of how trade unions use the media to engage with and influence the attitudes of young people, this article includes all forms of communication in its analysis.

In order to achieve this, one can fruitfully draw on the theoretical work of Manuel Castells. For the case study at hand, it is most pertinent to review the different forms of communication and their organisation.

2.3 *Theorising Communication*

Castells distinguishes between three types of communication in the twenty-first century (Castells 2009: 54–55):

(1) interpersonal communication (conversations between two people in person, over the phone or via email);
(2) traditional mass communication that is mostly one-directional (as with books, newspapers, films, radio and television);
(3) and mass self-communication, a historically new form of communication in which a large audience can be reached at little or no cost to the individual through the Internet and social media.

Trade unions, like any other large collective organisation, engage in all these forms of communication simultaneously when conducting campaigns. They have also begun adapting to the trend in communication technology towards multi-media systems; facilitated through the

Internet, individuals are increasingly using it to access, consume and share mass media (television, radio, newspapers) as well as any form of digitised cultural or informational product (films, music, magazines, books, journal articles, databases) (Castells 2009: 64). Unions are therefore increasingly required to be present on an increasing number of communication platforms with digital content to reach existing and potential members and engage with the public and mainstream media.

In order to analyse the 'Are you OK?' campaigns use of media it is also necessary to understand the media consumption patters of the target group (Crane 1986) and explore how young people compare to other age groups. Analysis from the latest annual report of the Danish Association of Interactive Media (FDIM 2012) shows that the Danes love the Internet, which continues to increase its share of the average minutes per day spent on media (totalling 6 hours and 40 minutes in 2011) from 80 minutes in 2008 to 100 minutes in 2011. Contrasted with the continued dominance of TV with 140 minutes and the steady decline of print and radio. A related trend is the mobile phone which has also increased its share to 40 minutes in 2011 with 55% of Danes between 16 and 74 using it to access the Internet; its' most common use being navigation (41%), apps (39%), email (37%) and news (32%).

If one breaks down the average minutes spent per day on media and compares young people to the other age groups, the data in Fig. 1 reveals marked differences in media consumption.

The most notable differences between age groups are:

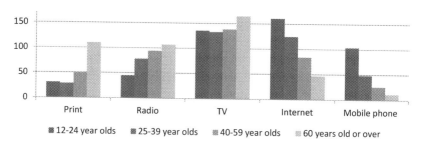

Fig. 1 Average time spent daily on media platforms according to age (*Source* FDIM [2012, p. 8])

(1) *Print:* young people between 12 and 39 use just 30 minutes on print whereas those over 60 used 110 minutes
(2) *Radio*: the upward slope reveals a clear generational shift in popularity, with the 12–24-year-olds spending just half the time consuming this medium relative to the other age groups
(3) TV: at a high level of 140 minutes for all age groups except those over 60, its continued dominance as a form of medium is clear
(4) Internet: the 12- to 24-year-olds spent more time on the Internet (160 minutes) and mobile phones (100 minutes) than TV, radio and print combined (210 minutes). Similarly those between 25 and 39 used 170 minutes on the former and 135 minutes on the latter.

The implications of these trends in media consumption are that while young people can still be reached through traditional mass media, the Internet has clearly become the most important form of communication for the youngest generations. While all age groups are heavy users of social media, young people between the ages of 15 and 34 are the heaviest users with the two most popular platforms being Facebook and YouTube[10] (FDIM 2012: 22). Consuming and sharing content (news, culture) in a variety of digital forms through these mediums has also become mainstream (DR 2014), supporting Castells argument outlined earlier. Given that this sharing is socially driven (see Lee and Barry 2014) and social contacts play an important role in shaping attitudes (Griffen and Brown 2011: 97), an effective union campaign should strive to tap into these networks of young people and provide information in a way that can be easily shared.

It is also important to consider how different organisations use these forms of communication. In Castells' (2009) theoretical work on communication power, the network is becoming the dominant mode of organising communication and power increasingly lies in the capacity of actors to shape these networks of communication to disseminate their own values in the battle for hearts and minds. From this perspective, it is commonly argued that the hierarchically organised labour movements will struggle to adapt to the new media environment. Compared to the

---

[10] YouTube is one of the most well-known and widely discussed sites of participatory media in the contemporary online environment, and it is the first genuinely mass-popular platform for user-created video. For an overview, see Burgess and Green's (2009) book *YouTube: Online Video and Participatory Culture.*

new social movements such as Occupy and the Los Indignados movement (Castells 2012) whose horizontal network of grassroots organisations are structured around the logic of the Internet and organised through it, rendering their use of social media far more dynamic.

There is evidence, however, of unions adopting similar networked modes of organisation and communication. The most notable of which are Union Solidarity International (Geelan 2013a) and the Peoples Assembly Against Austerity in the UK and Working America in the USA. These new organisations suggest that a new form of networked labour unionism is emerging which fuses the power of the Internet and social media with the power of networks. The extent to which this will help foster a broader revitalisation remains to be seen, but it is certainly increasing their communicative reach to include the unorganised and disinterested.

But there are of course difficulties of achieving this type of networked unionism in practice. Hecksher and Carre (2006: 619–620) identify four key mechanisms needed for collaborative networks to succeed: shared information platforms; shared behavioural norms; a common mission; and (effective) governance. All of this must be coordinated by an actor which can be called the 'network orchestrator', with relatively little power or size, but with the credibility to coordinate wide ranges of independent players. In the labour movement, this role is typically played by the peak union, which draws on the power of its affiliated unions to organise, coordinate and campaign for their shared interests. Once established, however, such networks also have serious weaknesses. The most common is their tendency to fragment and splinter, and the difficulty of maintaining strategic unity over time (Hecksher and Carre 2006: 617). Each union has its own modus operandi and interests that render collaborative networks very difficult to establish and maintain in the long term.

Having reviewed the theoretical and empirical background of the study, the next section outlines the case study approach adopted and the data used to examine how Danish unions are using the media in the battle for the hearts and minds of young people.

3   Data and Method

A case study approach (Ragin and Becker 1992; Yin 2009) was utilised, drawing on data from two non-participant observations, semi-structured interviews with union officials and secondary analysis of survey data. The sample of organisations is the confederate actor, the LO (the FTF was excluded due to the lack of survey data), and four of its largest affiliated federate unions:

- The Danish Union of Public Employees (FOA)
- The Union of Commercial and Clerical Employees (HK)
- The Danish Metalworkers Union (Dansk Metal)
- The United Federation of Danish Workers (3F).

The sample of organisations was selected for a combination of reasons: first, because access had already been attained to three of the organisations during prior research; second, because including actors at both the confederate and federate level that are working together on a campaign allows for exploration of how unions use the media in a networked mode of coordinated action. This helps shed light on the coordinating role of peak unions and their strategy and fits well with Castells' characterisation of communication power and the importance of networks. The case study aims to provide a rich theoretical case that will further our understanding of how trade unions can, and do, use the mass media in their efforts to change the image of trade unions among young people.

Data collection began in October 2012 during a yearlong fieldwork trip to Copenhagen, Denmark, as part of a larger doctoral research project on the production and dissemination of discourse through the media within the context of austerity in Denmark and the United Kingdom. This gave me the opportunity to observe campaign pitches by prospective media consultancy firms at the LO's central office, providing first-hand insight into the complexities of developing coordinated union campaigns. Shortly after the launch of the campaign in the beginning of 2013, I also attended meetings with senior union officials and researchers discussing the campaign's concept and aims.

After returning to the UK, another round of data was collected during an intensive fieldwork trip in June 2014. This involved interviewing the Head of Communication at each of the sampled unions and senior officials in the organising department of the LO. The interviews focused on how each organisation was involved in the OK campaign, their use of media, and the challenges of reaching the different demographic segments of the workforce with specific attention given to young people.

Finally, survey data on public attitudes gathered by Gallup on behalf of the LO is used in order to provide an indicative analysis of the campaign's efficacy. 1,246 respondents were surveyed in four rounds: October 2012, June 2013, December 2013, and May 2014. The target group consisted of individuals in unions affiliated to the LO, members of ideological alternative unions and the unorganised. Demographic and labour market data was collected from all the participants. The survey questions focused on the medium through which individuals were exposed to the campaign, their opinions of it, their knowledge of collective bargaining and their capacity to distinguish between LO unions and the ideological alternative unions.

4 The 'Are you OK?' Campaign

This section analyses three dimensions of the campaign: the message, its organisational structure, and finally, its impact on young people's attitudes and their understanding of the labour market.

4.1 Message

The campaign concept draws on an existing phenomenon in Danish culture. In Denmark, restaurants are regularly inspected and the results (e.g. hygiene, work conditions, etc.) are displayed in the entrance. Depending on the findings, a smiley is awarded. It can be happy, satisfied or unhappy and is published on a green backdrop in the storefront. Customers can then base their decision to eat at the establishment on this information. The campaign essentially applies this concept to the labour market by branding the LO unions that engage in collective bargaining with the green 'OK' logo (see Figure 3 in the Appendix), something which is easily integrated into the existing communication and organisation efforts of the federate unions involved, each with different capacities, interests and political cultures. The title of the campaign also plays on the acronym used in the media when referring to a collective bargaining round in the public or private sector—OK 2014—or whatever the year may be. The question in the campaign 'Are you OK?' seeks to start conversations about whether one is unionised or not and to highlight the importance of collective agreements and organisation. As an excerpt from a flyer explains:

This question is important for Danish wage earners. It concerns collective agreements and collectivism at the workplace. And it is about spreading the message about what collective agreements are and why it is important. (LO 2014)

Finally, and perhaps most importantly, the campaign highlights the concrete benefits that collective agreements provide: namely, good wages, maternity, pension, an extra weeks vacation and possibilities for continuing education. All the interviewees felt that this was particularly important to do because young people always ask the question—what's in it for me? By informing them of the benefits of union membership, the hope is that it will help shift their decision-making process, considered to be more rational and short-term. The message, however, is uniform and never explicitly segmented according to age or any other category, although each form of communication used of course has a predominance of certain demographics as highlighted earlier. This is a surprising finding. It is not enough for unions to simply use the communication technologies that young people spend their time on; they must also communicate using language, visuals and messages that resonate with them (Bailey et al. 2010: 57). Focus groups could be especially helpful in this regard.

4.2   Organisational Structure

The campaign draws on a complex network of organisations and their existing communication capacities. Conceptually, one can distinguish between four levels: peak, federate, branch and workplace.

At the peak level, the LO is responsible for using its institutional mandate and legitimacy to coordinate and steer the campaign activities. This includes liasoning with the contracted consultancy bureau and overseeing a meeting of union officials from the organisation and communication departments of its affiliates every three months to discuss campaign strategy and development. The LO's full-time youth consultant and the LO network of federate youth consultants and student groups (see Geelan 2013a) have, however, not been very actively involved in the campaign as their efforts are focused on the more immediate issues of unemployment and the lack of apprenticeships. In terms of communication, the LO is responsible for managing the campaign Facebook group (with 20,000 likes as of July 9, 2014) and has taken the lead on developing campaign videos (discussed in detail in the following section).

At the federate level, the four sampled unions each use their communication channels (based at their headquarters) to reach existing and potential members. The forms of communication include two-way communication (email, phone), mass media (electronic newsletters to their members and shop stewards, union magazines which all members receive in print) and the Internet (website, Facebook and YouTube). They also disseminate electronic campaign materials to their branches as well as physical materials (beach balls, key rings and dummies). Similar to the LO, the youth consultants are not actively involved in the campaign.

Finally, and perhaps most importantly, are the union branches and their relation to the workplace through each trade union's shop stewards. All the interviewees felt that the campaigns success was ultimately dependent on the extent to which the campaign was able to generate awareness at the workplace, and regarded the two-way communication of their shop stewards at the workplace as by far the most effective form of communication in terms of achieving the campaign objectives and increasing recruitment.[11]

In terms of using the campaign as part of their daily operations, all the interviewees indicated that the campaign materials had been well integrated into their existing communication streams. The reason for this success was best summarised by the Head of Communication at HK: "There are three factors, a good concept, freedom of implementation and a long-term approach". By allowing each organisation to use the campaign as they see fit, and discarding the traditional top-down short-term approach of previous campaigns, the LO has managed to generate a large-scale commitment from its affiliates. Its implementation therefore varies considerably. At Dansk Metal, the Head of Communication stated that he inserted campaign materials into the union magazine and membership communication every chance he got, which helps explain why the union has been more effective than the other three federate unions in the sample.

---

[11] A recent study examining the impact of workplace union density on the likelihood of Danish union membership supports this shared sentiment (Toubøl and Jensen 2014).

4.3 Analysing the Campaigns Efficacy

This final section examines how successful the campaign has been in shifting the attitudes of young people and their understanding of the role union's play in the labour market.

In terms of awareness, the goal has been to increase the number that has heard of the campaign or seen the logo in the last three weeks from 26% in 2012 to 35% by the end of 2013 and 60% in 2015. The survey data shows that the OK campaign has fallen short of the set target, reaching slightly less than one-third of young people between 15 and 39 (Table 1).

A demographic breakdown of the survey data from May 2014 provides interesting insight into the reach of different forms of communication. The most common for 15–29-year-olds were the union magazine (27%), outdoor posters (21%), the workplace (16%), the web (13%) and radio (12%). Facebook surprisingly had very little reach (4%). As one would expect, the older generations were much more likely to have come across the campaign or logo via print (union magazine, newspapers).

In order to reach the 60% target for 2015, the LO was advised that it would be necessary to incorporate video into the campaign due to its unrivalled reach and powerful emotive effect. In 2013 the LO began the video production process with external consultants and the first videos were made public in May 2014. They consist of brief conversations with people in the streets of Minneapolis, USA and Vilnius, Lithuania, in which they are told about some of the benefits Danish workers are entitled to such as six weeks holiday or 11% in pension contributions. The two-minute clips remind the Danish audience of the value of their entitlements and how they were achieved—through collective organisation (Fig. 2).

Table 1 Have you heard of the campaign or seen the logo in the past three weeks?

	15–29	30–39	40–49	50+
November 2012	29%	27%	28%	23%
April 2013	25%	24%	19%	21%
June 2013	24%	30%	20%	22%
December 2013	29%	31%	28%	23%
May 2014	29%	27%	28%	23%

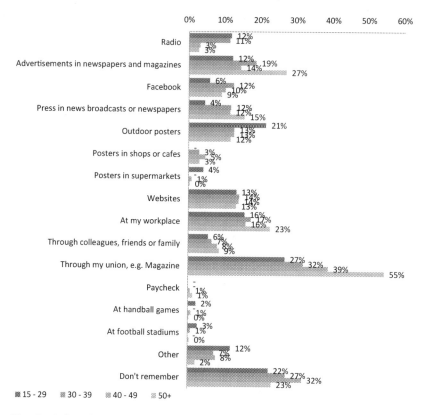

Fig. 2 Where have you seen or heard about the logo?/age

While Danish law prohibits unions from advertising on TV because they are political organisations, the unemployment insurance funds that are linked to them are not as they are promoting a product, insurance, and not a political worldview. To disseminate the videos the strategy has therefore been to enlist the LO's four largest affiliates sampled in this study—FOA, 3F, HK and Dansk Metal—using their own channels, a dedicated website[12] which allows individuals to explore which union best suits their needs, social media (as of August 1, 2014, the embedded YouTube videos have received thousands of likes on the OK-campaign

---

[12] www.fagforening.dk.

Facebook page and been shared 240 times), cinema and two national TV channels. The May 2014 survey was the first round to include questions on the reach of the videos and it reveals that these videos have been very effective at reaching young people. Asked whether they had seen the commercial in TV, cinemas or on the Internet, 65% of 15- to 29-year-olds and 59% of 30- to 39-year-olds answered yes, a quarter of whom thought the videos were very good. Compared to 42% for those 50 and older. This is twice the reach of all the other forms of communication examined earlier combined. Thus, while the campaign has failed to reach young people through Facebook, it has succeeded in its use of video and YouTube.

The final question, then, is what impact this dissemination has had on young people's attitudes and their understanding of union's role in the labour market? The survey data from May 2014 reveals that the impact has been somewhat limited. While approx 60% of young people agree or partly agree with the campaign's importance and almost half like it, less than 10% of 15–29-year-olds agree that they have a better understanding of collective agreements. The same is true of their awareness of the difference between LO unions and the ideological unions. Nevertheless, 7% of 15–29-year-olds answered that the campaign had made them consider joining a trade union and 39% answered maybe (see Tables 3–7 in the Appendix). In light of the existing research on positive union attitudes towards union membership and the increased propensity to unionise, this should be considered a success.

5   Some Conclusions

Using a combination of interviews and survey data the research has attempted to show how Danish trade unions are using the media in their attempt to engage and organise young people. Since the launch of the 'Are you OK?' campaign in 2012, it has managed to reach almost a third of all 15–39-year-olds, through traditional forms of union communication as well as new media. Its failure to reach young people on Facebook demonstrates the importance of integrating federate youth consultants and other youth groups into the campaign so that the message is shared through their social networks. The successful use of video and YouTube also suggests that this form of communication has enormous potential for union organising campaigns; it requires considerable resources and professionalism which trade unions often have in far more abundance than the network of grassroots organisations required to use social media most effectively.

The key to sustaining the collaborative campaign network that has harnessed the power resources of the LO labour movement was a clever concept, a peak-led campaign with freedom of implementation, and a long-term goal whose importance was recognised by everyone. Targeting the entire population, with a specific focus on young people, also helped ensure that it was not relegated to a 'youth effort' but instead involved union officials from both the communication and organisation departments of the sampled federate unions and each layer of their organisational structure all the way down to the branches and shop stewards.

While the campaign is very specific to the local industrial relations context, the case reveals the theoretical and empirical importance of taking a holistic approach to the analysis of union media efforts, if one is to understand the strengths and weaknesses of new and old media. Future research could explore the role of media in union organising efforts in different national and industrial relations contexts by adopting a similar approach as the one employed here. It remains to be seen whether the campaign will actually translate into an increasing level of union membership, but its success so far means that it is likely to continue and become an institutionalised dimension of trade union activity following the next LO Congress in 2015.

Appendix

See Tables 2, 3, 4, 5, 6, and 7 and Fig. 3.

Table 2 Danish Union Membership 1985–2014

	Trade Union Confederations (amount in thousands—union density in percentages)						
	1985	1995	2000	2005	2010	2013	2014
LO	1.119	1.208	1.167	1.142	955	895	867
FTF	309	332	350	361	358	349	346
AC	74	132	150	163	137*	146	203
LH	24	75	80	76	83	94	97
Ideological alternatives	13	53	68	94	173	229	236
Outside Confederations	161	62	55	57	98*	108	54
Total	1.700	1.862	1.870	1.893	1.804	1.819	1.803
Total (excl. alternative)	1.687	1.809	1.802	1.799	1.631	1.591	1.567
Employees and unemployed	2.434	2.547	2.614	2.640	2.676	2.614	2.605
Union Density	69,8%	73,1%	71,5%	71,7%	67,4%	69,6%	69,2%
Excluding alternatives Alternative	69,3%	71,0%	68,9%	68,1%	60,9%	60,9%	60,2%

Source Ibsen et al. (2014)

Table 3 The aim of the campaign is to inform the Danish public about collective agreements and their function. Do you agree or disagree that this is necessary?

	15–29	30–39	40–49	50+
Completely Agree	34%	25%	33%	44%
Partly Agree	28%	38%	33%	28%
Neither/Nor	19%	16%	18%	12%
Partly Disagree	3%	3%	2%	2%
Completely Disagree	1%	2%	2%	2%
Don't know	15%	15%	11%	13%

Table 4 What do you think about the trade union movement doing this campaign?

	15–29	30–39	40–49	50+
I like it	46%	42%	45%	50%
I have no opinion	38%	38%	37%	32%
I dislike it	2%	6%	8%	5%
I don't know	14%	14%	11%	12%

Table 5 The campaign has made me more conscious of collective agreements and their function in the labour market?

	15–29	30–39	40–49	50+
Completely Agree	1%	2%	1%	6%
Partly Agree	8%	6%	6%	8%
Neither/Nor	29%	27%	35%	31%
Partly Disagree	13%	10%	6%	5%
Completely Disagree	19%	21%	20%	14%
Don't know	30%	34%	32%	36%

Table 6 The campaign has made me more aware of the difference between LO unions and the ideological alternative unions?

	15–29	30–39	40–49	50+
Completely Agree	1%	2%	4%	10%
Partly Agree	7%	5%	4%	7%
Neither/Nor	24%	26%	32%	30%
Partly Disagree	13%	9%	6%	4%
Completely Disagree	24%	24%	21%	14%
Don't know	31%	34%	33%	35%

Table 7 Has the campaign made you consider joining a trade union?

	15–29	30–39	40–49	50+
Yes	7%	-	-	-
Maybe	39%	8%	-	12%
No	40%	87%	100%	86%
Don't know	14%	5%	-	2%

Fig. 3 The 'Are you OK?" Campaign Logo

Bibliography

Bailey, J., et al. (2010) "Daggy Shirts, Daggy Slogans? Marketing Unions to Young People", *Journal of Industrial Relations*, 52 (1): 43–60.

Blanchflower, D. (2007) "International Patterns of Union Membership", *British Journal of Industrial Relations*, 45 (1): 1–28.

Bryson et al. (2010) "Online Social Networking and Trade Union Membership: What the Facebook Phenomenon Truly Means for Labour Organizers", *Labor History*, 51 (1): 41–53.

Burgess, J., and Green, J. (2009) *YouTube: Online Video and Participatory Culture*, Cambridge: Polity Press.

Castells, Manuel (2009) *Communication Power*, Oxford: Oxford University Press.

Castells, M. (2012) *Networks of Outrage and Hope: Social Movements in the Internet Age*, Cambridge: Polity Press.

Chung, Heejung, et al. (2012) "Young People and the Post-recession Labour Market in the Context of Europe 2020", *Transfer: European Review of Labour and Research*, 18 (3): 301–317.

Crane, R. (1986) "Trade Union Advertising Campaigns: A Case Study", *Journal of Industrial Relations*, 28: 252–268.

Cregan, C., and Johnson, S. (1990) "An Industrial Relations Approach to the Free Rider Problem: Young People and Trade Union Membership in the UK", *British Journal of Industrial Relations*.

Danmarks Radio. (2014) Medieudviklingen 2013 [Media Development 2013].

Ebbinghaus, B., and Visser, J. (1999) "When Institutions Matter: Union Growth and Decline in Western Europe, 1950-1995", *European Sociological Review*, 15 (2): 135–158.

FDIM (2012) Danes Use of the Internet—2012. The Association of Interactive Media. May 2013. Available at: fdim.dk/sites/default/files/mediearkiv/rapporter/danskernes_brug_af_internettet_2012_rapport.pdf.

Geelan, Torsten. (2013a) "Responses of Trade Union Confederations to the Youth Employment Crisis", *European Review of Labour and Research*, 19 (3): 399–413.

Geelan, Torsten (2013b) "Union Solidarity International", *European Review of Labour and Research*, 19 (3): 419–424.

Griffen, L., and Brown, Michelle. (2011) "Second Hand Views? Young People, Social Networks and Positive Union Attitudes", *Labour and Industry*, 22 (1): 81–101.

Gumbrell-McCormick, Rebecca, and Hyman, Richard. (2013). *Trade Unions in Western Europe: Hard Times, Hard Choices*, Oxford: Oxford University Press.

Heckscher, C., and Carré, F. (2006) "Strength in Networks: Employment Rights Organisation and the Problem of Co-Ordination", *British Journal of Industrial Relations*, 44 (4): 605–628.

Hodder, Andy. (2014) "Organising Young Workers in the Public and Commercial Services Union", *Industrial Relations Journal*, 45 (2): 153–168.
Ibsen et al. (2014) *Fald i Organisationsgraden Igen* [A Decline in Union Density Again], Copenhagen: FAOS.
Jørgensen, Henning and Schulze, Michaela (2012) "A Double Farewell to a Former Model? Danish Unions and Activation Policy", *Local Economy*, 27 (5–6): 637–644.
Lee, Rainie, and Barry, Wellman (2014). *Network: The New Social Operating System*, Boston: MIT Press
Levesque, Christian, and Murray, Gregor. (2010) "Understanding Union Power: Resources and Capabilities for Renewing Union Capacity", *Transfer: European Review of Labour and Research*, 16: 333–350.
Lind, Jens. (2009) "The End of the Ghent System as Trade Union Recruitment Machinery", *Industrial Relations Journal*, 46 (6): 510–523.
LO (2010a) *Medlemsudvikling I LO-fagbeveagelsen 1990–2009* [Membership developments in the LO trade union movement 1990–2009], Copenhagen: Denmark.
LO (2010b) *Developments in Union Organization: Causes and Consequences for the Danish Model*, Copenhagen: LO.
LO (2011) New LO Version 2.0: Responsibilities, Roles, Tasks and Cooperation in the Congress Period, 2012–2015.
LO (2014) May Day Poll: Danes Support the Trade Union Movement. Accessed at: http://www.lo.dk/English%20version/News/may%20day.aspx.
O'Neill, Deirdre. (2007) "From Hunky Heroes to Dangerous Dinosaurs: Journalism-Union Relations, News Access and Press Coverage in the 2002-2003 British Fire Brigades Union Dispute", *Journalism Studies*, 8 (5): 813–830.
Oxenbridge, S., and Neathy, F. (2012) "Young People's Awareness and Use of Sources of Advice and Information on Problems and Rights at Work", ACAS Research Paper 19/12.
Panagiotopoulos, Panagiotis. (2012) "Towards Unions 2.0: Rethinking the Audience of Social Media Engagement", *New Technology, Work and Society*, 27 (3): 178–192.
Panagiotopoulos, Panagiotis, and Barnett, Julie. (2014) "Social Media in Union Communications: An International Study with UNI Global Union Affiliates", *British Journal of Industrial Relations*, published online: http://doi.org/10.1111/bjir.12060.
Philo, Greg (2014) *Seeing and Believing: The Influence of Television*, Oxon: Routledge.
Ragin, Charles, and Becker, Howard. (1992) *What Is a Case? Exploring the Foundations of Social Inquiry*, Cambridge: Cambridge University Press.

Reader, Susan, and Mathers, Andrew (2013) "Membership, Influence and Voice: A Discussion of Trade Union Renewal in the French Context", *Industrial Relations Journal*, 44 (2): 122–138.

Scheuer, Steen. (2007) "Dilemmas of Collectivism: Danish Trade Unions in the Twenty-First Century.", *Journal of Labour Research*, 28 (2): 233–255.

Scheuer, Steen (2011) "Union Membership Variation in Europe: A Ten-Country Comparative Analysis", *European Journal of Industrial Relations*, 17 (1): 57–73.

Schnabel, C., and Wagner, J. (2007) "Union Density and Determinants of Union Membership in 18 Countries: Evidence from Micro Data, 2002/03", *Industrial Relations Journal*, 38(1): 5–32.

Sullivan, Richard (2010) "Labour Market or Labour Movement? The Union Density Bias as a Barrier to Labour Renewal", *Work, Employment & Society*, 24: 145.

Toubøl, Jonas, and Jensen, Carsten. (2014) "Why Do People Join Trade Unions? The Impact of Workplace Union Density on Union Membership", *European Review of Labour and Research*, 135–154.

Walsh, G. (1988) "Trade Unions and the Media", *International Labour Review*, 127 (2): 205–220.

Yin, Robert. (2009) *Case Study Research: Design and Methods*, 4th ed., California: Sage.

CHAPTER 12

German Trade Unions and The EU Minimum Wage Debate: Between National Elite and Transnational Working Class

Mona Aranea

1 Introduction[1]

The European integration project is experiencing a deep and severe legitimacy crisis. High levels of socio-economic inequality both within and between member countries of the European Union (EU) have given rise to nationalist movements that are threatening not only the European common market but also the EU as a community of civil and intergovernmental peace (Standing, 2014). The reality of Europe's integrated

---

[1] I would like to thank Daniel Nicholson (Cardiff University) for encouraging me to operationalise, rather than simply assume labour interests. I am grateful to Martin Seeliger (Hamburg University) for important insights into labour class formation at European level. I sincerely thank everybody inside the "Brussels bubble" who has granted me their time and trust during interviews.

M. Aranea (✉)
Hans Böckler Foundation, Düsseldorf, Germany
e-mail: Mona-Aranea@boeckler.de

yet disembedded labour market stands in stark contrast to the promise of European integration as a regional project of shared prosperity. The common market has created growth, but no social cohesion (Crouch, 2015). The free movement of goods, capital and services has allowed production costs to fall, and profits to rise, but has in effect made the poorest sections of European societies poorer, and the richest sections considerably richer (Emmenegger et al, 2012; Piketty, 2013). Growing labour market dualisation and socio-economic inequality create a popular image of the EU as a class project that disproportionately benefits capitalist elites (Anderson, 2009; Meardi, 2013). The EU's "promissory legitimacy", based on the post-war compromise of shared prosperity between classes and nations, has reached the end of its tether. Social anomy—the disenchantment of individuals with social order—is on the rise across Europe (Beckert, 2020). The European Commission is under pressure to create a more inclusive pan-European employment regime in order to re-activate popular support for the European integration project.

The European Commission consultation on the challenge of fair minimum wages in Europe triggered dispute among the national organisations belonging to the European Trade Union Confederation (ETUC). The study uses two types of qualitative data to assess German trade unions' political agenda and advocacy work in Brussels between January and September 2020. The first set of data are trade unions' and employer groups' position papers and press releases in response to the European Commission consultation on minimum wages, as well as related European Commission documents and internal ETUC documents. The analysis included eighteen employer position papers and five position papers from European trade union federations (ETUFs) that were sent in response to the Commission consultation in early 2020, as well as two joint position papers from public sector social partners. The second set of data consisted of ten semi-structured expert interviews with trade union representatives in Germany and at EU-level. Interview respondents were policy officers working for the German unions IG Metall (metal sector), IG BCE (chemical and construction sector), ver.di (service sector) or the umbrella organisation *Deutscher Gewerkschaftsbund/* German Trade Union Confederation (DGB), as well as representatives of two ETUFs, industriAll and UNI Europa.

The research finds that German unions have to some extent emancipated themselves from the logic of national pacts for competitiveness and engaged pro-actively with the EU minimum wage initiative through the

ETUC. Based on Germany's positive minimum wage experience, German labour representatives advocate a more inclusive and less uneven European employment regime and adopt a strategy of recourse to binding law. Germany's most influential trade unions seem less focused on the particular interests of workers at the top of chemical and automotive value chains, and more sensitive towards a general worker interest in a European social floor. During interviews, German union officials took a clear stand against employers' deregulatory labour market agenda in Europe. During the ETUC debate, German unions abandoned their traditional role as members of a Nordic labour block against minimum wage regulation and aligned with other unions from the West, South and East in support of a more inclusive pan-European employment regime.

German unions' political advocacy work in Brussels is relevant for EU policy outcomes because of their influential position within the ETUC. The chapter argues that German support for pan-European minimum wage regulation has tipped the scale within the European trade union family in favour of labour demands from Europe's South and East. German unions' changing political alliances explain the differences between the ETUC response to the first stage Commission consultation on minimum wages and the ETUC response to the second-stage consultation. The ETUC response to the first stage consultation constituted a hard-won and fragile compromise between Eastern European labour movements in favour of the EU minimum wage initiative and Scandinavian trade unions who rejected the initiative. The second consultation response took a clear stand for a pan-European minimum wage regime. A major outcome of the ETUC minimum wage debate is the emergence of a pan-European coalition of class-conscious trade unions with powerful German organisations at their core. Scandinavian unions continued to narrowly defend Nordic labour's privileged position within Europe's uneven employment regime, resulting in an open rift in the European labour movement. The outcome of the EU minimum wage initiative remains open (as of early 2021). Alliances continue to shift. The research presents an in-depth snapshot of a dynamic process of class formation in Europe.

2 THE MINIMUM WAGE INITIATIVE IN THE CONTEXT OF THE EU SOCIAL PILLAR

The EU minimum wage initiative is situated in the context of the European pillar of social rights, or European Social Pillar for short. Under Commission President Juncker (2014–2019), the Commission made several attempts to re-establish legitimacy for Europe's integrated yet disembedded labour market. The Commission started off in 2015 with an attempt to re-launch European social dialogue as an instrument for social policy making. In their responses to the respective Commission consultation, European employer lobby groups such as the influential manufacturing organisation Ceemet demanded that "the European Commission does not use social dialogue as a tool for social policy making" (Ceemet, 2015). In 2017, the Commission launched a general consultation on social rights in the EU, followed by the official declaration of the European Social Pillar. BusinessEurope, EuroCommerce, and eleven other employer lobby groups jointly responded to the consultation, arguing that "the persisting social problems in Europe are not due to a lack of social policy measures, but to a lack of global competitiveness" (BusinessEurope et al., 2017). Between 2015 and 2018, the Juncker Commission undertook several legal initiatives in the area of social and employment policy, resulting in two Directives and one Council Recommendation.[2] The Juncker Commission's Social Pillar discourse constituted an unsuccessful attempt to create an EU-level elite consensus for social rights to complement the European free market.

> Juncker knows Europe's history, and understands why Europe is under attack from nationalist forces. (...) The EU is perceived as an actor who does not solve the social question but rather deepens the unfair market competition. Juncker understands the need for social policy to counteract this perception, and the need to bring employers in line for this. (interview with DGB, August 2020)

---

[2] The Directive on work-life balance for parents and carers (2019) replaced existing European Parental Leave regulation. The Directive on transparent and predictable working conditions in the European Union (2019) replaced the Written Statement Directive of 1991. The (non-binding) Council recommendation on social protection in all kinds of employment (2019) did not provide a clear definition of terms such as "worker," "employee" or "self-employment," in contrast to demands raised by labour organisations.

Decent wages for working people had not played any role in the Commission's social policy initiatives since the Social Charter had declared them a political goal of European integration in 1989 (Schulten, 2015). The Social Pillar Declaration of 2017 included a call to re-vitalise European Workers' right to a living wage. The Declaration stated under point six that "workers have the right to fair wages that provide for a decent standard of living" (European Commission, Council and Parliament, 2017, p. 15). The first draft of the European Parliament (EP) Resolution on the Social Pillar included support for setting national minimum wage levels at 60% of the national wage median.[3] Employers successfully lobbied for the removal of the respective paragraph in the final EP Resolution (European Parliament, 2017a).[4] An EP Resolution on poverty of late 2017 supported setting national minimum income schemes at 60% of the national median wage level and did not comment on minimum wage entitlements (European Parliament, 2017b, p. 14). Employers had successfully shifted the parliamentary debate around decent livelihoods from a focus on wages to a focus on welfare.

Workers' right to fair minimum wages re-entered the political debate when the new von der Leyen Commission took office in late 2019. In January 2020, the Commission launched a first stage social partner consultation on the challenge of fair minimum wages in Europe. The consultation named decent wages for workers as its core policy objective, in line with the 2017 Social Pillar Declaration. The first stage consultation document of January 14 stated that "[a]dequate wages are key for ensuring fair working conditions and decent living standards for European workers" and that fair wages and working conditions are "at the heart of a social market economy that works for people" (European Commission, 2020a). The second stage consultation document of June 2020 similarly emphasised that minimum wages "help sustain domestic demand, strengthen incentives to work, reduce wage inequalities and in-work poverty and contribute to closing the gender pay gap" (European

---

[3] On why this kind of minimum wage threshold makes sense and would have to be based on wage levels before taxes, rather than net wage levels, see Müller and Schulten (2020).

[4] The EP debate around the Social Pillar Resolution was characterised by strong regional conflicts of interest between debtor/creditor and high-wage/low-wage countries, overshadowing left/right cleavages in the Parliament. Minimum wage was one of the few issue where all centre-right groups were united in their quest for its removal. See Vesan and Corti (2019) for an insightful analysis of the EP voting behaviour.

Commission, 2020b). The second stage consultation was still ongoing at the time of research. The analysis focuses on the internal ETUC debate that took place between January and June 2020, between the first and second stage consultation.

The Commission consultation was open only to recognised EU-level social partner organisations representing employers and workers. Social partner consultations exclude national organisations, NGOs and individual citizens from the official policy debate. Employer responses usually outweigh labour responses in number and outperform them in unanimity. The Commission list of recognised social partner organisations includes around a dozen European trade union federations and close to seventy EU-level employer groups.[5] The Commission initially launched a public consultation on 13 January but withdrew this consultation within twenty-four hours, in response to pressure from employer lobby groups and trade unions in Brussels.[6] A closed social partner consultation replaced the public consultation on 14 January. In response to the first stage consultation on the challenge of fair minimum wages in Europe, the Commission obtained responses from eighteen European employer groups and seven European trade union federations (ETUFs). In June 2020, the Commission launched the second stage of the minimum wage consultation. The second stage consultation document was more ambitious than the first stage consultation document. The Commission named a Council Recommendation or an EU Directive as possible policy outcomes in the absence of social partner negotiations. The Commission later tabled a draft Directive in October. This chapter does not discuss developments after the tabling of the Directive in October. After a brief overview over responses to the first stage consultation, the analysis below focuses on the ETUC debate between the first and second stage consultation, between January and September 2020 (Table 1).

---

[5] See the list of European social partner organisations, last updated in September 2019: https://ec.europa.eu/social/main.jsp?catId=522&langId=en.

[6] Information obtained through confidential interviews in Brussels. The Commission deleted the original, public consultation, and the related Commission press release of 13 January from its website.

Table 1 Organisations responding to first stage EC consultation

Type of organisation	Independent response	Joint response	Total
European employer lobby groups	18	2	20
European trade union federations	5	2	7

Table 2 Labour responses to the first stage Commission consultation on fair minimum wages

	ETUC (affiliated)	Other
Cross-sectoral	ETUC	CESI
Public	EPSU (with CEMR)	TUNED (with EUPAE)
Managerial staff	-	CEC; Eurocadres
Sectoral	EAEA	-

3 Employer Responses to the Commission Consultation

Employer groups used the minimum wage consultation to once again declare their unanimous rejection of the European Social Pillar. Employer responses to the first stage consultation voiced general doubts about the rationale and proportionality of the minimum wage initiative. Employers found the EU-level inadequate for regulating core employment issues such as pay. Metal sector employers argued that the EU treaties excluded the issue of pay from EU competences and that higher wages would lead to further relocation of production away from Europe (Ceemet, 202, p. 3). The main employer lobby group representing small and medium employers, SME united, disputed low collective bargaining coverage in Europe as an accurate policy problem statement: "Taking into account the low level of low paid workers without collective bargaining coverage, a dedicated European initiative on minimum wage, would be disproportionate" (SMEunited 2020, p. 3).[7] Other employer groups questioned

---

[7] For an overview over the pan-European decline in national collective bargaining see for example Baccaro and Howell (2017) or Müller et al (2019).

the underlying policy objective of ensuring an adequate worker income. Retail sector employers argued that "issues such as income and poverty are better dealt with by national governments with the competence to redistribute wealth (…) than through blunt instruments such as minimum wages" (EuroCommerce, 2020, p. 1). BusinessEurope openly rejected the idea of linking workers' wages to their need for an income:

> It is important to remember that for employers and workers, wages exist to compensate the work performed, taking into account the way in which it is done and valued, including in the market and within the enterprise. This is an important difference with minimum income schemes, which pursue the social policy objective of ensuring an adequate minimum income to all that are considered to be legitimately eligible in a country in view of the costs of living. (BusinessEurope, 2020, p. 2)

In their refusal to recognise fair minimum wages as an essential labour right, employers continued the openly non-cooperative strategy adopted towards the Juncker Commission's re-launch of social dialogue, the Social Pillar Declaration and the ensuing legal initiatives since 2015. Their position papers are further evidence that employers across Europe are today more self-assured and less willing to respect the post-war class compromise of shared prosperity with labour (Baccaro & Howell, 2017). BusinessEurope and EuroCommerce argued in their position papers that ensuring an income to working people was a sole government responsibility. The Commission analysis of all responses to the first stage consultation recognised that none of the employer responses received favoured Directives. The Commission did not mention employers' openly voiced rejection of the policy objective behind the initiative (European Commission, 2020b).

4   Labour Response to the Commission Consultation

Labour responses to the first stage consultation represented the views of the ETUC, its affiliated ETUFs, public sector unions, independent unions, and managerial staff organisations. Five ETUFs responded individually to the Commission consultation while two ETUFs, representing public service workers, responded through joint positions with employers.

Table 2 gives an overview over trade union responses to the first stage consultation.

The ETUC response to the first stage consultation welcomed the EU initiative for fair minimum wages and voiced openness for social partner negotiations, while arguing for a protection of national collective bargaining systems and social partner autonomy (ETUC, 2020a). The position did not specify a desired policy outcome and thus avoided taking a stand for binding legislation on minimum wages. The ambiguity of the ETUC position paper reflected the ambiguity of the debate between ETUC member federations, discussed below. The ETUC position paper was the longest of all position papers analysed, and much longer than the second longest consultation response, the seven-page long European Arts and Entertainment Alliance (EAEA) position. The ETUC position was almost thirty pages long and included many graphs and tables as well as many repetitions. All other position papers analysed were shorter than five pages.

The European Confederation of Independent Trade Unions (CESI) responded to the Commission consultation with a call for support for national collective bargaining systems and demanded for trade union rights to be integrated into EU public procurement law. CESI also asked for clarification on how the Commission intended to improve the wages and working conditions of atypical workers and those in (bogus) self-employment who were not covered by minimum wage regulation, where it existed. CESI supported the idea of social partner negotiations with the aim to establish an EU framework for fair minimum wages and argued for ambitious legal action from the Commission in the absence of social partner negotiations (CESI, 2020). Both the ETUC position and the CESI position emphasised that a decent fair wage floor contributed to sustainable domestic demand.

Two ETUFs representing managerial staff responded to the Commission consultation. Both Eurocadres and CEC European Managers agreed with the basic problem stated in the Commission consultation with regards to wages being too low. Eurocadres emphasised the importance of collective bargaining in their position papers, arguing for a protection of national social partner autonomy: "Agreeing with ETUC, we want to emphasise that any action must fully respect the autonomy of social partners and safeguard well-functioning collective bargaining and industrial relation systems" (Eurocadres, 2020). Eurocadres was principally open to social partner negotiations on the issue. The CEC European Managers position paper also supported the basic problem statement: "Ensuring that every working person in Europe receives a salary that is sufficient to guarantee the basic living standards (and a meaningful participation in society) is in the first place a duty that our societies—which all share the common belonging to the "European social model"—need to fulfill" (CEC, 2020). The managerial staff organisation also emphasised the need to promote national collective bargaining and to protect social partner autonomy. CEC European Managers expressed readiness to participate in EU social partner negotiations.

Two public sector unions responded to the consultation via joint position paper with employers. According to the second stage Commission document, the Trade Unions' National and European Administration Delegation (TUNED) had responded to the first stage consultation together with the European Public Administration Employers (EUPAE). We did not have access to this position paper. One public sector ETUC member federation, the European Federation of Public Service Unions (EPSU), responded jointly with the Council of European Municipalities and Regions (CEMR) to the Commission consultation. Public social partners argued against EU wage regulation and for national social partner autonomy: "We as sectoral social partners underline that setting wages is a national competence and that this is done best through collective agreements between strong and autonomous social partners at the national level" (EPSU & CEMR, 2020: 1).

One sectoral ETUC member federation, the European Arts and Entertainment Alliance (EAEA) responded individually to the Commission consultation. The EAEA position focused on the concerns of atypical workers (self-employed, free-lance, project-based etc.) who are generally not covered by minimum wage regulation and enjoy limited union representation. The EAEA also demanded public procurement regulation that promotes collective labour representation but made no mention of a possible EU Directive on national minimum wage schemes (EAEA, 2020). Other sectoral ETUC member federations did not respond individually to the Commission consultation. The service sector union federation UNI Europa stated in a press release that minimum wage regulations, while desirable, were not enough to ensure fair wages in Europe. UNI Europa argued for legislation that would protect collective organising, such as ensuring union access to workplaces, and promote collective agreements, for example pro-union clauses in public procurement regulation (UNI Europa, 2020). The industrial sector ETUF industriAll Europe issued a press release in June 2020 in relation to the second-stage Commission consultation. The press release emphasised the need to promoting collective bargaining and to protect national social partner autonomy (industriAll, 2020). Both ETUFs supported the ETUC responses to the Commission consultation (interview with UNI Europa, July 2020; interview with industriAll, August 2020).

Of the organisations responding to the first stage consultation, only CESI spoke out clearly in favour of a binding legislative framework on fair minimum wages. All other ETUFs avoided favouring one policy outcome over the other, or openly criticised the idea of a binding EU Directive. The ETUC's second stage consultation response deviated from the first stage consultation response. The ETUC position had moved closer to the CESI position, in favour of binding legal action. The position paper took a clear stand for statutory minimum wages as a complementary policy instrument to national collective bargaining rights (ETUC, 2020b). This shift reflected political dynamics inside the European labour movement, playing out around regional conflicts of interests. The regional conflicts lay mainly, though not exclusively, between Eastern European trade unions in favour of a binding legal framework, and Nordic unions who remained strictly opposed to such legislation. The following section examines internal discussion and power dynamics during the ETUC's minimum wage debate between January and September 2020 from the perspective of German labour representatives. The analysis does not include other employer or trade union responses to the second stage consultation because of the focus on class formation within the ETUC during and after the first stage consultation.

5 The ETUC Debate During the First Stage Consultation: German Unions as Mediators

The ETUC response to the first stage Commission consultation on fair minimum wages in Europe constituted a hard-won and fragile compromise. The ETUC position of January 2020 neither argued clearly in favour of European minimum wage regulation, nor did it take a clear stand against such regulation from above. Most Eastern and some Western European trade unions were in favour of the EU minimum wage initiative, while most Scandinavian trade unions rejected the initiative as an interference with national wage-setting mechanisms. German trade unions were influential mediators in the debate that led to the fragile compromise between the two opposing fractions. German unions drew on their positive national experience with minimum wage legislation. Some Nordic unions deviated from the ETUC position in a separate letter to the European Commission in February 2020. Their refusal to be represented by the ETUC led to a marginalisation of Nordic positions in the ETUC during the second stage Commission consultation between June and September 2020.

The ETUC member federations engaged in long and controversial debates in late 2019 and early 2020 to reach a compromise position on the Commission initiative on fair minimum wages in Europe. Two regional factions within the ETUC were in favour of EU regulation towards a legally binding pan-European wage floor at around 60% of national medium wage levels (interview with IG BCE, August 2020). Eastern European trade unions viewed European minimum wage regulation as a way to address foreign multinationals' labour exploitation in dependent market economies such as Poland or Czech Republic (see also Adamczyk, 2018). Czech unions for example scandalised that fact that one Czech Volkswagen plant's productivity levels lay at around 80% of those in Germany—still workers' wages remained at around 20% of those earned in Wolfsburg. Some Western trade unions for example from France and Belgium, voiced their members' interest in German labour market regulation, including an increase in the German minimum wage (see also Seeliger 2017, p. 214). Germany's export-led production model reinforces a general tendency towards wage dualisation both within German plants and along pan-European value chains, to the benefit of a shrinking core of organised employees (Lehndorff 2012, p. 94; see also Schulten, 2018).

> Eastern European workers say there are being exploited as cheap labour. They strongly advocate for the minimum wage initiative. (…) Then there are some trade unions from Western Europe, for example France and Belgium, who view Germany's low-wage sector as an unfair competitive advantage. (interview with IG BCE, August 2020)

The ETUC had to find an almost impossible compromise between these Eastern and Western unions on the one side and several Nordic unions on the other, who strictly opposed binding legislation. An influential faction of Scandinavian unions inside the ETUC narrowly defended social partner independence and rejected any EU interference in the area of pay or employment conditions. This faction included national union federations from Sweden, Denmark, Norway and Iceland. Their position reflected the Nordic model of employment relations (interview with DGB, August 2020; see also Seeliger, 2017). Some German union representatives viewed the uncompromising Nordic position as an expression of an insider–outsider employment regime (interview with ver.di, July 2020). In such a system, the low wages of unorganised workers leave more room to negotiate higher wages for organised workers, making statutory minimum wages undesirable for the organised part of the workforce. According to some German labour representatives, Nordic unions showed little consideration for wider working-class interests beyond their narrow member constituencies. Their narrow organisational definition of interests-led Scandinavian unions to "reject anything that could weaken the organisations themselves – be it European regulation, minimum wages, or state interference in wage setting" (interview with IG Metall, July 2020).

German trade unions' position lay somewhere between the opposing regional factions. All German unions interviewed preferred collective bargaining rights over statutory minimum wages but evaluated positively the complementary function of minimum wage regulation to address wage inequality. According to a service sector representative interviewed, unions still viewed collective bargaining as the best way towards fair wages but had to acknowledge that half of Germany's working people were not covered by collective bargaining (interview with ver.di, July 2020). German unions did not share Scandinavian unions' legal arguments with regards to limited EU competences in the area of pay. Nordic unions disputed that wage regulation lay within the legal competences of the EU. Some German labour representatives lamented that Scandinavian unions focused solely on the content of EU Treaties and refused to engage in the political debate itself (interview with DGB, August 2020). German unions based their legal assessment on a German government report which found no legal barriers for EU-level minimum wage regulation (interview with DGB, August 2020). The report had been produced under German minister of employment Andrea Nahles around the time when she introduced minimum wage legislation in Germany.[8] Union

---

[8] The Commission recently appointed Nahles as advisor for social dialogue (European Commission 2020c, p. 3).

representatives interviewed saw the need for Western unions to show solidarity with Eastern and Southern labour movements (see also Czarzasty & Mrozowicki, 2018).

> For us this is question of solidarity with others. We see the need for solidarity with Eastern European workers. We understand that a European Directive can help balance out the wage differences between Germany on the one side and Belgium and France on the other. (...) Our position aligns with that of IG Metall on the matter. (interview with IG BCE, August 2020)

The DGB support for the EU initiative reflected German unions' positive experience with the national statutory minimum wage (interview with DGB, August 2020). When Scandinavian unions spoke out against European minimum wage regulation in the past, they had often enjoyed German support (interview with IG Metall, August 2020). The large manufacturing unions IG BCE and IG Metall were traditionally opposed to statutory minimum wages as an interference with the freedom for collective bargaining (interview IG BCE, August 2020, see also Behrens & Pekarek, 2020). During our interviews, both unions reported a learning effect form the German experience with minimum wage regulation (see also Seeliger, 2018). IG BCE and IG Metall had initially opposed the German minimum wage but shifted position in light of positive labour market effects in Germany (Behrens & Pekarek, 2020). Because of their positive experience with Germany's statutory minimum wage, labour representatives interviewed did not perceive the EU minimum wage initiative as a threat to Germany's collective bargaining system (interview with IG Metall, July 2020). They argued that minimum wages as a complementary policy instrument would help reduce wage inequalities in Germany and Europe. European minimum wage regulation had not been part of German unions' political agenda until the Commission took the initiative.

> Minimum wages would not have become a topic of interest for us without the Commission initiative. We would have focused on other issues. Minimum income from social benefits is an important topic for us. (...) From a German perspective, we do not need European minimum wage regulation. We have a statutory minimum wage in Germany. (...) But we

as trade unions have to make use of the opportunity now that the Commission has come forward with this initiative. (interview with DGB, August 2020)

The DGB and others worked together with the ETUC head office as influential mediators between the different interests involved. German unions hold considerable political weight in EU-level federations for their large member base and therefore significant financial contribution. IG BCE and IG Metall are the largest single unions inside industriAll, the umbrella organisation for industry trade unions in Brussels (interview with IG BCE, July 2020). IG Metall has an office location in Brussels in the same building with industriAll and the ETUC. At the time of research, German nationals held both the presidency and the position of General Secretary in the service sector union UNI Europa. The German DGB traditionally co-operated closely with Scandinavian unions on industry topics. At the time of research, the German DGB was sharing an office space with Swedish unions in Brussels (interview with DGB, August 2020). According to our interviews, Scandinavian unions' lack of willingness to reach a compromise with Western and Eastern European trade unions was immensely frustrating for German mediators (interview ver.di July 2020).

> As far as I know, the DGB tried to act as a mediator and to find a compromise to which, from our German perspective, the Nordics could agree. (…) Everybody involved in these discussions came back very frustrated, as the Nordics would not move a millimetre from their position. (interview with IG BCE, August 2020)

The difficult debates inside the ETUC resulted in a very long, partly repetitive and partly incoherent ETUC response. In the view of German labour representatives interviewed, the final ETUC position respected the Scandinavian interest in safeguards for social partner autonomy. The ETUC position argues that employers and trade unions should be able to set wages without state interference where their coverage is high enough. The position goes on to argue in favour of extension mechanisms for sectoral minimum wages to cover workplaces where collective bargaining is not functional. The setting of statutory minimum wages by the state remains an important "last resort" for decent wages (interview with ver.di, July 2020). One German labour representative interviewed explained the ambivalent ETUC position with the organisation's attempt "to build bridges, though without the desired effect" (interview with DGB, August 2020). Most ETUC member federations supported the final wording of the position, with the important exception of the Nordic bloc (interview with IG BCE, July 2020). German unions interviewed saw Scandinavian positions sufficiently represented in the ETUC response to the first stage consultation.

> The ETUC position clearly states that statutory minimum wages are not necessary where collective bargaining coverage it high. In this the ETUC position takes into consideration the interest of highly organised Scandinavian unions. (interview with IG BCE July 2020)

Scandinavian unions deviated from the ETUC response to the first stage consultation with a separate letter to the Commission in February 2020. For the first time in the history of the ETUC, national member organisations publicly spoke out against an ETUC position. In a letter to Commission president von der Leyen, a network of Nordic unions distanced themselves from the ETUC position. Signing parties were national trade union confederations from Sweden, Denmark, Norway and Iceland. In their letter to the Commission, Nordic unions declared their will to defend national social partner autonomy against state interference and asked the Commission not to come forward with proposals for binding EU legislation on minimum wages, quoted below. This dragged the rift in the European trade union family out into the open, making it visible to everyone wanting to see.

> [I]t is with regret that we need to inform the Commission that the ETUC reply [to the first stage consultation] is not representative for the undersigned Nordic trade unions. (…) We have always rejected proposals that are based on binding rules of wage floors on European level. (Nordic trade unions' response to first stage Commission consultation, February 2020)

6 The ETUC Debate During the Second Stage Consultation: German Unions Taking Sides

Scandinavian unions' refusal to be represented by the ETUC led to a marginalisation of Nordic positions in the ETUC debate from February 2020. German unions abandoned their mediator role and sided with the large Eastern bloc in favour of binding EU minimum wage legislation. The ETUC debate consequently shifted from a major focus on collective bargaining towards the promotion of minimum wages as a necessary complementary policy in national wage-setting systems. The ETUC response to the second stage Commission consultation, published in September 2020, argued in favour of a binding EU Directive on minimum wages to promote statutory minimum wages in countries without functioning wage-setting mechanisms. The final policy result of the EU minimum wage initiative may or may not help re-embed Europe's integrated labour market in society. An early result of this initiative is the long-overdue politicisation of ETUC debates. Now contemporary matching interests weigh heavier than old solidarity ties.

The continuously uncompromising Nordic position after the first stage consultation stood in stark contrast to the German labour perspective, which promoted a balanced approach between collective bargaining rights and minimum legal standards. An IG BCE representative interviewed lamented Nordic unions' "political affront" in writing a separatist letter to the Commission (interview with IG BCE, July 2020). An IG Metall representative agreed: "Differences of opinions and difficult debates are normal. (…) But to thwart a compromise reached is a different matter. (…) The Nordic intervention with the Commission is scandalous. (…) This will lead the European trade union family into real quarrels" (interview with IG Metall, July 2020). After experiencing the uncompromising attitude of unions from Sweden, Denmark, Norway and Iceland, German unions abandoned their role as flexible mediators, and ended their traditional solidarity with labour from Scandinavia. German unions decided to take a clear stand for a pan-European wage floor, as the following quote exemplifies.

> We want labour mobility. But we do not want poverty to force people to migrate to other European countries. Romanian workers prefer their shitty accommodations in Germany to the lives they endure at home. They even prefer sleeping in a subway station in Brussels to life in Romania. We have to support a living wage in Romania, and that is an issue of minimum wage regulation. (interview with DGB, August 2020)

The German opposition to further compromise with Scandinavian unions tipped the scale within the ETUC. German unions joined the large bloc of unions within the ETUC who viewed a European Directive as a viable means to address the pan-European race to the bottom in wages. The draft of the second stage consultation response promoted statutory minimum wages as a complementary policy to collective bargaining rights. In spring 2020, a crucial vote in the ETUC executive body determined the content of the ETUC response to the second stage Commission consultation. Most member organisations supported the ETUC position while the Nordics did not (interview IG BCE, August 2020). Unions from Sweden, Norway, Denmark and Iceland reiterated their position in a comment on the draft ETUC response to the second stage consultation, indicating renewed political deviation towards the employer camp.

> We find that ETUC's draft reply [to the second stage consultation] is presenting several proposals that interfere with the autonomy of the social partners. (...) It is (...) with great disappointment that we see that the ETUC is demanding a European Framework Directive on minimum wages as well as collective bargaining. In doing so, the ETUC risks creating a splitting division in the European trade union movement. (Nordic letter to the ETUC commenting on ETUC draft reply to second stage consultation, June 2020)

By September 2020, the new alliances were stable enough to issue the ETUC response to the second stage consultation without Nordic support. A renewed compromise between the different factions within the ETUC is unlikely. A large group of unions in favour of EU minimum wage regulation had marginalised a financially powerful but eventually small opposing group of unions from Europe's Scandinavian North in the debate. Some German representatives interviewed argued that Nordic unions' particularly good financial endowment generally allowed them to punch above their weight within the ETUC, because "the ETUC needs the Scandinavian member federations for their money" (interview with ver.di, July 2020). This is certainly an argument one could equally apply to the powerful German DGB. Other German labour representatives lamented that Swedish unions were defending the particular interests of Swedish multinational companies operating in European value chains, explaining the Swedes' "missionary zeal" when rejecting minimum wages (interview with IG Metall, July 2020). The ETUC practice of debates has now shifted away from consensus at all costs and towards issue-based conflicts and crucial votes. A DGB representative interpreted the minimum wage consultation as the beginning of a new era of majority decision-making within the ETUC.

> For the first stage consultation response, we tried to get the Nordics on board. We really tried to find compromises. (…) You won't find see anything of this in the second stage consultation response. The Nordics don't want a compromise. (…) We will now find, with the European pillar of social rights, that we cannot establish a consensus inside the ETUC and have to work via majority voting. (interview with DGb, August 2020)

7 Conclusion

The Commission's minimum wage initiative brought forward a nostalgic, if not utopian idea of Europe. It is the idea of a European regional integration project based on shared prosperity between capital and labour, and peaceful co-operation between free European nation states. The contemporary reality for European working people, including in Germany, is one of low wages, rising precarity and blatant managerial class war. In close alignment with national elites, multinational companies of predominantly German and American origin are establishing a highly profitable but socially unstable Wild West regime of self-employed workers, undeclared work, and forced labour across Europe, following their successful experiments in Europe's Eastern and Southern periphery (González Begega et al., 2018; Meardi, 2013). Management agency increasingly disappears behind online platforms, apps and bogus self-employment. Workers still know the difference between their interests and those of managers and shareholders. Working people throughout Europe demand social security and decent work. One aim of the edited volume is to identify ways in which unions can help to 'put the brakes' on the destruction of democracy in European workplaces and societies. Germany's system of co-determination, works councils and collective bargaining has turned German trade unions into the most resourceful and yet least class-conscious workers' organisations in Europe. The result is an enormous low-wage sector in Germany and a toxic collaboration between German unions and transnational business lobby groups in Brussels, euphemistically dubbed European social dialogue (González Begega & Aranea, 2018; Streeck, 2019).

The chapter presented an analysis of German trade unions' views and political alliances during the 2020 ETUC minimum wage debate. The results show that trade unions can find a balance between their close alignment with national capitalist elites and their role as class agents representing working people. German unions interviewed voiced high and unanimous support for the EU minimum wage initiative. All German unions interviewed preferred collective bargaining rights over statutory minimum wages but evaluated positively the complementary function of minimum wage regulation, especially for groups that are notoriously difficult to organise, like many service workers or outsourced workers in metal and chemical industries. Labour representatives did not perceive statutory minimum wages as a threat to Germany's collective bargaining system. Germany's most powerful industry unions, IG Metall and IG BCE, both reported a learning effect form the German minimum wage experience (see also Behrens & Pekarek 2020; Seeliger, 2017). German unions expect EU minimum wage legislation to help decrease both low-wage labour migration into Germany and low-wage labour competition from other parts of Europe. Labour representatives interviewed also saw the need for solidarity with labour in EU-member countries without functioning collective bargaining systems.

Class conflict is always a conflict within and across societies, not between societies. German unions' engagement with the EU minimum wage initiative indicates a new blossoming of class consciousness in the world's most co-opted national trade union movement. The German experience with effective national minimum wage regulation allowed the German labour discourse to emancipate itself from the dominant employer discourse of social partner autonomy and free collective bargaining. IG Metall and IG BCE understand that their members' interests clash essentially with those of employers, be they German or American, and not so much with those of other workers, be they outsourced temporary agency workers, self-employed migrant workers or workers in competitor or supplier companies in other parts of Europe. The German position stands in stark contrast to Scandinavian labour attitudes towards the EU minimum wage initiative. In open deviation from the ETUC response to the second stage consultation on minimum wages, Scandinavian unions defended national social partner autonomy against state interference in an independent consultation response. Trade unions from Sweden, Denmark, Norway and Iceland remain important paying members within the ETUC but increasingly struggle to translate monetary power into political influence. Nordic unions suffered a political marginalisation in the minimum wage debate with the final loss of their German allies.

The erosion of Germany's hegemonic bloc has made room for new cross-national alliances. German trade unions' disenchantment with national and European capitalist elites may be a hopeful sign for the future of a pan-European labour movement. The ETUC now promotes binding EU legislation on minimum wages, effectively positioning itself as a countervailing power against the transnational business project of a purely market-led pan-European employment regime. For the first time in its history, the ETUC is pursuing a political agenda in open conflict to some of its richest and most powerful member federations. The open rift between Scandinavian unions and the rest has drawn the ETUC's long-time clash of interest between different regional factions out into the spotlight (Adamczyk, 2018). The different factions hold different views on the future of Europe. The EU can be a regional union of democratic nations with peace between classes and countries, or a regional empire with stark socio-economic inequalities between capital and labour, and between the democratic countries at the centre and the dependent countries in the periphery (Czarzasty & Mrozowicki, 2018). It cannot be both. The EU minimum wage debate shows that trade unions' national competitive alliance with employers makes pan-European working-class organisation more difficult but does not render it impossible.

The future is bleak for the EU minimum wage initiative as a social democratic countermovement from above (Harriss, 2010). Elite support for a socially embedded market needs both labour and employers as classes for themselves, organised into enlightened federations (Swenson, 2002). This chapter has outlined some progress on the labour side. The recognised EU social partner organisations from the employer side continue to be predominantly transnational business lobby groups. These groups are unenlightened by design. Their positions reflect the particular interests of the American and German multinational companies who fund them, rather than any general collective employer interest. Unlike small and medium employers, multinational enterprises are notoriously oblivious to the need to embed markets into societal rules. Employer responses to the EU minimum wage initiative openly argued that wage-labour does not have to provide workers with the means to make a living. The employer positions show once more that small and medium employers are structurally unable to influence large business groups' political positions

(Traxler & Huemer, 2007). The EU-level employer practice of undisguised class war and the opening of cracks in Germany's hegemonic bloc are not unrelated. German unions seem to have now abandoned their strategy of national alliance with employers, along with their strategic partnership with Nordic unions. As one German labour representative soberly noted during our interviews, German unions are coming to grips with the simple fact that "the era of social democracy has come to an end."

Bibliography

Adamczyk, S. (2018). Inside the trade union family. The 'two worlds' within the European Trade Union Confederation. *European Journal of Industrial Relations* 24(2), 179–192.

Anderson, P. (2009). *The new old world*. Verso Books.

Baccaro, L., & Howell, C. (2017). *Trajectories of neoliberal transformation: European industrial relations since the 1970s*. Cambridge University Press.

Beckert, J. (2020). The exhausted futures of neoliberalism: from promissory legitimacy to social anomy. *Journal of Cultural Economy* 13(3), 318-330.

Behrens, M., & Pekarek, A. (2020). Divided We Stand? Coalition Dynamics in the German Union Movement. *British Journal of Industrial Relations*. Online first. https://onlinelibrary.wiley.com/doi/abs/10.1111/bjir.12565.

Czarzasty, J., & Mrozowicki, A. (2018). Is a new paradigm needed? A commentary on the analysis by Sławomir Adamczyk. *European Journal of Industrial Relations* 24(2), 193–199.

Crouch, C. (2015). *Governing Social Risks in post-crisis Europe*. Cheltenham: Edward Elgar.

Emmenegger, P., Häusermann, S., Palier, B., & Seeleib-Kaiser, M. (Eds.). (2012). *The age of dualization. The changing face of inequality in deindustrializing societies*. USA: Oxford University Press.

González Begega, S. & Aranea, M. (2018). The establishing of a European Industrial Relations system. Still under construction or chasing a Chimera? *Employee Relations* 40(4), 600–616.

González Begega, S., Guillén, A., & Alonso Domínguez, A. (2018). Europa como recurso de autoridad. La reforma del mercado laboral español durante la crisis. Conference Paper. VII Congreso REPS, Panel 4 Hacia un nuevo estado de bienestar.

Hardy, J. (2014). Transformation and crisis in Central and Eastern Europe: A combined and uneven development perspective. *Capital & Class*, 38(1), 143–155.

Harriss, J. (2010). Globalization(s) and Labour in China and India: Introductory Reflections. *Global Labour Journal* 1(1), 9–10.

Höpner, M. (2007). Ist Politik gegen Verbände möglich? 25 Jahre Mancur Olsons "The Rise and Decline of Nations". *Leviathan*, 35, 310–347. https://doi.org/10.1007/s11578-007-0020-8.

Lehndorff, S. (2012). *Ein Triumpf gescheiterter Ideen. Warum Europa tief in der Krise steckt. Zehn Länder-Fallstudien.* VSA.

Meardi, G. (2013). *Social failures of EU enlargement: a case of workers voting with their feet.* Routledge.

Müller, T. & Schulten, T. (2020a). *The European minimum wage on the doorstep.* ETUI Policy Brief 1/ 2020.

Müller, T., Vandaele, K., & Waddington, J. (2019). *Collective bargaining in Europe: Towards an endgame.* Brussels: ETUI.

Piketty, T. (2014). *Capital in the twenty-first century.* Cambridge.

Schulten, T. (2015). Konturen einer europäischen Mindestlohnpolitik, in: von Alemann, U., Heidbreder, E.G., Hummerl, H., Dreyer, D., Goedde, A. (eds) *Ein soziales Europa ist möglich.* Springer VS, Berlin 2015, 159–182

Schulten, T. (2018). Wie hoch ist der Tarifabschluss in der Metallindustrie tatsächlich? *Makronom* 13 February 2018, available at https://makronom.de/ig-metall-tarifpolitik-wie-hoch-ist-der-tarifabschluss-in-der-metallindustrie-tatsaechlich-25316.

Seeliger, M. & Sommer, B. (2019). Trade union politics as a countermovement? A Polaniyan perspective. *Culture, Practice & Europeanization*, 4(1), 5–23.

Seeliger, M. (2018). Why Do (Some) European Trade Unions Reject Minimum Wage Regulation?. *Culture, Practice & Europeanization*, 3(1), 37–46.

Seeliger, M. (2017). Die soziale Konstruktion organisierter Interessen: gewerkschaftliche Positionsbildung auf europäischer Ebene (Vol. 89). Campus Verlag.

Standing, G. (2014). The precariat. *Contexts*, 13(4), 10–12.

Streeck, W. (2019). Progressive Regression: Metamorphoses of European Social Policy. *New Left Review* 118, 117–139.

Swenson, P. (2002). *Capitalists against markets: The making of labor markets and welfare states in the United States and Sweden.* Oxford University Press on Demand.

Traxler, F., & Huemer, G. (Eds.). (2007). *Handbook of business interest associations, firm size and governance: A comparative analytical approach.* Routledge.

Vesan, P. & Corti, F. (2019). New tensions over Social Europe? The European Pillar of Social Rights and the Debate within the European Parliament. JCMS: Journal of Common Market Studies 57.5 (2019), 977–994.

Official documents and position papers

BusinessEurope. (2020). Response to first phase social partner consultation on a possible action addressing the challenges related to fair minimum wages. https://www.businesseurope.eu/sites/buseur/files/media/position_papers/social/2020-02-19_response_first_stage_consultation_minimum_wages_final.pdf.

BusinessEurope, UEAPME, Ceemet, COPA, ECEG, EFCI, Euratex, EuroCommerce, FIEC, HOTREC, InsuranceEurope, IRU and WEC. (2017). More competitiveness to sustain the social dimension of Europe. Employer key messages.

CEC European Managers. (2020). First phase consultation of Social Partners under Article 154 TFEU on a possible action addressing the challenges related to fair minimum wages. 25 February 2020.

Ceemet. (2020). Response to first phase social partner consultation on a possible action addressing the challenges related to fair minimum wages. https://www.ceemet.org/positionpaper/ceemet-reply-first-phase-social-partner.

Ceemet. (2015). Relaunch of European social dialogue has to get basics right.

CESI. (2020). CESI Position on an EU minimum wage framework. Brussels: February 2020.

EPSU & CEMR. (2020). EPSU-CEMR joint reaction to the First phase consultation of Social Partners under Article 154 TFEU on a possible action addressing the challenges related to fair minimum wages. Undated.

ETUC. (2020a). ETUC REPLY to the First Phase Consultation of Social Partners under Article 154 TFEU on a possible action addressing the challenges related to fair minimum wages. 26 February 2020.

ETUC. (2020b). ETUC Reply to the Second Phase Consultation of Social Partners under Article 154 TFEU on a possible action addressing the challenges related to fair minimum wages 03 September 2020.

Eurocadres. (2020). First phase consultation of Social Partners under Article 154 TFEU on a possible action addressing the challenges related to fair minimum wages. 24 February 2020.

EuroCommerce. (2020). Comments on the first stage social partner consultation on EU Action on Minimum Wages. 24 February 2020. Available at https://www.eurocommerce.eu/resource-centre.aspx#PositionPaper/11758.

European Arts and Entertainment Alliance. (2020). EAEA Response to the First phase consultation of Social Partners under Article 154 TFEU on a possible action addressing the challenges related to fair minimum wages. Undated.

European Commission. (2020a). Consultation document. First phase consultation of Social Partners under Article 154 TFEU on a possible action addressing the challenges related to fair minimum wages.

European Commission. (2020b). Consultation document. Second phase consultation of Social Partners under Article 154 TFEU on a possible action addressing the challenges related to fair minimum wages.

European Commission. (2020c). European Social Dialogue e-newsletter. Issue No 11.

European Commission. (2019). List of EU social partner organisations. September 2019. Available at: https://ec.europa.eu/social/main.jsp?catId=522&langId=en.

European Parliament. (2017a). Resolution of 19 January 2017 on a European Pillar of Social Rights (2016/2095(INI))

European Parliament. (2017b). Resolution of 24 October 2017 on minimum income policies as a tool for fighting poverty (2016/2270(INI)).

industriAll. (2020). European Commission launches second consultation on fair minimum wages. Press release. 04 June 2020. Available at https://news.industriall-europe.eu/Article/456.

SMEunited. (2020). Reply to first phase social partner consultation on a possible action addressing the challenges related to fair minimum wages. https://smeunited.eu/publications/smeunited-reply-to-the-first-phase-consultation-of-social-partners-under-art-154-tfeu-on-a-possible-action-addressing-the-challenges-related-to-fair-minimum-wages.

UNI Europa. (2020). Minimum Wage: EU in danger of missing the point. Press Release. 14 January 2020

CHAPTER 13

Workplace Democracy in the UK: Reviving Voice Institutions in Unpromising Times?

David Coats

> In accepting trade union rights and freedoms, we are doing no more than accepting, in the industrial sphere, the basic principles of our society.
> —Alan Fox (1966)

1 Human Rights and Trade Union Voice

The decline in trade union membership and influence in the UK is, arguably, the most striking and far-reaching change in the labour market over the last 40 years (Fig. 1). In 1979 one in every two employees was a member of a trade union and almost four in every five had their pay and conditions of employment determined by a collective agreement. Today, fewer than one in four employees (23.4%) is a trade union

---

D. Coats (✉)
Centre for Sustainable Work and Employment Futures, University of Leicester, Leicester, UK
e-mail: dcoats@workmattersconsulting.co.uk

© The Author(s), under exclusive license to Springer Nature Switzerland AG 2022
B. Colfer (ed.), *European Trade Unions in the 21st Century*, St Antony's Series, https://doi.org/10.1007/978-3-030-88285-3_13

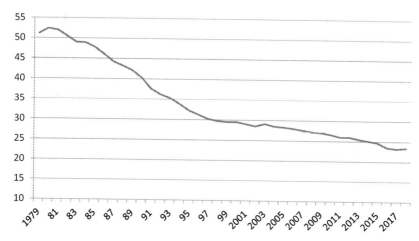

Fig. 1 Trade union density in the UK 1979–2018 (% employees) (*Source* BEIS, Trade Union Statistical Bulletin)

member and collective bargaining covers a similar proportion of the workforce. Trade union members tend to be older than the general working population and are concentrated in the public sector. Fewer than one in seven employees in the private sector is a trade union member (13.2%). Contrary to the established stereotypes, most trade union members are women (56%), largely because professionals and associate professionals in the public sector are relatively well organised (BEIS 2019).

Many countries across Europe can tell a similar story of trade union decline, but while membership may have fallen, collective bargaining coverage remains high. France is a case in point; trade union members constitute 8% of the workforce but collective bargaining coverage is 98%. Other countries (Germany for example), with union membership levels lower than the UK but much higher than France, are also characterised by the widespread observance of collective agreements. To that extent, the UK remains an outlier in the EU15 (those countries that were members before the 2004 enlargement), with a particularly low level of collective bargaining coverage.

Union membership decline is widespread and affects countries with diverse institutional arrangements. Beyond the Nordic countries, it seems that public policy designed to support workplace democracy has had little positive impact on trade union membership. What is most surprising, perhaps, is that the retreat of workplace collectivism is not generally viewed as a problem even though trade union rights are, in principle, seen as fundamental human rights. The UN's Universal Declaration, adopted in 1948, is explicit:

> Everyone has the right to form and to join trade unions for the protection of his (sic)interests. Art 23 (4)

Similar provisions are to be found in the European Convention on Human Rights, the Council of Europe Social Charter and in Article 12 of the Charter of Fundamental Rights in the EU. Alan Fox, in the epigraph to this essay asserts what was, in the 1960s, accepted as a central feature of a democratic society—that workers do not surrender their rights as citizens at the point they cross their employer's threshold.

And yet, in many countries, including the UK, it can be argued that merely *formal* guarantees are believed to be sufficient to prove that these fundamental rights are being respected. In other words, so long as there are no legal impediments placed in the path of trade union membership and organisation it can be asserted with confidence that no further action is needed to promote industrial democracy. Moreover, the UK makes dismissals for trade union membership and activities automatically unfair, generating claims for compensation that are not subject to the usual financial limits on remedies.

The principal argument of this paper is that merely formal guarantees are in no way sufficient. If workers lack the capability, resources or organisational capacity to vindicate fundamental rights, then those rights are *not* being respected. There *is* a policy problem to be solved and a strong case for a dispassionate assessment of current arrangements to identify weaknesses and develop a programme of reform.

One might say that the position in the European Union is somewhat different from the UK. After all, trade unions (alongside employers) have a role in developing legislation through the social dialogue process. The Economic and Social Committee is designed to provide a direct link between the EU's decision making and the interests of labour and capital and social dialogue is often described as a fundamental feature of the European social model.[1] Again, in formal terms, all this is true. But the

---

[1] The Treaty of Amsterdam (1997) created a unified framework for social dialogue in the EU, resulting in framework agreements between the social partners on part-time work,

social partners have made little progress with the development of framework agreements in recent years and, despite the constitutional guarantees entrenched by the various EU treaties, there must be a serious question whether the status quo can be sustained if trade union membership decline continues.

Despite these emerging weaknesses, however, it is worth recalling the rationale for social dialogue and the involvement of the social partners. Jacques Delors, former president of the European Commission, in making the case for social Europe, observed that the completion of the single market would generate a wave of restructuring across the EU as businesses sought to reap economies of scale and as technological change destroyed old jobs and created new employment opportunities (Delors 1988). Workers would, in the absence of practical alternatives, be resistant to any change that threatened established patterns of employment. The purpose of social Europe was to give everybody a voice in the process and a stake in the outcome. New forms of worker participation in corporate governance (the notion of the European company), would be matched by commitments to lifelong learning and a renewed dedication to improving social protection and the scope of collective bargaining.

From the standpoint of a sceptical observer in 2020, this position can look quaint, out of time and out of step with the realities of Brexit, austerity across the EU and the monetary and fiscal policy constraints of the Eurozone. But there is an equally strong case for saying that the case for industrial democracy (and social Europe) is, if anything, stronger today than in 1988. Indeed, one might say that the Delors argument was just as much focused on the fundamental features of capitalism—disruption, dislocation and "creative destruction" (Schumpeter 1943)—as it was on the completion of the single market and the consequent restructuring. The interaction of capital, technology and competition is an unavoidable feature of economic life, no matter what policymakers may do. And it is clear from historical experience as well as recent empirical analysis that markets, left to themselves, do not and cannot create inclusive prosperity (Piketty 2014).

Much commentary in recent years has focused on the supposedly revolutionary implications of robotics and the development of artificial

---

fixed-term work and parental leave, all of which were enshrined in EU directives. The Treaty of Lisbon emphasised the role of the social partners, recognising the importance of social dialogue while respecting the autonomy and diversity of the parties.

intelligence (AI). Most notorious perhaps is Frey and Osborne's suggestion that 47% of jobs in the US could be automated by the middle of the 2030s (Frey and Osborne 2013). The OECD has offered a more measured analysis, suggesting that no more than 10% of jobs in the UK will be affected by automation, although it is also suggested that lower skilled and lower paid workers will bear the brunt of restructuring (Arntz et al. 2016). Economic geography has become an increasingly salient issue and there is little doubt that recent political developments can be explained by the failure to create high quality jobs in areas that have witnessed a fall in industrial employment. The phenomenon can be observed across the EU—declining industrial towns in France of Germany look much like their counterparts in the UK. An accelerating pace of industrial change intensifies rather than undermines the case for social dialogue and industrial democracy, even though the scope and scale of these developments may be less challenging than Frey and Osborne suggest.

There is a strong case for saying too that a determined programme of action to tackle climate change will have a much bigger impact on the structure of employment than the supposed rise of the robots and the advance of intelligent machines. Some industries may disappear completely and others may change quite fundamentally as they seek to reduce their carbon footprints. Radical upheavals can be anticipated in manufacturing, agriculture, transport, finance, construction and retail. Indeed, it is arguable that no sector of the economy will remain untouched by the imperative to respond to climate change. Precisely how the economy can be reshaped without the involvement of workers and their representatives is more than a little mysterious. To that extent, the international trade union movement has a stronger grasp of the issues than many policymakers in calling for a *just transition* (Burrow 2015). In other words, it is recognised that there will inevitably be winners and losers from a climate action programme; the priority for the unions is to ensure that the costs and benefits are shared equitably.

Business decisions (and their wider social implications) must, therefore, be justified and legitimised if they are to be accepted, just as political decisions must be made through due process. This is what Alan Fox meant when he said that respecting the role of trade unions is nothing more than the application of the basic principles of our society in the workplace. It explains too why trade union rights are described as fundamental human rights, essential if a democratic polity is to be sustained.

2 The State of Worker Voice in the UK Today

Some readers may argue it is tendentious to suggest that the UK does too little to give practical effect to voice in the workplace. Fortunately for the argument presented in this paper, there is a wealth of social science confirming that the rights for workers to speak up, be heard and receive a reasoned response from their employer are honoured more in the breach than the observance. Neil Millward, in his analysis of the UK's 1990 Workplace Industrial Relations Survey (WIRS), drew the following striking conclusion:

> Britain is approaching the position where few employees have any mechanism through which they can contribute to the operation of their workplace in a broader context than that of their own job. There is no sign that the shrinkage in the extent of trade union representation is being offset by a growth in other methods of representing non-managerial employees' views. There has been no spontaneous emergence of an alternative model of employee representation that could channel and attenuate conflicts between employers and employees. (Millward 1994)

Seventeen years later, the 2011 Workplace Employment Relations Study (WERS) confirmed Millward's judgement.[2] Joint consultation through formal mechanisms was a minority pursuit; fewer than one in ten workplaces had a joint consultative committee in operation bringing together workers representatives and managers to discuss the problems of the day. More disturbingly, perhaps, almost two thirds of employees were disappointed by their level of involvement in workplace decision making and half of all employees said that managers could not be trusted to keep their promises (van Wanrooy 2013).

The HR profession has invested much time and energy in promoting employee engagement over the last 15 years. There has been a government sponsored task force, *Engage for Success*, and a good deal of promotional activity (MacLeod and Clarke 2009). One of the critical indicators of engagement is whether employees are willing to offer extensive discretionary effort. In other words, are they willing to "go the extra mile", undertaking tasks with enthusiasm that are above and beyond

---

[2] The WIRS/WERS series began in 1980 and was the product of a collaboration between the government and a number of other agencies. It is hard to detect any enthusiasm on the part of the present government for a new survey.

contractual requirements. A useful source of data is the Skills and Employment Survey 2017 (SES), which is part of a series that began in the early 1990s. The SES records a fall in discretionary effort over time, especially in the private sector (Green et al. 2018). Moreover, this fall in discretionary effort has taken place in a context of more extensive employer controls over the organisation of work, falling autonomy and task discretion, and an increase in work intensity (Green et al. 2018; Gallie et al. 2018). The quality of employment appears to be falling despite the considerable rhetorical investment in the case for "good work".

Consistent with the WERS series, the SES suggests there has been no increase in effective organisational participation over the last 25 years despite the emphasis on employee engagement. The researchers examined the extent of quality circles and consultative meetings, both of which have fallen in usage, alongside a composite measure of organisational influence, which again shows no significant change over the period (Fig. 2). At first glance, it seems that there was an increase in organisational influence between 2012 and 2017 *despite* the decline in consultative

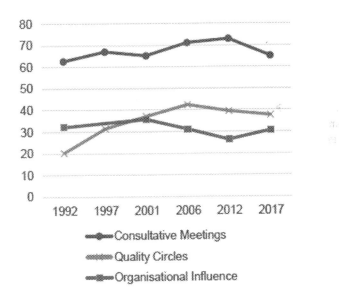

Fig. 2 Trends in organisational influence 1992–2017 (% employees) (*Source* SES 2017)

institutions. This is explained, however, by the fact that those organisations valuing organisational participation were making more effective use of these arrangements than was previously the case. While 65% of the employees surveyed reported the use of consultative meetings, only 30% believed they could influence organisational decisions affecting their work—the same result recorded by WERS 2011 (Gallie et al. 2018). The conclusion is clear: there had been no significant improvement at all over a six-year period; no more voice overall, but slightly more effective voice in the minority of workplaces where it exists.

The UK's productivity gap with other major economies has been well-documented elsewhere and will, if not addressed, affect living standards and overall prosperity (BEIS 2017). Part of the productivity story is about investment, skills, innovation, entrepreneurship and competition. But what happens inside the workplace matters too; much innovation is incremental rather than transformational and depends on suggestions from workers about how to do their jobs more effectively. The SES found a relatively weak level of workplace innovation, with fewer than one in five workers making successful proposals for positive change in their workplace (Felstead 2018). Moreover, the conditions under which workers were encouraged to contribute appeared to be weakening; lower autonomy, less supportive management, more intrusive or less useful systems of performance management and appraisal, less effective worker voice.

The decline of worker voice institutions in the UK has had a negative effect on the link between wages and productivity. In conventional economic theory, rising wages depend on rising productivity and exemplify the principle that employers will share the fruits of growth with their employees. What we have learned over the last 40 years is that the process is not automatic and the balance of power between capital and labour matters.

The Resolution Foundation, for example, have documented how wage growth for all those on median earnings and below became disconnected from productivity growth in the early 1990s (Pessoa and van Reenen 2012; Commission on Living Standards 2012). Those countries that had preserved the coverage of collective bargaining, despite union membership decline, experienced a much weaker delinking of pay and productivity (Bailey et al. 2011). From the workers' standpoint, or at least for anybody below the middle of the distribution, the sense of unfairness is palpable—a falling back throughout the 1990s and the early 2000s when productivity was growing quite rapidly, followed by stagnant wages or sluggish wage growth in the wake of the global crisis.

The labour economist Richard Freeman has suggested that the current realities are best viewed as a form of feudalism, where employers are able to behave with baronial authority and workers have no choice but to obey (Freeman 2012). Historically, the absence of institutions to manage conflict has generally produced an organisational response—trade unions were inspired, at least in part, by the gross economic inequalities that existed in the nineteenth and early twentieth centuries, which led in turn to an upsurge in industrial conflict.[3] There are two aspects of the current conjuncture that are worthy of comment: first, the scale of strike action in the UK has been set at a historic low for most of the past two decades; second, trade unions have failed to make the most of the opportunities available to rebuild membership and collective bargaining coverage.

3 Policy Responses

This is not to suggest, of course, that trade unions have been idle. From the early 1990s until the early 2000s the Trades Union Congress (TUC) had a practical agenda for the reform of labour law that would, ostensibly, make it easier to rebuild workplace organisation. Indeed, given what has been said so far, the TUC's programme was successful to the extent that many of the proposals found their way onto the UK's statute book.

3.1 Statutory Arrangements for Trade Union Recognition

The UK now has a well-established statutory procedure, supervised by the Central Arbitration Committee (CAC) in Great Britain and by the Industrial Court in Northern Ireland, to establish employer recognition for collective bargaining.[4] Following an award of recognition by the CAC the trade union concerned has a right to negotiate a collective agreement with the employer on pay, hours and holidays.

In part, the impulse for legislative action flowed from the TUC's view, subsequently shared by the 1997–2010 Labour government, that

---

[3] In the period before the First World War (more precisely between 1910 and 1914) the level of industrial conflict was higher than at any time later in the century.

[4] Originally enacted in the Employment Relations Act 1999. The powers and duties of the CAC were set out in Schedule 1.

employers could, in principle, defeat a claim for voluntary recognition, no matter what level of membership a union may have achieved. From the government's standpoint the objective was to ensure the orderly conduct of industrial relations, so that unions had other options than simply organising a strike in pursuit of a recognition claim. For the unions, a statutory framework for the conduct of collective bargaining added weight to the argument that organised labour had a role in a modern economy.

It is surprising, nonetheless, given the vigour of the TUC's campaign, that the recognition procedure has been used so sparingly. In the year 2018–19, for example, the CAC received only 37 applications for trade union recognition of which 29 were accepted for further consideration (CAC 2019). The numbers of workers covered by CAC awards remains small and it is hard to sustain the argument that the statutory procedure has had any *direct* effect on the level of union membership or collective bargaining coverage in the UK.

A more positive assessment might point out that there could be a *demonstration* effect at work, albeit that causation is hard to prove and the impact is hard to quantify. Employers know, for example, that the statutory procedure exists and it may therefore provide a breakwater against even more hostile attitudes towards trade unions. After all, the big declines in union membership and bargaining coverage took place from the 1980s through to the middle 1990s and the decline since the recognition procedure was introduced has been muted in comparison (Fig. 1).

A critic of the CAC process would say that it is deliberately designed to constrain the capacity of trade unions to secure recognition. To begin with the application must be accepted by the CAC and this is a process subject to two quite stringent tests: first, the union must demonstrate that it has the support of at least 10% of the workers in the bargaining unit; second the union must show that it would be likely to win a ballot for recognition were a ballot to be ordered by the CAC. Moreover, the employer is able to challenge the union's preferred bargaining unit and can call for a ballot of the workforce to determine support for recognition. There are some examples too (although few in number) of employers using union busting consultants to ensure that recognition ballots are lost.

But if the procedure really were fundamentally flawed then one might anticipate a *higher* level of applications from unions to expose these weaknesses and a more assertive public campaign to secure changes in the law.

Most trade unions today either pretend that the statutory procedure does not exist or are unaware of the possibilities that it creates. Certainly, it is hard to detect any trade union organising strategy behind the applications that have been submitted in the last year. If unions were only using the statutory system *in extremis*, once all other options have been exhausted, one would expect to see collective bargaining coverage rising as a result of voluntary agreements—a phenomenon that cannot be observed. As things stand, applications to the CAC appear to be random, dependent on the enthusiasm or knowledge of individual union officials rather than a national strategy co-ordinated by the TUC.

3.2 *The Information and Consultation of Employees Regulations 2004 and the EU Directive*

Once the recognition procedure was in place, the focus of union attention moved on. The European Commission had brought forward proposals to create a common framework for the provision of information to workplace representatives and worker involvement in robust consultative processes. To begin with the UK government was resistant to this initiative, but eventually embraced the idea on the grounds that more extensive worker participation could boost productivity and increase the number of high performance workplaces (DTI 2002).

EU Directive 2002/14 is transposed in the UK by the 2004 Information and Consultation of Employees Regulations (ICE). Workers can vindicate their rights by presenting a petition signed by at least 10% of the employees in the undertaking triggering the election of workplace representatives—the 10% threshold was reduced to 2% of employees in the undertaking in April 2020.[5] These representatives are then empowered to negotiate a framework for information and consultation with the employer, which includes the option for consultation with individual employees as an alternative to consultation with elected representatives.[6] To date the 2004 regulations have been used even more sparingly than the

---

[5] This forms part of the government's response to the report of the *Taylor Review of Modern Employment Practices* (Taylor 2017).

[6] In principle, therefore, representatives can be elected to negotiate an ICE agreement that dispenses with the need for workers' representatives. There is a serious question whether this is consistent with the intention of the EU directive.

recognition provisions. Once again the CAC is responsible for the application of the regulations and in 2018–2019 received only two complaints. Since the provisions became effective in 2005, the CAC has received only 21 applications.

It could be argued that the ICE regulations are drafted to place insurmountable obstacles in the path of workers seeking to establish new consultative arrangements. The 10% threshold is a very high barrier and in large undertakings may be difficult to achieve. Certainly, this explains why a government generally viewed as sceptical about the case for worker participation reduced the threshold in 2020. But even with this change it is not entirely clear that there will be an upsurge of ICE related activity. The regulations are either unknown or poorly understood and, despite the TUC's efforts in the early 2000s, a change in the leadership of some large unions means that ICE is seen as a second best alternative to collective bargaining, deserving little or no attention.

In addition to ICE, EU law makes provision for consultation with workers' representatives on business transfers (the Acquired Rights Directive), collective redundancies, working time and health and safety at work. Some commentators (not least the present author) have suggested that there is a strong case for bringing all these rights together in a coherent body of law, establishing in the UK something analogous to the German model of workplace codetermination. But works councils in the EU depend for their effectiveness on the enthusiastic involvement of the trade unions. There must be an organised presence in the workplace to both establish the institutions and provide training, advice and support to elected representatives. In the absence of a decisive change in trade union strategy, reinforced by the promotion of the regulations by government, it is unlikely that even an integrated framework of ICE rights will lead to a significant increase in workplace participation.

It would be plausible to conclude that the relatively limited impact of both the recognition procedure and the ICE regulations proves that public policy alone cannot ensure that formal rights will be vindicated in practice. As the Anglo-German labour lawyer Otto Kahn-Freund argued almost 50 years ago, the law is simply not equipped to transform industrial relations realities (Kahn-Freund 1972). Certainly, the law can play a reinforcing role, extending the coverage of collective agreements negotiated by the parties—see, for example, the extension mechanisms that are commonplace in continental Europe—but statutory intervention is most effective when it cuts with the grain of well-developed industrial relations cultures.

This was certainly true in the UK until the election of the Thatcher government in 1979. The state embraced the belief that collective bargaining was a collective good with beneficial economic consequences. Measures were taken that allowed for the extension of collective agreements to non-signatory employers (a policy most recently found in Schedule 11 of the Employment Protection Act 1975) until the Thatcher government repealed them. And the state took seriously its responsibility only to do business with reputable organisations when procuring goods and services. The Fair Wages Resolution 1946 fixed the principle that all government contractors should observe the relevant collective agreements before they could gain access to the public service market.

The Thatcher government's trade union reforms support Kahn-Freund's assessment. By the end of the 1970s employer opinion had changed quite fundamentally, largely in response to price inflation and industrial conflict over the course of the decade. Trade unions may not have been seen by many employers as "the enemy within", but unions were certainly viewed as over mighty, out of control and in need of legal restraint. In the absence of employer and wider public support, the Conservative government's programme would have proved ineffective.[7]

Unions became an estate of the realm not simply because they enjoyed government support but because membership and collective bargaining coverage were rising *before* public policy offered any support at all—indeed, until 1906, when trade unions were given immunity in tort, it is arguable that public policy was either neutral or hostile to the role of organised labour; trade unions were operating at and sometimes beyond the margins of lawfulness.

We are left, therefore, at the end of this discussion, with a series of dilemmas. Rights to trade union voice are established as human rights but, so far as the UK is concerned, these rights are formal rather than effective. Governments of varying political colours over the last 20 years have created new opportunities for trade unions and workers to assert their rights to voice, but these legislative efforts have proved inadequate to the

---

[7] As was the case with the 1970–1974 Heath government's programme of reform, the Industrial Relations Act 1971, which was met with unremitting trade union hostility and employer indifference.

task. As a practical matter, workers in the UK today have fewer opportunities for voice than in the past (as WERS and the SES demonstrate) despite the existence of more extensive rights. Technological change and a necessary response to the climate crisis are likely to prove hugely disruptive to settled patterns of work, reinforcing the case for dialogue between workers, employers and government if painful processes of change are to be justified and legitimised with an equitable sharing of the costs and the benefits. It is not unreasonable to conclude that the status quo is unfit for purpose. What then should be done?

4   Possibilities for the Future?

Two decades ago, British commentators often looked with envy at the strength of collective bargaining in other EU countries, at the legal guarantees of information and consultation and at the involvement of workers in business decision-making. Today, while continental European systems still offer advantages over arrangements in the UK, many of these institutions are under pressure, union membership is falling and organised labour is playing a less important role in the community. The challenges facing the UK outlined in this paper are to be found, in similar forms, across continental Europe.

The purpose of this discussion is not to outline a detailed programme of reform but to highlight some possibilities for the future. Perhaps the most important initial conclusion is that British trade unions should stop their search for an instant legislative solution and recognise, assuming public policy is not hostile, that they have no choice but to be agents of their own resurgence. Trade union membership is an experience good—it is hard to place a value on the potential advantages of being a trade union member unless you are already a member or know others who have benefited from trade union membership.[8] There are now more people at work in the UK who have *never* been members of a trade union than are current or former members. In other words, trade unions are seeking to recruit in a labour market where most workers have no precise idea of the trade union role beyond media coverage of struggle, strikes and strife.

These unavoidable realities place a premium on the development of a persuasive trade union story about the role of organised labour in a

---

[8] On the notion of union membership as an experience good see Bryson et al. (2001).

modern economy. This paper has briefly described the phenomenon of declining job quality in the UK, much of which can be explained by the retreat of effective voice institutions. Alan Fox offered some wise insights on this matter too:

> The preoccupation with the unions' economic role in labour markets [wage formation] has meant that **an even more important role** [my emphasis] has been neglected and insufficiently understood. This is the role of union organisation within the workplace in regulating managerial relations ie the exercise of management authority in deploying, organising and disciplining the labour force after it has been hired. (Fox 1966)

We can see from the results of the SES that workers are concerned about work intensification, declining autonomy and control, intrusive performance management systems *and* an absence of voice in the workplace. Trade unions have drawn attention to the exploitation of workers with zero hour contracts, the rise of the gig economy and the persistent problems of low pay. But rather than focus on the minority of workers in precarious situations, trade unions would be well-advised to recognise, drawing on the findings of the SES, that those in mainstream, apparently secure employment can have a troubling time at work too. The challenge, perhaps, is to craft a narrative and an agenda that appeals to the majority of people at work, identifies shared interests and enables the strong to support those at the margins. Solidarity is a more effective organisational tool than altruism.

So far as public policy is concerned, although it may be right to abandon the quest for instant solutions, there is still a strong case for interventions that support a process of institution building. Trade unions could be given rights of access to workplaces so that they can organise without impediment. The terms of reference of the Advisory, Conciliation and Arbitration Service (ACAS) could be revised to impose a duty to promote collective bargaining. The various ICE rights contained in EU directives could be brought together in a coherent framework, laying the foundations for workplace institutions analogous to works councils. The government could sponsor a dialogue between unions and employers in low paid sectors with a view to raising labour standards. And, drawing on Kahn-Freund's insight that it had a bigger impact on the observance of collective agreements than any other measure, the government could adopt a new Fair Wages Resolution.[9] More than anything, however, making industrial democracy a reality depends on people having the courage to organise themselves, speak up and assert with confidence that rights to voice are human rights, deserving universal respect.

Bibliography

Arntz, Melanie et al. (2016), *The Risks of Automation for Jobs in OECD Countries: A Comparative Analysis*, OECD Social, Employment and Migration Working Papers No. 189, OECD

Bailey, Jess et al. (2011), *Painful Separation: An International Study of the Weakening Relationship Between Economic Growth and the Pay of Ordinary Workers*, Commission on Living Standards/Resolution Foundation

BEIS (2017), *Industrial Strategy: Building A Britain Fit For The Future*, Department for Business, Enterprise, Innovation and Skills

BEIS (2019), *Trade Union Statistical Bulletin*, Department for Business Enterprise, Innovation and Skills.

Bryson, Alex et al. (2001), *Youth-Adult Differences in the Demand for Unionisation*, Centre for Economic Performance, London School of Economics.

Burrow, Sharan (2015), *Sharan Burrow's Speech to the Oslo Climate Change Conference*, Oslo, 13 March 2013, ITUC, available at: https://www.ituc-csi.org/sharan-burrow-s-speech-to-the.

CAC (2019), *Annual Report 2018/19*, Central Arbitration Committee.

Commission on Living Standards (2012), *Gaining from growth: Final report of the commission on living standards*, Resolution Foundation.

Delors, Jacques (1988), *Address to the Trades Union Congress*, Bournemouth, 8 September 1988, available at: https://ec.europa.eu/commission/presscorner/detail/en/SPEECH_88_66.

DTI (2002), *High Performance Workplaces: The Role of Employee Involvement in a Modern Economy*, Department of Trade and Industry.

Felstead, Alan et al. (2018), *Insecurity at Work in Britain*, LLAKES.

Fox, Alan (1966), *Industrial Sociology and Industrial Relations*, Research Paper 3, Royal Commission on Trade Unions and Employers' Associations.

Freeman, Richard B (2012), *Toward Economic Feudalism? Inequality, Financialisation and Democracy* available at: http://www.lse.ac.uk/assets/richmedia/channels/publicLecturesAndEvents/slides/20120502_1830_towardEconomicFeudalism_sl.pdf.

---

[9] The first Fair Wages Resolution was adopted in 1891 by Lord Salisbury's Conservative government.

Frey, Carl Benedikt and Osborne, Michael (2013), *The Future of Employment: How Susceptible are Jobs to Computerisation*, Oxford Martin School.
Gallie, Duncan et al. (2018), *Participation at Work in Britain*, LLAKES – UCL Institute of Education.
Green, Francis et al. (2018), *Work Intensity in Britain*, LLAKES – UCL Institute of Education.
Kahn-Freund, Otto (1972), *Labour and the Law*, Stevens and Sons.
MacLeod, David and Clarke, Nita (2009), *Engaging for Success: Enhancing Performance Through Employee Engagement*, Department for Business Industries and Skills.
Millward, Neil (1994), *The New Industrial Relations*, PSI.
Pessoa, Joao and van Reenen, John (2012), *Decoupling of Wage Growth and Productivity Growth: Myth and Reality*, Resolution Foundation.
Piketty, Thomas (2014), *Capital in the Twenty-First Century*, Belknap Harvard.
Schumpeter, Joseph (1943), *Capitalism, Socialism and Democracy*, Unwin paperback edition 1987.
Taylor, Matthew (2017), *Good Work, The Taylor Review of Modern Working Practices*, BEIS.
Van Wanrooy, Brigid et al. (2013), *Employment Relations in the Shadow of Recession*, Palgrave Macmillan.

CHAPTER 14

Polish Unions Towards Populism: Strategies and Dilemmas

Jan Czarzasty and Adam Rogalewski

1 Introduction

Over recent years, Polish trade unions have operated under the auspices of the right- wing populist government of Law and Justice Party (Prawo i Sprawedliwość/PiS) that was first elected in 2015. The PiS government succeeded the liberal-conservative coalition of the neo- liberal Civic Platform (Platoforma Obywatleska/PO) and the Polish People's Party (Polskie Stronnictwo Ludowe/PSL), a farmers' party (from 2007 to 2015). Furthermore, the 2015 election saw the complete elimination of left-wing parties from the parliament and led to, unprecedented in the history of Polish politics, a one-party government. This victory was repeated again by PiS at the end of 2019, but this time the parliament

J. Czarzasty (✉)
Warsaw School of Economics, Warsaw, Poland
e-mail: jczarz@sgh.waw.pl

A. Rogalewski
European Federation of Public Service Unions (EPSU), Brussels, Belgium

was more balanced, with the upper chamber dominated by the opposition and with social democratic parties returning to parliament. The absence of left-wing parties from power for the last 16 years, and the 8 years of domination by a neo-liberal government during this period, put Polish unions in a very difficult situation as far as PiS is concerned. The party was not only elected on the basis of a robust social agenda, mirroring to a large extent many core union policies, but it also successfully implemented them in the first months of being in power. Yet this is the party which, ever since it formed a majority government, has shown strong authoritarian tendencies. This begs the question of how the Polish unions have dealt with this dilemma. What strategies and methods have the unions deployed to challenge the government's populism and authoritarianism? This chapter seeks to answer these questions.

We will examine the response of the three national trade union centres s in Poland and their affiliates, which are formally recognised as representative worker organisations in the national-level tripartite Social Dialogue Council (Rada Dialogu Społecznego), namely: Trade Unions Forum (Forum Związków Zawodowych/FZZ), All-Poland Alliance of Trade Unions (Ogólnopolskie Porozumienie Związków Zawodowych/OPZZ) and NSZZ 'Solidarność' (Solidarność).

In our analysis we focus on two of the most important events in the recent history of Polish trade unions which put them in a position of formal disagreement—or even outright dispute—with the government. First, their position regarding the revision of the EU's directive concerning the posting of workers and the important role of the European-level trade union movement in supporting Polish unions' positions against the government. This is an example of how changes in the European Union (EU) legal environment can promote solidarity. Secondly, we will look at recent protests by public service workers, including among the uniformed services (i.e. police officers and firefighters), as well as teachers and civil servants employed by the Ministry of Justice. In particular, the teachers' strike was successful in maximising opportunities associated with the network society, as we shall see.

In keeping with Mueller (2017), we understand the sort of right-wing populism that we observe under the 2015-PiS government as involving a blend of anti-elitism and anti-pluralism. Right-wing parties often embrace populism and use it as a vehicle to advance various sets of postulates, that can be eclectic, but that typically share a common denominator, albeit a fuzzy one. For Pelinka (2013, pp15-16) *'European right-wing populism tends to be pro-state, tends to criticize the absence of a strong role of government in the realm of the economy,* [and] *tends to lament the decline of the national welfare state'.*

Finally, we believe that right-wing populist policies and politics is not only a challenge for Polish unions but, as reality shows, it can also become a reality for more unions around the world, as Visser (2019) suggests. We hope that recounting the experiences of Polish unions during this period can serve as a lesson for other unions, as well as interesting research material for scholars in the field of industrial relations.

2 Polish unionism in the context of a power resources approach

In recent years we have witnessed growing interest in the power resources approach within the industrial relations literature. The approach is rooted in classic sociological thought, such as that of Max Weber, followed by the Twentieth-century debates that focused mainly on collective action (see: Korpi, 1985). For a number of years it fell into relative obscurity. Its rise from the ashes, as far as labour studies is concerned began in the 2010s, and is reflected by a stream of literature addressing the weakening position of trade unions in many contexts (e.g. Levesque and Murray, 2010, 2013; Lehndorff et al. 2018, Schmalz et al., 2018; Doellgast et al., 2018).

Power resources should not be mistaken for power. Rather, power resources reflect *'fixed or path-dependent assets that an actor can normally access and mobilize'* (Levesque and Murray, 2010, p. 335). So, power resources are actually capacities (or a potential) which may transform into power only if put into effective use by influencing the behaviour of other actors within a given field; in the case of trade unions, this would be the state and employers. The power resources of trade unions are diverse, and thus translate into various categories of power. The major categories of union power are: associational, structural, institutional and societal. Associational power is not entirely related to unionisation levels. It is defined by Wright (2000, p. 962) as *'the various forms of power that result from the formation of collective organizations of workers.'* So, the associational power of trade unions depends not only on the absolute number of members (i.e. the rate of density), but also on the composition of union membership (i.e. the relative importance of major occupational groups that are organised by unions in the labour market), and worker participation in decision-making structures (i.e. worker voice) (see Levesque and Murray, 2010). Structural power *'results simply from the location of workers within the economic system'* (Wright, 2000, p. 962). At the macro-level, structural power is also determined by the *'specific incorporation of a country into global capital accumulation'* (Schmalz et al. 2018, p. 124). In other words, it reflects the place of a country in the global division of labour and value chains or, more generally, its position vis-a-vis the centres of the global economy (see the post-Wallerstein core-periphery debates, in the context of Central and Eastern Europe, especially Bohle and Greskovits 2012 and Rapacki et al. 2019).

Institutional power stems from 'struggles and negotiation process based on structural power and associational power' (Schmalz et al., 2018, p. 121). In general, institutional power involves using institutional arrangements such as collective bargaining and social dialogue by unions to achieve their ends by completing collective agreements, social pacts and favourable legal regulations.

Societal power, on the other hand, comes from the usage of some less tangible assets described as *'the latitudes for action arising from viable cooperation contexts with other social groups and organisations, and society's support for trade union demands'* (Schmalz et al. 2018, p. 122). As Bernaciak and Kahancová (2017, p. 13) argue, the accumulation of societal power resources can be accomplished through various actions and means such as *'protests and demonstrations, advocacy campaigns and media appearances as well as the innovative use of different types of media and information and communication technologies to present unions' claims, opinions and concerns'*. Or in other words, societal power also comes through the maximisation of opportunities associated with the network society.

As we apply the power resources approach to the situation of trade unions in the Central and Eastern European (CEE) countries (Poland included), it becomes evident that, while suffering from the evaporation of associational, structural and—to a lesser degree—institutional power, unions have managed to accrue some successes through building societal power resources and by translating them into societal power, especially following the 2008-series of crises (see: Butkovic et al. 2021). Trade unions in Poland and other CEE countries have been shifting from the 'logic of membership' to the 'logic of influence' (Schmitter and Streeck, 1981). However, considering the apparently deliberate attempt by the populist government in Poland to capture the trade union agenda since 2015, the prospects for organised labour to further develop their societal power become blurry.

3 SETTING THE SCENE

Jan Guz, the late OPZZ president, used to say that it is difficult for the unions to challenge the PiS government on their social policies because the party pledged to greatly extend and implement many of the unions' own flagship social policies (reduction of pension age or increasing the coverage of minimum wage to all types of workers). It is maybe an oversimplification, but at first glance, PiS have indeed introduced many core trade unions demands over recent years. This has included: the reinstatement of the retirement to 65 years of age, from the previous level of 67 years that had been introduced by the previous PO government. The party also implemented an old demand of the OPZZ and Solidarność by introducing the minimum wage for workers on civil law contracts (including freelancers) and by significantly increasing the minimum wage for all employees. In 2016 the government even went further and increased the minimum wage by an amount that exceeded the unions' demands. Obviously, this was a political decision which, among other things, shows the level of the party's ignorance vis-à-vis social dialogue processes and trade unions, but it was very well received by the Polish population and by many union members. Nonetheless, the minimum wage already increased by one third from 1750 PLN (390 euros approx.)[1] per month in 2015 to 2250 PLN (500 euros approx.) in 2019. Additionally, the party introduced a children's allowance payment through the now infamous '500 + policy' (which saw an allowance of 500 PLN (110 euro approx.) for a second and any subsequent child, which later becomes a synonym for the party's core social policy. Thanks to PiS, all retired workers received and an additional 13th pension payment, and some pensioners also received an additional care allowance of 300 PLN (65 euros approx.).[2] As a result of these interventions, the living

---

[1] In December 2020 1 PLN had a value of approximately 0.22 Euros.

[2] For public relations and political reasons PiS chose to name their policies after the sum of money they relate to, with the addition of 'plus'.

and working conditions of the poorest sections of Polish society were significantly improved (Rogalewski, 2020).

Contrary to PiS, the previous PO government's policies were embedded in the party's liberal identity and aimed to support the agenda of employers and business. Furthermore, PO did not conduct genuine dialogue with trade unions and left them with no choice but to leave the tripartite committee and suspend their participation in social dialogue (Czarzasty, 2019). Eventually, at the end of its term in office, PO appeared to loosen their liberal policies and came to appreciate the importance of cooperation with trade unions. For instance, it created the Social Dialogue Council which would have more competences than the previous national social dialogue body had (Czarzasty, 2019).

Aside from challenges related to neoliberal and later populist policies, industrial relations in Poland are decidedly neoliberal (Prosser, 2019) and the corporatism that exists is 'illusory'. Over recent decades, Polish unions have been confronted with falling rates of membership and collective bargaining coverage, which were both already among the lowest in the EU. As of 2017, trade union density was 12.7 per cent, and coverage stood at 18 per cent (Czarzasty, 2019). Since the end of communism, union density has steadily decreased as has the number of collective agreements (Czarzasty, 2019). Currently there is no sectoral collective bargaining in Poland although this possibility is permitted under the Labour Code. Collective agreements, where they exist, are concluded at the company-level which has further contributed to the fragmentation of the unions. For instance, at the national post office, there are now about 90 trade unions. Fragmentation of the unions went hand-in-hand with the fragmentation of the workforce, with many workers being employed on fix-term contracts or performing jobs on different than employment contracts. For instance, during the time of the PO government, a new form of precarious employment appeared, given the emergence of a service contract (umowa zlecenie), which is the equivalent of a zero-hours contract in the UK, was based on the regulations of the civil code rather than the labour code. As a consequence, workers employed this way, become quasi self-employed with almost no protection i.e. without sick or holiday pay. Fortunately, as a result of union pressure the legal situation of this group was gradually improving, and PO had already provided workers on service contracts, with obligatory social insurance coverage. In 2015, the Constitutional Tribunal, in a case involving a claim submitted by OPZZ, decided that workers employed on civil contracts cannot be prohibited from joining a union (Constitutional Court, 2015). The court's decision was eventually implemented in Polish law by the revision of the Trade Union Act, which came into force at the beginning of 2019 and confirmed the right for all workers to join or form a trade union (Czarzasty, 2019). Although the situation of people employed on civil contracts was indeed improved, this is still one of the most precarious group of workers with only limited protection against dismissal or access to health and safety regulation. Finally, the fragmentation of the Polish labour market increased due to the recent inflow of migrant workers from Ukraine, who in the vast majority were employed in the precarious working conditions (Duda, 2020).

However, not all of PiS' social policies were supported without contestation, and the unions were particularly unsatisfied with the level of social dialogue. Unions complained about the lack of consultation with social partners and about the introduction of bills via the initiative of members of parliament (MPs) rather than via the government. Notably, bills introduced by MPs do not require submitting it for consultation with social partners, and doing so excluded the social partners from the decision-making process.

With regard to the social policies that have been introduced by PiS, including those that were generally in line with the unions' positions, Polish unions chose to approve their objectives but were more critical of specific details or of the ways in which they were implemented. For instance, while OPZZ supported the introduction of children's allowance, they argued that the income threshold was too low for receiving it for one child. Furthermore, OPZZ welcomed the introduction of free medicine for pensioners, but was critical that money allocated for this initiative was not sufficient to cover prices of many important medicines. In the same statement, that assessed the early of days the PiS government, OPZZ raised its concerns about shifting the priorities of the government from socio-economic issues to those related to the political system (OPZZ, 2016). It quickly became clear that focusing on the government's socio-economic polices was much more difficult task than criticising the government outright. For example, OPZZ raised its disapproval regarding the unconstitutional changes in the judiciary,[3] and it was

---

[3] https://www.opzz.org.pl/opinie-i-analizy/opinie-i-analizy-opzz/zdaniem-zwiazkowca/nie-dla-niszczenia-dialogu-i-sadownictwa.

also vocal in joining civil society organisations when protesting against attacks on women's and LGBT rights.

It is important to underline that PiS was not the only party which has successfully 'hijacked' the trade unions' social agenda. The incorporation of trade union polices by right-wing parties has been a phenomenon in a number of Western European countries including in France with *Le Rassemblement National*, and its predecessor *Le Front National*, in Italy with the Lega in the UK with the United Kingdom Independence Party (UKIP). An archetypical populist party is the Swiss People's Party (*Schweizerische Volkspartei/ Union démocratique du centre*), which since 2000 has formed part of successive Swiss governments. Many union members in Western Europe have supported these parties against the advice of their own unions. For instance, in Germany where the extreme right-wing *Alternative für Deutschland* (AfD) has been gaining support at the expense of social democrats, particularly in the East of the country. Similarly, a crisis of social democrats is not only a Polish phenomenon and can be observed in many European countries including, and as already mentioned, in Germany or France, and also in Austria, the Netherlands and the UK. This is partly because, as Pelinka (2013) rightly argues, the European right-wing populists now disproportionally represent the lower classes, which were traditionally the core constituency of the European trade union movement.

4 Using the European Trade Union's Solidarity to Tackle Populism

One of the first example of clear divergence between the unions and the government in Poland was the revision of the posting of workers directive (Directive (EU) 2018/957). The revision came into force on 30 July 2020 and significantly improved the situation of posted workers in Europe—among whom Polish workers were the largest group (Eurofund, 2020)[4]—by extending the coverage of the collective bargaining agreements and the remit of the definition of 'payment' (i.e. remuneration). The revision was opposed by the Polish government and employers' representatives but was supported by the unions. The main argument

---

[4] In 2017 out of 2,8 million issued declarations required for posting of workers, 573,385 were issued for Polish citizens followed by 399,745 for Germans (Eurofund, 2020).

used by the government was that the revision would not only lead to job losses but also loss of income for the Polish authority that was responsible for collecting social security contributions (for example, according to the revision, pension contributions after two years had to be paid to the relevant authority of the country where work is performed, and not in the country of origin).

Polish unions' support for the revision was embedded in the context of broader European industrial relations. ETUC along with Western European trade unions had been lobbying for a revision of the directive for years, whose loopholes were used by employers to lower workers' wages and this to engage in 'social dumping'. Furthermore, the now infamous Viking and Laval cases in 2007 had previously given precedence to the economic freedoms of employers over the collective bargaining rights of posted workers, which represented a real threat to collective barging in Europe.

The main argument used in Poland by unions for supporting the revision was the importance of the introduction of the principle of 'equal pay for equal work in the same workplace' in relation to posted workers. The introduction of this principle could be seen as the first step towards increasing the wages of all Polish workers. For instance, OPZZ, in its letter to the Prime Minister, insisted that the revision of the posting of workers directive provides the unique opportunity for Polish workers—or at least those working abroad—to finally receive 'European wages' and, as such, the directive delivers the government's promise of wage increases for Polish citizens (OPZZ, 2018a). Similar arguments for supporting the revision were used by Solidarność and FZZ.

It should be said that, given the limited number of Polish workers who will benefit from the revision of the directive, and because many of them were employed only to be posted abroad and as such were not members of the unions, OPZZ, FZZ and Solidarność did not have an important interest in supporting the revision. Furthermore, the unions could have afforded to support the PiS position, and by doing this would have received some concessions from government. However, the unions decided to support the revision and used ETUC's position and the European context as a leverage against PiS. By doing this, the unions not only exposed the hypocrisy of the Polish government, which called for the EU wages but did not support their implementation for the Polish posted workers, but they also expressed their solidarity with the European trade union movement. In other words, the unions used the European context as a way to tackle the populism of PiS. This was also the reason why the Polish unions decided to initiate the adoption of a statement from the Visegrad group (i.e. Czechia, Hungary, Poland and Slovakia) at its meeting in Warsaw 2017, which called on their governments to support the revision (Trade union V4 Group, 2017).

5 Actions for Increased Pay for Public Service Workers

Although PiS significantly increased the minimum salary within four years of taking power, the wages of public service workers stayed frozen since the economic crisis, following a decision of the previous PO government. This led to a paradoxical situation whereby some government employees or local authority workers, including employees of courts, teachers, or social workers, had salaries that were close or even below the minimum wage. Since the PiS government came to power by promising wage increases for all workers, the unions used these promises to develop strategies aimed at increasing the salaries of public service workers. For instance, OPZZ borrowed from the motto of the ETUC 'Europe Needs a Pay Rise' campaign to launch its own campaign under the slogan of 'Poland Needs a Pay Rise' in 2018.

As part of OPZZ's campaign, the union organised a demonstration in Warsaw on 22 September 2018. The demonstration was convened under the motto of 'We have enough- Poland Needs a Pay Rise'[5] involved almost 20,000 participants. The union's demands, apart from a pay increase for public sector workers of 12.1 per cent, included a call for an increase in the minimum wage to 50 per cent of the average national wage, improvements in the functioning of social dialogue, changes to the tax system which would allow for lower wage workers to pay less taxes while increasing their salaries and with pension rights to be linked to the number of years spent working as opposed to age (specifically to 35 years of employment for women and 40 years for men) (OPZZ, 2018b). The government did not respond to OPZZ's demands.

Actions calling for pay increases were also organised by trade unions representing uniform services, including the largest among them, the

---

[5] In Polish ' Mam Dość', https://www.opzz.org.pl/aktualnosci/kraj/mamdosc.

Independent Self-Governing Trade Union of Policemen (NSZZ Policjantów[6]), affiliated to FZZ. It should be stated that these services had been neglected by all previous governments in terms of wages increase. Since workers employed in uniform services are not legally permitted to participate in industrial action,[7] unions needed to find some other ways of presenting their grievances. One of them saw coordinated action where ~~members of the public~~ uniform services employees donated blood, which allowed them not only to get time off from work but aimed to gain a higher public sympathy towards their demands. In Poland, donating blood is free and can be carried out during the working time. Given that blood is in high demand, donors are perceived with the high esteem by the society. As such union members aimed to symbolically present themselves as those who did not only risk their lives at work to protect the society but as those who 'gave' the blood for the society. On 2 October 2018, uniform service unions organised a national demonstration in Warsaw along with other unions representing uniform services such as including Trade Union of Firefighters 'Florian' (ZZ Strażaków 'Florian'). The protest attracted almost 30,000 participants effectively mobilised pressure on the government, and PiS on the 8 November 2018 agreed to increase monthly wages by on average 655 PLN from 1 January 2019 and by 500 PLN from 1 January 2020.[8]

The OPZZ campaign for increased wages and the successful action by uniform services' unions took place against a background of growing demands from teachers led by the Polish Teachers Union (Związek Nauczycielstwa Polskiego, ZNP), the largest education union. The arguments used by the union to call for pay increases were based primarily on the fact that the government had found money for many of its social policies, including the aforementioned children's allowance, the additional pension payments and increased wages for those working in uniform services, but were unwilling to improve the wages of teachers. Following

---

[6] See https://nszzp.pl/aktualnosci/federacja-zwiazkow-zawodowych-sluzb-mundurowych-domaga-sie-pilnego-spotkania-z-ministrem-spraw-wewnetrznych-i-administracji/

[7] On the margin it needs to be said that the legal situation regarding a ban for strike for some public servants and uniform services was challenged by Solidarność in ILO and by lodging the claim to the Constitutional Tribunal. As of August 2020, the court did not decide about the claim (Gardawski, Surdykowska 2019).

[8] Text of the agreement could be found here: https://nszzp.pl/wp-content/uploads/2019/09/porozumienie_z_mswia_1_.pdf.

the failure of negotiations with the government, in January 2019, ZNP initiated a ballot of its members for strike action. With the majority of its members supporting industrial action of unlimited duration, a strike was called on 8 April 2019. The turnout for the ballot was one of the highest in the history of the union, with teachers in almost 80 per cent of schools taking part, and with several hundreds of thousands of teachers confirming their willingness to strike (ZNP, 2019).

This would be the largest strike by teachers Polish since the fall of communism. Furthermore, the dispute was not only conducted by ZNP, although this was indeed the largest teachers' union, but also with a smaller union representing teachers, namely Free Trade Union 'Solidarity- Education' (Wolny Związek Zawodowy "Solidarność-Oświata", WZZSO),[9] affiliated to FZZ. Solidarność, which also represents teachers, did not take part in the industrial action and signed the agreement with the government on 7 April. ZNP and WZZSO demanded a pay increase for teachers employed in schools and nurseries 1000 PLN monthly (220 euros approx.). This sum was the difference between the average salary of qualified teachers and the average salary in Poland. The conflict between the unions and the government was also fuelled by recent reforms to the education system which had been implemented by PiS a year earlier without the consent of teachers, which had reorganised the secondary education system and had strongly politicised the curriculum.

The strike resonated with large parts of public opinion, and received support from parents and local authorities. A strike fund was set up to collect money to support striking workers. Within a couple of days the union had collected 7.8 million PLN (1.74 million euros approx.).[10] Furthermore, many celebrities supported the teachers, as did the liberal media, which was historically at odds with the trade unions. Furthermore, opposition politicians, including many within PO, publicly applauded teachers and many local authorities announced that they would pay workers' wages even though they were on strike.

It can be argued that the industrial action grew beyond the confines of the dispute over teachers' grievances, and developed into a broader public

---

[9] http://forum.wzzso.pl.

[10] https://wyborcza.pl/7,75398,24715517,jak-podziela-7-8-mln-zl-zebranych-dla-str ajkujacych-nauczycieli.html.

protest against the government. The teachers were able to effectively channel public anger into a form of a strike action that received support from all opposition parties, much of the media and many local authorities. In many cities, demonstrations that expressed support for teachers were organised by parents or NGOs. Some popular internet memes were circulated widely on social media that sought to underline the government's hypocrisy, with one of the most famous comparing teachers to livestock, with the former being worth less to the government. This was done in the context of PiS politicians attempting to attract farmers' votes in advance of the European elections in May 2019 announcing that the government would provide subsidies to be paid according to the number of heads of cattle and pigs that farmers owned (with 500 PLN for a cow and 100 PLN for a pig, or 110 and 22 euros approx. respectively).

The strike lasted 18 days but, notwithstanding high levels of support among the public, the government did not greatly moderate its position regarding pay increases. Instead, it offered a pay increase of 10 per cent for teachers from the following year, but with extended working time. The proposal, which was already approved by Solidarność, was unacceptable to ZNP and WZSSO. The exams period for pupils was approaching which exerted moral pressure on teachers. Furthermore, ZNP was concerned about its strike fund which would not be able to sustain the action much longer. As a result, ZNP and WZZSO had no choice other than to suspend strike action on 27 April 2019.

It should also be said that, regardless of the strike suspension and the fact that it has never been re-initiated, the dispute yielded positive results for the unions. The strike clearly elevated the debate regarding the importance of investment in education in the public discourse, and also showed that the mobilisation of workers and the garnering of public support and media coverage for trade unions is still possible in Poland. This case clearly shows that unions are able to increase their social power. Furthermore, as mentioned by the president of ZNP in his statement of 25 April 2019 to the prime minister—for many people, the strike was similar to the Solidarność's protests in the 1980s, which turned into a social movement that eventually overthrew the country's communist government:

> I will tell you more Mr Prime Minister, as a trade unionist, who remember the 1980s. Then we also begun with individual actions. But all action, such as the strike of teachers gives people the power. This creates a snowball

effect, which you would not be able to stop. Because people know that that the situation is bad and feel the contempt showed to them.[11]

A 'snowball effect' was also observed on a small scale, and only during the protest of civil servants at the Ministry of Justice held the following month, which yielded a more unambiguously positive outcome. Similar to the teachers, administrative employees in Polish courts were for a long time among the most forgotten group of public workers with some salaries being even below the national minimum wage. An action short of industrial action was coordinated by nine trade unions, including one representing Solidarność: NSZZ Solidarność of Employees of Courts and Prosecutor Offices (NSZZ Solidarność Pracowników Sądownictwa i Prokuratury), one affiliated to OPZZ, NSZZ of Employees of Justice Administration (NSZZ Pracowników Wymiaru Sprawiedliwości RP), and another to FZZ (Ad Rem). Negotiations between court workers' representatives and the government started already at the end of 2018 without sufficient results, with the government offering only a 200 PLN monthly pay increase (45 euros approx.), and the representative unions opted to intensify the dispute. The main demand from the unions was similar to that from the teachers, namely: a monthly pay increase of 1000 PLN (220 euros approx.), which again was the difference between the average wage and the wage of clerks employed at the Ministry of Justice. As was the case with uniform services, civil servants are not allowed to go on strike and, as such, unions needed to use some other, more innovative forms of action to express their grievances. This involved the organisation of demonstrations during lunch breaks or wearing black cloths to work as a sign of support for the unions' demands. Furthermore, the unions erected a campsite in front of the Ministry of Justice from 7 May 2019 to 4 July 2019 to highlight their demands.[12] It was visited by celebrities and the Warsaw citizens wanting to express the support for workers. The campsite was similar in its intention to an occupation strike, albeit

---

[11] Full statement of ZNP regarding the strike's suspension: https://znp.edu.pl/prezes-znp-dzis-zawieszamy-strajk-ale-walka-trwa-i-bedzie-trwala-do-skutku/ Original version: 'Powiem Panu więcej, jako związkowiec, który pamięta lata '80. Wtedy też zaczynało się od pojedynczych akcji. Ale każdy taki zryw, jak wielki strajk nauczycieli, daje ludziom siłę. Tworzy się kula śniegowa, której nie będzie Pan w stanie powstrzymać propagandą. Bo ludzie wiedzą, że jest źle i czują okazywaną im pogardę.

[12] See: http://www.solidarnosc.org.pl/aktualnosci/wiadomosci/branze/item/18777-pracownicy-sadow-wywalczyli-podwyzki.

outside the work premises, which is a common form of protest in the Polish labour movement. This was seen for example in the case of the successful protest by nurses in 2007 when workers set up a campsite in front of the prime minister's office (Kubisa, 2014). Likewise, in the case of the nurses' protest, the justice workers' campsite was visited by many citizens, celebrities, journalists and others wanting to express their support. After almost two months, the dispute was settled on 4 July with unions accepting a wage increase of 1100 PLN (245 euros approx.) monthly, albeit to be paid in two instalments, with the first being paid immediately and the second after a year.

The analysis of these disputes—the protest of court and uniform workers along with the strike by teachers—demonstrates how important it is for unions to mount a unified front vis- a- vis the government, especially in the fragmented union landscape in Poland. The industrial action by teachers was met with strong support from celebrities (including artists and musicians, who even organised on 17 April a public concert supporting teachers[13]) and elements within the media, including from outlets that had traditionally not been friendly towards the trade union movement. One of these was a largest daily newspaper 'Gazeta Wyborcza', which historically supports liberal parties including PO. Both outlets provided daily briefings supporting the strike action and their readers and listeners endorsed teachers.[14] This was not the case in the action by court employees and uniform workers where the unions decided to act together. The unity between the unions turned out to be the most effective factor in convincing the government to meet their demands. However, when analysing the unions' actions, we should not only assess them in relation to their influence over government policy, but also on attitudes in wider society, in the context of the unions' social power. While the teachers' strike was ultimately not successful in meeting the unions' demands, the episode brought some other less visible victories for the labour movement. It could be argued that for the first time since 1989 the unions received significant support from artists, celebrities and from

---

[13] See: https://wiadomosci.radiozet.pl/Polska/Koncert-Artysci-dla-nauczycieli-w-Warszawie.-Gwiazdy-zagraly-dla-strajkujacych.

[14] See the article of Gazeta Wyborcza from 23 April 2019 'Readers of Wyborcza to protesting teachers: We are with you!' (Czytelnicy Wyborczej do nauczycieli: Jesteśmy z Wami!)': https://wyborcza.pl/7,162657,24692687,16-dzien-strajku-czytelnicy-wyborczej-do-protestujacych.html.

liberal politicians. That is the groups, in particular liberal politicians, who were historically less supportive for the workers' movement in Poland. The unions took a firm stand in the fight for the dignity of workers, and also the Polish citizens, as well as respect for democracy. In particular, in underlining the importance of respecting the views of those who did not support the government, and to protect justice system, uniform services and education from the right-wing populist politicisation. In other words, by combining economic demands for with political ones, unions were able to successfully articulate latent demands and grievances by presenting them in the form of a strike action. As such, numerous groups in society unsympathetic to the PiS government had seen the union as their agent of change.

6 Conclusion

Since being elected in 2015, we have seen that the PiS government 'hijacked' many of the core policies of the Polish unions which, as we have argued, is not a phenomenon that is unique to Poland. However, the unions were able to successfully deal with this challenge by identifying the weakest points in the current government's social policies. In the Polish case, the current government's policies seem to be *prima facie* social in nature, but in reality, are deeply neoliberal in character, and are designed to delude workers and trade unions. The unions exposed the contradictory attitudes of the government towards workers' wages and regarding the discriminatory treatment of workers across different sectors and locations. For instance, PiS was explicitly in favour of increasing the minimum wage but was against increasing the wage for posted Polish workers through its opposition to the revision of the relevant EU directive. When it wanted to increase the wages for workers paid by private companies, especially those paid the minimum wage, the government did not want to increase salaries for workers employed by its own government, such as those working in uniform services, education or the justice system. Consequently, the unions focused their efforts on tackling the government's right-wing populism by initiating a combination of both lobbying activities, as was the case with posted workers, and industrial action, as was the case with teachers. In terms of the strategies the unions deployed, their connections with the European-level trade union movement were also important. Unions used the revision of the posted of workers directive aiming to increase wages of Polish posted workers, supported by the Western European trade unions and rejected by the government, to revel the populist, neo-liberal face of PiS and to show its hypocrisy towards workers' rights.[15] In Poland, the unions' strategy was based on moving their repertoire of action from a 'logic of membership' to a logic of influence' and by building up their campaign strategies by focusing on societal power. The teachers' strike in particular showed the importance of gaining support from the public and, as such, the union was able to turn the strike into a nation-wide protest against the government. Although it was not ultimately successful, as opposed to the successful actions by uniform service workers and court clerks, all of those actions, regardless of their results, increased the societal power of the unions, as they received much support from even those opposition parties that traditionally opposed them, including from PO which has close ties with the interests of employers and businesses.

Polish trade unions suffered considerable losses across all the aforementioned major types of power resources over the last 30 years, with the exception of societal power. Struggling with falling density, ageing membership, deteriorating collective bargaining and 'illusory corporatism', to name just the key challenges, unions have recently managed to regain some influence over public opinion with campaigns that sought to address issues that resonated with both members, supporters, and citizens in wider society. Despite the moderate successes in building societal power, trade unions still face a serious threat, as their agenda is being 'hijacked' by government policies, with society receiving an unspoken message of *'what do you need trade unions for?'* from government. It is exactly the pessimistic case of union substitution by populist parties that Visser (2019) lists among possible major challenges for trade unions worldwide. The cases explored in this chapter suggest, however, that Polish unions are aware of the threat and are ready not only to protect their territory but also act as emissaries of the wider public in their defence of public services suffering further deterioration resulting from the policies ushered in by the current government.

---

[15] On the margin it should be added that the same anti- workers approach was revealed by the government in November 2020 (Government RP, 2020) by rejecting the proposal for the directive on the European adequate minimum wages presented by the EU Commission at the end of October 2020 (COM(2020) 682). The directive aims to support introduction of minimum wages in the EU as well as encourages Member States to promote sectoral collective bargaining.

Bibliography

Bernaciak, M., Kahancová, M. (2017). Introduction: Innovation against all odds? In: Bernaciak M and Kahancová M (eds) Innovative Union Practices in Central and Eastern Europe. Brussels: ETUI, pp. 7–20.

Bohle, D., Greskovits, B. (2012). Capitalist Diversity on Europe's Periphery. Cornell University Press.

Butković, H., Czarzasty, J., and Mrozowicki, A. (2021). Societal Resources as Sources of Trade Union Power in Croatia and Poland (in review). European Journal of Industrial Relations.

Constitutional Tribunal. (2015). Decision K1/13. Available at: https://trybunal.gov.pl/postepowanie-i-orzeczenia/komunikaty-prasowe/komunikaty-po/art/8073-zasady-tworzenia-zwiazkow-zawodowych (Accessed: 12 August 2020).

Czarzasty, J. (2019). Collective bargaining in Poland: a near-death experience. In: Müller, T. Vandaele, K., Waddington, J. (eds.) Collective bargaining in Europe: towards an endgame. Vol. II. Brussels: ETUI, pp. 465–482.

Directive (EU) 2018/957 of the European Parliament and of the Council of 28 June 2018 amending Directive 96/71/EC concerning the posting of workers in the framework of the provision of services. (2018). OJ L 173, 9.7.2018, pp. 16–24.

Doellgast, V, Lillie, N, and Pulignano, V. (2018). Reconstructing Solidarity. Labour Unions, Precarious Work, and the Politics of Institutional Change in Europe. Oxford University Press.

Dörre, K, Holst, H. and Nachtwey, O. (2009). Organizing—A Strategic Option for Trade Union Renewal? *International Journal of Action Research* 5(1): 33–67.

Duda, K. (2020). Organizacje wspierające migrantów na polskim rynku pracy" Friedrich-Ebert-Stiftung, Przedstawicielstwo w Polsce oraz Ogólnopolskie Porozumienie Związków Zawodowych.

Eurofound (2020) *Improving the monitoring of posted workers in the EU*, Publications Office of the European Union, Luxembourg.

Gardawski, J., and Surdykowska (Ed.). (2019). Ku kulturze dialogu: geneza i dzień dzisiejszy dialogu społecznego w Polsce. Warszawa: Rada Dialogu Społecznego.

Government RP. (2020). The project of the opinion on the EU directive on adequate minium wage.

Korpi, W. (1985). Power resources approach vs. action and conflict: On causal and intentional explanations in the study of power. *Sociological Theory* 3(2): 31–45.

Kubisa, J. (2014). Bunt białych czepków. Analiza działalności związkowej pielęgniarek i położnych.

Lehndorff, S, Dribbusch, H., and Schulten, T. (2018). European trade unions in a time of crises—An overview. In: Lehndorff S, Dribbusch H and Schulten T (eds) Rough waters: European trade unions in a time of crises. Brussels: ETUI, pp. 7–37.

Levesque, C., and Murray, G. (2010) Understanding union power: Resources and capabilities for renewing union capacity. *Transfer: European Review of Labour and Research* 16: 333–350.

Levesque, C., and Murray, G. (2013). Renewing union narrative resources. How union capabilities make a difference. *British Journal of Industrial Relations* 51: 777–96.

Müller, J. W. (2017). What is populism?. Penguin UK.

OPZZ (2016) Stanowisko Rady Ogólnopolskiego Porozumienia Związków Zawodowych z dnia 9 marca 2016 roku w sprawie oceny 100 dni rządu Beaty Szydlo.

OPZZ (2018a) List OPZZ do premiera w sprawie rewizji dyrektywy o pracownikach delegowanych z dnia 7 marca 2018 roku (OPZZ/P/760/218).

OPZZ (2018b) Petycja do premiera z dnia 22 września 2018 roku.

Pelinka, A. (2013). Right-wing populism: Concept and typology. Right-wing populism in Europe: Politics and discourse, 3–22.

Prosser, T. (2019). *European labour movements in crisis: From indecision to indifference* (1st ed.). Manchester University Press.

Rapacki, R. (Ed.). (2019). Diversity of Patchwork Capitalism in Central and Eastern Europe. Routledge.

Rogalewski, A. (2020). Right Wing Populism in Poland: A Challenge for Trade Unions. *International Union Rights*, 27(1–2), 8–9.

Schmalz, S., Ludwig, C., and Webster, E. (2018). The Power Resources Approach: Developments and Challenges. *Global Labour Journal* 9(2):113–134.

Schmitter. P, C., Streeck, W. (1981). The organization of business interests: A research design to study the associative action of business in the advanced industrial societies of Western Europe. Discussion Paper IIM/LMP 81/13. Berlin: IIM/LMP.

Trade union V4 Group, 2017.

Visser, J. (2019) Trade Unions in the Balance. Available at: https://www.ilo.org/wcmsp5/groups/public/---ed_dialogue/---actrav/documents/publication/wcms_722482.pdf. (Accessed: 29 September 2020).

Wright EO (2000) Working-Class Power, Capitalist-Class Interests, and Class Compromise. *American Journal of Sociology* 105(4). University of Chicago Press: 957–1002.

ZNP (2019) Information for foreign trade unions about the strike.

CHAPTER 15

Conclusion: Multiple Challenges Confronting European Trade Unions

Richard Hyman

The previous chapters have offered a rich and diverse picture of recent developments in industrial relations in Europe, and of the efforts by trade unions to respond to increasing challenges. The introductory chapter presented a clear overview of the varied contributions, and I see no need to repeat the exercise. Rather than attempt to provide a conventional conclusion, I therefore offer my own reading of the European context in the third decade of the twenty-first century. I will discuss, first, how far 'varieties of capitalism' persist, and the implications of changes in industrial relations regimes for trade unions. Second, I will consider some of the ambiguities of EU regulation. Is 'Social Europe' (still) a bulwark against market liberalisation? Third, I draw on Polanyi to examine the rise of precarious work situations, including the emergence of the 'platform economy'. Fourth, I comment on the impact of Covid-19 and the climate crisis, before some brief final remarks about trade union responses.

R. Hyman (✉)
London School of Economics, London, UK
e-mail: R.Hyman@lse.ac.uk

1   All Liberal Market Economies Now?

In the introductory chapter, the 'varieties of capitalism' thesis was clearly presented. What I would stress is that, at least in its initial formulation, this was not simply a taxonomy for cross-national comparative analysis but also an assertion of institutional resilience. CMEs and LMEs each possessed a system of institutions which tended to 'cluster' over time according to an underlying structural logic. As Hollingsworth and Boyer (1997: 2–3) put it, 'the industrial relations system; the system of training…; the internal structure of corporate firms; the structured relationships among firms…; the financial markets of a society; the conceptions of fairness and justice held by capital and labor; the structure of the state and its policies; and a society's idiosyncratic customs and traditions as well as norms, moral principles, rules, laws and recipes for action' tend to be 'tightly coupled with each other' and thus 'coalesce into a complex social configuration'. Each element in the configuration was thus supported by the others, inhibiting piecemeal change.

This assumption of functional integration has been increasingly challenged (Crouch 2005; Streeck 2008; Streeck and Thelen 2005). Institutional regimes are as likely to be internally contradictory as complementary, providing scope for 'institutional entrepreneurs' to transform their workings. Their functioning may be hollowed out by incremental adjustments, each on its own of minor significance. In effect, the meaning of the rules which regulate the power and status of labour market actors is constantly reconstructed and renegotiated. As recent experience demonstrates, it is often easier for those who wish to weaken employee rights to erode their practical effect rather than to attack them frontally The Introduction notes the argument of Baccaro and Howell (2011, 2017), who focus in particular on Britain, France, Germany and Sweden, that Western Europe has seen a sustained process of 'institutional convergence'. They insist (2017: 15) that 'resilience and continuity of institutional form is perfectly compatible with convergence in institutional functioning' so that 'institutions can appear largely unchanged but in fact come to perform in quite different ways from before'.

This is of crucial importance for trade unions, for in most of western Europe they have long enjoyed extensive institutional power resources which have insulated them from the need for high membership density and mobilisation capacity. This can result in what Hassel (2007) terms 'the curse of institutional security': if institutional supports lose their effects, unions may no longer possess the capacity to deploy alternative power resources. This is particularly the case when institutional supports are eroded, so to speak, by stealth. Some years ago, in research for our book on European trade unionism (Gumbrell-McCormick and Hyman 2018), we interviewed a leading Swedish union official who explained with some dismay that the unions had long been prepared to mobilise against attacks on the legal and institutional foundations of the Swedish industrial relations system, but the more subtle changes to the labour market and social security supports for this system had left them unprepared. In the 15 years since this interview, union density in Sweden has fallen from roughly 80 to 65%. So a crucial question for trade unions is what new power resources they can fashion (or what old resources they can rediscover) in order to survive and thrive in hard times.

2 The European Union: An Ambiguous Ally?

For most of their history, trade unions were first and foremost actors in nationally bounded industrial relations systems. In many respects, their status as national interlocutors (or 'social partners') was reinforced by the post-war socio-political compromises reached across most of the countries of western Europe. Employers were primarily national in terms of corporate ownership and production strategies and in most countries were willing to act collectively. Governments were to a large degree autonomous in social and economic policy and encouraged the rise of the Keynesian welfare state. Even conservative regimes tended to endorse the institutionalisation of social dialogue.

Of course, the world has changed. Globalisation—a concept often deployed unthinkingly but which certainly designates a real transformation in ownership structures, production strategies and cross-national value chains—has removed the dominant capitalist agglomerations from national control. The liberalisation of financial markets has increasingly subordinated what used to be termed the 'real economy' to the priorities of casino capitalism. It is now possible, and indeed more effective, to generate a surplus without producing value: money can be expanded without the production of commodities as traditionally understood. Employing organisations have themselves become commodities, increasingly bought and sold, creating new modes of insecurity: for growing numbers of workers (and their unions), it is no longer even clear *who* is the employer. Governments with reduced room for manœuvre in shaping economic and social policies now often claim that 'there is no alternative' to a neoliberal regime. This dynamic, Peters (2011) has argued, is the key reason for trade union decline across the world.

It has commonly been assumed, not least within European trade unions, that the EU could provide a defence against neoliberal globalisation. Indeed several of the contributors to this book detail instances where workers and their unions have been beneficiaries of 'Social Europe'. The discourse of the 'European social model' can be seen, first, as a celebration of the features of CMEs in which workers are assigned both individual and collective rights and status. Second, the term implies the goal of generalising and extending these rights and protections through the harmonisation and upward standardisation of outcomes across the EU.

However, the notion of a 'European social model' is inherently ambiguous. At its strongest, it may mean an equivalence of the rights of labour and of capital: in effect, a system of dual power. More modestly, it can mean what is known in Germany as *soziale Marktwirtschaft* or social market economy. Here, the key question is whether the emphasis is on 'social' or 'market'. When the term was popularised by post-war Christian democrats, it was a slogan for 'free' markets with limited social regulation; subsequently, more weight was given to the social regulation of markets, and in particular labour markets. At its weakest, the idea of a social model approximates to a system in which social solidarity is subordinated to market competition. Given these incompatible meanings of 'social Europe', the concept is essentially contested: it possesses iconic status as an abstraction, but there is no consensus on its content. It is possible to endorse the label without signing up to any specific policy outcome.

This means that its function is often cosmetic: in recent years, the rhetoric of 'social Europe' has often served as a disarming accompaniment to Euro-liberalism. In the uphill struggle for a meaningful social Europe, trade unions confront not only the gravitational pull of the existing constitutional framework, but also the force of weighty opponents. There is the familiar imbalance within the institutions of the EU itself: the Parliament, the most 'popular' (directly elected) element in the decision-making architecture, and the most reliable supporter of an effective social dimension to European integration, is also the most limited in its powers. The Commission, while dependent for its own status on the extent of EU regulatory capacity, is at best an ambiguous ally. While the

Directorate-General for Employment and Social Affairs (DG EMPL) may be sympathetic to many trade union aspirations for social regulation, its own influence is subordinate to that of the many others with a primarily market-making mission. Note than in recent years, DG EMPL has always been assigned a Commissioner from a small or 'peripheral' country, after the more influential briefs have been carved up among the heavyweights.

To these biases is of course added the imbalance of influence between labour and capital. This is not simply a matter of organisational resources. In many respects, the European Trade Union Confederation (ETUC) is organisationally more robust than Business Europe, though we should not forget the ranks of lobbyists and representatives retained in Brussels by individual companies and national associations, vastly outnumbering the European officials of national trade unions. Far more than veto power is exercised by the European Round Table of Industrialists: the single market project of the 1980s, and the more general commitment to liberalisation of European societies, was largely the outcome of its strategic initiative (Balanyá et al. 2003; van Apeldoorn 2000). But the issue is also structural: employers and industrialists work with the grain of entrenched EU policy, while trade unions (if they are serious about 'social Europe') seek a major change of course. In such a context, veto power is typically more effective as well as more discreet. Recall the argument of Offe and Wiesenthal (1985: 191–193) concerning the 'structural asymmetry' of capital and labour in their relationship with the state: since governments are dependent on the investment decisions of a multiplicity of individual firms, capital exerts political pressure without the need to mobilise collectively. The normal economic rationality of company decision-makers has a political significance which may not even be intended.

At national level, employment regulation typically takes the form either of collective agreements between unions and employers (in many countries, with binding status) or of legislation, the two commonly operating in conjunction. In the EU, the analogue to national collective bargaining is the social dialogue, only exceptionally resulting in anything more than 'joint opinions', with the number of agreements reached under the Maastricht social partners' route still minimal; while the analogue to national legislation is the directive, an instrument which is always slow (that on European Works Councils was first proposed in 1980 and finally adopted in 1994), and rarely does more than codify existing practice in the great majority of member states. Over and above this, there has been a marked shift in recent years away from regulation by directive to 'softer' methods.

Indeed, economic integration, and in particular the single market project, has pointed in a diametrically opposite direction to an extended social dimension. In one sense, Europe can be seen as a particularly strong instance at continental level of globalisation, involving transnational product market integration, corporate restructuring and financial liberalisation—threatening the traditional basis for autonomously created national socio-economic regimes. As Scharpf (1999) has argued, the preferred mode of Europeanisation has been 'negative integration', the elimination of national regulations which constitute obstacles to free movement. Negative integration reflects the priority of economic over social and political integration: a common market can be understood primarily in terms of freedom *from* regulations which inhibit cross-national exchange, whereas the creation of a social community depends on *rights* which are entrenched in new regulatory institutions. The Treaty of Rome established Community competence primarily in market terms; the Single European Act was most mandatory and specific in the field of market-making (with the formalisation of qualified majority voting primarily directed to this end); the Maastricht Treaty, though celebrated by the trade union movement for its social chapter, was most binding in outcome in respect of the notorious deflationary convergence criteria for economic and monetary union (EMU); the Stability and Growth Pact of 1999 reinforced the commitment to budgetary restraint (Gill 1998); and the Lisbon Treaty of 2007 reaffirmed neoliberal economic imperatives in unambiguous terms while giving far more diffuse approval to social goals. This conception of 'anti-social Europe' has been brutally asserted by the Court of Justice of the European Union (CJEU) in a series of landmark decisions. In the Viking and Laval cases in 2007 it adopted the principle that, irrespective of national law, industrial action which interfered with freedom of movement was legitimate only if it satisfied a 'proportionality' test. These were followed in 2008 by the Rüffert and Luxembourg cases, which set very strict limits on the extent to which public authorities could prescribe minimum employment standards if these interfered with the freedom to provide services. Despite formal commitments in 2017 to a 'European Pillar of Social Rights', market 'freedoms' are still assigned priority over social and employment protections; while the hollowing out of companies through outsourcing and subcontracting of previously 'core' activities accentuates labour force fragmentation and insecurity.

The economic crisis of 2008–09 was followed by the austerity packages imposed on the 'programme' countries by the Troika of European

Commission, European Central Bank (ECB) and International Monetary Fund; and by the adoption of the 'new economic governance', which 'gave the Commission wide-ranging policy intervention and sanctioning powers, not only in order to counter "excessive" budget deficits of EU member-states, but also to ensure the '*proper functioning* of economic and monetary union' (Jordan et al. 2021: 192). This new regime increasingly targets social welfare and employment protection. Schmidt (2021: 139–140) comments that current EU policies are increasingly dominated by 'ordoliberal ideas about macroeconomic stability, the dangers of deficits and debt and the benefits of austerity…; and neoliberal ideas about the need for ever freer markets and a smaller and smaller state, the glories of competitiveness and the advantages of labour market flexibility'. As Lehndorff (2015: 13) argues (and the introductory chapter notes), 'austerity policy in combination with so-called "internal devaluation" is the hard core of EU crisis policy'. Trade unions which for so long have looked to the EU for their salvation are now disoriented (Erne 2015, 2018). Yet 'more Europe' is often still the default option for European trade union leaders, despite their criticism of actually existing EU policies (Kuhlmann and Scherrer 2019). Not surprisingly, however, it has become increasingly difficult to mobilise membership enthusiasm for the EU project, as the 2016 Brexit referendum clearly demonstrated.

3 The Re-commodification of Employment Relations

As a number of the previous contributions highlight, work and employment have become increasingly precarious, a trend which poses multiple challenges for trade unions. The longer-term erosion of (more or less) permanent employment contracts, with increased temporary or fixed-term employment, the growth of agency work, the outsourcing of what were once core activities and the rise in dependent self-employment, has been reinforced by the emergence of the platform (or 'gig') economy, in which workers are in theory rendered self-employed entrepreneurs, often competing for brief, one-off tasks (as in the case of Uber taxi drivers), but in practice are often subordinated to the platform owner (Drahokoupil and Fabo 2016). I draw on Polanyi to examine the rise of such precarious work situations.

For Polanyi (1944), the rise of industrial capitalism in the late eighteenth and early nineteenth centuries imposed a commodity status on workers; but he argued that the resulting social dislocation necessarily precipitated a counter-movement through 'a spontaneous reaction' (1944: 149), eventually establishing a new framework of social rights. Subsequently, Esping-Andersen (1990) wrote of 'decommodification', the protection of workers from the vagaries of market forces (and the imbalances of social power which they embedded).

In post-war Europe, a range of regulations ensured that 'labour markets' constituted markets only in limited respects. Across the countries of what became the EU, varieties of institutional structures entailed that the employer-employee relationship was no longer primarily determined by market forces. Labour became recognised as a collective 'stakeholder' with rights analogous to those of capitalists and shareholders.

Decommodification was often imposed through elaborate employment legislation which prescribed a wide range of substantive employment standards such as minimum wages, holiday entitlements and maximum working hours, as well as extensive provisions regarding health and safety. Likewise, legislation restricted the employer's right to hire and fire, in contrast to the long-established US doctrine of 'employment at will'. In essence, employment was treated as a *status* rather than a mere *contract*, and could be terminated only for good cause and through due process.

Public policy typically encouraged collective bargaining, and collective agreements usually had priority over individual employment contracts, further limiting the 'freedom' of individual labour market actors. Moreover, centralised agreements and in some countries legal extension mechanisms resulted in high levels of bargaining coverage (even when union density was low). And almost universally, there were standardised national systems of workplace representation at least partially independent of management: a reflection of the principle that a company is not simply the private property of its owners, that employment by a firm entails membership of a workplace community and requires a form of 'industrial citizenship' of a democratic character.

This process was reinforced by extensive public welfare. In the view of Marshall, this created a 'social citizenship' by establishing the right to at least minimum standards of 'economic welfare and security' and hence to enjoy 'the life of a civilised being' (1950: 10–11). The 'social safety net' served to strengthen all employees in their relationship with the employer.

Where did these workers' rights come from? Though Polanyi regarded a 'counter- movement' to commodification as inevitable, it would be very mistaken to assume that national labour regimes were the outcome of some historical consensus on the architecture of employment regulation. In general, workers' rights were established in an uneven, sedimented and contested process, with reverses as well as advances in decommodification. The systems emerging in each country reflected a contingent historical balance of class forces: rights were usually achieved as a negotiated accommodation between class interests or as a set of concessions by those in power to dampen protest from below.

The institutionalisation of workers' rights at a time when the balance of class forces was particularly favourable to labour movements was a major social achievement. But this could not prevent regression when circumstances changed. One reason, as argued above, is that formal rights acquire substance only through a process of interpretation and application, and these compromises always involved a contradictory and hence unstable synthesis of status and contract, as many writers noted long ago (Fox 1974; Hyman 1987; Supiot 1999). The meaning of the rules which embody these rights is constantly reconstructed and renegotiated; as I indicated above, it is often easier to weaken such rights by eroding their practical effect rather than attacking them frontally.

Recent trends can be understood, within Polanyi's framework, as a *counter*-counter-movement, a *third* phase involving the deliberate unravelling of the regulatory web constructed in previous decades. The norm of insecurity, widely believed to have been overcome in the mid-twentieth century, is increasingly re-imposed. For many, and in some countries most, new labour market entrants, the only available employment opportunities are precarious: short-term contracts, bogus self-employment, agency work, zero-hours contracts.... What was once considered 'atypical' employment is now increasingly typical. This has been one cause of growing income inequality and the expanding proportion of the workforce afflicted by the structural violence of no work on the one hand, overwork on the other; by increasingly precarious work; often by indecent work in its many guises; or as Wood (2020) calls it, 'despotism on demand'. Needless to say, this confronts unions with challenges which in most countries they have not previously experienced, at least since the nineteenth century.

The rise of the 'platform economy' has brought a return to spot contracting in the labour market. Huws et al. (2019: 8) summarise recent developments as the latest stage in a longer-term trend: 'on the one hand, there is a growing tendency for people to piece together patchwork livelihoods from multiple sources of income while on the other technological change is leading to a growth in the use of digital means for the organisation and management of work, especially in service industries. Platform work sits at the apex of the intersection between these two trends and is the most visible manifestation of larger trends affecting significant proportions of the European workforce'. As Flanagan (2019) insists, platform work involves an extreme of subordination (discipline and surveillance) and insecurity which has long been characteristic of (largely female) personal service work.

Most platform workers lack any kind of collective representation (de Groen et al. 2018). Despite the obstacles, however, it would be wrong to imagine that effective collective resistance is impossible. Joyce et al. (2020), in an extensive global survey of platform worker protests between 2015 and 2019, document almost 150 such actions in Western Europe. The main focus of such protests is pay, working conditions and employment status. The primary organisers are mainstream trade unions (which tend to give priority to legal challenges to the platform owners) and unofficial unions (which often mobilise strikes), in roughly equal numbers. Many of these forms of protest achieve results, as the case studies presented by Johnston et al. (2020) clearly demonstrate.

4 Covid and the Climate Crisis

Finally, I comment on the impact of Covid-19 and (as some would argue, its origin), the ecological crisis. Most of the contributions to this volume were written before the spring of 2020, when the world—and the world of work—was transformed. 'Labour markets around the world were disrupted in 2020 on a historically unprecedented scale', with workplace closures (temporary or permanent), job losses and reduced working hours for many of those still in employment. 'Working-hour losses in 2020 were approximately four times greater than during the global financial crisis in 2009' (ILO 2021: 1). In the EU, nearly 6 million workers were laid off in the first half of 2020. Surprisingly, official unemployment rates barely altered, largely because most of those who lost their jobs were registered as inactive rather than unemployed. Job losses would have been far higher but for government schemes to mitigate economic disruption. These were evident in LMEs as well as CMEs: for example, the British government has spent roughly €70bn on a 'furlough' scheme to compensate employers who retained workers on their books. In the EU27, 37% of workers had reduced hours in 2020, but there were major cross-national differences. Job losses and reduced hours were particularly high in 'contact-intensive' sectors (Eurofound 2021: 1–2).

So far, policy responses in Europe show a marked contrast from the previous crisis over a decade ago. Then, most government funding was directed to avoid the collapse of the banking sector. In 2020, however, the EU launched a 'Support Mitigating Unemployment Risks in an Emergency' (SURE) programme, allocating €100bn euros for loans to Member States to support short-time work and job retention schemes. Far greater resources were subsequently allocated to a Recovery Plan for 2021–27. Moreover, again in contrast to the previous crisis, this funding 'would appear to be devoid of any demands for greater labour market flexibility or the decentralisation of wage-setting'. And there seems to be far more involvement of trade unions in the design of the recovery policies (ETUI and ETUC 2020: 6–9).

The impact of Covid on workers has been extremely uneven: across countries, across sectors and across different types of employees. Pre-existing inequalities, for example in terms of gender and ethnicity, have been intensified. Some occupational groups, including many professionals and other white-collar workers, were able to work from home in relative security (though often subject to new forms of stress) and sometimes gained financially through saving on the cost of commuting and other expenses. At the other extreme, 'national research evidence shows that the pandemic exacerbated the disadvantages of those groups that were considered marginalised before the outbreak of the pandemic' (Kyzlinková 2021: 13). Many of those who were already poorest and most precarious suffered dramatically. Hence 'if any doubts lingered over the vulnerability of platform workers in hard times, COVID-19 surely dispelled them. When government orders restricted the public to accessing essential services only, large numbers of platform workers doing customer-facing tasks, such as giving lifts or cleaning houses, lost their access to work overnight. Those operating as independent contractors – which is most – were unlikely to have been covered by social protection insurance, and how they fared financially depended on the catchment of the emergency benefit schemes instituted by governments. On the other hand, platforms that provided services designated as essential – food and parcel delivery, for instance – saw escalating demand, and many broadened their offerings to take advantage of the changed climate. The workers providing these services helped to keep society ticking over during lockdowns, yet they cannot be said to have had a "good pandemic". For some, competition for work intensified as other newly unemployed workers swelled their ranks, and so take-home pay dropped, or they experienced long and unsocial working hours, higher work intensity and stress. For all, there was the risk of exposure to the virus to contend with, and the prospect of unpaid self-quarantine if confirmed as a close contact of someone with the virus. For those who fell ill with COVID-19, the refusal of platforms to cover sick pay left them reliant on their own resources or forced them to return to work before they had fully recovered' (Eurofound 2021: 16).

Similarly, Purkayastha et al. (2021: 4) note that 'workers in sectors declared essential by state authorities have been mandated to continue working in physical settings during the pandemic. Several such sectors involve many face-to-face contacts with colleagues and clients, meaning that workers face a higher risk of exposure to Covid-19. Unregulated safety measures, a lack of personal protective equipment and crowded settings further increase the risk in these sectors. Persisting inequalities are exacerbated by the pandemic, as low-wage workers, workers from ethnic minorities, migrant workers and women are overrepresented in these sectors. They also face intersecting factors, including precarious contracts, job insecurity, inadequate paid sick leave, a lack of bargaining power and low socioeconomic status.... Studies show that there is also a gender dimension..., with women facing a higher exposure to the disease, a higher care burden and an increased risk of domestic violence. These patterns of inequality play a significant role in a health crisis, determining who is at greater risk of becoming infected, and whether or not they will have access to healthcare and self-isolation'.

'Well-being across Europe plummeted during the lockdowns of spring 2020' (Eurofound 2021: 56). Among those contracting the disease but surviving, a significant proportion developed 'long Covid', with symptoms persisting for a duration as yet unknown. Stress and insecurity damaged mental health. Even among those who did not suffer economically (for example by switching to home-working), damaging psychological effects were common. 'Early evidence suggests many have suffered from a growing expectation to be available online on a near-constant basis – leading to longer hours, shorter breaks and burnout (Vargas Llave and Weber 2020). This has often been coupled with remote surveillance and, especially for women, the shouldering of household and caring roles previously performed by others during working hours' (McGinnity 2021; Countouris and De Stefano 2021).

A key challenge for trade unions is how to manage the long-term consequences. New forms of flexibility in work and employment which developed during the pandemic may be used to benefit employers or workers, but not necessarily both. Many scenarios for 'recovery' are likely to pose continuing threats to physical and mental health. And the looming political issue for the coming years is who will pay for the economic costs of Covid. Experience after the crisis of 2008–2009 is far from encouraging. There could be major battles ahead if workers and their unions are not to be the long-term losers.

Covid is a novel development; the climate crisis has been evident for decades. Yet the two are intimately linked. 'Habitat destruction and an ever-increasing pressure on natural resources (especially food production) have clearly emerged as a breeding ground for pandemics.… The assault on ecosystems that allowed the novel coronavirus to jump from animals to humans shows that sustainable use of Earth's resources and biodiversity protection have a key role in preventing similar diseases from emerging in the future' (ETUI and ETUC 2020: 78).

Despite growing recognition that humankind is careering towards disaster, there are major conflicts in perspectives and interests—across countries, between capital and labour, between different sections of the working class—and any resolution confronts multiple collective action problems. Trade unions, both national and international, have paid increasing attention to the climate crisis, and have adopted often imaginative policies; but the process has been slow and uneven.

There is by now a substantial literature on unions and the climate crisis (for example, Brecher et al. 2014; Hampton 2015; Laurent and Pochet 2015; Räthzel and Uzzell 2012; Stevis and Felli 2015; Stevis et al. 2018), and there is no need to rehearse the discussion in detail. The traditional trade union view in most countries was that the environment was not a trade union issue (as with many other questions which are now centrally on the union agenda), and that there was inevitably a trade-off between pollution and jobs.

Much has changed in recent years. Thomas and Doerflinger (2020) identify a shift from opposition to policies to mitigate climate change to what they term 'hedging' and eventually support. Some unions have not moved beyond opposition: notably, in Europe, Polish unions (with a strong basis among coal-miners), which in some cases still deny the reality of human-induced climate change. 'Hedging' involves acceptance of the scientific evidence and hence agreement in principle to decarbonisation policies, but resistance (often in collaboration with employers) to 'over-ambitious' goals which are seen as a threat to jobs. More proactive policies accept the need for fundamental change to the existing economic model and seek new socio-ecological policies to assist workers.

Increasingly trade unions, especially at international level, have adopted the position that there can be no simple technological 'fix' to the climate crisis; that de-industrialisation is not the solution, rather a targeted change in industrial policy; that there is a need for a new growth model which is both socially and ecologically sustainable; and that the workers should not be the main victims of restructuring. Often this is encapsulated in the demand for a 'just transition' (Clarke and Lipsig-Mummé 2020). As Coats argues above, there will inevitably be winners and losers from a climate action programme; so the priority for trade unions must be to ensure that the costs and benefits are shared equitably. Or as Laurent and Pochet put it (2015: 35), what is required is 'protection rather than castigation'. Nevertheless, any shift by trade unions from rhetoric to practice faces major obstacles: the Italian study by Tomassetti (2020: 448) demonstrates 'how controversial the implementation of [just transition] policies is, and how union positions can diverge when confronted with economic and institutional constraints that transitionary practices involve'.

5 What Is to Be Done?

The balance of class forces in Europe has shifted dramatically towards employers, and capital has increasingly escaped the constraints painfully constructed in previous decades; while the dominant approach of the EU is seemingly to reinforce rather than to resist this trend. Is the juggernaut of capital now irresistible? The starting point for any sober assessment of alternative trajectories is that structural forces are powerful, but that agency is also important. To explore the tension between structure and agency we need to focus on social relations. These relations are in turn always uneven and contradictory, creating openness to historical contingency, since material contexts impose constraints but also create opportunities. The organisational capacities and strategic competence of the key actors shape the outcomes, perhaps producing the difference between success and failure.

The cross-national differences in the dynamics of institutional change and regulatory reconfiguration can be understood in terms of the concept of variable geometry. Any discussion of possibilities for resistance to attacks on workers' conditions and the rights of collective organisation needs to address in particular three aspects of unevenness: the relationship between the global and the local; that between trade unions and other vectors of protest; and the challenge of crafting common interests and action from diversity. To fight back against the odds requires strategic imagination, new alliances and transnational learning and solidarity.

Trade unions confront almost unprecedented challenges when their traditional power resources are in most countries seriously depleted (Gumbrell-McCormick and Hyman 2018). Structural power is severely weakened by globalisation, and associational power has declined with falling membership density. In much of Western Europe, institutional power remains superficially robust, which can induce complacency, as was long the case with German unions; but without other supports, institutional status can be fragile (Hassel 2007). One part of a response must be to develop new forms of 'resourcefulness' (Ganz 2000): to focus on the strategic deployment of those resources which remain. Another, as I discuss below, is to develop 'softer' types of power resource.

There is a long history of mutual suspicion between trade unions and more spontaneous, often activist-led social movements and NGOs; yet neither form of resistance can succeed alone. Unions are almost universally weak among the younger workers who have been particularly seriously affected by the erosion of labour market security. Many of the victims of insecurity see trade unions as part of the problem. Yet if protests against austerity, unemployment and precarious work have commonly been led by more radical social movements, their very spontaneity obstructs sustained resistance; and in some cases they become captured by highly politicised 'orchestrators'. Organisational divisions and rivalries can seriously weaken the capacity for effective action. Where these divisions are transcended, important synergies can be created between the different types of collective actor. As Ibsen and Tapia (2017) show, there is growing evidence of successful attempts by unions to build 'coalitional power' with other social movements.

Globalised 'neo-entrepreneurial' capitalism, as Jenkins and Leicht (1997: 379) term it, 'produces a more fragmented labor market as it also shrinks the number of established places for members of the working class'. Different social and economic groups have been affected in significantly different ways by crisis and austerity, and not least by Covid, and these differences can create new divisions and antagonisms, not the supposed unity of the '99%'. A sense of mutuality, of a common fate and common interests, is not objectively given but is a task requiring a difficult struggle. Unity cannot be built by a linguistic sleight-of-hand—'the people united'—but requires sustained dialogue and debate, otherwise the interests of the weakest are easily submerged beneath a spurious assumption of commonality. As Coats puts it in his contribution, 'the challenge, perhaps, is to craft a narrative and an agenda that appeals to the majority of people at work, identifies shared interests and enables the strong to support those at the margins'. As Doellgast et al. (2018) document, many trade unions across Europe are successfully confronting this challenge.

One of the consequences of the 'institutional security' long enjoyed by unions in much of Western Europe has been a loss of mobilising capacity: social partnership appeared a more cost-effective route to success than contestation. Union strength appeared independent of membership numbers and of workers 'willingness to act' (Offe and Wiesenthal 1985). This is less and less the case; revitalisation requires a rediscovery of unions' representative capacity and of their ability to inspire and motivate. Above all, this means a need to strengthen their democratic mandate and to ensure the reality of the old slogan, that the members *are* the union (Gumbrell-McCormick and Hyman 2019).

After the pandemic, will there be a return to business as usual, or is there a possibility of 'building back better' Sisson (2021)? If unions are to be among the leaders of such a process, they must be able to articulate a convincing vision of an alternative. The challenge, as always for those pursuing a different socio-economic order, is to formulate alternatives which are concrete, comprehensible and attractive. The issue is partly one of language, to simplify without trivialising; but it is also to provide concrete examples of economic solidarity outside the market. Those who drive neoliberal globalisation, the hegemony of finance capital, the politics of insecurity and austerity and the destruction of the natural environment rely on the demoralisation of their victims. Resistance may well draw its inspiration from anger, but to be translated into constructive action it requires self-confidence in the capacity to initiate change. In dark times, to build hope is perhaps the most difficult challenge, and not only because hopes can so easily be disappointed. But fatalism and surrender should not be the only options. Another world is possible.

Bibliography

Baccaro L and Howell C (2011) 'A Common Neoliberal Trajectory: The Transformation of Industrial Relations in Advanced Capitalism', *Politics & Society* 39(4): 521–563.

Baccaro L and Howell C (2017) *Trajectories of Neoliberal Transformation: European Industrial Relations Since the 1970s*. Cambridge: Cambridge University Press.

Balanyá B, Doherty A, Hoedeman O, Ma'anit A and Wesselius E (2003) *Europe Inc.*, 2nd edition. London: Pluto.

Brecher J, Blackwell R and Uehlein J (2014) 'If Not Now, When? A Labor Movement Plan to Address Climate Change', *New Labor Forum* 23(3): 40–47.

Clarke L and Lipsig-Mummé C (2020) 'Future Conditional: From Just Transition to Radical Transformation?', *European Journal of Industrial Relations* 26(4): 351–366.

Countouris N and De Stefano V (2021) 'The "Long Covid" of Work Relations and the Future of Remote Work', *Social Europe* 14 April.

Crouch C. (2005) *Capitalist Diversity and Change*. Oxford: Oxford University Press

de Groen WP, Kilhoffer Z, Lenaerts K and Mandl I (2018) *Employment and Working Conditions of Selected Types of Platform Work*. Luxembourg: Publications Office.

Doellgast V, Lillie N and Pulignano V, eds (2018) *Reconstructing Solidarity. Labour Unions, Precarious Work, and the Politics of Institutional Change in Europe*. Oxford: Oxford University Press.

Drahokoupil J and Fabo B (2016) *The Platform Economy and the Disruption of the Employment Relationship*. Brussels: ETUI Policy Brief 5/2016.

Erne R (2015) 'A Supranational Regime that Nationalizes Social Conflict. Explaining European Trade Unions' Difficulties in Politicizing European Economic Governance', *Labor History* 56(3): 345–368.

Erne R (2018) 'Labour Politics and the EU's New Economic Governance Regime (European Unions): A New European Research Council Project', *Transfer* 24(2): 237–247.

Esping-Andersen G (1990) *The Three Worlds of Welfare Capitalism*. Cambridge: Polity Press.

ETUI and ETUC (2020) *Benchmarking Working Europe 2020. Covid-19 and the World of Work: The Impact of a Pandemic*. Brussels: ETUI.

Eurofound (2021) *Living and Working in Europe 2020*. Luxembourg: Publications Office.

Flanagan F (2019) 'Theorising the Gig Economy and Home-Based Service Work', *Journal of Industrial Relations* 61(1): 57–78.

Fox A (1974) *Beyond Contract*. London: Faber.

Ganz M (2000) 'Resources and Resourcefulness: Strategic Capacity in the Unionization of California', *American Journal of Sociology* 105(4): 1003–1062.

Gill S (1998) 'European Governance and New Constitutionalism: Economic and Monetary Union and Alternatives to Disciplinary Neoliberalism in Europe', *New Political Economy* 3(1): 5–26.

Gumbrell-McCormick R and Hyman R (2018) *Trade Unions in Western Europe; Hard Times, Hard Choices*, 2nd edition. Oxford: OUP.

Gumbrell-McCormick R and Hyman R (2019) 'Democracy in Trade Unions, Democracy through Trade Unions?', *Economic and Industrial Democracy* 40(1): 91–110.

Hampton P (2015) *Workers and Trade Unions for Climate Solidarity: Tackling Climate Change in a Neoliberal World*. London: Routledge.

Hassel A (2007) 'The Curse of Institutional Security: The Erosion of German Trade Unionism', *Industrielle Beziehungen* 14(2): 176–191.

Hollingsworth JR and Boyer R, eds (1997) *Contemporary Capitalism: The Embeddedness of Institutions*. Cambridge: CUP.

Huws U, Spencer NH, Coates M and Holts K (2019) *The Platformisation of Work in Europe: Results from Research in 13 European Countries*. https://www.feps-europe.eu/resources/publications/686-the-platformisation-of-work-in-europe.html

Hyman R (1987) 'Strategy or Structure? Capital, Labour and Control', *Work, Employment and Society* 1(1): 25–55.

Ibsen CL and Tapia M (2017) 'Trade Union Revitalisation: Where Are We Now? Where to Next?', *Journal of Industrial Relations* 59(2): 170–191.

ILO (2021) *ILO Monitor: COVID-19 and the World of Work. Seventh edition: Updated estimates and analysis*. Geneva: ILO.

Johnston H, Caia A, Silberman MS, Ceremigna M, Hernández D and Dumitrescu V (2020) *Working on Digital Labour Platforms: A Trade Union Guide for Trainers on Crowd-, App- and Platform-Based Work*. Brussels: ETUI.

Jenkins JC and Leicht K (1997) 'Class Analysis and Social Movements: A Critique and Reformulation' in JR Hall, ed, *Reworking Class*. Ithaca: Cornell UP, 369–397.

Jordan J, Maccarone V and Erne R (2021) 'Towards a Socialization of the EU's New Economic Governance Regime? EU Labour Policy Interventions in Germany, Ireland, Italy and Romania (2009–2019)', *British Journal of Industrial Relations* 59(1): 191–213.

Joyce S, Neumann D, Trappmann V and Umney C (2020) *A Global Struggle: Worker Protest in the Platform Economy*. Brussels: ETUI Policy Brief 2/2020.

Kuhlmann R and Scherrer P (2019) 'Yes to More Europe – Now !' in P Scherrer, J Bir, W Kowalsky, R Kuhlmann and M Méaulle, eds, *The Future of Europe*. Brussels: ETUI, 11–25.

Kyzlinková R (2021) *Working Life During the COVID-19 Pandemic as Observed through National Research Data*. Dublin: Eurofound.

Laurent E and Pochet P (2015) *Towards a Social-Ecological Transition: Solidarity in the Age of Environmental Challenge*. Brussels: ETUI.

Lehndorff S, ed (2015) *Divisive Integration: The Triumph of Failed Ideas in Europe Revisited*. Brussels: ETUI.

Marshall TH (1950). *Citizenship and Social Class*. Cambridge: Cambridge University Press.

McGinnity F (2021) 'Work-Life Conflict in Europe', *Social Europe* 26 March.

Offe C and Wiesenthal H (1985) 'Two Logics of Collective Action', in C Offe, *Disorganized Capitalism*. Cambridge: Polity, 170–220.

Peters J (2011) 'The Rise of Finance and the Decline of Organised Labour in the Advanced Capitalist Countries', *New Political Economy* 16(1): 73–99.

Polanyi K (1944) *The Great Transformation*. New York: Rinehart.

Purkayastha D, Vanroelen C, Bircan T, Vantyghem MA and Gantelet Adsera C (2021) *Work, Health and Covid-19: A Literature Review*. Brussels: ETUI Report 2021.03.

Räthzel N and Uzzell D, eds (2012) *Trade Unions in the Green Economy: Working for the Environment*. London: Routledge.

Scharpf F (1999) *Governing in Europe: Effective and Democratic?* Oxford: Oxford University Press.

Schmidt V (2021) 'European Economic Governance: Key Issues to Assess its Recent Past and its Desirable Evolution' in MJ Rodrigues, ed, *Our European Future: Charting a Progressive Course in the World*, 139–144.

Sisson K (2021) *Building Back Better: The Why and Wherefore of the 'New Social Contract' Agenda*. https://docs.google.com/document/d/1K55H4qGkogv uYtedL9cJ8bUNIrIBfj9vPeosKte1KCs/edit

Stevis D and Felli R (2015) 'Global Labour Unions and Just Transition to a Green Economy', *International Environmental Agreements: Politics, Law and Economics* 15(1): 29–43.

Stevis D, Uzzell D and Räthzel N (2018) 'The Labour-Nature Relationship: Varieties of labour Environmentalism', *Globalizations* 15(4): 439–453.

Streeck W (2008) *Re-Forming Capitalism: Institutional Change in the German Political Economy*. Oxford: OUP.

Streeck W and Thelen K, eds (2005) *Beyond Continuity: Institutional Change in Advanced Political Economies*. Oxford: OUP.

Supiot A (1999) *Au-delà de l'emploi*. Paris: Flammarion.

Thomas A and Doerflinger N (2020) 'Trade union Strategies on Climate Change Mitigation: Between Opposition, Hedging and Support', *European Journal of Industrial Relations* 26(4): 383–399.

Tomassetti P (2020) From Treadmill of Production to Just Transition and Beyond, *European Journal of Industrial Relations* 26(4): 439–457.

van Apeldoorn B (2000) 'Transnational Class Agency and European Governance: The Case of the European Round Table of Industrialists', *New Political Economy* 5(2): 157–81.

Vargas Llave O and Weber T (2021) 'Telework and the "Right to Disconnect"', *Social Europe* 8 December.

Wood A (2020) *Despotism on Demand: How Power Operates in the Flexible Workplace*. Ithaca: Cornell University Press.

Index

A
'Are you Ok?' campaign, 212, 216, 220, 225
Authoritarianism, 278

B
Bullying, 96, 98

C
CCOO case, 47, 57, 58
Charter of Fundamental Rights of the European Union, 9, 22, 45
Collective action, 191, 196, 199
Collective agreement(s), 131, 133, 136, 139, 141, 142, 145, 259, 260, 267, 270, 271, 273
Collective bargaining, v, vi, 6, 7, 9, 10, 13, 14, 19–24, 26–36, 38–44, 110, 114, 119, 124
Collective dismissals, 96, 98, 100, 101, 106
Comisiones Obreras/Workers' Commissions (CCOO), 194
Communication, 212, 214–217, 219–223, 225, 226
Competition, 236, 252
Court of Justice of the EU, 46, 48, 50–58, 60–62
Czech trade unions, 187

D
Daily and weekly rest periods, 56, 58, 60
De-unionisation, 110, 113
Direct effect doctrine, 47, 52, 57
Discrimination, 113, 122
Distributional coalition, 14, 235

E
Economic dependence, 20, 21, 29, 33, 39–42, 44
Employee representatives, 130, 131, 133, 134, 137, 141–144
Energy sector, 134, 136
EU competition law, 30, 32, 33, 38, 39, 41, 43

318   INDEX

European Commission, 234, 236–238, 240, 244
European Committee of Social Rights, 21, 33–36, 39–42, 44
European single market, 5

F
Fluid organisations, 151, 166, 167
Freedom of association, 9, 22, 23, 29, 39, 48, 174
French labour law, 101
French trade unions, 113, 117, 123, 124
Fundamental social rights, 46, 48, 51, 52, 62–64

G
Gilets Jaunes (yellow vests), 158, 159, 167

H
Harassment, 97, 98, 100, 102–104
Health and safety, 96, 98, 102, 104–106, 130, 133, 142, 145

I
Individualism, 114

J
Judges, 106
Judicialisation, 51, 58

L
Labour migration, 72–75, 77–81, 83–85, 87–89
Laval-quartet, 50, 62
Leadership, 150, 151, 159, 163

Limitation of maximum working hours, 58
Litigation strategies, 46, 47, 64

M
Macron, Emmanuel, 129, 149
Marea Pensionista, 191, 195, 200
Media, 210, 212–220, 222, 225, 226
Miners, 179–183, 187
Minimum wage, 234–253

N
Network society (networks), 5, 15, 185, 191, 205, 278, 280

O
Occupational safety, 175, 178
Online trade unions, 186

P
Pension(s), 179, 180, 182, 187, 191, 192, 194, 195, 200–204
Poland, 278, 280, 282, 284–289, 291–293
Popular legislative initiative, 191, 196–199, 205
Populism, 278, 284, 286, 292
Posted workers (Posting of workers), 9, 81, 278, 284, 285, 292
Preliminary ruling procedure, 47, 51, 54, 55
Primacy, 52, 53, 64
Privatisation, 95, 98
Professionalisation (of trade union officers), 121, 124
Public sector, 260
Public service, 278, 286, 293

R
'Race to the bottom', 9, 250
Raids on new members, 184
Right to strike, 9, 48–50

S
Self-employed, 29, 31–40, 42–44
Social dialogue, 280–283, 286
Social media, 150, 214, 215, 217, 218, 224, 226
Social movements, 150–152, 160, 164, 165, 167–170
Social policy, 281
Solidarity, 4–6, 8, 9, 12–14, 64, 71, 73, 78, 105, 106, 157, 158, 161, 191, 205, 246, 249, 252, 273, 278, 285, 300, 312
Strike, 150–152, 154, 156–158, 160, 163, 166, 169, 170
Supervisory boards, 13, 251

T
Toledo Pact, 192–195, 200, 204, 205
Trade union density, 260

U
Union elections, 131
Unión General de Trabajadores/the General Workers' Union (UGT), 194
Union participation, 191, 192, 195, 197, 205

V
Varieties of capitalism, 2, 15, 297, 298

W
Wages, 74, 75, 78–80, 82–84
Welfare state, 2, 4, 12, 79, 115–117, 299
Worker voice, 5, 97, 264, 266, 280
Working conditions, 74, 75, 77–79, 82, 83, 85, 88, 89
Workplace teams, 123
Works councils, 175, 178, 179

Y
Young people, 210–221, 223, 225, 226